Common Ground

Dutch-South African Architectural Exchanges 1902–1961

Common Ground

Nicholas J. Clarke, Roger C. Fisher, Marieke C. Kuipers – editors

LM PUBLISHERS

Pretoria, DR Church Pretoria North; photo 2020

Content

1 **In Search of Shared Heritage** – *Marieke Kuipers* 7

2 **The Netherlands – Country of Emigration** – *Marieke Kuipers* 23

INTERLUDE Educating the Dutch architect – *Lizette van der Wal and Marieke Kuipers* 49

3 **Two Waves of Dutch Immigration to South Africa** – *Annie Antonites* 55

INTERLUDE Cross-continental Careers – *Nicholas Clarke and Marieke Kuipers* 67

4 **Public Service and Community Buildings** – *Nicholas Clarke* 75

INTERLUDE Celebration and Commemoration – *Marieke Kuipers* 93

5 **Building for Communities of Faith** – *Nicholas Clarke* 99

6 **Building for Banking and Industry** – *Catherine Deacon and Marguerite Pienaar* 119

7 **Evolution of the Pretoria Dwelling** – *Arthur Barker* 139

INTERLUDE Kitchen: Heart of the Home – *Esther de Haan* 157

8 **Model Township Atteridgeville** – *Mathebe Aphane and Kees Somer* 163

9 **Technological Trajectories from North to South** – *Michael Louw* 181

INTERLUDE Water and Concrete/Cape Town Foreshore Harbour – *Roger Fisher* 199

10 **Tectonic Archives** – *Johan Swart* 207

11 **Constructing Stories** – *Mary Lange and Roger Fisher* 229

12 **Reflections and Projections** – *Ben Mswinga* 241

Sources 247

Acknowledgements 256

Authors 259

Image credits 261

Register 263

Colophon 272

Promotional poster of the Holland Afrika Lijn showing people onboard the VZN ocean liner 'Randfontein', designed by Jan Michels, 1960

1 In Search of Shared Heritage
General Introduction

Marieke Kuipers

Introduction

'Oh, now I am part of history', exclaimed sister Elizabeth gladly, after we had explained to her the reasons for our visit to the Fort Savage Assisi Mission farm, church and school in the Free State. Similar reactions of pride and surprise were received at other South African places of which we knew (from archives, literature or oral history), on hearing that these buildings, such as schools, churches, factories, offices, social institutions, technical installations and a wide range of houses, were designed by Dutch-born architects during the first six decades of C20.

Most of those we visited proved personally attached to the places where they live, work or gather—because, in the main, these buildings are extant and still accommodate their activities in a rapidly changing environment. What mattered to them was the scholarly recognition of these cherished buildings as something valuable for a community broader than just their own; thereby also adding value for themselves. Being part of a wider history, beyond their own generation and beyond their own community, and being acknowledged as worthy custodians by external researchers made all our temporary hosts proud and helpful to our ambitious mission to find and identify these places. The same is true for the families of some Dutch-born architects that we had been able to trace by way of various sources and through contemporary media. These people were most generous in sharing their family stories and archives with us, for which we are most grateful. Some of their photographs are included in this book.

Brixton, Johannesburg, Dutch Reformed Church in use during a Sunday service in 2018; architects: Geers & Geers, 1940

Assisi, Church of St Francis at the Assisi Catholic Mission, Fort Savage mission farm, designed by Edy Payens in about 1940; photo 2020

All such interactions are at the core of the Shared Heritage programme of South Africa and the Netherlands that has been running since 2009. In 2013, and again in 2017, this agreement was revisited, based on the 2004 memorandum signed by the two countries. This programme, among its other goals, aims at building and exchanging knowledge on the more recent, though barely recognised legacy of Dutch architects and engineers in South Africa, as well as advancing 'integrated planning' of urban conservation and development.[1]

This current book is one of the tangible results that received financial aid from this Shared Heritage programme. Its progenitor is the similar transcontinental research and dissemination project 'Tectonic ZA Wilhelmiens'. This current project was initiated in 2017 by the University of Pretoria, with collaboration from other parties, including the University of Cape Town, the Erfenisstigting [Heritage Foundation], the Delft University of Technology and the Netherlands Cultural Heritage Agency. It relates to the preceding project, 'Eclectic ZA Wilhelmiens', that is dedicated to the historicist late C19 legacy of Dutch émigré architects (differing from 'Victorian') and resulted in the acclaimed book with the same title.[2]

The term 'Wilhelmiens' refers to the Dutch Queen Wilhelmina who reigned over the Netherlands and their colonies from 1898 until 1948. 'Tectonic' is a reference to Kenneth Frampton's seminal studies and the profound impact of new technologies on the construction and aesthetics of modern architecture of the Machine Age. 'ZA' is the international country code for South Africa, but is historically associated with the former Zuid-Afrikaansche Republiek (ZAR), forged by Paul Kruger as an independent Boer Republic in the 1880s. Dutch architects were invited to modernise the ZAR and, likewise, Dutch engineers to construct railroads and bridges at that time.

While retaining the same focus, the title of the book has nonetheless been changed during the course of the project into '*Common Ground / Dutch-South African Architectural Exchanges / 1902–61*', in order to appeal to an audience broader than a merely academic one and to underline the aspect of exchanges. It is also a more suitable reflection of the great stylistic diversity of the Dutch-related C20 contributions to the vast built environment of South Africa. Often, the 'Dutchness' of a building or design is somewhat hidden in particular details, at times the 'shared heritage' is a hybrid resulting from the architectural adaptation to the differing climatological and socio-political circumstances of the two countries.

Sharing heritage?

In South Africa, the socio-cultural appropriation of relatively recent artefacts with Dutch connections as *shared* heritage, be it a particular Dutch Reformed Church building or suchlike, is often more complex than elsewhere in the world due to the contested history of South Africa, with its diverse population and its uneven representation in the official records and collective memories. For instance, the Kruger Memorial in Pretoria/Tshwane, designed by the Dutch-born sculptor Anton van Wouw to commemorate the ZAR's freedom, is today fenced off and hardly recognized anymore as a typical late C19 work of art that can be linked with multiple stories of a shared, however controversial, past.

1 Corten, 2015; www.dutchfootsteps.co.za.
2 Bakker *et al.*, 2014.

Yet, it is undeniable that there are strong ties between South Africa and the Netherlands, of which the Afrikaans language and the C17 and C18 'Cape Dutch' architecture from the Dutch East Indies Company (VOC) are widely known and prevailing legacies. After the Cape capitulated to British rule, tensions arose between the Brits and the Boers, culminating in the South African War. During this conflict, not only did the Boers receive sympathy and support in and from the Netherlands, but also many Dutchmen, including several architects and builders, joined the voluntary *Hollanderkorps* [Dutch Corps] to fight with the Boers against the Brits.[3] After the hostilities were ended in 1902, with the signing of the Treaty of Vereeniging, the Dutch expertise in public works, civil engineering and construction was needed for the rebuilding of the country, especially in the Transvaal and Orange Free State, though they were only accepted under British conditions. The establishment of the Union of South Africa in 1910 brought the four provinces together as a

3 Schoeman, 2011.

Pretoria, the Kruger Memorial by Anton van Wouw on Church Square as a popular photo-spot, with the Ou Raadsaal by Sytze Wierda in the background; photo 2016

Johannesburg, late C19 fort on Constitution Hill; photo 2018

unitary, self-governed dominion of the Commonwealth until 1961, when the Republic of South Africa was founded.

Against this backdrop, the historic dates of 1902 and 1961 mark the period of our research on the Tectonic ZA Wilhelmiens architecture in all its diversity. During this period, thousands of Dutch immigrants embarked for South Africa to start a new life. Counted amongst these many immigrants were dozens of architects and builders. The purpose of our focus on these Dutch connections is to reveal that they, though hitherto unrecognised, indeed exist. This lack of awareness is a consequence of the dominance of English, particularly in the scholarship and historiography of the built environment of the time. This related built residue might otherwise be forgotten or neglected, although its major portion is nowadays also covered by the '60 years rule' of the South African Heritage Resources Act (1999). In order that our research enterprise is further shared, the collected data of our findings is deposited in, and substantially augments, the South African Heritage Resources Information System (SAHRIS).[4]

Today the concept of 'shared heritage', successor to the previous terms of 'mutual heritage' and 'colonial heritage', might be severely criticized, particularly in view of colonial history and the study on 'dissonant heritage'.[5] Recent movements against the monuments that were erected to honour the colonial powers, such as the 'Rhodes must fall' protest, indicate that the mutuality is not always shared or supported. On the other hand, there is a growing interest in the 'places of pain and shame' or the 'difficult heritage' associated with painful events and periods, such as Robben Island, now inscribed on Unesco's World Heritage List.[6] Studies as to how heritage values are socially, culturally and politically 'constructed' is of more recent concern. Such studies provide insight into the evolution of 'shared heritage' as a complex, if not contradictory, assemblage of projected identities and mixed values. Initially these were directed by a renewed interest, from both the decolonized countries and the Netherlands, in their shared colonial legacies of the C17 and C18, which were aimed at raising awareness as well as collecting technical expertise for conservation and adaptive reuse.[7]

Without knowledge and without seeking the traces of history from different vantages, even if they are the result of a contestable past, it is difficult to develop useful strategies for the preservation of a built heritage. The tangible residue can act as a multivocal instrument to aid mutual understanding of sometimes painful episodes, by evoking various stories from different perspectives, as is done, for instance, with

4 www.sahris.co.za.

5 Tunbridge & Ashworth, 1994; www.atlasofmutualheritage.nl.

6 Logan & Reeves, 2008; MacDonald, 2008.

7 Fienieg, 2006; Oostindië, 2008.

the former prison at Constitution Hill in Johannesburg, or the German bunkers in the Netherlands. In the latter case, it should be noted that for a long period of time such traces of World War 2 (WW2) had been disregarded and wilfully demolished, thereby aspiring to erase the traumas of the German occupation. Yet this strategy of destruction did not result in forgetting. On the contrary, in recent years, these former 'places of guilt' have gradually become places of commemoration and reflection for diverse generations and various communities, as a means for deepening understanding and promoting reconciliation.

An uncomfortable, if not confrontational, aspect of this shared heritage is its connection with the apartheid policy, which the Dutch-born Hendrik Verwoerd (though raised in southern Africa) was instrumental in implementing after WW2, though building on prevailing discrimination and segregation in place since the Union had been established, and even before. The 1960 Sharpeville massacre, in particular, has cast a long shadow over the country as well as international exchanges. The event resulted in a strong anti-apartheid movement in the Netherlands.

Only since the installation of Nelson Mandela in 1994 as the first fully democratically elected president has there been a renewal of activities for strengthening cultural ties and supporting bilateral cooperation in the field of cultural heritage conservation – in particular the heritage associated with the endemic populations. This resulted, among other initiatives, in the rehabilitation of the C18 settlement Genadendal [Valley of Grace], a Moravian mission post in the Western Cape, realised with financial support and expertise from the Netherlands as well as the direct involvement of the local community.

When president Mandela decided to rename the official residence in Cape Town from Westbrooke to Genadendal in honour of this oldest mission settlement in the country, a place blessed with a rich tangible and intangible heritage, he noted: "a place associated with the coming together of people from different racial groups: in addition to being the first permanent Khoi settlement at the Cape, it was also a place of sanctuary for more than a thousand slaves when slavery was abolished in 1838. It boasts of vernacular architecture, musical traditions and language and a long tradition of humanitarian efforts and political struggle." He acknowledged the combined efforts of restoration and providing infrastructure to improve the quality of inhabitants' lives, and wished that the history of Genadendal may continue to inspire.[8]

The Genadendal project did not only demonstrate the merits of the 'integrated conservation' approach, but also led to the establishment of the permanent scientific committee for Shared Colonial Architecture and Town Planning of ICOMOS in 1998. In fact, it also laid the foundations of the later Shared Heritage programme of the Dutch government and South Africa, and other countries.

As already indicated above, the aim of this book is neither to provide a critical assessment of the concept of 'shared heritage', however useful this would be for academia or policies, nor to re-introduce a certain Dutch-related colonialism. Rather, it seeks to identify the—often unknown and increasingly endangered—contributions by the dozens of C20 Dutch architects to the built environment of South Africa. We further wish to show how they have deployed their expertise to adapt

8 Du Preez *et al.*, 2009.

Genadendal, C18 Main Assembly Hall (currently museum) of the Moravian Mission; photo 2018

their designs to the different circumstances in their new homeland. Nevertheless, many of their works often also contain aspects of cultural resilience inherited from their Dutch architectural education, such as an intense interest in careful planning, orientation and ventilation for residential and other buildings.

This aspect in itself would merit another study for further investigating the influences and experiences of building in the 'tropical Netherlands'; at the time–Surinam, Antilles and the Dutch Indies–on the Dutch-related (sub)tropical architecture in South Africa. These might also eventually be related to the emergence of the 'Streamline Moderne', partly inspired by the aerodynamic design of the ocean-liners, that was applied in commercial buildings, combined with apartments, such as the former OK Bazaars and Amanda Court, both in Pretoria.

Pretoria, former OK Bazaars Building, designed by Burg Lodge & Burg in the 1930s; photo 2020

From the passengers lists of the intercontinental shipping companies, then published daily, and subsequent archives we learned that many Dutch families criss-crossed the globe for their work or personal visits. Several Dutch-born civil engineers practising in South Africa certainly had first-hand familiarity with the tropical conditions, but we have not, as yet, come across such evidence for Dutch architects, although it is likely that they were informed through journals, stories and pictures shared by family and friends who had been abroad.

Historiography and fieldwork

The Dutch archivist JC Overvoorde, founder of the Netherlands Archaeological Association and honorary member of the Royal Commission for the Recording of Monuments, had, in 1910–11, together with his wife Johanna Gordon, already undertaken a self-funded tour. His aim was to identify the historic buildings and monuments overseas that had been created by Dutchmen or under Dutch influence. This venture was triggered by similar English initiatives. He considered such identification in the field, as well as the inspection of the condition of the local archives, as being a necessary extension of the broader task of surveying the Dutch Monuments of History and Art in the Netherlands.[9] South Africa, being on the route to the then still colonised Dutch East Indies, was the first country he explored. Apart from his reports, he also brought various photographs to illustrate his findings and to open Dutch eyes to the beautiful setting and architecture of their *stamverwante*

9 Overvoorde, 1910 and 1911; Overvoorde, 2018.

Pretoria, Amanda Court with shops and apartments, designed by Burg Lodge & Burg in the 1930s; photo 2020

[brethren] pioneers in the southern hemisphere, such as Groot Constantia at Wynberg.

That the Cape Dutch architecture continued to inspire Dutch-born architects and clients can be noted in, for instance, the Pretoria Engelenburg House (with richly furnished interior restored) and House Grobler ('Lydia', now somewhat refurbished internally). However, under the influence of the British architect Herbert Baker, the 'Cape Dutch Revival' would become widely applied by British architects and by Public Work Departments in the early C20.

This current project is primarily focused on Dutch-related buildings that were erected after Overvoorde's mission was completed and his inventory created, but in its combination of field work and bibliographical research it can be considered a follow-on study, methodologically speaking. The preceding Eclectic ZA Wilhelmiens research can be considered the project that fills the gap. An initial scoping exercise had already identified more than fifty Dutch-born and educated architects active in the Union of South Africa, but in the course of researching the project many more have been discovered. A number of highly influential manufacturers and contractors have also been found, such as Bruynzeel/BruPly.

Yet, we had often to tackle the problem of the relative obscurity of the 'Tectonic' architects, lack of data about the location of the buildings and the renaming of places and practices. Some were associated with private practices run by a British-born architect, others worked more or less anonymously in public service. As we discovered during our research, some were involved in the design of townships and (sub-) economic housing, thus implicitly supporting the segregation of black and white people, like Atteridgeville in Pretoria for the 'black' middle class inhabitants, its equivalent, nearby Danville, for the 'white' working class, and the Iscor [Iron and Steel Corporation of South Africa] company town on Proclamation Hill.

For various reasons, these Dutch-born architects did not extensively publish their works or ideas, the usual gateway for research by architectural historians. Therefore, in addition to the scarcity of available publications and diverse archives (public and private), we also developed another approach by combining the results of oral history, modern media and many digitised sources.

Wynberg, Groot Constantia, photographed by Jacob Overvoorde in 1910 during his inventorying travels

Pretoria, Engelenburg House designed by Frans Soff in 1903, shortly after completion

Pretoria, House Grobler, 'Lydia' designed by Kraan & Wijers in 1931; photo 2016

Stellenbosch, abandoned site of the former Bruynzeel wood ply factory; photo 2016

When we started this project, we were able to make use of the independent and interactive web-based resource, www.artefacts.co.za. This aims to make information of interest about the Built Environment of Southern Africa readily accessible for anyone who can access the World Wide Web. For reasons of compactness we have omitted the possibly numerous references to this essential website and, instead, made a general reference in our list of consulted sources. Meanwhile, the reader is kindly invited to consult the steadily updated and expanded database, for which a special section has been created in the Lexicon under the heading 'Tectonic ZA Wilhelmiens'.

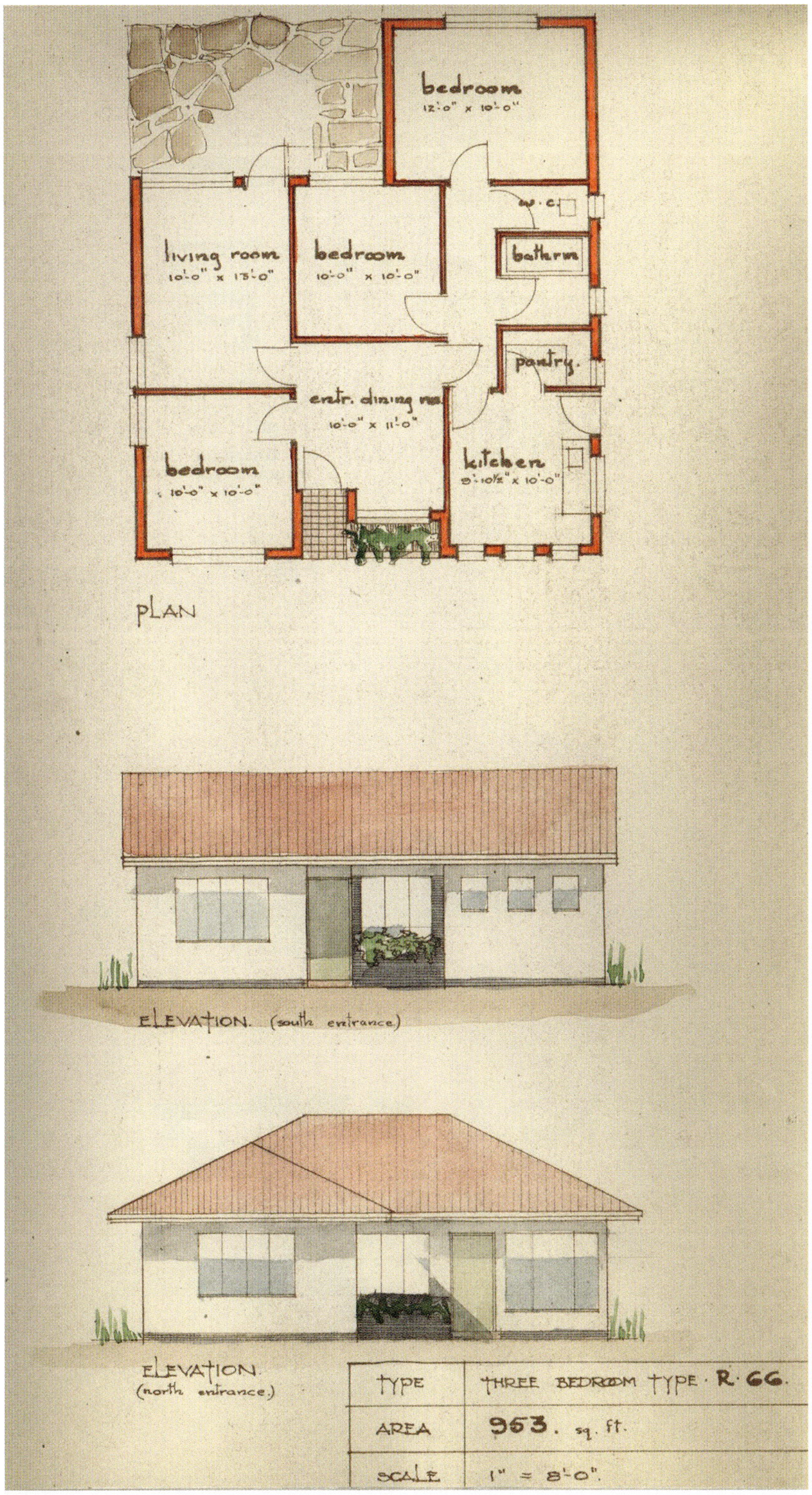

Danville, 3-bedroom type house design by Pretoria City Architect Jan de Jong, 1952

At the core of this resource is the electronic data set compiled by Joanna Walker (at the time librarian of the Human Science Research Council) for the South African Biographical Dictionary of Architects. This data set is now lodged with the archives of the Department of Architecture, University of Pretoria. In turn, this dictionary was begun in 1984 by Gerhard-Mark van der Waal, Arie Kuijers and Joanna Walker under the auspices of the Human Sciences Research Council, attempting to include the biographical data of the architects and their works. To this end, various sources were systematically researched and scanned, including files from the Royal Institute of British Architects and the Institute of South African Architects, South African architectural and building periodicals, theses and suchlike.

As for hard-copy publications, the input of the Dutch-born publisher Guus Balkema has been vital in the South African book industry and for architectural publications in particular, while he managed to improve the printing and layout by engaging qualified people from overseas.[10] He migrated in 1946 and was entrusted with the official publication of the three volumes of Van Riebeeck's *Daghregister* in 1952, on the occasion of the Tercentennial celebration of his landing. Six years later he published the first Afrikaans anti-apartheid novel, Jan Rabie's *Ons, die Afgod*, which suited his own critical stance towards the Nazi regime in the Netherlands. However, he also invited scholars to publish about the South African heritage and published Désirée Picton-Seymour's *Victorian Buildings in South Africa*.[11] It was, in fact, this still-valuable book which triggered the search for the 'Wilhelmiens' buildings that were designed by Dutch immigrant architects in late C19 and early C20 as a counterpart to the 'Victorian' legacy.

While most of the published resources are written in English or Afrikaans, many Dutch sources, lying dispersed in archives, libraries, or personal collections, concerning the Dutch origins and education of C20 immigrant architects, were also investigated. This integrated approach to research also issues the challenge that the historiography of C20 architecture in the Netherlands, which is still very much dominated by the almost mythological story of the triumph of the Modern Movement, be re-assessed. In fact, there was a much more varied palette of styles, technological trends and interaction between architects, engineers and artists than is usually posited in the secondary literature. Such (re)discoveries also enrich the history of migration and cultural exchanges between South Africa and the Netherlands during the first six decades of C20.

10 Human, 1999.
11 Picton-Seymour, 1989.

Danville, two semi-detached sub-economic type houses; photo 2019

Unexpected Discoveries

When drafting the research project, we opted for ten major themes that marked the evolvement of the Union and the context of the Dutch-related architectural contributions. However, during our research we also discovered unexpected sub-themes, as well as almost forgotten, though interesting, architects and seldom-told stories of their experiences as practitioners and of post-occupancy practices.

To our surprise, several Roman-Catholic architects of Dutch descent had migrated to South Africa and settled in all provinces. An intriguing figure like Mello Damstra, who was very much inspired by Italian Renaissance and Baroque styles, designed magnificent houses in Cape Town and Stellenbosch. Villa Palermo is just one of the luxurious homes he had created for his family, but as his grandsons told us, he also designed the cottages for the caretakers of the Oranjezicht gardens and multi-storeyed Breda Court. Although the Roman Catholics form a minority in the country, they are present in the urban and rural landscapes through their churches, schools, hospitals, homes for miners or the elderly.

The province of Orange Free State was largely part of the Catholic Archdiocese and a major area of missionary work. It was no coincidence that the pious Dutch immigrant architect Edy Payens had established his practice at Bloemfontein (in 1936). From there he designed not only the aforementioned church in Assisi, but also many other churches, as well as various mission schools and hospitals throughout neighbouring Lesotho, while he built the new Cathedral (1960) in the provincial capital of the then Orange Free State. Similarly, Anton Voorvelt, migrated c. 1937 to Johannesburg, designed remarkable Catholic churches in the expanding towns of Gauteng (then Transvaal) in a relatively advanced architectural vocabulary.

Unknown place, architect Jan Zeger Schuurmans Stekhoven in front of his aeroplane

Building a new church, sometimes genuinely in 'the middle of nowhere', was always an important step for further town development, meant as a draw-point for the local community, and often the Dutch Reformed Church was the instigating denomination.[12] At the same time, general public facilities were required to serve the local communities, such as school buildings, sometimes in very distant locations. Therefore,

12 See also Chapter 5.

Cape Town, Oranjezicht, House Palermo designed by Mello Damstra for his family, with his car parked in front; photo c1925

Unknown place, probably Vrede; architect Edy Payens' 1959 photograph of a dome being placed on the tower of a church of his design

the Dutch émigré architect, Jan Zeger Schuurmans Stekhoven, an adventurous man, acquired a small aeroplane with which he could visit remote construction sites, like Springbok in the Northern Cape.

In larger towns, public libraries were also built for education. The 1936 North End library in Port Elizabeth is an interesting example, designed by Gertruida Brinkman when she was working in the practice of her Dutch immigrant father, Hendrik Siemerink; she was one of the early formally qualified female architects in South Africa. By then, the classicist eclecticism was still fashionable for such culturally esteemed buildings like libraries, but the firm Siemerink & Brinkman was among the first to deploy modernist designs for factories and villas in the eastern Cape.[13]

Stylistic diversity within one architect's oeuvre was not uncommon during the 1930s and 1940s, albeit that most Dutch immigrant architects were no longer applying historicist style ornamentation, but rather searching for contemporary architectural expression while incorporating modern comfort. For instance, John van de Werke, who emigrated in 1935, designed, alongside his distinctive houses, the modernist girl's dormitory (1940) on the campus of the University of Pretoria and the Pretoria College of Education (1955), which is closer to the post-war 'Shake-Hands' architecture in the Netherlands. This dual idiom was similarly deployed by the Johannesburg-based immigrant architect, Jaap Van Niftrik; for example, his design for a medium high school at Schweizer-Reneke or in the private bungalows he designed.

13 See also Chapter 6.

Port Elizabeth, North End Public Library designed by Siemerink & Brinkman in 1936; photo 2020

Pretoria, Huis Voortrekker, (now University of Pretoria Xayata Hostel, also known as 'Glaskas') on the University of Pretoria campus, designed by John van de Werke in 1940; photo 2020

Design for the Pretoria Teachers College by John van de Werke, 1955

Schweizer-Reneke, Hoërskool Schweizer-Reneke public high school, designed by Jaap Van Niftrik in 1960, shortly after construction

Worcester, the Hextex textile factory in its picturesque setting, designed by Henk Niegeman of Andrews & Niegeman in 1940

Truly functionalist design was, however, brought to South Africa by the well-travelled Dutch-born architect Henk Niegeman, who had been a member of the CIAM-affiliated avant-gardist group 'de 8' before he permanently settled in Cape Town. He started there in practice with ED Andrews in 1939 but was certainly the main designer of what is probably the most renowned clothing factory building, Rex Trueform. Lesser known, though also noticeable is his design for the Hextex textile factory at Worcester, where the local wool is processed for clothing and carpets, even to this day. The first processes were documented in images which reveal that Black people also had a great responsibility for the quality of the products at that time.

Such discoveries were only enabled by the photographs and oral histories that were so generously shared with us by the descendants of these Dutch-born architects or current custodians of their legacy.

We were also surprised to discover that for particular buildings, at least two different Dutch artists had travelled to South Africa from the Netherlands for the express purpose of creating, locally, works of

Johannesburg, the refurbished KLM booking office with interior architect Jaap van Niftrik and artist Jan Dijker in front of the mural 'Holland' in 1950.

applied art, done in similar fashion to the early post-war activities of monumental art in their home country. The first was Marinus Schipper, who was invited to provide a painting for the newly built clothing factory Rex Trueform at Cape Town in 1948.[14] The second, Jan Dijker, was specially flown in by KLM, to execute a mural on 'Holland' on site, inside the refurbished booking office of this air company for which Van Niftrik had made the interior design at Johannesburg in 1950.[15] Dijker expressed both the long historic ties that connect South Africa and the Netherlands and the contemporary connections that could be maintained by modern means of transportation and suchlike. The figurative mural is now only known through photographs. Parts of the scenes can be easily associated with the episode of Van Riebeeck's arrival, an event that was strongly revived in the 1950s among the Dutch and Afrikaans speaking communities of South Africa, as well as in the Netherlands, as a marker of a shared past.

Narrowly related to the history of the Huguenot community is the public monument at Franschhoek, inaugurated in 1948 and designed in the main by the Dutch immigrant architect Jaap Jongens after winning the preceding competition of 1938.[16] Jongens had been in public service with

14 Anon. 1948, *Zuid-Afrika Maandblad*, May: 78. No further details known.
15 A&B. 1956, July: 42–43; Locarno House, Loveday Street, Johannesburg; www.jandijker.nl.
16 See also the interlude on Celebration and Commemoration.

Franschhoek, Huguenot Monument, architectural design by Jaap Jongens (1938–45), sculpture by Coert Steynberg, inaugurated in 1948; photo 2016

Cape Town City since 1940, both as designer and draughtsmen of an impressive portfolio, but incidentally, he was allowed to work on private projects, as will be discussed later in this book.

All in all, it can be concluded that the concept of 'shared heritage' can not only lead to surprising, sometimes uncomfortable, discoveries, but also unfold a wider engagement than merely Dutch-related communities and practitioners in C20 built South Africa.

Reading guide

Though far from a complete and comprehensive overview, the richness of the 'shared heritage' of South Africa and the Netherlands from 1902–61, or 'Tectonic ZA Wilhelmiens', is broadly reflected in the following chapters. They are, in general, theme-based and partly alternated by shorter interludes on a particular topic.

Firstly, a historical overview is provided of C20 Netherlands as the country of emigration. Here, *Marieke Kuipers* sketches the geographical, political, economic and socio-cultural context as well as the push factors that had influenced Dutch architects when they decided to migrate. Two major periods, punctuated by WW2, each have their own character and dynamic that informed their South African operations.

The interlude on the education of the Dutch architect, by *Lizette van der Wal* and *Marieke Kuipers*, addresses the great diversity of educational institutions and various paths that could be followed to become an architect in the Netherlands. The vocational school was the lowest of the four levels of technical education, the Delft Institute of Technology (precursor of the current University of Technology) the highest, with the technical colleges and academies in between.

Why it was that South Africa was a desirable choice for Dutch immigrant architects in C20 is explained by *Annie Antonites* in her chapter about the pre- and post-WW2 waves of migration. It considers the typical conditions of the country of arrival and the relevant state policies on migration. Also influential were the three Afrikaner reformed sister-churches, especially for their cultural integration. The majority of newcomers settled in the former Transvaal, and Pretoria in particular, which became home to the largest Dutch community in the country.

The interlude on the surprising cross-continental careers of some architects is briefly sketched by *Nicholas Clarke* and *Marieke Kuipers* on the roles of six Dutch-born architects who had worked both in the Netherlands and South Africa, and often also in other countries. The small yet representative selection includes JE Ferguson, JC Jongens, JC Meischke, HTO Niegeman, AJC Voorvelt and C Wegerif.

Building for civic works and communities was a great challenge in the South African context as *Nicholas Clarke* demonstrates. Several Dutch émigré architects have contributed considerably to the civil infrastructure, but most of their work remains obscure as they were produced in the name of the municipal departments they served, such as Pretoria, Bloemfontein and Cape Town. Some other Dutch-born architects working in private practice were commissioned by specific organisations for designing schools, hospitals and other community facilities.

The interlude on celebration and commemoration, by *Marieke Kuipers*, only briefly addresses a selected series of purpose-designed memorials as well as specific fairs, in which Dutch designers, products and special relations were involved, such as the statue of Maria de la Quellerie and the Van Riebeeck Festival/Tercentenary, or the Rand Easter Show.

The multi-faceted topic of building for communities of faith is explained by *Nicholas Clarke*, who signals not only that there were a great variety of denominations for which Dutch-related designs were made for buildings and applied arts, but also that these places have exerted a great influence in the local community and town development.

In building for banking and industry, the Netherlands Bank of South Africa (NBZA, today Nedbank), has played an important role as *Catherine Deacon* and *Marguerite Pienaar* show. Various architects of Dutch origin conceived architectures of exchange and enterprise, but renowned local architects have also been commissioned. The dissemination of rational and flexible planning based on Dutch experience and knowledge has resulted in many extant buildings still being used, including the Hollandia House in Johannesburg and the Rex Trueform factory in Cape Town.

The evolution of the Pretoria dwelling is discussed by *Arthur Barker* in the context of a localised regionalism and particularly in relation to the picturesque and the practical. The largely unrecognised influences of six Dutch immigrants on C20 domestic architecture in the suburbs of the South African capital are demonstrated by a surprising selection of examples, ranging from Erasmus Castle to the (now demolished) House De la Hunt.

The interlude on the kitchen as the heart of the home by *Esther de Haan* notes the differences in the living conditions between the Netherlands and South Africa, both climatically and socially. Three examples illustrate how the South African kitchen as a working space in the household was organized in different categories.

Such differences are also evident in the planning and design of Atteridgeville as a model-township for the 'urban native', which was partly Dutch influenced as *Mathebe Aphane* and *Kees Somer* reveal. The new settlement evolved under the leadership of the Dutch-born JJ de Jong, who was in municipal service of Pretoria and had to deal with the severe conditions of racial segregation in C20, while, at the same time, attempting to improve the living conditions of the black population. After discussing the development, urban characteristics, amenities and housing types, the chapter concludes with an evaluation of 'old' Atteridgeville based on testimonies from past and present residents.

Pretoria, Savelkoul Building with shops and (originally) offices; designed by Burg Lodge & Burg in 1949; photo 2020

The technological trajectories and influences of immigrant Dutch-born architects, contractors, suppliers and educators who practiced in the Union of South Africa, are explored by *Michael Louw* along themes such as adaptation, daylighting, efficiency, labour, urgency, industrialisation, and innovation. The technological trends of C20 Netherlands clearly exhibited tensions between tradition and modernity. Their overseas transfer, however divergent, to southern Africa was further influenced by differences in climate, the availability of skill and labour or the lack thereof, available materials and socio-political circumstances. Yet, their influence can still be noticed today, partly due to the immaterial legacies.

The interlude on the Cape Town Harbour and Foreshore Project, by *Roger Fisher*, sheds light on the large involvement of Dutch civil engineering technology in the making of the Duncan Docks and Sturrock Graving Dock, and the ambitious land reclamation completed in 1945. In creating the harbour there was opportunity for extending the available land to build the infrastructure required for the developing industry and commerce of Cape Town.

The chapter on the 'Tectonic' Archives by *Johan Swart* introduces the relevant archival collections, architectural records and paper based evidence as a significant component of the concept of 'shared heritage' of both the Netherlands and South Africa. Various valuable and insightful records were uncovered from already established archives, while a number of entirely new collections have also been discovered and added during the research project. These are all very supportive in identifying and giving value to the hitherto hardly recognised contributions by Dutch-born architects to the built environment of C20 South Africa.

The essay by *Mary Lange* and *Roger* Fisher on the construction of stories is based on interviews with two Dutch immigrant architects at Pretoria, Gerrit Brink and Hans Wegelin. The oral history of these case studies adds new insights not only to the immigrants' struggle to adapt to a different country, climate and society, but also to the history and the cross-continental exchanges of architectural practice in general.

Finally, *Ben Mwasinga* presents his valuable reflections and projections related to the findings of the 'Tectonic ZA Wilhelmiens' project and the concept of sharing heritage in the dynamic turmoil of South Africa's built environment and society. His critical observations are important lessons for the building of a mutual understanding of the values of heritage, even if this can be associated with a controversial past.

During three years of research we have identified far more buildings, structures and archival material than previously anticipated, because many Dutch-born professionals and their achievements were hitherto unrecorded. We have also learned that some of those architects in public service have contributed to a contentious heritage (including low-cost housing, schools and administrative buildings) as it relates to the time of the entrenchment of apartheid. Yet, the built residue is an undeniable part of South Africa today and in daily service, like the Savelkoul Building by Burg Lodge Burg in Pretoria, or the Newlands Public Swimming Pool at Cape Town by Jongens.

Cape Town, Newlands Public Swimming Pool in use, grandstand designed by Jaap Jongens in 1955; photo 2015

Thaba Nchu, Roman Catholic Church, designed by Edy Payens for Father Frans Claerhout, c1964; photo 2019

What follows aims at a broadening of the knowledge on the architecture of the period 1902–61 in general, and the Dutch contribution to this legacy of South Africa's built environment in particular. This book also aspires to a deepening of understanding, and valuing of this legacy, so that what remains may be purposefully and sympathetically utilized in enriching the environment, and thereby the lives of the peoples and communities they serve.

The Netherlands, country of emigration, promotional poster of booking office Ruysch & Co, indicating South Africa as one of the destinations, approximately 1955

2 The Netherlands

Country of Emigration

Marieke Kuipers

Introduction

When the young princess Wilhelmina was festively inaugurated as the Queen of the Netherlands, in 1898, there was great support for the cause of the Boers in South Africa. Attempts were also made to mediate in the conflict, though they proved fruitless.[1] Hundreds of new streets were named after the Transvaal, and various monuments were erected in the Netherlands to commemorate important figures of the South African War.

After this war ended in 1902, new waves of emigration into South Africa would follow those of the late C19, in which many architects, carpenters, contractors, engineers and craftsmen (and their families) were involved. This huge country in the south held for them more apparent promise than the Dutch colonies (Dutch Indies, Surinam and the Antilles) or their home country. So far, we have identified over seventy Dutchmen who practiced as architects in South Africa during the period 1902–61. Their typologically diverse projects, executed in various styles, stretched from the Cape to the Rand and beyond.

This chapter will sketch a general picture of the country from which those 'Hollanders' emigrated and will pinpoint some push factors for leaving.

1 Bossenbroek, 2012.

Amsterdam, view of the Kraaipan Street in the Transvaal district, designed by HP Berlage, Gratama & Versteeg in 1916–19, postcard, 1924

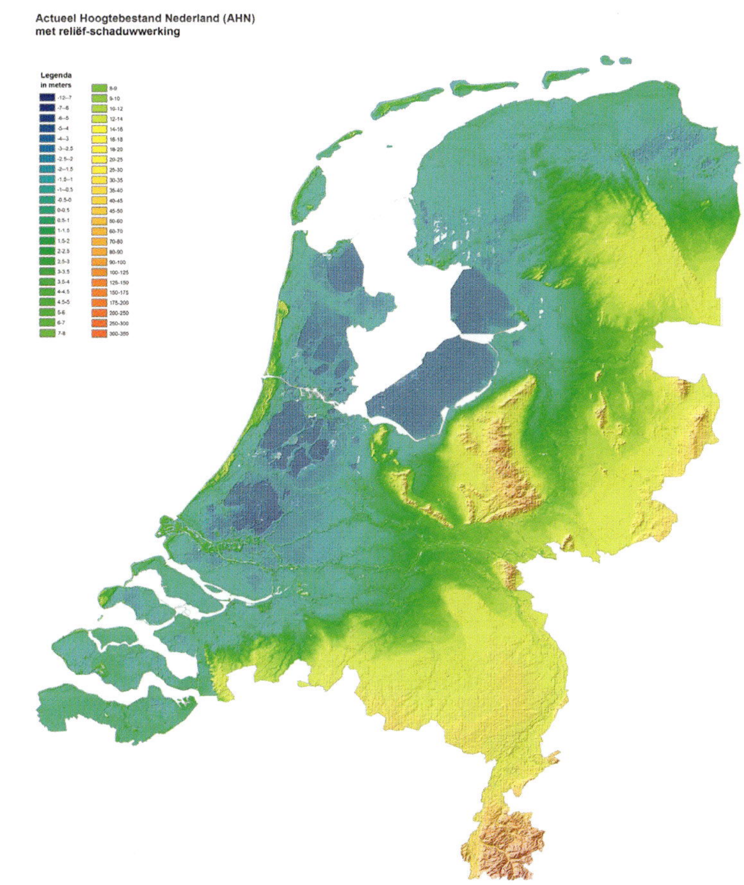

Contour map of the Netherlands indicating the heights below and above sea level

Geography[2]

The main part of the Dutch Kingdom is located in the northwest corner of the European continent, along the North Sea, and is thus blessed with a moderate seaboard climate. The country's name, the Netherlands or 'Low Lands', refers to the unique situation that about half of the terrain lies below sea level, in the flat deltas of the rivers Rhine, Maas and Scheldt, protected by natural dunes. This has led to the establishment of a long tradition of water management, supported by windmills, dykes, sluices and canals. It is by all means a man-made environment, being frequently restructured–also in the higher eastern areas. Around 1900 there was still about one third of 'uncultivated' land, but due to the rapid growth of the population and urbanisation, particularly in the post-WW2 period, the country has become almost entirely built up or cultivated (except for the specially designated nature reserves).

The Netherlands is strongly characterised by its great variety of both cultural landscapes and carefully spread towns of relatively small to medium sizes. These result partly from communal efforts to 'tame the waters', and partly from an age-old tradition of balancing political powers. Ever since the C11, the Dutch have reclaimed land for agriculture and settlements; first from wetlands, thereafter from the lakes, and in the C20 also from seas. Over time, these reclamations increased in scale and scope, culminating in the closing off of the *Zuiderzee* (1932) and the creation of the IJsselmeer polders (1930–76). In response to the disastrous sea flood of 1953, in the South-West, the spectacular Delta Works were made as advanced mega-structures for coastal defence and infrastructure. Most iconic of the traditional hydraulic engineering works are the C18 windmills at Kinderdijk, east of Rotterdam, meant to keep the *polders* dry. The marshy meadows serve for cattle-rearing. Arable fields are located mainly in the eastern provinces. The rivers and canals are

2 See for this section: De Mulder et al., 2019.

still important waterways connecting the *hinterland* with the (sea)ports and the many towns in the densely populated country. Only after the 1860s, due to state interventions, did a large network of railroads come into being after the first steam-powered line between Amsterdam and Haarlem was realised by private initiative (1839). The first *Rijkswegenplan* for national highways was approved as late as 1927, when the first airport, Schiphol, had already been functioning for ten years.

Natural resources were abundantly available for traditional construction works and building materials (for example timber, clay, reed, and sand), whereas natural stone and iron were relatively scarce. However, marl was dug out of the Pietersberg at Maastricht, where commercial production of cement started in 1926. While the usual resources for fuels such as wood and peat were locally exhausted by the end of the C19, the need for alternatives spurred on huge investments. Coal, necessary for steam-powered production and artificial gas, was largely imported from abroad but was also extracted from the southernmost soils of the country in Limburg. Here the Dutch government actively advanced local coal mining from 1900 onwards, partly in reaction to the undesirable effects of allowing private mining activities in Johannesburg. The first State Mine (active 1906–69) was named after Queen Wilhelmina and followed by four others. The 'carbon colonisation' of south Limburg, like the exploitation of resources in the Dutch colonies, brought drastic changes to the regional scenery and created a demand for many new settlements and amenities for the miners.[3] For the production of supporting pitwood, new forests were established by the newly created State Forest Service. Oil was mainly imported from the Dutch East Indies by private Dutch companies, which then also built refineries near the port of Rotterdam. Oil and natural gas were accidently discovered in the North-East of the Netherlands in 1943 (Schoonebeek) and 1959 (Slochteren), respectively. These new discoveries in the motherland were very welcome since the loss of its colony through the independence of the Republic of Indonesia in 1949, but the exploitation of these newfound resources also led to great transformations.

3 Tummers, 1974.

Kinderdijk and environs, aerial view of the ensemble of hydraulic works for the drainage of land for agriculture with windmills; photo 2007

Society and culture until 1940[4]

The Dutch population was about 5 million people by 1900 but it had grown to 11,5 million by 1961 (over 17 million today), accompanied by the on-going process of urbanisation. Despite their egalitarian spirit, rooted in the age old tradition of water management and the bourgeois culture of the late C16/early C17 Republic, a certain class consciousness and a tendency towards parochialism remained influential in Dutch society and culture during Queen Wilhelmina's fifty-year reign. In her time, not only did the emancipation of labour take shape, but there was also a fundamental cultural turn towards modernity in the arts and culture, as well as the political shift towards full parliamentary democracy.

In 1913 the Peace Palace at the Hague was inaugurated by the queen as the international Court of Justice with Library. Its idealistic peace-oriented intentions were fully embraced by the Dutch government, albeit largely for economic reasons. As a global trading nation, it proclaimed a strictly neutral position in foreign policy. Unlike many other European countries, the Netherlands was not directly engaged in the military conflict of the Great War, but it suffered from economic blockades and the torpedoing of her shipping vessels. About 200 000 men were called to arms and stayed mobilized for four years. Hence, these many side effects had a huge impact on daily life, such as the influx of one million Belgian refugees and increasing shortages of materials, housing, food and fuel. In part, but only temporarily, women could take over the vacant positions of the absent men. Immediately after the demobilisation the male breadwinners were again at work and the patriarchal family values reinstated, led by the dominant Christian democratic parties.

Apart from class, religion often played an important role in the populace's sense of belonging, at least until the 1960s. However, different belief systems also led to many disputes and splits. In general terms, the major rivers divide the country socio-geographically into the Protestant north (the Zeeland archipelago included) and the Catholic south. After the Reformation during the revolt against the Spanish (1568-1648), Noord-Brabant and Limburg did not then belong to the 'golden' Republic of the Netherlands where Calvinism had become the dominant religion.

There was, in fact, a richly differentiated and complicated patchwork of Dutch communities with different world-views – including liberals, Lutherans, Jewish and other – spread across the country. This diversity became increasingly visible in the built environment from the late C19. After the reinstatement of the Catholic episcopal hierarchy in 1853, the Catholics built many new churches, monasteries, schools and other institutions to manifest their regained power. The Gothic Revival style was often applied as a reference to the pre-Reformation period, particularly by the prominent architect of the time, Pierre Cuypers. At the same time, Protestant communities dynamically split into a great number of denominations, each establishing its own church building, often designed by local architects. The new build went on into the C20, mostly in more contemporary styles and in parallel with the (planned) extensions of towns and villages.[5]

Holland 1913, promotional poster with the Peace Palace in The Hague, issued by the Dutch Central Bureau for Tourism in 1913–14

The so-called Bible Belt emerged as a south-west-north-east transitional zone from Zeeland to Overijssel, with a high concentration of several orthodox Dutch Reformed communities critical of modernisation and secular state-funded education. These neo-Calvinists (or *Anti-Revolutionairs*) preferred the use of the pre-revolutionary *Statenbijbel* [State's bible] in church, schools and daily life. In response to the strict separation between Church and State in government, imposed since Napoleonic rule (1798), they had become engaged in an enduring *Schoolstrijd* [School conflict]. Just as the Catholics, they strove for the right to create denomination-based education and to also receive public financial support for the building of their own schools – which they finally achieved in 1917.

This outcome is part of the phenomenon of the *Verzuiling* [Pillarisation], by which the Dutch typified society that was practically organised and voluntary subdivided into all kinds of socio-culturally cohesive groups, each of whom then founded their own institutions. These varied from political parties and unions to housing corporations, hospitals, schools, universities and sports clubs, and suchlike. Unifying worldviews for these 'pillars' were either religious (Catholics, Protestants, Jews) or political (socialists, liberals). The communities were informed by associated

4 See for this section: Frijhoff & Spies, 2004; Wielenga, 2009.
5 Steensma & Van Swigchem, 1986.

Kollum, Dutch Reformed Church, Oosterkerk, interior, designed by Egbert Reitsma in 1924–25; photo 2017

newspapers, periodicals and, from 1924 on, also by broadcasting associations. For direct communication with the Dutch overseas colonies, a special interference-free radio station was built–exceptionally by the state–near Kootwijk (1918–22).[6]

Besides religious or political events, people could meet in public places such as libraries, theatres, cinemas, museums, art galleries, tearooms and pubs and occasionally in all kinds of clubs, both for debate, education and pleasure. Almost every town had such facilities and associated organisations, varying from local to regional or (inter)national, and from general to charitable, amateur, or professionally oriented. Their number is strikingly high in comparison with other countries, and they present important nodes in the complex network of social, cultural or trade connections in the Netherlands. Some of those societies already had a long history and a permanent location. In contrast, various progressive artists formed their own groups. They often manifested their existence and ideas through (alternative) exhibitions and illustrated magazines, such as *De Stijl* (1917–31) or *De Ploeg* (1918–28).[7]

Similarly, numerous local, regional or national associations and pressure groups were formed that dealt with history, heritage, landscapes and nature.

6 Weltens et al., 2002; Van der Pluijm, 2014.
7 Overy, 1991; Van der Ploeg, 2017.

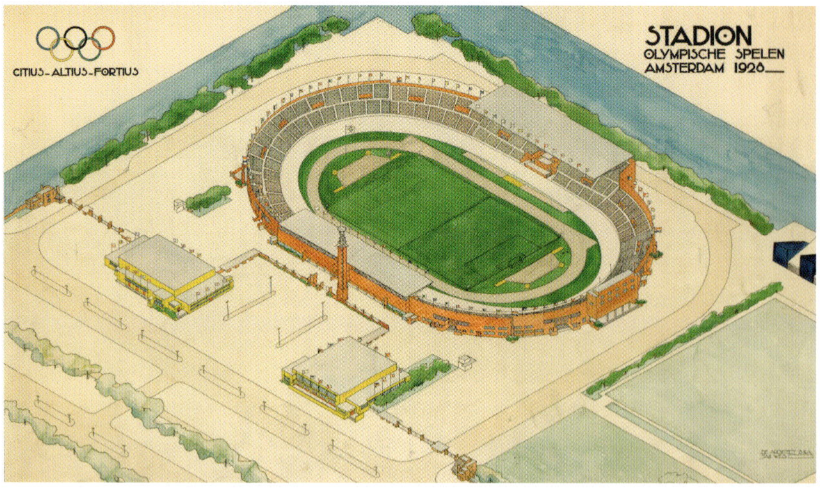

Amsterdam, Olympic Stadium, Marathon tower and side buildings, eye bird's view by Jan Wils, 1928

Leisure time became, incrementally, within reach of the labouring classes after the eight hours working day was introduced in 1919 by the Labour Act. Sunday was maintained as the weekly day-off for the whole of society, during which almost all shops were closed. Respect for the Lord's Day is still an issue in Dutch public life, although more exceptions were gradually allowed for cultural and sporting events, such as the 1928 Olympic Games held in Amsterdam.

Megen environs, unemployed workers digging for the partial canalisation of the river Maas, under supervision of the Heidemij in the 1930s

Poster advocating for women's suffrage, designed by Theo Molkenboer for the Women's Suffrage Association about 1912

In 1929 the country was not only unsettled by a strike in the Dutch agricultural sector but also by the immediate effects of the Wall Street Crash on the economy and daily life. Hundreds of thousands of workers lost their regular jobs. Poverty led to social unrest, culminating in the 1934 Jordaan riot in Amsterdam that was violently suppressed. A multitude of unskilled labour projects for public benefit provided the unemployed with work, though this was often arduous and located far from home, like the digging of canals, ponds and harbours; land reclamation and cultivation, or preparing airfields. Many facilities for recreation, public green spaces and infrastructure date back to this period of economic depression and are still in use.[8]

Politics and economy until 1940[9]

The first prime minister of the C20 in the Netherlands was the Anti-Revolutionary journalist/reverend Abraham Kuyper, who was fundamental in establishing the 'pillarisation' in both politics and society. He was the spokesman of the so-called *kleyne luyden*–orthodox reformed middle-class people–farmers, workers and petty-officials. At that time, under the census rule, they were deprived of their right to vote for parliament. Kuyper applied an ambivalent policy based on his antithesis of religious and secular parties.[10] On the one hand, he aimed at reducing state power as much as possible in family, education, or labour affairs, pleading for 'sovereignty in one's own circle'. On the other hand, he wanted to sustain the unity of the nation–the Dutch East Indies included–and to keep control over the labour class. Workers had started to build trade unions and collective funds and claimed civic rights. Initially, Kuyper reacted oppressively to the 1903 Strikes of Railroad Workers but later on he supported the formation of denomination-based trade unions and other organisations.

Nonetheless, it was under the liberal minority cabinet led by Pieter Cort van der Linden that the internal 'Pacification' was achieved, to resolve both the schooling question and the suffrage issue by way of revising the Constitution in 1917. The constitutional right to equal funding for worldview based schools was further elaborated in the 1920 School Act. Universal suffrage was introduced in two steps: first only for male voters and in 1919 also for women, together with party-list based proportional representation in government and compulsory voting.

Just as in church affairs, there was a large number of political parties and these did not agree at all about social-economic issues. In view of the contemporaneous outbreak of the Russian Revolution (1917), they had to search for compromises while communist ideals and a revolutionary spirit were also being bolstered in the Netherlands. Such a compromise regarded the support by the–predominantly pacifist–social-democratic workers party (SDAP) for the national policy of 'armed neutrality' during the Great War and consequently for mobilizing the army for defence of the Dutch territory.[11]

8 Van Balen, 1936.

9 See for this section: Griffiths & Van Zanden, 1989.

10 Bratt, 1998.

11 Lijphart, 2007.

Cartoon-like New Year's card depicting prime minister Hendrik Colijn relying on the Bible and the 'oil money', drawn by Patrick Kroon, about 1930

In November 1918, inspired by the recent events in Germany/Weimar Republic and taking note of social unrest among soldiers and workers, SDAP leader Pieter Jelles Troelstra called for a 'proletarian revolution' in the House of Representatives, finally without success. His action rather reinforced the position of the confessionals in national government during the following interwar period. In local politics, however, the social-democrats had substantial influence, specially favouring the construction of affordable housing for workers. The associated youth movement, AJC, found broad support, aiming at the cultural upliftment of working class youth through diverse common activities.[12]

As for (inter)national politics and the economy, the Anti-Revolutionary Hendrikus Colijn, a man with a remarkably chequered career and international experience, had become a major player in a variety of roles.[13] When prime minister in the 1930s, facing the economic crisis and increasing tensions, his austerity policies proved difficult to maintain. State investments were made for employment, supervision, infrastructure and military defence. Most conspicuous was the execution of the *Zuiderzee* works (further discussed below).

Meanwhile, Colijn took a firm stand against the emerging anti-democratic movements, such as the National Socialist Movement (NSB). This fascist party was led by a former engineer of the Utrecht Provincial *Waterstaat*, Anton Mussert, and modelled on the Nazi party in neighbouring Germany. Against the backdrop of the depression, the NSB quickly attracted thousands of followers and had several representatives in Parliament and provincial councils through democratic elections. Since late 1933, however, NSB-membership was formally prohibited for civil servants; some years later serious democratic parties, trade unions and churches took prohibitionist measures when they became aware of the dangers of fascism.[14]

12 Woltjer, 2001.
13 Colijn was a former military officer in Dutch East Indies, former Minister of War, ad interim of the Navy and since 1914 director of the Bataafsche Petroleum Maatschappij (BPM, later part of Shell) and led various delegations; Langeveld, 2004.
14 Van der Heijden, 2009.

July 1939 saw an end to Colijn's last cabinet, due to the huge governmental dilemmas raised by the economic crisis, the influx of German refugees and contrasting priorities. The new centre-left coalition was headed by Dirk Jan de Geer (Christian Historical Union). Confronted with the grim international developments around the neutral Netherlands, he prompted a general mobilization in August and reinforcement of defensive works, still trusting that this strategy would save the country from war.[15]

WW2 and partial decolonisation[16]

Despite the carefully sought neutrality between the United Kingdom and Nazi Germany, the Netherlands was brutally invaded on May 10, 1940. The attacks were part of Adolf Hitler's military strategy to prevent Allied forces from coming closer to his *Third Reich*. The fierce resistance of the Dutch caused, unintentionally, the successive devastations of the inner cities of Rotterdam and Middelburg by bombardments. The great losses forced the Dutch army to capitulate, but Queen Wilhelmina and her ministers had escaped to London and formed an anti-German government of the Netherlands in exile. Just before the Dutch Commander-in-chief, Henri Winkelman, was captured, he had issued two important orders for the *wederopbouw* [reconstruction/rebuilding] and appointed civil engineer Johan Ringers as the government commissioner in these matters.

Meanwhile, the general secretaries (heads of state administration) were charged with the implementation of Dutch national policy in daily affairs. At provincial and local government level, the administration initially remained more or less intact. After the installation of the Austrian Nazi governor Arthur Seyss-Inquart as the *Reichskommissar for the Occupied Netherlands* (29 May 1940), two parallel administrative systems reigned for the next five years, with increasing pressure from the Nazi party–and NSB–on the Dutch population.

The Nazi ideology aimed at incorporating the Low Lands into the Greater Germanic Reich, based on supposed similarities in culture and race. Soon harsher measures were imposed to advance the 'nazification' of society, its press and administration; non-nazist organisations were forbidden.

15 Nuij, 2000.
16 See for this section: Barnouw, 2017.

Rotterdam, aerial view of the wartime devastation in the historic city with partially surviving Laurens Church in 1940

Most horrendous was the systematic oppression and persecution of the Jewish people, ending in the Holocaust. Resistance was cruelly countered, but it continued underground.

Forced labour for German factories was introduced in two stages; hiding was the only way to escape, and it was not easy. While food and other goods became scarce (being diverted to Nazi Germany), a rationing system was applied, only accessible to those who were officially registered. Architects, artists and journalists often decided to hide, since it had become compulsory to register in the Dutch *Kultuurkamer* (a Nazi institution) to get a licence to work.

From 1 July 1942 on, hardly anything could be built anymore in the Netherlands due to the German building ban. This rule aimed at collecting all construction materials and workers for the building of the *Atlantikwall* as a German defence system along the North Sea coast. To make way for this broad military zone, 300 000 people were forcefully evacuated and their homes and buildings were torn down; the national Dutch civil administration was forced to move to the east of the country.[17]

17 Bosma & Wagenaar, 1995; Mellink et al., 2017.

Scheveningen coastal zone near The Hague with concrete works of the German *Atlantikwall*, shortly after the liberation in 1945

After the Allied invasion on the Normandy coast, in June 1944, the southern Netherlands was, by the autumn, liberated from German occupation. In contrast, the subsequent battles of the Liberation offensive added the harshest war-time year to the Dutch population north of the major rivers, since the Allies had failed to cross the river Rhine at Arnhem by Operation Market Garden. The accompanying rail road strike was perpetuated, and consequently, the scarcity of food, fuel and materials increased. In the western cities in particular, people suffered severely during the Hunger Winter. Intensive air raids, field battles and summoned inundations hit both towns and agricultural areas, causing great casualties.

At long last, the German army in the Dutch mainland surrendered on May 5, 1945. This date is still the national festive day of the Netherlands to celebrate the Liberation. For people in the Dutch East Indies, however, WW2 went on until the pro-German Japanese army, that had hastily occupied this colony from 1942, capitulated on August 15, 1945. Two days later, the leader of the National Indonesian Party, Sukarno, proclaimed the independence of Indonesia from the Netherlands. This unilateral action was met with a furious response from the reinstated Dutch government in the motherland, that ordered two military actions against the local revolt but also agreed to negotiate their decolonisation.

Finally, the long-awaited transfer of Dutch sovereignty to the recognized Republic of Indonesia (excluding New Guinea) took place in December 1949 under the reign of the new Dutch Queen Juliana, who had succeeded her mother after Wilhelmina's abdication in September 1948. However, another conflict arose in the former colony after the declaration of independence of the Republic of Malaku South (RMS) in Ambon in April 1950. Here, the majority of the population consisted of Christians; many had professionally served the Royal Dutch East Indies Army (KNIL) and fought for the Dutch cause. While the RMS did not receive recognition, the Dutch government had to take care of the former KNIL officers and their families. So, about 12 500 South Moluccans were transported to the Netherlands, where their arrival put yet more pressure on the huge housing shortage. In anticipation of their later return, they were provisionally accommodated in 90 *woonoorden* [assigned places for living] and kept more or less in isolation.[18]

18 Freriks, 2015.

Westerbork, overview of the 'transit camp' during the Nazi occupation, 1944

Westerbork, 'repatriated' families from the South Moluccan islands living in the former camp barracks, then renamed as *woonoord Schattenberg*, in 1951

In fact, they could not return, and the Dutch government gradually developed new policies to tackle the inland effects of decolonisation, with mixed success in integration and housing. The continued dispute on the transfer of West Guinea to Indonesia was finally resolved in 1962 through the intervention of the United Nations.[19]

Post-war politics and economy until 1961[20]

The first post-war cabinet, an 'emergency' coalition of Christian democrats and socialists, was tasked with reinstating Dutch order and making a start with the reconstruction of the heavily devastated and totally depleted country. For this huge challenge, a centrally devised *Bouwplan* [Construction plan] was presented for the construction of public works and buildings, as well as central guidelines for the design of subsidised dwellings.

Unlike the interwar situation, the Dutch government now wanted to keep close control of the national economy, including prices and wages, but not without consultation with the 'social partners'. Due to the scarcity of food, goods, construction materials and houses, the centralised rationing system from the war-time period was maintained. A radical monetary reform was implemented, together with new banknotes, to render all circulating black-market money worthless. Special courts and tribunals were installed to judge traitors and collaborators with the Nazi regime and to have the guilty ones punished after trial, including some architects.[21]

A similar policy of major state engagement for common revival was continued by the next–democratically elected–cabinet of Catholics, socialists, and non-affiliated notables. The reconstruction of the main infrastructure was a top priority, as was the revival of the major economic sectors and of international connections. Tackling the immense shortage of housing and other accommodations proved a long-term affair for the growing Ministry of Reconstruction and Housing. Initially, provisional solutions were sought, such as constructing 'emergency dwellings' and implementing the 1947 Act on Dwelling Spaces to enforce 'living-in' in other people's houses, particularly those of the elderly. The use of standardisation and pre-fabricated elements for mass housing and farm buildings was encouraged but also bound to the approval of the central Foundation *Ratiobouw* (established in 1944).[22]

As for foreign affairs, the Dutch government decided to join new international organisations, such as the United Nations and NATO. The Netherlands emphatically sided with the western alliances at the onset of the Cold War. The American Marshall Plan (1948–51) was instrumental in (re)building large-scale industries and fostering the mechanisation of agriculture. Modern American equipment was provided to extract petroleum in South-East Drenthe. The associated programme of technical assistance and specific study trips to the United States gradually stimulated a wider acceptance of the American way of life and a more consumerist orientation of the populace.[23] However, the socialist prime minister, Willem Drees, who stayed on until December 1958, was known for his sobriety in every respect.

19 Penders, 2002.
20 See for this section: Schuyt & Taverne, 2004.
21 Keuning, 2017.
22 Siraa, 1989.
23 Ibelings, 1997.

Arnhem, rebuilding the destroyed Rhine bridge (that was "too far" for Operation Market Garden) in 1949

Oil drilling in the rural region of South East Drenthe near Schoonebeek in 1945

Goeree Island with flooded houses after the Great Flood Disaster of 1 February, 1953

Besides the physical reconstruction, the coalition also considered the restoration of public morality an important task, to be based on generally shared spiritual values in which Christianity held a greater share. The 'pillarisation' was thus re-established, even in public television broadcasting. Both public and 'special' education was fully supported at all levels. Hundreds of new, often temporary, school buildings were erected for increasing numbers of children, caused by the post-war 'baby boom'. Much attention was paid to the formation of craftsmen and the extension of higher economic and technological education, as well as to the liberal arts. In 1951 a special regulation was established that 1,5 % of the construction costs of new government buildings (ranging from tax offices to schools) be applied for their artistic decoration. Widespread support was given to countless cultural facilities, performances, educational and art exhibitions. One of those was the national Jan van Riebeeck festival held in 1952 at his birthplace, Culemborg, to commemorate the Dutch landing on the Cape of 300 years before.[24]

Just when the post-war reconstruction began to show substantial progress, the South-West part of the Netherlands was hit by the disastrous North Sea flood in early 1953. In the aftermath of the country's war-damage recuperation, the 'Delta Plan' was conceived by a special committee as a national project to construct a series of dams, sluices, and storm surge barriers to prevent future floods in the Rhine-Meuse-Scheldt delta, and to control both the dynamic levels and water quality of these rivers. Five years later the Delta Act was approved and its subsequent execution would give an enormous boost to Dutch civil engineering.

Almost at the same time, the government built on general social security by introducing government pensions for all Dutch residents aged 65 or older and advancing the construction of new retirement homes. Drees had a great part in this preparation, but he stepped down after disagreement with his coalition partners about the national budget.[25] In the next cabinets up until 1965, the socialists were no longer represented, and the central control of wages became gradually loosened. Yet the creation of the social welfare state went on, which could be partly financed by the exploitation of the newly found natural gas resources in the north of the country. In 1961 the 'free Saturday' was collectively introduced for factory and office workers and civil servants. The extra leisure time brought a consumerist turn towards a 'consumption society' after the preceding period of extremely hard work and moderation.

24 Van Ledden, 2005.
25 Brouwer & Van der Heiden, 1995.

Amsterdam, dinner hall of the Willem Drees retirement home for (socialist) elderly people, designed by Tuynman & Snellebrand in 1957 (recently demolished)

Civil engineering[26]

The typical geographical conditions of the 'Lowlands' require intensive civil engineering, not only (proverbially) to 'keep Dutch feet dry', but also for all sorts of infrastructure. The term *civil* engineering was introduced as the counterpart to the military discipline after the Royal Academy was founded at Delft (1842) and the formation of professional engineers received a boost after the *Technische Hoogeschool* was established as its academic successor (1905).[27] Historically, works related to the construction and management of waterways, flood defences and polders, belonged to the domain of 'wet' civil engineering. The 'dry' civil engineers dealt mainly with the construction of railways and roadways. Both branches developed in the C20, their professional competencies narrowly intertwined with the expanding knowledge of reinforced concrete and the emergence of private companies besides the State or Province run *Waterstaat* departments. Steel (and later aluminium), is also applied in many civil engineering works, such as bridges, roof constructions, frames and masts.[28]

One pioneering project was the *Hofpleinlijn* viaduct (1904–08) in Rotterdam, constructed in reinforced concrete for the first electrified railroad in the Netherlands. Other civil works stretched from silos to water towers, houses and even a church cupola. The innovative hyperbolic form of concrete cooling towers was conceived by State Mines director Frederik van Iterson in 1917–19 and found following world-wide.

The completion of the 30 km long Afsluitdijk [Enclosure Dyke], in 1932, with two sets of sluices crowned by concrete lift towers at either end, was the key work for all other audacious South Sea Works. These

26 See for this section: Van der Ham, 1999; Heerding, 1971.
27 The precursor of the current Delft University of Technology, the Military Academy moved to Breda; Baudet, 1992; see also the interlude on Educating the Dutch architect.
28 Den Ouden, 1994.

Rotterdam, part of the 1901 reinforced concrete viaduct for the ZHESM rail connection with The Hague/Scheveningen; photo 2003

Brunssum, hyperbolic cooling towers, originally built for State Mine Emma about 1918; photo 1977 (since demolished)

Closure Dyke under construction, with the discharge sluices to the right, 1932

Lock in the newly dug Lek Canal near Nieuwegein, named after the new-born princess Beatrix, photographed shortly after the inauguration in 1938

included the reclamation of the *Wieringermeer* in North Holland and the creation of 'New Land' with the North-East polder and two Flevopolders on the former sea bottom, as well as the building of pumping stations (designed by Dirk Roosenburg), bridges and temporary camps for the workers.[29]

To improve the navigability and water supply quality of the major waterways, various new or reworked canals, sluices and weirs were realised under the supervision of State and Provincial Waterstaat departments, partly as employment projects during the 1930s; for instance, the newly dug Lek Canal and the 'twin pair' of the Princess Beatrix Lock (1938).

29 Ministerie van Verkeer en Waterstaat, 1959.

Hagestein, visor weirs in the river Lek near Hagestein with (covered) hydro power installation to the left, designed by RWS and Wouter Hamdorff; photo 2010

The new southern stretch of the Amsterdam-Rhine Canal was finally accomplished in 1952, together with the Prince Bernhard Lock. Meanwhile, the first Dutch subaquatic tunnel, underneath the Nieuwe Maas River, was opened in 1942 in Rotterdam.

The 1953 flood in the South-West Netherlands led to the impressive Delta Works, intended for the closing off the estuaries in Zeeland with dams and dykes and the control of the salinity and levels of the major rivers. This started with the Storm Flood Barrier in the river Hollandsche IJssel, at Capelle, near Rotterdam (1954–58). In addition, the Lower Rhine was reshaped by canalised short-cuts and three pairs of visor-like weirs near Hagestein, Amerongen and Driel (1953–69, Pieter Blokland and Wouter Hamdorff). The Hagestein ensemble contained an in-built hydro power installation in the centre to deliver electricity to the residents of Utrecht.[30]

At the time, they were built almost in the middle of nowhere. The same applies for the first series of five tall concrete radio transmitter towers by Anton Auer, that were constructed for national television reception in the Netherlands and a connection with the Eurovision network. They all brought, by function and appearance, modernity to remote areas.

Central part of garden village 't Lansink at Hengelo, designed by Karel Muller and Pieter Wattez for machine factory director Charles Stork in 1911; photo 1979

Physical planning[31]

The Dutch tradition of making towns and polders was largely based on military and civil technological considerations. The 1901 national Housing Act marked a new era of growing government intervention regarding the quality of (social) housing and physical planning after decades of liberalism that had precipitated the rise of slums. Municipalities counting over 10 000 inhabitants were now required to draw up urban extension plans, indicating the new infrastructure, functional zoning and location of

30 Bosma, 1995.

31 See for this section: Wagenaar, 2015.

Een-kamer woning, Huurprijs f 1.50 à f 1.70 per week.

Twee-kamer woningen. Huurprijs f 2.60 per week.

Drie-kamer-woningen. Huurprijs f 3.— per week.

Differentiated typology of subsidised low-cost housing in Leeuwarden from: *Friesland en de Woningwet*, 1913

(semi-) public facilities. They were entitled to expropriate land for such urban planning, without which further building was prohibited, but in practice this proved frequently problematic.

Construction sites often had to be raised by pumping sand slurry, as well as the adaption and/or creating of waterways and infrastructure. Over and above considerations of safety and hygiene, the development of greenery and aesthetics came into play, though there were few Dutch architects and engineers available for such a complex task, since initially not many had specific training in urban design. The procedures for the new extensions, to be approved by the provincial authorities and city council, usually took several years. Some municipalities invited private architects for envisioning the urban design, others commissioned their own staff of Public Works for which architects were also appointed.

Meanwhile, some enlightened industrialists, inspired by English and German examples, established company towns for their workers, like 't Lansink (1910–23) at Hengelo for Stork's machinery factory, Heyplaat (1914–18) for the Rotterdam Dry Dock Company and Heveadorp (1916–19) for the rubber factory near Renkum. The independent garden village Vreewijk, in Rotterdam South (1916–42), was initiated by three socially engaged men and intended for all workers in need of affordable rented houses. They engaged architects Hendrik Berlage for the core's lay-out and Marinus Granpré Molière for the adjacent parts and housing. Special attention was paid to the public green, differentiated street profiles and incorporation of pre-existing landscape elements like watercourses, ditches and dykes. The low-rise terrace houses, with small front and back gardens, made Vreewijk a key reference for other small-scale extensions elsewhere in the Netherlands.[32]

For larger urban extensions with higher densities in (semi-) closed blocks, Berlage – trained at Zürich and a convinced socialist – was greatly influential. He pleaded for coherent townscapes as a collection of 'rhythmic spaces', articulated by well-situated community buildings, unified multi-storeyed housing blocks and differentiated streets. His reworked design for the Amsterdam South extension (1915, approved 1917) was exemplary (though executed by expressionist architects), as was his monumental Mercator Square project in Amsterdam-West.[33]

The inter-war extensions of Spangen, Bergpolder and Blijdorp at Rotterdam were developed by the Public Works Department. Granpré Molière and Pieter Verhagen had worked there before they started a private practice in 1916 and collaborated on Vreewijk. Both were trained at Delft and strove for a human-orientated built environment, with carefully designed streetscapes filled with public greenery and gardens. Molière was a great promoter of integrated planning–from housing to landscaping–and vice-chair of the Urbanism Council of the Netherlands Institute of Housing and Town Planning. He was appointed professor in architectural design in 1924 at Delft and converted to Catholicism three years later, but remained associated with his firm. With Verhagen, Molière was also involved in regional planning, showing a great concern for the scenery of the rural areas. They fully designed the landscapes and villages of the new IJsselmeer polders, in a mixture of modern analytics and traditionalist forms. Each village was laid out around a green and provided with churches of three denominations, community buildings, schools, shops and terraced houses in the main.[34]

All designs for the Northeast Polder (dry by 1942) – including its infrastructure, vegetation, villages, farm buildings and even the selection of farmers – particularly reinforced the Dutch idea of *maakbaarheid* [makeability] as a conceptual framework for planning, that became increasingly important in the C20 as a professional discipline in both the built environment and society. Whereas Molière and his followers sought continuity and familiarity in their three-dimensional planning, the Dutch members of the *Congrès Internationaux d'Architecture Moderne* (CIAM) promoted functionalist planning schemes with separated zoning for living, working, traffic and recreation, and an abundance of public greenery. These principles were first applied in the 1934 General Extension Plan for Amsterdam (AUP) by Cor van Eesteren, head of the Municipal Urban Development Department and chairman of the CIAM. By way of exception, the Dutch CIAM members, associated in *de 8* and *Opbouw*, were allowed to draft a modernist polder village, Nagele (1947–54) and later a new town, Lelystad (1950–67) in eastern Flevoland – both with orthogonal patterns and flat-roofed buildings.[35]

32 Korthals Altes, 2004.
33 Polano, Fanelli, De Heer, & Van Rossem, 1989.
34 Kuiper, 1991; Steenhuis, 2007.
35 Van der Wal, 1997.

Plantation plan of the North East Polder with Emmeloord in the centre, 1947

Promotional poster for the 'ruilverkaveling' [land consolidation], issued by the Cultuurtechnische Dienst Utrecht in 1946

Sadly, the War had caused great destruction and delays in construction. Post-war reconstruction was an unprecedented challenge of physical planning in the Netherlands, apart from the need to create large new neighbourhoods. The plans were locally developed but nationally steered by the Ministry of Reconstruction, Housing, Building Industry and Spatial Planning, for which Ringers had laid the foundations during the War and immediately thereafter as minister. In the name of progress, huge interventions took place in both urban fabric and the countryside. After comprehensive consultation, many farmers were forced to move to modern farms and reconfigured plots in the framework of land consolidation programmes that were directed to mechanized agriculture, better drainage, modern facilities, and cultural elevation.[36] To this day, the Dutch are constantly busy in shaping and reshaping their environment.

Housing[37]

Even before the national Housing Act came into effect in 1902, some charities and corporations had provided affordable and qualitatively reasonable housing for workers, albeit often on small scale. The act allowed for governmental financial support, diversity in drafting local building codes as well as for slum clearance and substitution programs. It implied an increasing control, at all administrative levels, of budgets and the constructive, hygienic and architectural qualities of the housing. For instance, so-called back-to-back houses and box beds were now forbidden. Based on detailed norms and sizes, a great variety of dwelling plans were developed within a restrictive classification system related to income-groups and number of rooms. In the north-western province of Friesland, family dwellings dominated, terraced or (semi-)detached. In the southern mining region collective bachelor homes were also built amidst the new company towns of the State Mines, for which special housing associations were in charge (mainly Catholic).[38]

36 Andela, 2000.
37 See for this section: De Vreeze, 1993; Huisman et al., 2000.
38 Van Welderen Rengers, & Faber, 1913; Hofstee et al., 1978.

The quickly growing village of Hilversum appointed Willem Dudok Director of Public Works in 1915, thus bringing the design of the urban layout, public facilities and public housing more or less in one hand, like his first municipal housing scheme, with an overarching public library building between the terraced dwellings. These were built in brick, with wooden doors and window frames, crowned by high pitched tiled roofs. Variation was sought in emphasizing corner houses and mirroring normal dwelling types in between, with living rooms at the front, kitchens at the back and bedrooms in the attic.

Similar principles of subtly varied small-sized family houses were frequently applied in the suburban neighbourhoods built between 1910 and 1930 throughout the Netherlands. In the major towns, however, higher densities were urgently required to accommodate the thousands of working-class families, of whom a great many lived in shacks.

In Amsterdam, multi-storeyed mass housing in closed or semi-open urban blocks was facilitated by the extension plans for South and West, but without a–costly–elevator it was not permitted to build higher than four upper floors. Common well-lit stairwells were located just behind the façades, sometimes partly at street level to provide more individuals access to the dwellings on the upper floors.

Most housing schemes were executed by the–pillarised–housing associations and their particular preferences–be it a separate kitchen, a parlour or individual access–were mainly hidden by the collective street fronts of the urban blocks. Such differentiation can be noted in the Zaanhof ensemble opposite the famous *Eigen Haard* [Own Hearth] scheme 'Het Schip' (by Michel de Klerk) during and shortly after the Great War. The Protestant association 'Patrimonium' built the outer ring with outer stairs, the socialist 'Het Westen' the inner ring with public green and playgrounds, accessible through arches, and a lower section was built by the Railroad Workers Association.[39]

39 Stieber, 1998.

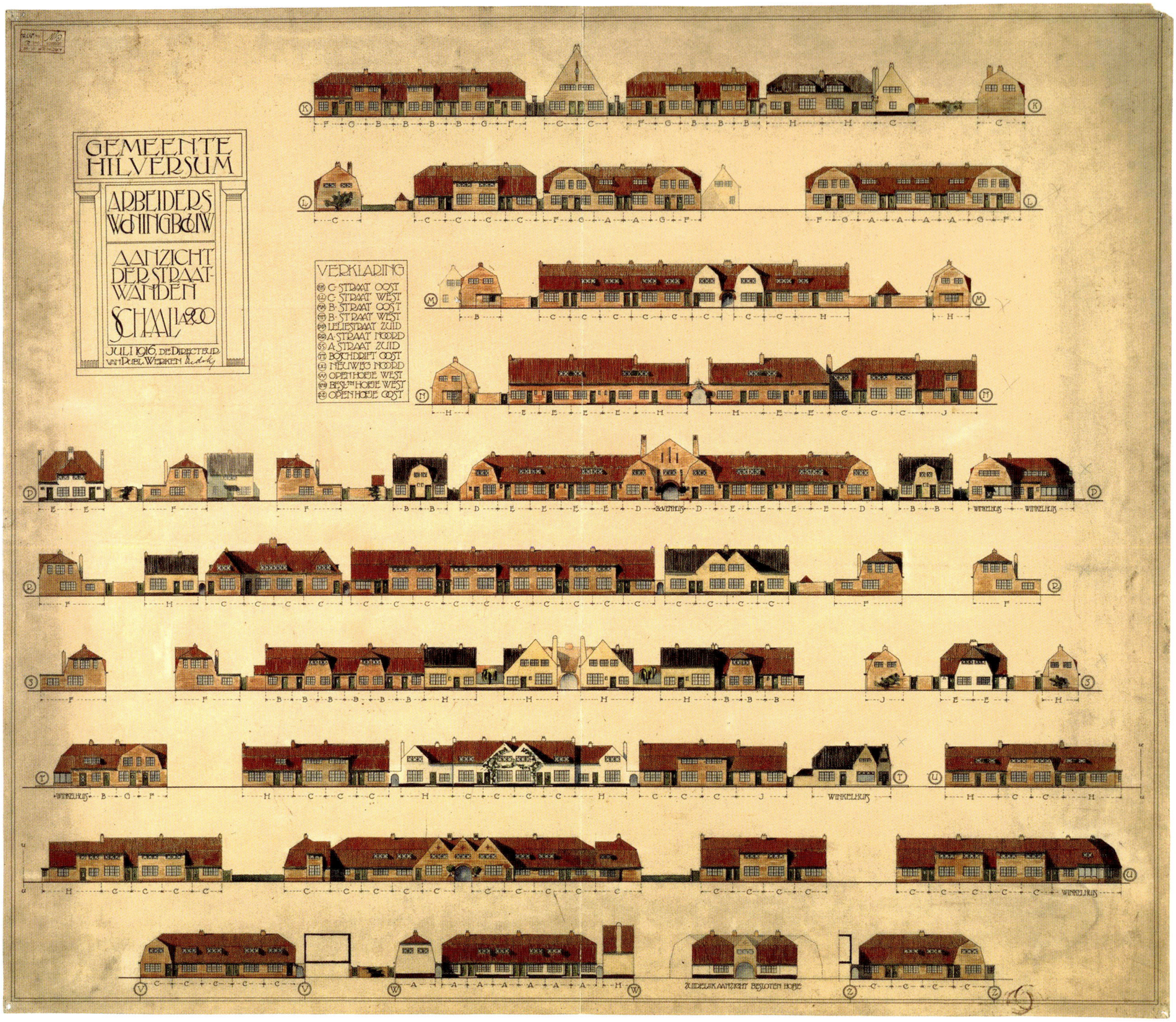

Hilversum, first scheme for subsidised housing, designed by city architect Willem Dudok in 1915–19

Nevertheless, for reasons of cost effectiveness, the central government tried to encourage architects and housing associations to adopt standardization (in plans and types) and normalisation (of measures and construction elements) by issuing regulations and conditional state support. This was met with still serious reservations, as both designers and clients feared a restriction of their freedom of choosing forms, materials, and layouts.

Amsterdam, Concrete Village, concrete housing constructed with the Bims Beton Bouw system and geometric ornaments in tar, all designed by JB van Loghem; photo 1926

In response to the immediate shortage of housing and raw materials in those days, coupled with rising wages for bricklayers, some municipalities with socialist aldermen had initiated remarkable experiments of building houses in concrete. The best-known example is the Amsterdam *Betondorp* [Concrete Village], part of the larger 'Garden Village Watergraafsmeer' and built in 1922–25 as the testing field for ten different concrete systems. The 900 tiny dwellings had flat roofs (at the time unusual) and two floors, partly and temporarily subdivided as 'duplexes' for accommodating two families in one unit. Governmental support implied far reaching maternalistic control over way of life, both for public health, economic and moral reasons. The families were carefully selected amongst skilled labour groups and civil servants, and the homes' cleanliness was regularly controlled by municipal inspectors who collected the weekly rents.[40]

Even larger control was exerted over so-called 'asocial' families, considered undesirable renters and incapable of inhabiting their homes properly. Dozens of *woonscholen* were developed to teach the elsewhere inadmissible families 'living well' between 1914 and 1970, as a complementary governmental engagement with the socially disabled in society, together with slum clearance and relocation in new housing schemes.[41]

40 Kuipers, 1987.
41 Dercksen & Verplanke, 1987; www.canonsociaalwerk.eu/1918 - woonschool Zeeburgerdorp.

The majority of rented housing, however, was built by private companies (just as the private houses for the well-to-do clients). They preferred the traditional construction methods and plans, but some also developed new types, such as apartments for single women. During the interwar period few tower-blocks were built for labour families. The modernist Bergpolderflat in Rotterdam, the first with outer corridors, is the major exception (1933-34, Van Tijen, Brinkman & van der Vlugt) and this prototype would be extensively followed in the post-war neighbourhoods. After the traumatic War, the housing shortage was called public enemy number one. Previous reservations about repetition, normalisation, standardisation, prefabrication and high-rise in subsidised housing were put aside in order to speed up production. New experiments with non-traditional construction methods were broadly stimulated, often in combination with open urban planning, for example Pendrecht in Rotterdam. Compact units with a living room, three bedrooms (for parents, girls and boys), kitchen, toilet, bath cell and balcony or loggia were built in vast numbers, alternated by small dwellings for singles and elderly people. All were orderly arranged for receiving sun, light, and fresh air, with great views onto public greens and works of art.

Amsterdam, aerial view of the Spaarndammerplantsoen and Zaanhof housing ensemble, built for different housing corporations in 1915–20; photo about 1999

Rotterdam, Bergpolderflat, the first gallery flat block in the Netherlands, designed by Brinkman, Van der Vlugt & Van Tijen for the *N.V. Volkswoningbouw*, in 1933; photo 1934/35

The idealistic organisation *Goed Wonen* [Good Living] propagated the use of light furniture and modern living by means of magazines and model homes, for which interior architects delivered designs. Despite the constant claim of modernity, the traditional role division of outdoor working men and indoor nurturing 'housewives' persisted during the post-war reconstruction period.[42]

42 Kuipers, 2019.

Architecture[43]

For centuries Dutch architecture was defined by the use of load-bearing brick walls and pitched roofs covered by–for the most part, ceramic–roof tiles in all sorts of variations. The rationalist Stock Exchange by Hendrik Berlage (1898–1903) in Amsterdam, generally acclaimed as the first modern building in the Netherlands, also has these characteristics. The bare bricks are not only shown in the elongated façades, but also in the solemn interiors as a deliberate expression of the honest use of materials, in contrast to the preceding period of neo-styles and imitations. With the incorporated art works it forms a ground-breaking *Gesamtkunstwerk* for new community ideals. As a convinced social-democrat, Berlage applied the same design principles in the simultaneously erected diamond workers union building (ANDB), which evoked less controversy than the Beurs did with its capitalist clients. As a counter-piece, a new exchange building was opened nearby (1911–14, Jos Cuypers), with an innovative reinforced concrete construction and a classicist inspired exterior suitable for the historic streetscape.

This new historicising or '*um 1800*' style, forging reinterpretations of Louis XVI-like elements (pilasters, frontons, bay windows, garlands, rustication, towers) with modern, yet partially hidden technology and comfort, was favoured for commercial buildings, like banking offices and department stores, but also for the country houses of their directors.[44] The former office of the Co-operative Central Farmers Bank in Eindhoven (1909, Jan Stuyt) and the Van Thiel House at Helmond (1930, Jan Hanrath) are typical examples of this retrospective movement.

43 See for this section: Buch 1993; Groenendijk & Vollaard, 2006.
44 This term was coined after Mebes, P. (1908), Um 1800: Architektur und Handwerk im letzten Jahrhundert ihrer traditionellen Entwicklung, Munich: F. Bruckmann.

Rotterdam, Pendrecht, view of Plein 1953 square with subsidised housing in apartment blocks on 'pilotis', urban planning designed by Lotte Stam-Beese in 1949–53; photo 2002

Amsterdam, two Stock Exchange buildings, left designed by H.P. Berlage in 1897–1903, right designed by Jos.Th. Cuypers in 1911–14; photo 2017

Eindhoven, former Central Co-operative Farmers Bank building designed by Jan Stuyt in 1909–12; photo 2009

Meanwhile, new directions were explored to combine custom-made functionality with an architectural expression of the early C20 period, initiated by the a-historicist *Art Nouveau* or *Jugendstil* designs with curved lines and floral motifs, as well as the rationalist renewal based on well-considered proportioning and an emphasis on constructive elements. One trend regards the expressionism of the 'Amsterdam School', full of fantasy in forms, ornamentation, plans and application of materials. The picturesque *Scheepvaarthuis* at Amsterdam (1913–16), built for several shipping companies and in every detail another *Gesamtkunstwerk*, is the earliest example. Remarkably, two of its designers, Joan Melchior van der Meij and Piet Kramer, were then affiliated with the municipal Public Works department as aesthetics advisors besides their private practice. Their engagement was part of the ambitious policy of the capital city to present itself as a similarly beautiful city in the contemporary era as it was in the Golden Age, by means of nicely designed bridges, municipal offices and service buildings, public schools and 'street furniture'.[45]

Housing corporations were encouraged to commission talented architects like De Klerk, Kramer, Margaret Kropholler and Henk Wijdeveld for their multi-storeyed blocks, elaborated with plasticly shaped street fronts and originality in detailing. This artistic trend also spread to other towns and was partly adopted for various state buildings, too.

Fundamentally different was the *Nieuwe Bouwen* [New Building], that focused on functionality, transparency, hygiene and efficient use of advanced construction methods with industrial materials like steel,

45 Van Schaik, 2018.

Amsterdam, former shipping companies' office, designed by Joan van der Meij, Michel de Klerk and Piet Kramer with JG and ADN van Gendt in 1913–15; photo about 1925

glass and reinforced concrete. The modernist architects embraced prefabrication and standardization for the sake of cost reduction and equality. They hardly allowed ornaments, preferred geometric forms and flat roofs, and wanted materials, surfaces, and varied colours to speak for themselves in 'pure' architecture (like Jan Gerko Wiebenga's Technical school at Groningen, 1922–23).

With the 'constructivist' Schröder House in Utrecht (1924), painted in primary colours and non-colours, architect/cabinet-maker Gerrit Rietveld gave expression to the abstract ideals of the *De Stijl* movement, while also introducing new ways of living in inner spaces (sliding doors, light furniture, corner windows). He was among the first CIAM conference participants (1928), but the functionalist concepts were most actively spread in the Netherlands by the members and journal of *de 8* and *Opbouw*. Both concrete and brick façades were often whitewashed to express cleanliness and lightness, just as the large portions of glass and balconies meant openness and access to fresh air and healing sunshine – very important in view of the continuous threat of tuberculosis (such as Jan Duiker's Nirwana tower block at The Hague, 1927, Open Air

Utrecht, Schröder House, designed by Gerrit Rietveld in 1924; photo 2012

School at Amsterdam and Zonnestraal sanatorium at Hilversum, both 1928–31).[46] The lucid Van Nelle Factory in Rotterdam (Brinkman & Van der Vlugt, 1928–31), commissioned by the theosophist Kees van der Leeuw, was created as a healthy working environment inside and outside. Its modernist architecture widely appealed due to the curtain walls of steel and glass, mushroom columns of reinforced concrete, dynamic overhead bridges and circular viewing pavilion on top.[47]

However well-intentioned, the 'new builders' met with much criticism, both for their sometimes rather sterile designs, rigid opinions about 'good' or 'bad' architecture and radical rupture with the past. Internal tensions made 'Group '32' split off, and their members, including Albert Boeken, Arthur Staal, Sybold van Ravesteyn and others, were not shy to apply curved lines and ornaments inspired by baroque creations.[48]

46 Molema *et al.*, 1996.
47 Kuipers, 2017.
48 Bock et al., 1983.

Truly traditionalist was the 'Delft School', named after its foreman Granpré Molière's teachings about eternal values, harmony, and beauty at the Polytechnic. The simplicity of traditional rural architecture and their local materials was an important source of inspiration for modestly designed houses. Yet, a solid monumentality was sought for public and religious buildings in their masses and volumes (like Enschede Town Hall, 1933, Gijsbert Friedhoff) to underline their prominent functions for society and townscape.

As a side-branch, artisanal regionalism took shape, modelled on local cottages and alike but larger in size and more comfortable inside, as demonstrated by the brick-built villas with impressive undulating roofs of reed in '*Gooise landhuisstijl'*. The emphasis on the *streekeigen* (region specific) character as a strong quality, often supported by heritage champions, became unintentionally compromised in other regions when it was appropriated by adepts of the Nazi *Blut und Boden* [blood and soil] ideology.[49]

49 Bond Nederlandse Architecten, 1941.

Rotterdam, Van Nelle Factory, designed by Jan Brinkman and Leen van der Vlugt in 1925–31; photo 2011

Hilversum, Town Hall, designed by Willem Dudok in 1928–31; photo 2020

Laren, villa *De Rietvink*, designed for Leo Polak en Julliët Groen by HF Smit in 1926; photo 2020

Traditionalism prevailed, initially, in the rebuilding of the ruined towns, both during the first years of the German occupation (until the mid-1942 construction ban) and the first post-war decade, in attempts to restore the lost identities of Dutch cities (Middelburg, Rhenen). While in the south hundreds of churches were destroyed and in need of rebuilding, a three-year ecclesiastical architecture course was organised at 's-Hertogenbosch (1946–73) guided by the ideas of Dom Hans van der Laan on spatial proportioning and the 'plastic number'. The resulting 'Bossche School' is mostly used for Catholic churches and monasteries, but also for town halls (Heusden, 1955, Nico van der Laan).

Next to that, so-called 'Shake Hands' architecture emerged, blending traditionalism and modernism like a 'marriage between brickwork and concrete', as Van Tijen termed it and applied in the National Aerospace Laboratory at Amsterdam (1939–41, with Hugh Maaskant). It was also adopted for new government buildings, in combination with specially subsidised artistic decoration, like the Provincial Administration Building of Gelderland in Arnhem (1950–54, Jo Vegter and others) or the former Geodetic Lab at Wageningen (1953, Frants Roentgen).

Halfway through the 1950s, new international trends – particularly from the USA – became influential in Dutch architecture and the modernists obtained more chances to build for post-war revival, both in inner cities (like Lijnbaan and Groothandelsgebouw, Rotterdam) and extensions

Enschede, Town Hall, designed by Gijsbert Friedhoff in 1931–33, shortly after completion

Arnhem, aerial view of the Provincial Administration, designed by Jo Vegter with Jan Brouwer, Teun Deurvorst and 25 artists in 1950–54, connected with the similarly restored Sabelspoort (city gate); photo about 1970

Wageningen, former Geodetic Laboratorium, designed for the University of Agriculture by Frants Roentgen in 1953; photo 2007

Vaals-Lemiers, Abbey church Sint Benedictusberg with original furniture, all designed by Dom Hans van der Laan in 1962–66; photo 2017

Aerdenhout, Advent Church interior, designed for the Dutch Reformed Church by Karel Sijmons in 1956–58; photo 2007

(Hengelo, Klein Driene) and (almost) entirely new towns (Emmen, Nagele; Lelystad). The housing shortage and the war-time studies on efficient plans had prompted a much wider acceptance of pre-fabrication and standardization than in the interwar period. The 'nakedness' of exposed concrete was no longer disliked in prestigious buildings, but sometimes part of wilful architectural expression in bold forms (Technical School Patrimonium, Amsterdam; Adventskerk, Aerdenhout), influenced by Le Corbusier. A new generation of architects within CIAM, including Aldo van Eyck, started to criticize the rigidity of post-war modernism. He pleaded for another–more humane–approach and found for his multi-domed Orphanage in Amsterdam (1958–60) inspiration in traditional settlements built in northern Africa.[50]

Push factors for emigration[51]

At first sight, the growing demand of utility works, housing and other building types seemed to offer sufficient opportunities for architects to practice their profession in the Netherlands since the Housing Act was implemented in the C20. Stricter building codes and upcoming 'Beauty Committees' stimulated the engagement of adequately trained architects instead of self-made builder-designers. Various professional organisations had advanced both a wider training, knowledge exchange and better fee conditions for their architect-members.[52] Yet, the architect's title was not legally protected until 1988 and diplomas and membership of a professional association were usually considered sufficient. Competition could be hard, because all architectural designers and practitioners were dependent on the willingness of clients, companies and governments to receive commissions, and budgets were sometimes very small. The fluctuating state of the economy, the reach of reputation and personal networks–often related to a certain 'pillar'–played an important role.

Leaving the Netherlands to build an architectural career elsewhere was, therefore, not an easy step, apart from the requirements that the foreign countries imposed on newcomers and the need to learn a new language. Architects and construction workers were, generally, regarded as indispensable by the Dutch government, but in periods of wide-spread unemployment they were allowed to migrate permanently. Such periods of economic decline were the late C19, the 1930s and the first years after WW2.

50 Kuipers, 2002.
51 See for this section: Gosselink, Holtrop & Ross, 2017; Ploeger, 1994.
52 Schilt & Van der Werff, 1992.

Amsterdam, the municipal Orphanage under construction, designed by Aldo van Eyck, in 1959

Amsterdam, departure of the oceanliner 'Tabinta' with emigrants towards South Africa, with remaining families and friends on the Javakade, in 1948

For other sectors, particularly agriculture, emigration was strongly stimulated and increasingly regulated (for instance by the 1936 and 1952 Emigration Acts), albeit mainly for the United States, Canada and Australia. Although the Dutch government did not directly subsidise interested *landverhuizers* during the pre-war decades, it supported the 'pillarised' organisations that were founded to provide information and advice on emigration.

The private *Nederlandsch-Zuid-Afrikaansche Vereeniging* (NZAV, founded in 1881 by Kuyper and others) held a special position in this regard, aiming at both cultural exchanges and practical help – first in response to the agony caused by the South African War and afterwards for repatriation and rebuilding the South African country.[53]

In 1951 a bi-lateral cultural convention was agreed between the Netherlands and the Union of South Africa to strengthen the old ties between the two nations after the previous tensions among the Boers and the Brits, Dutch and Germans.[54] The following Van Riebeeck festivities in both countries made these intentions publicly manifest. By then, governmental subsidies were also partially granted to those emigrants who could otherwise not afford their travel costs to South Africa.

Nevertheless, pragmatic personal reasons prevailed among the Dutch architects who decided to emigrate, often accompanied by their (just married) spouses. It was mainly because of the economic crises in the Netherlands and, for some, the fear of another world-war. Ideological arguments, like *stamverwantschap* [being cognate] or familiarity with the Dutch Reformed church, had become less appealing, certainly after 1940, but the similarity of the Afrikaans language and the sunny climate were still positive factors for most emigrants. Other motivations were the assumed perspectives to widen their scope and, eventually, to deploy their artistic aspirations more in their architectural designs. First-hand news from relatives and acquaintances or direct invitations to come to work in the Union of South Africa, when part of the British Commonwealth served as further motivating factors.[55] Some architects knew each other from their Dutch architectural education, but the majority went individually.

Before the Dutch architects were formally entitled to set up a private practice, they had to pass a British professional exam (which most did). Other options were to join an already established practice or to work in public service. Whatever their choice, they stayed and built, although they sometimes also struggled with the special conditions of a deeply divided society. Their multi-facetted legacy is thus far hardly known, yet it shows a great variety of styles, materials and typologies, often with a noticeable Dutch flavour.

53 This organisation is now part of the foundation Zuid-Afrika Huis that is housed at Amsterdam (www.zuidafrikahuis.nl).
54 It was effectuated in 1953 and unilaterally dissolved in 1982 as an official act against the Apartheid policy.
55 Interviews held by Nicholas Clarke and this author with descendants of MG Damstra, JC Jongens, JJ van Niftrik, EHA Payens, JZ Schuurmans Stekhoven and AJC Voorvelt in 2018 and 2019.

Amsterdam, HP Berlage's 1915 Extension Plan for South, drawn by Public Works and approved in 1917

SARPHATI PARK
CEINTUUR BAAN
ACADEM. ZIEKENHUIS
A
AMSTEL
SPOORBAAN
PARK
BEGRAAFPLAATS
ZORGVLIET
NIEUWE SLUIS
HET GEMAAL

Amsterdam, Dongestraat, detail of mural titled 'The old makes way for the new' by Leo Visser in the Municipal Technical College (MTS), in 1931

Educating the Dutch architect

Lizette van der Wal and Marieke Kuipers

Introduction

Those Dutch architects who migrated to South Africa in C20 had differing backgrounds and diverse levels of education. Some were not even formally trained in construction and architecture but had gained their knowledge in practice with a recognized architect, complemented by their attendance of additional evening classes. Only in 1988, after eighty years of lobbying by the Association of Dutch Architects (BNA), was the title of 'architect' granted legal protection in the Netherlands for those who have successfully completed their training at an accredited institution. There is, moreover, a distinction in the Dutch language between that of a *bouwkundige*, associated with construction, and that of an architect trained in *bouwkunst,* which includes developing artistic design skills.

Various paths existed to becoming an architect, depending on the level of preceding education and the opportunity (or lack thereof) of being able to study by day. Due to the rapid developments in construction methods, materials, machinery and equipment, the demand for theoretical training increased. This was met by a growth in the number of institutions over time offering such studies. Most of these institutions went through several relocations and reorganising. Some principal teachers moved from one school to another; often teaching (evening) classes while being active in practice. Apart from the levels of study, main focus (arts, technology or architecture) and type (private or public, secular or worldview based), the dynamics in legislation, programming and financing were also influential, leading to a great diversity of educational institutions. Occasionally, new purpose-designed schools were erected in which both theoretical and practical lessons could be taught.
In the main, four levels of technical education can be distinguished: primary, secondary, post-secondary and tertiary, all of which went through a succession of name-changes. While only a few were focused entirely on architectural education, the balance between theory and practice, technology and arts, science and humanities, past styles and new design approaches were frequent topics of discussion and adaptation. Before sketching the major levels of civil architectural education below, it should be noted that many pupils had already been introduced to the building scene through their fathers' occupation.

Vocational training

The *Ambachtsschool* [Crafts school] was a vocational schooling method initiated by the professional body and open to boys who had completed their primary school education. In 1930 more than eighty craft schools offered day-time courses, where carpenters, furniture makers and the like were trained over a period of two to four years, depending on the local institution and its time. In general, both theoretical and practical classes were followed during wintertime, alongside a general education, including courses in Dutch and mathematics. Most of the morning hours were spent on drawings, which would increase in complexity as the course progressed. Pupils developed their spatial skills initially by drawing compositions of straight lines, circles and other geometric

The Hague, carpentry workshop with Crafts School students showing their work, c1928

shapes, as well as doing freehand drawing and sketching. In the next stage they worked on representing simple wood joints, and finally they were able to produce complete views and cross-sections of window frames, pile foundations, staircases, and roof timbers.[1]

Practical exercises took place in the workshops, where all kinds of architectural elements were made on the basis of detailed working drawings.[2] Most manufactured pieces were commissioned by municipalities or charities, but some orders were executed for local craftsmen (for a small fee), or for application in the school building itself.[3] Vocational training gained more homogeneity at a national scale when the Lower Technical School (LTS) was introduced through legislation in 1949.

After completing the *Ambachtsschool*, young craftsmen could further develop their skills by attending additional evening classes or through training at a Technical College.

Technical Colleges

From 1910 onwards, technical education at secondary school level was provided at the *Middelbare Technische School* [MTS, Technical College] for students who were already trained at the crafts or general secondary schools. In this year, the first new purpose-built MTS for construction and civil engineering education was inaugurated in Utrecht. It was largely financed by the Dutch Contractors Association and designed by the first director, civil engineer Adriaan Dwars, who created multifunctional and well-lit classrooms to be used for both theory and practical courses.[4]

1 Verhoeven, 2007.
2 Breman, 1983: 6.
3 Van Essen, 1902: 64, 68.
4 Dwars, 1909: 583–85.

Utrecht, Croeselaan, class room with architectural students of the Technical College, 1920

Groningen, view of the modern Technical College annex Crafts School designed by director-structural engineer Jan Gerko Wiebenga and architect Leen van der Vlugt in 1922

Amsterdam, Dongestraat, Municipal Technical College for architecture, designed by Public Works director Nicolaas Lansdorp in 1931; photo 2005

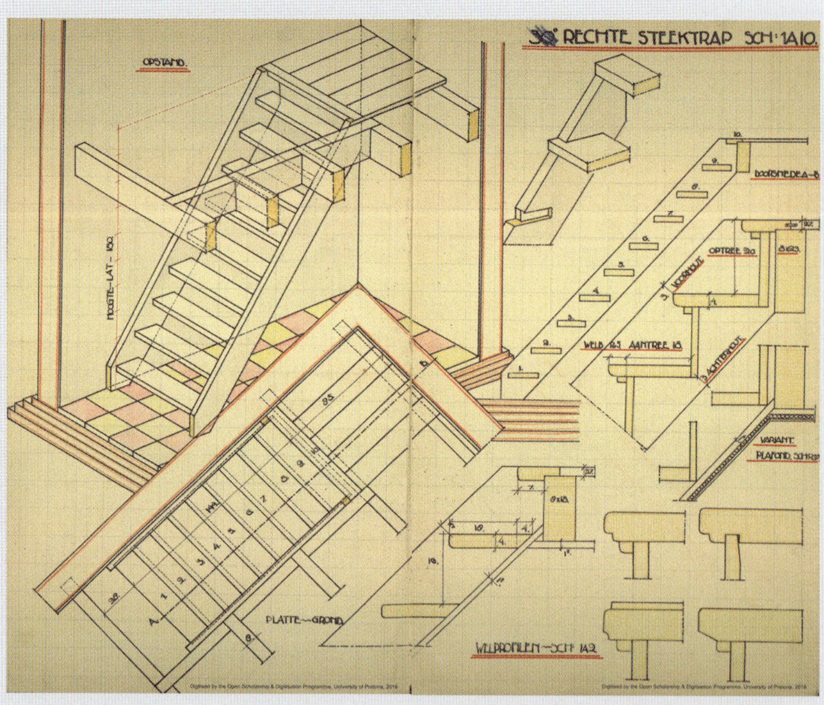

Study on stair construction drawn by John van de Werke at the Technical College in Utrecht in 1927

Ten other Technical Colleges offering education in construction were established between 1914 and 1931 in Dordrecht, Rotterdam, The Hague, Leeuwarden, Haarlem, Den Bosch, Heerlen, Sneek, Groningen and Amsterdam, most of these publicly funded.[5] Their aim was to train 'well-developed and civilized *burger- en waterbouwkundigen*' [civil engineers] who were able to design independently, execute simple structures and, as professionals, be intermediaries between the craftsmen and the more qualified architects or engineers.[6]

A three-year theoretical curriculum included algebra, physics and chemistry, English language, accounting, specifications, budgets and social economy alongside architectural theory, styles, and ornaments. Great emphasis was laid on (technical) drawing, both for (construction) details and full-scale designs, but architectural and freehand drawing were also taught. A year of apprenticeship was often mandatory for acquiring practical training. Most lecturers at the Technical Colleges taught part time and were mainly active in the field, assuring a rapid transfer of knowledge on the latest technological developments. Guest teachers were invited to present short courses. Numerous field trips were made to local construction sites, factories and companies. Through all these exchanges strong ties were maintained with the field, where the professional future of the Technical College students lay.[7]

Several new Technical Colleges were founded after WW2, spurred by the immense challenge of the post-war rebuilding of the country and need for skilled labour in construction and architecture. In 1957 all Technical

5 Schippers, 1989: 33–59.
6 Lijdsman, 1920: 210.
7 Lijdsman, 1920: 206–30.

Rotterdam, Coolsingel, classroom with young pupils of the Academy of Arts and Technical Sciences; photo c1925

Haarlem, Dreef, school building for Drawing and Applied Arts, designed by Jac. van Lokhorst, in use 1884–1930; photo c1900

Colleges were upgraded to Higher Technical School (HTS) status, with an extended curriculum which, after completion, allowed for access to the academic institution at Delft.[8]

Academies

After expanding their educational programs, some historical art schools and academies also provided architectural training, even though the Royal Academy at Amsterdam had forfeited this option to the Polytechnic School (PS) in Delft in 1870. To bridge the gap to this secondary level education, the Rotterdam Academy of Visual Arts and Technical Sciences offered preliminary education for thirteen-year-old aspirant architects, as a foundation for its four-year architectural training (alternating day and evening courses). In addition to designing buildings and making construction calculations, students were taught specifications, budgets, architectural history and styles. The students completed their studies by designing private houses, commercial and industrial buildings.[9]

8 Schippers, 1989: 109.
9 Maas, 1951: 24.

Interior drawing by a 2nd year student of the Quellinus School at Amsterdam as published in *Architectura*, 1915

Remarkably, the Haarlem Drawing school for Applied Arts introduced an independent architectural department in 1914, and evolved in 1918 into the School for Building, Decorative Arts and Crafts, with leading architects as senior lecturers. Its general aim was to achieve a unity in architecture, visual and applied arts, encouraged by optional courses in metal and woodworking, etching and batik-work. So as to develop an 'understanding of building', architectural students were taught to design based on knowledge, skill and art. The whole building, not separate elements, was considered the basis of design classes. The proper relationships between construction, function and form were taught through tuition that reflected the practice of building. In addition to drawing, painting and sculpting activities, attention was paid to art history, colour theory, materials and proportion. In addition, field sketches were made and trips undertaken to construction sites, brickworks and laboratories where new building materials were tested. Yet however innovative its architectural education, the school had to close in 1926 because, unlike the local MTS (founded in 1920), it was no longer being subsidized by the State. Nevertheless, this training remained influential in the evolution of modernist architecture.[10]

The multidisciplinary artistic education at the Amsterdam Quellinus Applied Arts School (founded by architect Pierre Cuypers and reorganised in 1909 and 1917) did not aim for the technical training of architects, but presented four-year courses in decorative, architectural and furniture drawing, together with courses in theory. Interior design was thus an integral aspect of the programme. After its fusion with two other institutes, the Institute of Applied Arts Education was formed in 1924.[11] Under the directorate of Mart Stam (1939–48) the educational programme was modelled after Bauhaus teachings, though without training in architectural construction techniques.[12]

10 Pijzel-Dommisse, 1989; Ringer, 1980.
11 Martis, 1980.
12 In 1968 the institute was relocated and renamed as Gerrit Rietveld Academy; Van Adrichem, 2016.

The Hague, Prinsessegracht, entrance section of the 1937 Academy of Arts, designed by director-structural engineer Johan Plantenga and architects Jan Buijs & Joan Lürsen, shortly after completion

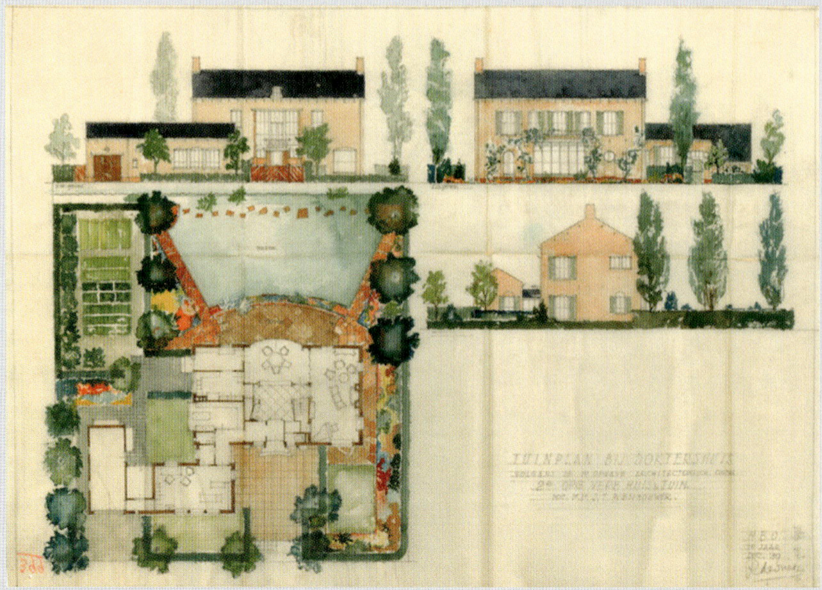

Amsterdam, VHBO final study drawing for a medical doctor's house, interior and garden, designed by Romke de Vries in 1939

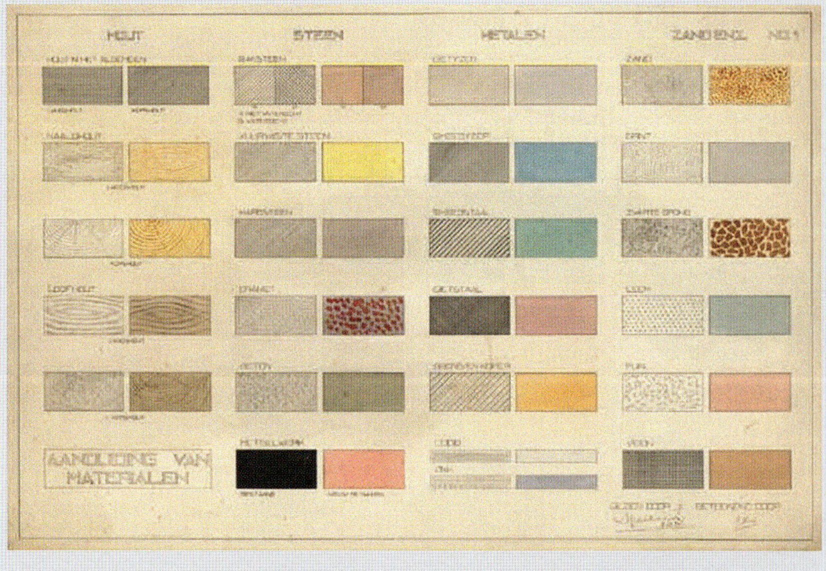

Delft, study drawing indicating construction materials by TH student Jannie Kret, 1924

By contrast, the age-old Academy of Arts at The Hague had been offering an architectural education since 1821, as well as, in subsequent years, courses in interior design and applied arts. After the first Act on *Nijverheidsonderwijs* [education for industry] was implemented in 1920, the day-time architectural education at this academy was brought up to the level of the MTS. In 1929 Jan Hendrik Plantenga was appointed as director (trained, like Dwars, as civil engineer at Delft). Not only did he advance modern concepts with the teaching staff, he also demonstrated these through his design, with Jan Buijs and Joan Lürsen in 1937, of the Institute's academy building, to replace the 1839 neoclassicist 'temple'.[13]

The four-year evening course, *Voortgezet en Hoger Bouwkunst Onderricht* [VHBO, further and higher architectural education], founded in 1908 in Amsterdam with an emphasis on architecture as an art, was important in its offering of a post-secondary-level education (later Academy of Architecture). During these studies, the students, who had often completed technical training, had to work at an architectural firm. The multi-facetted curriculum focused on aesthetics, but also dealt with specific fields like reinforced concrete, statics, urban planning, housing and legislation. The technical subjects were concentrated in the first two years. In the final year, students focused on the so-called *groot ontwerp*, which was a monumental architectural project in which all details, calculations and decorations had to be fully worked out.[14]

Similar Academies of Architecture were established in other cities and often adapted to regional needs, for example at Tilburg (1918), where the curriculum also contained symbolism, iconography and liturgy. These topics were considered indispensable for the training of a Catholic architect in the southern Netherlands.[15]

Institute of Technology Delft

The tertiary level of architectural education was (until 1966) solely offered at Delft, where the *Technische Hogeschool* (TH, Institute of Technology) was formally established in 1905 as the academic successor of the Polytechnic School (PS). Architecture was, by then, one of the six fields of training for engineers and the only one with a five-year curriculum (instead of four for the others). This consisted of a 'harmonious composition of

13 Plantenga, 1938: 64–70, 84.

14 Wendt, 2008: 27–35.

15 Tuinstra, Petermeyer, 1987: 22; Remery, 2011.

Delft, axonometric projection of a church design by TH student Jannie Kret, 1927

Delft, new drawing room of the *Bouwkunde* faculty in the former VOC warehouses as reproduced in Bouwkundig Weekblad, 1933

disciplines' allowing for training in both the technical and aesthetic considerations of the *bouwkundig ingenieur* [b.i., architectural engineer] or architect.[16] On the one hand, construction-oriented lessons similar to civil engineering were taught (including mechanics, knowledge of construction materials and technologies), on the other, much attention was paid to historic and contemporary architecture, history of art and various drawing techniques as well as modelling.

Among the first *Bouwkunde* professors were Jacob Klinkhamer (previously at the PS and also the designer of the Park Halt station at Johannesburg, 1895/1897) and Henri Evers (previously with the Rotterdam Academy and later designer of the Rotterdam Town Hall, 1914–20).[17] A special collection of objects and building elements was assembled by professor Karel Sluyterman and his predecessors for use in developing artistic skills through drawing.[18] These 'decorative treasures' were partly incorporated into the historic Portugal House on the Oude Delft, which was purposely refurbished in 1917, in a range of styles and with lecture, reading and drawing rooms.[19] Drawing from objects, models or existing buildings (visited and measured during excursions) was seen as a vital part of the architects' artistic formation.

The students' design assignments were initially directed at contemporary needs, such as housing and railways buildings, always prioritising construction.[20] In their concluding (fifth) year students could eventually specialize in monumental architecture, non-residential building, or urban design. A specialisation in utilitarian buildings was an option, particularly meant for those students who intended to work in what was then the colonized Dutch East Indies (today Indonesia). New professors were appointed for both directions in 1924: architect-town planner Marinus Granpré Molière and structural engineer Richard Schoemaker, who had previously taught at the Bandung Institute of Technology, and who was Klinkhamer's successor.[21]

The former warehouses of the Dutch East India Company in the city centre were transformed by architect-professor JAG van der Steur in 1932 to accommodate the burgeoning number of architectural students, averaging 100 until 1940.[22] An entirely new faculty building would not be inaugurated until 1970, located outside of the historic core, which became the home of an increasingly expanding community of students and professors in architecture. This concrete tower-block, designed by part time professors Van den Broek and Bakema, then came to symbolize the radical change in architectural education from the post-war era into the dominant modernity.[23]

16 Roelofs Heijermans, 1906; Westendorp, et al.,1930.
17 Timmer, 1997.
18 Hilkhuijsen, 2001; Crijns, 1994: 90, 120.
19 Sluyterman, 1917.

20 Technische Hoogeschool Delft, [1925]; Kooijman, 1995: 15–18.
21 Schoemaker, 1924; Technische Hoogeschool [1925].
22 IJperlaan and Van der Steur, 1932; B(ruin), 1933.
23 Annema, 1973; Kaper et al., 1994; Van Es, 2018; the *Bouwkunde* building burnt down on 13 May 2008.

Cover of an issue of the Dutch Emigratiekroniek showing emigrants departing for South Africa

3 Two waves of Dutch immigration to South Africa

Annie Antonites

Introduction

South Africa and the Netherlands have a historic connection stretching back to the arrival of Jan van Riebeeck and the Dutch East India Company at the Cape of Good Hope in 1652. During the late C19, presidents Burgers and Kruger encouraged Dutch citizens to immigrate to the *Zuid-Afrikaansche Republiek* (ZAR; South African Republic), specifically to be deployed as civil servants. Many of these Dutchmen—known as the *Hollanderkorps* (Dutch Corps)—fought on the Afrikaners' (Boers) side against Britain in the South African War (1899–1902). Those Dutchmen who returned after exile or decided to stay were instrumental in the rebuilding efforts after the war. The revived nostalgic ties with the previous Dutch-related settlers had no small part to play in the choice of South Africa as immigration destination and the South African government's attitude towards Dutch immigrants in the C20.

Among an estimated 37 000 Dutch-born immigrants arriving between 1902 and 1955 were dozens of architects and builders who chose South Africa as their new homeland. These *landverhuizingen* can be divided into pre- and post-WW2 waves.[1] This chapter contextualises the reasons behind Dutch emigration in the C20 as well as why South Africa was a desirable immigration choice. It considers the underlying immigration policies that created the opportunities for Dutch citizens to immigrate to South Africa and characterises the Dutch immigrant community in terms of their experience in South Africa and efforts to maintain their Dutch heritage.

South Africa, country of arrival[2]

Modern South Africa is in large part a political construct, shaped by historical factors rather than a clearly defined geographical area. The area covered by the Union with its formation in 1910, was *circa* 1.22 million km^2. This is large by European standards, approximately the size of Great Britain, France and Germany combined. Historically, it had a low population density (*circa* 6 000 000 in 1910), which covers the spectrum from sparsely settled regions in the arid western half of the country to the more densely settled areas to the east.

Geographical map of South Africa, 1949; from *Eerste Afrikaanse skoolatlas*

South Africa is bounded to the west by the Atlantic Ocean and to the south and east by the Indian Ocean. Despite having more than 3 000 km coastline, there are only a few good natural harbours. Throughout most of its history, the two major ports were Cape Town and Durban. Substantial amounts of cargo also passed through Port Elizabeth and East London. To the north, the country is bordered, from west to east, by Namibia, Botswana, Zimbabwe and Mozambique, with the boundaries formed primarily by the Orange, Molopo, and Limpopo Rivers. None of South Africa's rivers are navigable and none of the river mouths has sufficient depth for sea-going ships to enter.

1 Loedolff, 1960; Ploeger, 1994.
2 Partial summary of (Feinstein, 2005); see (Bokhorst, 1953) on Iscor Jubilee.

Dutch farewell scene before emigration to South Africa, c1950

Port of Cape Town in the early 1940s

The South African population at the turn of the C19 can broadly be divided along racial, linguistic and ethnic lines. While it is today recognized that these categories are fluid, and in many cases social constructs, they did form the foundation of race-based classification that underpinned colonial and apartheid legislation. Within this context, the term "African" is typically used to refer to indigenous Bantu-speaking people, without implying that other groups are not equally rooted in the continent. Historically, they make up the majority of the South African population and are comprised of different ethnic and linguistic groups. Communities of San hunter-gatherer ("Bushmen") and Khoi pastoralists—both part of the non-Bantu cluster of click-language speakers—also have a long settlement history in the country. By the C20, smallpox epidemics led to a massive drop in their population size and encroachment by African and European farmers had pushed them to the margins of society. Colonial (and present day) governments classified them under the generic term "Coloured"—a term that also includes the descendants of Malay slaves brought to the Cape by the Dutch, black slaves freed at the Cape in the decades after Britain abolished slavery in 1808, as well as people of mixed race descent. "White" is typically used as a generic term to refer to European immigrants and their descendants. This group is itself comprised of Afrikaners—the Afrikaans-speaking descendants of mainly Dutch, French and German immigrants—and English-speakers descending from Great Britain. There is also a sizable Asian population, mostly descending from C19 indentured Indian labourers whom British authorities brought to work in the sugar plantations. The social and cultural divide between these different segments of society ran deep throughout the C20 and stood in contrast to the relatively homogenous Dutch (and European) society.

Prior to the discovery of gold and diamonds in the late C19, South Africa can be regarded as having had a relatively backward economy, almost entirely dependent on agriculture. Despite the importance of agriculture, the relatively low rainfall throughout most of the country means that even this economy was characterised by slow growth. However, the development of the diamond and gold fields in the interior transformed this situation overnight.

From the late C19 onwards, all commercial activity was focused on mining operations concentrated around volcanic pipes, which contained diamonds and the gold bearing layers of the Witwatersrand and the northern Highveld. Gold mining was complemented by the discovery of shallow coal deposits in the eastern Highveld and KwaZulu-Natal. The development of a domestic iron and steel industry in the inter-war period was based on the presence of large reserves of high-grade iron ore, and other base metals found in significant quantities such as chromium, manganese, vanadium, titanium, antimony and copper, which occur mainly in the northern and north-eastern parts in what is today the Limpopo and Northern Cape Provinces. Dutch-born immigrant, Cornelis Delfos, was a key figure in the development of the iron and steel industry in South Africa and responsible for the establishment of the South African Iron and Steel Industrial Corporation (Iscor) in 1928.

A citrus plantation in the environs of Rustenburg, 1957

A Witwatersrand gold mining production site with shaft and labour accommodation

Pretoria, ISCOR steelworks, aerial view, 1956

State policies of migration

In early C20 South Africa, immigration policies were linked to local tensions between Afrikaner and English (British) communities in the aftermath of the South African War. Following the war and the forming of the Union (1910), the government attempted to ease these tensions by creating an immigration policy that 'reflected a shared sense of colonial identity based on a racial ordering of society.'[3] European immigration—though prioritising British and discouraging Eastern European and Jewish immigrants—was promoted as a collective means to develop the country in a "civilized" way while at the same time limiting black South Africans' rights.

Unity in maintaining the status quo was, however, always fleeting and the Afrikaner/British schism remained deeply embedded in society. To this end, immigration policies were drawn further into underlying conflict between Afrikaner Unionists and Nationalists (pro- versus anti-British sentiment), especially leading up to and following the National Party's victory in 1948.

3 Henkes, 2016: 645.

Cover of the information book on a 'Dutch family in sunny South Africa' by H. Bloem, office manager of the NZAV, published in 1949

The appeal of Dutch immigrants derived from the urge to maintain white dominance and a Protestant ethic in South Africa. This also meant that only a small proportion of the immigrants were Catholic. Here, the involvement of the three Afrikaner reformed sister-churches—the *Nederduits Gereformeerde Kerk, Gereformeerde Kerk* and *Nederduitsch Hervormde Kerk*—in immigration policies and cultural integration were particularly influential. *Stamverwantschap* or "kinship ties"—the historically cultural and genetic link between Afrikaners and the Dutch and Germans—gave Dutch immigrants an additional immigration advantage at times, especially during the 1950s. Even during this time, however, prospective immigrants still had to be approved by the selection board of the South African embassy in The Hague. Criteria included having a work permit, health certificate and sufficient financial means. The South African government did not pressure immigrants to change nationalities for fear of political consequences, and most retained their European citizenship.[4]

As a symbolic event to signal improved cooperative relations between the two countries, South African Prime Minister JBM Hertzog, through engineering ingenuity, remotely launched the MS 'Bloemfontein' in Amsterdam from Pretoria in 1934. Thousands of people watched the ship slide into the IJ, including Dutch Prime Minister Hendrikus Colijn.[5] The building of this passenger/cargo vessel and other ships for the *Vereenigde Nederlandsche Scheepvaartmaatschappij* (VNS) enabled the subsequent waves of *landverhuizers* [emigrants] to South Africa, who mostly travelled by sea. Shortly afterwards, the MS 'Jagersfontein' and other new ships followed. Only after WW2 were direct flights serviced by KLM on a regular basis.

Soon after WW2, the then Prime Minister of South Africa, Jan Smuts and his United Party, pushed for European immigration to fill the skills and labour shortage but also to counter the growing agitation for black emancipation. Citizens from Allied nations—especially from Britain and specifically excluding Germans—were encouraged to come to South Africa. This policy resulted in a significant increase in general European

4 Donsky, 1989: 59; Henkes, 2016; Loedolff, 1960; Slater, 2005.
5 Anon. 1934. *De Ingenieur*, Jun: 239–40.

Amsterdam, remote-controlled launch of the MS 'Bloemfontein', 1934

immigration in 1947 and 1948, within which Dutch numbers steadily increased up until 1948. When the Afrikaner National Party came into power in 1948, they imposed their ideological aims onto immigration policies, sowing greater racial divide and discouraging immigration—except from those of Germany—to put their "own people" first. British and Jewish immigrants were particularly unwelcome. The result was a sharp decrease in overall immigration from the Netherlands and other European countries.[6]

By 1949 efforts to resolve the strained diplomatic relationship between South Africa and the Netherlands were underway. The Dutch government had also, by this time, lifted the temporary ban on the emigration of skilled citizens who had to remain in the Netherlands after the War to help rebuild the country. Many Dutch citizens wanted to leave their war-torn country for a better economic future in countries like the United States, Canada, Australia and New Zealand. An influx of people returning and migrating from recently independent Indonesia and fewer opportunities for migration to the Dutch East Indies contributed to the economic and social pressure to make an alternative life elsewhere. In addition, the Netherlands experienced a housing shortage, rising unemployment and over-supply of labour in certain sectors (such as agriculture) as well as difficulty in obtaining training or a professional qualification. This situation led the Dutch government to actively encourage and facilitate emigration to relieve the pressure of economic overpopulation. Drawing on *stamverwantschap* and turning a blind eye to the Nationalists' Apartheid policies, they convinced the South African government to lift their restrictions against Dutch immigrants.

6 Donsky, 1989; Henkes, 2016; Loedolff, 1960: 13.

Cartoon by Kees van Lent, depicting how restricted Dutch families felt in their development, published in the booklet *Van emigrant tot immigrant* (1960)

By the early 1950s, in an ideological effort to strengthen the minority white Afrikaner community, Dutch immigrants were once again welcomed to South Africa. Of the quarter of a million Dutch citizens who emigrated between 1946 and 1955, almost 23 000 came to South Africa.[7] Lists of passengers reveal that not only were places of origin and destination registered but also personal data like religion and profession. For instance, the Dutch Reformed architect Wim van Wijngaarden migrated from The Hague, with his wife, to work with architect Henk de Bie in Bloemfontein, in 1955.

After peaking in 1952, numbers steadily declined in line with a general drop in emigration from the Netherlands. From the early 1960s onwards, Dutch immigration to South Africa was no longer encouraged due to continued global pressure against the Nationalist government's racist policies. The gradually improving economic milieu in the Netherlands further lessened the appeal to emigrate.

Push and Pull Factors

Shortly after the South African War came an economic depression between 1903 and 1909, which ultimately lifted, ameliorated by a revival in the gold mining industry. In the early decades of the C20 there was a relatively small inflow of Dutch immigrants, which included some returning Dutch-born architects who had been members of the *Hollanderkorps*. The promulgation of the Immigration Quota Act of 1930 introduced stricter immigration measures, yet the economic domino effect of the global Great Depression "pushed" many to emigrate. The ever present "poor white problem" also served to curtail numbers. By 1934, however, South African mining, commerce and construction had recovered, followed by industrialisation and urbanisation. As a result, the need for skilled professionals grew, compounded by legislation aimed at preventing blacks from filling this labour shortage.[8]

After WW2, however, emigration became a national concern in the Netherlands as a way to deal with the economic problems caused by the factors outlined in the previous section. In addition, the strong involvement of religious emigration organs lent a missionary aspect to immigration policies. Under the centralised auspices of the *Nederlandse Emigratiedienst* [Netherlands Emigration Service], the Dutch government assisted migrants in terms of guidance and preparation, subsidies, transportation costs, housing, money transfer, credit services and even repatriation.[9]

Returning WW2 servicemen were easily absorbed into the South African labour market but an acute shortage of skilled artisans and technicians remained, which could, considering the legal strictures on the local black population, only be immediately filled by immigrants.[10] This situation is clearly reflected in the number of immigrants, which, within the twelve years between 1925 and 1938 saw only 6 500 Dutch citizens come to South Africa, compared to around 8 000 from 1947 to 1950.[11] The majority of newcomers settled in the former Transvaal, and Pretoria in particular, which became home to the largest Dutch community in the country.

7 Donsky ,1989; Haveman, 1958 as cited in Slot 2003: 19; Henkes 2016; Loedolff 1960: 13, 44.
8 Donsky, 1989; Henkes, 2016; Katzen, 1963; Ploeger, 1994.
9 Hofstede, 1964: 12-15, 74–95, 185-190; Loedolff, 1960: 12–16.
10 Donsky, 1989: 21–22.
11 Ploeger, 1994: 25, 34.

Pretoria, family house in a new suburb, designed by Dutch-born architect John van de Werke; the photograph was used to promote Dutch migration to South Africa, 1940s

Who immigrated to South Africa and why?

People migrate for several interrelated reasons and the most decisive for Dutch immigrants, especially post-WW2, were economic. In the pre-war decades, immigrants wishing to improve their quality of life were drawn to South Africa because of similarities in language, law and religion. As a growing industrial nation, South Africa provided abundant opportunities. There was a skilled labour shortage—partly aggravated by the Job Reservations Acts, which prohibited black people from filling this shortage—and those willing to work could earn higher wages. The 1950s saw many Dutch citizens come to South Africa because of job opportunities for skilled professionals, to start their own businesses, to provide a better future for their children and to join family or friends. This choice was fuelled in no small part by the agreeable climate, *stamverwantschap,* and positive reports from friends and family who had already settled in South Africa.[12] These factors certainly influenced Dutch immigrant architects, although the prospect of practicing seems to have been the main motivation.

Information on immigrants' place of origin for the period before WW2 is scant. However, after the War, the majority of immigrants came from the provinces of North and South Holland. These were the most densely populated provinces in the Netherlands and home to major cities such as Amsterdam, Haarlem, The Hague, Rotterdam and Delft. What can be gathered from the available sources is that between 1903 and 1909 Dutch immigrants to South Africa comprised mainly teachers for the *Christelik Nasionale Onderwys* [Christian National Education] schools, trained administrative personnel, masons, carpenters, tradesmen and women (with and without children) who joined their husbands and fiancées.[13]

In the early C20, those who settled in Pretoria, for example, could do business with their fellow countrymen through several Dutch companies such as the *Nederlandsche Bank voor Zuid-Afrika* [Netherlands Bank for South Africa], *Nederlandsche Zuid-Afrikaansche Landbouw Maatschappij* [Netherlands South African Agricultural Company] and the *Algemeene Maatschappij van Levensverzekering en Lijfrente* [General Life Insurance Company] as well as businesses, such as wine merchants, butchers, bakers, opticians, shoemakers, accountants, architects,

12 Henkes, 2016; Loedolff, 1960:47; Ploeger, 1994: 29; Wentholt, 1961 as cited in Slot, 2005: 21

13 Hofstede, 1964; Loedolff, 1960: 36; Ploeger, 1994: 25.

Pretoria, staff and pupils of the CNO Oost-Eindschool, 1904

Wonderfontein, the new Adorp cooperative cheese factory, established by Dutch immigrants, 1934

Wonderfontein, the rondavel-house of the Dutch immigrant Jan Blauw, 1934

contractors, florists and general dealers.[14] There were also Dutch firms with branches in South Africa, including Philips (lighting), Bruynzeel (wood) and De Vries Robbé (steel).

Farmers were especially encouraged to emigrate because of the oversupply of agricultural labour in the Netherlands. As early as the 1920s, a group of Dutch farmers—unable to continue farming independently in the Netherlands—settled on the farm Wonderfontein 65, in what is today the West Rand district of Gauteng. These farmers introduced the concept of the cooperative and supplied dairy products and vegetables to Johannesburg, Pretoria and Potchefstroom. The cooperative only ceased to exist as a Dutch settlement in 1965. Given the already established agricultural sector and availability of cheap local labour, South Africa eventually only attracted a small number of Dutch farmers.[15]

During the 1930s and throughout the 1950s, South Africa was a popular destination for those working in the building industry. According to the Dutch-born architect Jan Zeger Schuurmans Stekhoven, the development boom of the mid-1930s in the gold mining capital of Johannesburg and also in Cape Town created favourable employment opportunities for

14 For example, De Beurs, 1938; Ploeger, 1994: 167–68; Anon. 1936b, Hollands Weekblad voor Zuid-Afrika, 27 June 1936; see also Chapter 6.

15 Hofstede, 1964; Loedolff ,1960; Ploeger, 1994; Schutte, 2020.

architects and draughtsmen.[16] In the mid-1950s, Willem Botbijl, a building contractor who came to South Africa in 1935 as a mason, described the conditions for building contractors in a promotional immigration magazine as follows:

De ontwikkeling van de Unie heeft zulk een razend-snel tempo aangenomen, dat het bouwbedrijf onmogelijk de behoefte aan gebouwen en huizen kan vóór blijven. Er is een nijpend tekort aan geschoolde vaklui. Eerstdaags ga ik beginnen aan twee grote panden ... en ik heb voor de werken nog een heel aantal vakmensen nodig. De kwaliteit van ons werk behoort tot de hoogste ter wereld en ik kan dus alleen mensen gebruiken, die degelijk opgeleid zijn. De bouwvak-arbeider geniet in de Unie een sociale bescherming, die even goed is als die in Nederland.
[The Union has developed at such a fast pace that it is impossible for the building industry to keep up with the supply of buildings and houses. There is a pressing shortage of skilled craftsmen. I will soon start on two large buildings... and I still need a number of professionals to do the work. The quality of our work is world class and I can only use properly trained people. The construction worker enjoys social protection in the Union equal to that in the Netherlands.][17]

Prospective immigrant architects had to have a good command of the English language, as drawings and building specifications were usually written in English. They would only be allowed to practice in South Africa, in the 1930s at least, if they:

...als lid zyn ingeschreven by de, door de wet vasgestelde, Architekten Genootschappen, waartoe een diploma noodig is. Ter verkryging van dit diploma wordt een zwaar examen afgenomen. Vrystelling van dit examen hebben zy die het analoge (doch m.i. minder zware) Engelsche A.R.I.B.A examen hebben afgelegd. Dezerzyds wordt niet over gegevens beschikt of, en dan in hoeverre, buitenlandsche graden, als byvoorbeeld het Delftsche Ingenieurs diploma, voor gelykstelling in aanmerking kunnen komen.
[... were registered as a member with the, legally determined, Architects Associations, which require a diploma. Obtaining such a diploma depends on the completion of a difficult exam. Those who have passed the similar (but in my view easier) English A.R.I.B.A. exam are exempt [from the diploma exam]. It is not known if, and to what extent, foreign degrees, such as the Delft Engineers' diploma, qualify for recognition].[18]

In addition, Dutch people worked in industry and commerce related professions, while scientifically and administratively trained professionals were also amongst the immigrant work force. In Pretoria, several Dutch professionals were employed at the Council for Scientific and Industrial Research (CSIR), the South African Bureau of Standards (SABS) and as civil engineers at the Transvaal Provincial Administration. Women who immigrated as "housewives" needed permission from the Minister of Home Affairs to find formal employment; when allowed, they worked mainly in offices and shops or in the personal services industry as hairdressers, housekeepers and boarding house owners.[19]

Johannesburg, view of Rissik Street with high-rise buildings, 1936

Life in South Africa

'For more than a hundred years, the Dutch and their descendants have proven themselves ... as skilled workers, entrepreneurs, faithful residents, decent citizens and respected culture bearers, stalwarts in many fields, in church, education, government, art and the sciences', according to GJ Schutte.[20]

State and civic organisations provided useful information to prospective emigrants. The *Nederduitse Hervormde Kerk* [Dutch Reformed Church], for example, distributed an immigration booklet in the 1950s, which gave a short historical and cultural overview of the Unites States, Canada, Australia and South Africa.[21] In addition to providing the necessary spiritual support and resources, church members were encouraged to learn the English language and to take books on religious life, educating children, and ones that would promote the Netherlands to new contacts and friends. Medical insurance was to be taken out as soon as possible and pregnant women were advised not to immigrate prior to giving birth,

16 Letter to the Dutch Consul-General in Cape Town, 6 March 1935 (Dutch National Archive, The Hague, ARA, Z-A Kaapstad/CG 1860-1939, inv.nr. 00096); author's translation; see also Anon. 1937, Zuid-Afrika Maandblad: 150-151.

17 Thuis in Zuid-Afrika, 1955: 20; author's translation.

18 Letter by Jan Zeger Schuurmans Stekhoven (see note 16); author's translation.

19 Loedolff, 1960; *Thuis in Zuid-Afrika*, 1955.

20 Ploeger, 1994: 156 '... de Hollanders en hun nakomelingen hebben zich hier ... al meer dan honderd jaar ... doen kennen als vakbekwame werkers, goede ondernemers, trouwe ingezetenen, achtenswaardige burgers en gerespecteerde cultuurdragers.' Quote by GJ Schutte, former chairperson of the *Nederlands Zuid-Afrikaanse Vereeniging* [Netherlands South African Association].

21 Hervormde Emigratie Commissie, 1960.

due to high medical costs in their new home countries. The first few months would be difficult and lonely but it was important to preserve the Dutch character and insight and to adapt to a new way of life in a rational manner. People intent on settling in South Africa were specifically advised to learn both English and Afrikaans and to affiliate themselves to a church for a more welcoming experience. They had to prepare for immediate "exposure" to racial segregation but were cautioned to refrain from critique until becoming true citizens and to contribute towards a solution for this difficult problem in a thoughtful and sensitive manner.[22] Similarly, the Catholic organisation for Emigration published information for their community, in line with the 'pillarized' society in the Netherlands.[23]

Life in South Africa was more affordable than in the Netherlands. Housing and entertainment were more expensive but groceries and fabric were cheaper. Salaries were higher and personal income tax lower. There were opportunities to start one's own business—an especially appealing prospect for architects once they were registered after passing the exam—and even to save enough to go on holiday. Unlike the situation in the Netherlands, many immigrants could own a free standing house with a large yard and garden. They boasted of the enjoyable climate and the absence of *standsverschil* [class difference] in society, albeit obviously just among the white segment of the population.[24]

Churches played an important role in the integration of immigrants into their local communities. Although this was not the case for all, many Dutch people could, to a greater or lesser degree, relate to the theology of Afrikaans reformed churches and found spiritual comfort in their new surroundings through the church. Immigrants were encouraged to join a church as soon as possible. Churches, in return, provided social, spiritual and sometimes even financial support. Fulfilling its mandate to welcome and assimilate immigrants into Afrikaner society depended on the congregation and varied in its effectiveness. In addition, not all religious immigrants were satisfied with the nature of South African church-life and found the preaching somewhat superficial. Because of the preference for Protestant immigrants, the Dutch Roman Catholic community remained fairly small and these immigrants tended to assimilate more into the local English segment of society.[25]

Maintaining a Dutch heritage

Assimilation and integration did not happen immediately—many immigrants, even after a few years, still only mingled with their fellow countrymen. In addition, the lack of entertainment, compared to what people were used to in Europe and, in later years, the slow adoption of television, contributed to a general sense of boredom amongst immigrants.[26] As such, the diverse range of associations and clubs became the social glue that held the Dutch community together, especially in the interwar decades.

Large cities such as Pretoria, Johannesburg, Cape Town and Bloemfontein had their own *Nederlandse Vereeniging* [Dutch Association] and these were affiliated with several smaller independent associations and clubs.[27] The *Nederlandse Vereenigingen* brought those with a Dutch connection together, catered to their interests and provided entertainment.[28] In the pre-War years, events included dance evenings, food-centred evenings (where *hutspot* and *erwtensoep* were served), gymnastics classes, English conversation evenings and amateur theatre productions. They regularly held fundraisers—drawing on other Dutch connections such as theatre companies—to support community initiatives like *Ons Tuis*, a Dutch retirement home in Pretoria. Many chapters had a library with original Dutch books and a local reading circle. *Nederlandse Vereenigingen* also assisted immigrants in finding work and sometimes even supported members financially. There was usually a special portfolio to address the needs of the increasing number of Dutch immigrants to South Africa. They further served to maintain ties with the "homeland" through, amongst other things, contact and collaboration with the *Nederlands Zuid-Afrikaanse Vereeniging* in Amsterdam (which had an emigration desk).[29]

Johannesburg, shop window displaying Dutch produce, presented by the Dutch Chamber of Commerce, 1919

During the early C20, Dutch clubs and associations in Pretoria, for example, catered to any and all interests—politics, economics, education, charity, literature, dance, theatre, music and sport (including football, chess, fencing and gymnastics). From the 1930s onwards, Dutch veterans of the South African War and former employees of the *Nederlandsche Zuid-Afrikaansche Spoorwegmaatschappij* or NZASM [Netherlands-South African Railway Company] had their own associations as well. Dutch sports clubs brought sport and socialising together and the ones in Pretoria were especially successful in achieving this balance. The *Pretoria Gymnastic Vereeniging* (gymnastics) and *De Vrije Wapenbroeders* (fencing) clubs survived the South African War and, together with the *Hollandsche Voetbal Vereeniging* (football),

22 See also *De Unie van Zuid-Afrika*, 1939.
23 Smits, 1989.
24 *Thuis in Zuid-Afrika*, 1955; SLN/NZAV. 1939; Van Ginkel, 1936: 22.
25 Loedolff, 1960.
26 Donsky, 1989: 53; Loedolff, 1960; some considered the Dutch community (in Pretoria at least) to have been somewhat cliquey, see Meek, 1967.
27 These associations occasionally reconfigured and regrouped themselves, sometimes involving a name change; see Anon.1936c; De Jong, 1980; the Cape Town chapter was known as *De Hollandse Kring*.
28 De Jong, 1980; Loedolff, 1960: 104–08; some even had a few Afrikaner and non-Dutch members, see Meek 1967; Schuur, 1913.
29 Anon. 1936b; Anon. 1936c; Cremer, 1936; De Jong, 1980: 60-66; Loedolff, 1960; Schuur, 1913.

actively contributed to Dutch cultural life in early C20 Pretoria. The fencing and gymnastics clubs often held public performances, followed by very popular balls.[30] The membership composition and character of associations and clubs varied those with older members tended to be more formal than those with younger members; some had members of diverse backgrounds and professions, while others were comprised of people from specific professions or companies.[31]

Weekly and monthly newsletters or magazines, such as the *Hollands Weekblad voor Zuid-Afrika* and *Nederlandse Post*, provided the Dutch community with news from the Netherlands, discussion of current local and global events and regular updates on the social activities of the various associations and clubs in the large cities and small towns across the Union. In the personalia sections, one could keep up to date with the lives of fellow countrymen—from their health status and travel itineraries to weddings and graduations. Advertisements promoted mostly Dutch-owned businesses. The Pretoria-based *Hollands Weekblad* printed schedules for shipping companies and church services which were distributed to unemployed subscribers free of charge.

Maintaining a sense of Dutch identity through food and language continued to be important to the immigrant community, at least in the decades prior to WW2. There were butchers specialising in familiar meat cuts, while Dutch delicacies such as smoked eel, rollmops, *rookworst* [smoked sausage], dried *Boerenkool* [kale] and *spekulaas* [spiced biscuits] were imported and seemingly available throughout the Union.[32] The preservation of the Dutch language in the face of increased Afrikaans and English influence can be seen in the frequent complaints of its deterioration penned in Dutch magazines and newsletters.[33]

30 De Jong, 1980; Ploeger, 1994: 27.

31 (Meek, 1967) recalled this difference in age/formality between the music and theatre groups *Onze Taal* and *Amicitia*. The *Hollandse Voetbal Vereeniging* (football club) comprised mainly of staff members from the Nederlandse Bank; the popular *Hollandse Mannenkoor* (men's choir) had members from diverse backgrounds and professions; see also De Jong, 1980.

32 As seen in advertisements by, for example, *Afrik. Handelsmaatschappij*, and *Pretoria Meat Supply* in the *Hollands Weekblad*, 27 June 1936.

33 Anon. 1936a; Geefu 1936; Schuur 1913.

The Dutch-born immigrant architect Mello Damstra with his extended family outside Cape Town

Dutch festivities such as *Koninginnedag* [Queen's Day] and *Sinterklaas* continued to be celebrated.[34] Several larger events were organised over the years for fundraising or to celebrate Dutch heritage and achievements. In 1944, for example, the *Studiegenootschap voor Nederlandsche Belangen* [Society for the Study of Netherlands Interests] organised an exhibition "Vrij Nederland" in Cape Town. The aim of the exhibition was 'to illustrate the activities and aims of the Free Netherlands and Netherlands Indies in modern times' and was opened by Prime Minister Smuts.[35]

During WW2, Dutch immigrants were at first allowed to fight in the South African forces; however, this decision was later reversed in favour of strengthening the Netherlands' forces. This decision left many immigrants who saw South Africa as their new homeland disgruntled. Many, including Dutch-émigré architects and builders, joined the Princess Irene brigade in England. Several volunteers from South Africa were also imprisoned in Japanese camps in the Dutch East Indies. On the South African side, the Administrator of the Transvaal, JJ Pienaar,

Architect Anton Voorvelt (with spectacles) and his Dutch comrades of the Princess Irene Brigade performing for the BBC broadcasting programme 'Songtime in the Laager', c1943

34 Anon. 1930a; De Jong 1980; Posthumus, 2019.
35 Anon. 1944a, *Cape Times*, 11 February 1944; Anon. 1944b. catalogue and photos of the Exhibition 'Vrij Nederland', 1944 (both in National Archive of the Netherlands, NL-HaNA, Consulaat-Generaal Kaapstad, 2.05.125, inv.nr. 118).

Cape Town, the crowded *Hollandse Bazar* with replicated Dutch gables, 1938

Van Riebeeck commemorative stamps and envelope, issued for the Tercentenary, 1952

established a fund for children in the Netherlands, and several supportive committees in Pretoria and Johannesburg were formed, including a War and Women's Committee.

Van Riebeeck Days were commemorated annually from the 1920s on a small scale, with the tercentenary in 1952 celebrated on a massive scale nationally in South Africa and in the Netherlands. Not merely serving as a commemoration of Van Riebeeck's arrival at the Cape, the festival served a broad political, economic and cultural agenda for both countries. Moreover, Dutch-born architects, like Jaap Jongens and Willem van Beijma, were directly involved in the design of the infrastructure and organisation of the festival.[36]

Conclusion

Rapid industrial and commercial development during the C20 created opportunities for Dutch architects and builders in South Africa. Yet their built heritage legacy cannot be removed from the broader socio-political context in which race, religion and *stamverwantschap* played a determining role. Waves of Dutch migration were influenced by local and international factors—economic depression, war, poverty, unemployment, political alignment, industrialisation, urbanisation and national labour practices—that dictated periods of increased and decreased movement of people. Colonel-historian Jan Ploeger, who himself immigrated in 1936 from the Netherlands and studied the successive waves of immigration to the Transvaal, observed in 1999: 'Geen enkele Nederlandse immigrant ... het hom in Suid-Afrika kom vestig met die doel om niks te doen nie. Elkeen het oor ervaring en kundigheid beskik wat hy ... toegepas het om 'n vaste en dikwels floreerende bestaan te voer'. [Not a single Dutch immigrant ... settled in South Africa with the aim of doing nothing. They applied their expertise and skills ... to make a secure and often prosperous living.] [37]

Cover of the promotional immigration magazine *Thuis in Zuid-Afrika*, 1955

As the following chapters will reveal, the immigrant Dutch-born architects, engineers, builders and contractors are no exception to this observation. In various ways they had, with their families, created a home in South Africa.

36 Henkes, 2016; Rasool & Witz, 1993, Rosenthal 1952–53; JC Jongens Collection, see also the interlude on Celebration and Commemoration.
37 Ploeger,1994: 3–4.

Rotterdam, interior of the Prinsekerk with transferred C18 organ, designed by Meischke & Schmidt, 1932–33; photo 1997

Cross-Continental Careers

Nicholas Clarke and Marieke Kuipers

For a Dutch-born and educated architect it was a serious challenge, certainly in the early C20, to establish a professional career outside of the Netherlands. Working abroad implied adapting to another language as well as other social, cultural, practical and climatological conditions. In addition, measurements and construction materials could be totally different from what they were used to, and before starting a private practice they had to pass foreign exams. Yet, various Dutch émigré architects already had international experience before they relocated to South Africa, literally at the other end of the world. Only very incidentally did some architects like Coenraad Meischke return to their country of birth and continue to practice, enriched by their experiences in South Africa.[1] His career and that of five other remarkable compatriots who had worked in both the Netherlands and South Africa are briefly sketched in this interlude. These are JE Ferguson, AJC Voorvelt (both in Johannesburg), JC Jongens, HTO Niegeman, and C Wegerif (all in Cape Town). They all emigrated in c1936, for private and economic reasons, probably without knowing each other.

JC Meischke

Johan Coenraad Meischke was born in 1889 in Rotterdam into a family of carpenters and building contractors. His father was Chief Inspector of the Rotterdam Building Inspectorate. Two of his uncles, Jo Vixseboxse and Matthé Meischke, worked as architects/builders in South Africa. The latter called his nephew to Pretoria in 1910 to assist with the construction of the huge Union Buildings that had just begun.[2] Coenraad, recently qualified at the Rotterdam Academy (1908), had also attended courses at the Delft Institute of Technology. In Johannesburg he designed the commercial Meischke's Building (1913) for his uncle.[3] Typical of his interest in heritage, he incorporated the pre-existing Guildhall Pub into the new office block. He may have designed more buildings during his three years' stay and won the design competition for the 1911–12 banner of the architectural monthly *The African Architect*.[4] He next went to Prague, where, in 1915, he qualified as Academic Architect at the Academy led by the modern architect Jan Kotera, and subsequently returned to Rotterdam and worked on the construction of the new Town Hall. In 1916 he succeeded Willem Kromhout as the head teacher of his former school (until 1920). A year later he established a joint practice with Pieter Schmidt. This firm realised a rich portfolio, ranging from social housing to churches, offices, schools and the Academy Building (with BJK Cramer, 1939–40), alongside the restoration of the war-damaged Laurens Church. Meischke published frequently on a large range of topics, from concrete to Constantia.[5] He remained interested in

1 Amongst others were Klaas van Rijsse and Dirk Wentink; see Bakker, *et al.*, 2014.
2 De Bruin, 1982: 124–27.
3 Van der Waal, 1987: 132.

4 Anon. 1911, *The African Architect*, Aug: 56; www.theheritageportal.co.za.
5 For instance, Meischke, 1912, 1914, 1915, 1923, 1926.

The 1911 banner of the journal *The African Architect* designed by the annual competition winner, Johan Meischke

Johannesburg, Meischke's Building with incorporated Guildhall Pub, designed by Johan Meischke, client and contractor: Matthé Meischke, built in 1913; photo 2018

Rotterdam, Academy for Visual Arts and Technical Sciences, designed by JC Meischke & BJK Cramer, built in 1939–40; photographed in mid-1945, with war-time barriers of reinforced concrete still in place.

South Africa, organised an exhibition on photographs by Arthur Elliott, and served on the *Nederlands Zuid-Afrikaanse Vereniging* board. He died in 1966 in Rotterdam.[6]

JE Ferguson

Shanghai is where Johanna Eleanor Ferguson was born in 1900, into a Dutch family with ties to both colonial administration and Theosophy. Her father, though trained as a civil engineer, was at the time the director of the Chinese customs services. In 1912, she moved with her mother and siblings to the Netherlands, and six years later Joop, as she was then called, started studying architecture at the Delft Institute of Technology. While just a candidate-engineer, she published her pieces for do-it-yourself furniture in a women's magazine.[7] When she graduated in 1926, she was one of the first female architectural engineers in the Netherlands. Her first built projects were for her mother, an expressionist house at Wageningen (1926), and for her father, a flat-roofed house at Bosch en Duin near Utrecht (1928).[8]

6 Tillema, 1967; www.stadsarchief.rotterdam.nl.
7 Ferguson, 1926.
8 Th[unnissen?], 1931: 13–21.

Wageningen, 'De Huif', house for Willemine Ferguson-Boerrigter, designed by her daughter, Joop Ferguson and built in 1926; photo 2019

Johannesburg, August House, designed by Ferguson & Stakesby Lewis in 1946, with façade art installation by R1 in c2019

After she emigrated to South Africa, she registered there as an architect in 1937. She set up a joint practice with her third husband, Stakesby Lewis, in Johannesburg in 1938. They were joined by Conrad Sayce in 1948 and according to the firm's letterhead, its joint office was then in the modern Washington House. Apart from numerous private houses in Westcliff, Orchards and elsewhere, the firm was responsible for the Diamond Cutting Works (1943), Belen Bakery, (1944), the Bienvenue Shelter (1944), August House (1946) and Sterling House (1951), all in Johannesburg and all executed in a modernist brick aesthetic.[9]

Besides her architectural practice, Eleanor Ferguson was president of the South African Theosophical Society in Johannesburg (1946–53), for which she lectured and published internationally.[10] In 1953 she relocated with her family to Salisbury (now Harare, Zimbabwe), and in around 1961 moved to Camberley (United Kingdom), where she died in 1982.

9 The Heritage Register; Guerney, 2017.
10 Stakesby Lewis-Ferguson, 1953.

AJC Voorvelt

Antonius Johannes Cornelis Voorvelt was born into a Catholic family in Schoten near Haarlem in 1906, where his father was director of Public Works.[11] Anton trained as a carpenter and became an architect by practice in various offices.[12] He was still in his twenties when he designed the parish church Onze Lieve Vrouw van Zeven Smarten in Schoten (Haarlem) in collaboration with GJM Simons. Now known as the Maria Church, this monumental Romanesque Revival basilica (completed 1936) is enlivened by artwork, including stained glass windows by Joep Nicolas.[13]

By 1935, work was so scarce in the Netherlands that Anton's brother Theo set out from Haarlem for South Africa *by bicycle* in search of new prospects.[14] En-route, he opted to settle in Kenya. Anton visited Theo soon afterwards. Here he learnt that the South African Railways and Harbours (SAR&H) were hiring, and by 1937 Voorvelt was employed in its Johannesburg office.

11 www.noord-hollandsarchief.nl
12 Anon. 1954b, De Tijd, 26 July: 4.
13 Simons, 1937.
14 Anon. 1935b, *De Tijd*, 10 Aug: 10.

Haarlem, interior of the Onze Lieve Vrouw van Zeven Smarten Church, designed by GJM Simons & AJC Voorvelt in 1936; photo 2019

Baptismal font of the Onze Lieve Vrouw van Zeven Smarten Church, designed by GJM Simons & AJC Voorvelt; photo 2019

Pretoria, WW1 memorial to fallen soldiers, part of the Pretoria Station Gardens, all designed by Anton Voorvelt for the SAR&H; photo 2016

Design for a stained glass window, The Stained Glass Studio, Anton Voorvelt, 1970; photo 2019

He remained in the SAR&H office—designing, inter alia, the Pretoria Station gardens—until he was drafted to serve in the Princess Irene brigade, during WW2.[15] After his discharge, Voorvelt took the Special Qualifying Exam at the University of the Witwatersrand to establish himself as an independent architect in Johannesburg. He worked alone, but completed large complicated projects. The Catholic Church was his most important client. He even remotely designed an altar in Bolsward, Netherlands (1953), where another brother was priest and school director.[16]

Locally, Voorvelt designed churches and chapels, seminaries, and schools, including the Catholic Centre (1954) and St Benedict's College (1957), both in Johannesburg and an education building in Roma (now National University of Lesotho). He also worked for other denominations and private clients (Royal Court, 1949). For government he designed the Daeraad School, Wolmaransstad, and the Keetmanshoop Primary School (Namibia), Johannesburg, as well as the Keetmanshoop State Hospital (Namibia).[17] In 1961 he established himself as a stained-glass artist. His glass-art can be found in schools and churches throughout South Africa.[18] Anton Voorvelt passed away in Maastricht while visiting the Netherlands in 1985.

JC Jongens

Jacob Cornelis Jongens was born in Amsterdam in 1898, where he trained at the Kunst-Nijverheid-Teekenschool Quellinus. After qualifying in c1922, Jaap was employed in the office of DF Slothouwer, whose practice continued after he was appointed as professor in Delft in 1926.[19] Over ten years, Jongens took the lead in many of the Slothouwer office's most prestigious projects, including the restoration of the historic estate De Wiersse in Vorden (1921–25) and 'De Neude' in Nijkerk (c1927).[20]

Jongens was retrenched in 1932 when work in Slothouwer's office dried up. He now busied himself with design competitions, designed Scandinavian-inspired furniture and completed three duplex-houses in Heemstede (1934–36) and a shop-house in Amsterdam-Watergraafsmeer. To escape hardship, Jongens seriously considered going to Russia where work for architects was plentiful, but a letter from friends in South Africa convinced him to opt for Cape Town.[21]

After his arrival in 1936, Jongens first worked for Walgate & Elsworth, designing amongst other buildings, the Stellenbosch Town Hall (1938–41).[22] He entered the City of Cape Town's service in 1940 and remained there until his retirement, but also continued to design for others. Because he was not legally registered as an architect in South Africa, he executed these private works under the name of Walgate & Elswoth. These included private residences, many for Dutch emigrants like himself, and the Huguenot Monument in Franschhoek.[23]

After retiring, Jongens associated with the practice of his compatriot Hessel Spoor, Chapman & Spoor.[24] He passed away in Cape Town in 1986, leaving a great but hitherto obscured legacy.

15 See also Chapter 3.
16 Anon. 1953b. *Leeuwarder Courant*, 24 Mar: 3.
17 Personal communication with Antony and Denise Voorvelt, 17 February 2019.
18 Oxley, 1994: 35.
19 Mieras, 1946.
20 Personal communication with Elsbeth Jongens, 26 October 2018.
21 Jongens, 2010; augmented by information from the Jaap Jongens drawing archive and personal communication with the Jongens family, Cape Town and Haarlem (NL).
22 See also Chapter 4.
23 See the interlude on Commemoration and Celebration.
24 See also Chapter 9.

Claremont, Cape Town, House Sorensen, 'Bakebo' designed by Jaap Jongens, 1950, working under the name of Chapman & Spoor; photo shortly after completion

Nijkerk, 'De Neude' manor house, designed by Jaap Jongens in the office of DF Slothouwer and built in 1927; photo 1999

Perspective drawing of a department store for a city of 200 000 people, by Jaap Jongens for the 1931 competition organised by the Rotterdam-based association 'Bouwkunst en Vriendschap'; photo 2020

HTO Niegeman

Of these Dutch-South African architects, Hendrik Theodoor Otto Niegeman (born in 1905 near Haarlem) had the widest cross-continental career. Like his elder and better-known brother Johan, he was trained at the Arts and Crafts Academy in Haarlem; both became active in the Modern Movement. Henk was named after both his maternal grandfather, who had worked for the NZASM in South Africa, and his versatile uncle, Henk Wijdeveld, expressionist architect, and international networker.[25]

In the early 1920s, the Niegeman brothers went to work in Germany for Erich Mendelsohn and stayed at the Bauhaus in Dessau. While Johan next joined Ernst May's brigade in Russia, Henk was contracted by the Soviet Building Trust to design heavy industry buildings (Yarolslavl), a locomotive factory (Lublinov), a workers' club (Grosny), a theatre (Moscow) and a railway station (Vladivostok). In 1932 he went to Kazahkstan but, after several months, he left the republic with his Russian wife.[26]

25 Biographic notes in Wijdeveld archive at Het Nieuwe Instituut, Rotterdam (WIJD 168).

26 Niegeman, 1938, 1939 and Andrews & Niegeman, 1944.

Grosny (former Soviet Union), Workers Clubhouse, built c1931 to the design of Henk Niegeman, as published in the *SAAR*, 1938

Cape Town, Foschini Building, built c1940 to the design of Henk Niegeman, as published in *Cape Town*, 1963

Hout Bay, interior of the bungalow 'Alma Ata' with tubular furniture all designed by Henk Niegeman for himself and his wife, c1943

Paris, Bois de Boulogne, the first Dutch East Indies pavilion built to the design of PAJ Moojen and WJG Zweedijk for the 1931 International Colonial Exhibition under the supervision of Chris Wegerif (soon destroyed by fire)

In late 1933, he assisted Wijdeveld in establishing the short-lived European Mediterranean Academy project at Cavalière, attended by Max Policansky, a Liverpool-trained architect born in Cape Town. In 1934 each returned to his home country, while Niegeman also worked and lectured abroad. On the invitation of Policansky, Niegeman settled in Cape Town in 1936, collaborating on the Judge clothing factory.[27]

He established the independent practice Andrews & Niegeman with Edwin Andrews, whom he knew from Policansky's office, in 1939. Niegeman was the main architect of the Rex Trueform Factory and the proximate clothing factory for Bertish & Co.[28] He designed his own modernist house 'Alma Ata' at Hout Bay with bespoke tubular furniture—for which he also received outside commissions.[29] The practice also worked in the Congo. With interests in shaping a healthy environment and a concern for hygiene, ventilation and logistics, the firm designed modernist apartment blocks, factories, the Shell Training Centre (1957, now SA Naval College) and healthcare institutes. The largest project, Tygerberg Hospital, commenced in 1956, was only completed four years after Niegeman's retirement and subsequent death.[30]

27 Van Graan, 2011: 133–34, 137–38.
28 Personal communication with Bernard Shapiro, 13 February 2019.
29 Niegeman, 1944.
30 See also Chapters 4 and 6.

C Wegerif jr.

Chris Wegerif was born in 1898 in Apeldoorn, where his parents were active promoters of the Arts and Crafts movement and designed furniture for the Dutch royal family. They were central to an international circle of designers and thinkers, including the Anthroposophist Rudolf Steiner. His well-travelled mother Agathe was a famous batik textile designer and teacher. Unlike his father (also Chris), elder brother and cousin, who were all contractors and self-taught architects, Chris jr. trained as an architect at the Delft Institute of Technology. He qualified in 1927 and soon collaborated with his study-mate Frits Gerretsen on plastic-organic architecture (House 'Winjewanje', 1927 and the Vrije School, 1929, both at The Hague, House 'Schermbloem' at Voorthuizen, 1928, and Villa 'Cradalis' at Laren, 1929). In 1930 he supervised the building of wooden constructions for an Anthroposophist summer camp with 1,000 international participants on the Veluwe.[31]

Chris subsequently oversaw the construction of the impressive contribution from the Dutch East Indies for the 1931 International Colonial Exhibition near Paris, the pavilion in Balinese style designed

31 Anon. 1930b, *Het Vaderland*, 7 August: 1 [Avondblad].

by the Java-based architects Pieter Moojen and Willem Zweedijk. Unexpectedly, this richly decorated building burnt down shortly after the opening. A second, more modest pavilion was quickly built under Wegerif's technical supervision.[32]

Back in Holland, he did some work for Anthroposophical clients, but, as times got worse, he emigrated with his family to South Africa in 1936. There he designed various other Anthroposophy-inspired buildings at the Cape, such as Camphill Village, schools and private houses. Around 1950 he associated with Jan Zeger Schuurmans Stekhoven, and later inherited that practice.[33] He passed away while visiting his step-son in Switzerland in 1984.[34]

Surprising links and legacies

The cross-continental careers of Meischke, Ferguson, Voorvelt, Jongens, Niegeman and Wegerif are not unique, but they speak to the talent, training and tenacity of these architects. They became important links in the intercontinental transfer of expertise in times when intercontinental travel was time-consuming and communication challenging. Their legacy is surprisingly rich and varied.

Laren, Villa Cradalis, garden side; built to the design of Gerretsen & Wegerif based on Anthroposophist principles for Chris' sister, Aagje van Houten-Wegerif, in 1929; photo 1983

32 Wegerif was knighted for these efforts, just like Moojen and Zweedijk; see also Anon. 1931a, *De Hollandsche Revue*: 59–63; Bloembergen, 2001: 220–59, Schoemaker, 1931 and Zeijlstra, 1931.
33 Personal communication with Michael Stekhoven, 12 February 2019.
34 Personal communication with Julian Stekhoven, 7 January 2020.

Cape West Coast, chapel of Camphill Village built according to the design of Chris Wegerif based on Anthroposophist principles in the 1960s and still in use in 2019

Pretoria, University of Pretoria, first Agriculture Building, designed by the Public Works Department, completed in 1921; photo 2019

4 Civic Works and Community Buildings

Nicholas Clarke

The creation of the built environment of South Africa dates, for the most part, to the C20. At the start of that century, much-needed care and community facilities for specific population groupings or the general good were often commissioned and constructed by community and charitable institutions. Over time these tasks were then taken over by governmental institutions. Surprisingly, many Dutch émigré architects made a significantly large contribution to these public works and community buildings. This chapter presents both pragmatic and emblematic projects from 1902–61, with the focus on what was formerly the Transvaal and Cape, the economic and administrative epicentres in this period.

At the outset it must be noted that this period was also coloured by contemptible preconceptions of European superiority over other groups, which resulted in the formalisation of racially based apartheid policies. This led to unjust and inequitable provisioning for communities, unfortunately still reflected in the country's built landscape today.

Accommodating Government

British hegemony was established over southern Africa in 1902 when the surrender of the independent South African (ZAR) and Orange Free State Republics to the British forces ended the South African War (1899–1902). The C20 birthed a three-tiered administrative system in the country, with powers delegated from national to provincial and local level. New accommodation was required as the administration and its services grew.

During the C19 many architects and builders from the Netherlands worked in the large and well-oiled ZAR Department of Public Works (DPW).[1] Its successor, the Transvaal Colony Public Works Department (PWD), already established during the South African War in 1901, was initially staffed by military engineers. At the end of the War in 1902, the PWD became a civil service, counting eighteen members of staff, but grew to 150 men by the end of the same year. Amongst its new employees were a surprising number of former DPW employees who had vehemently fought against the British invasions during the War, some of whom had been incarcerated in exile. A significant number were returned to their former postings in the districts, but then under British superiors. Former Netherlands South African Railways Company (NZASM) drawing office staff also entered the PWD, some remaining there for their entire careers.[2] In this way the PWD subsumed the tacit knowledge of the ZAR DPW and the NZASM.

Herbert Baker was commissioned to design a new administration building in 1909 to accommodate a growing government, and as a symbol of an envisaged new Union of South Africa. All of the detailing, the technical design, contract management and construction supervision was

Pretoria, Union Buildings, celebratory photo taken at the placing of a statue of Atlas on one of the two towers utilising Meischke's construction equipment; photo 1913

undertaken by a specially constituted project team in Pretoria District PWD, dominated by Dutch-born practitioners.[3] Hendrik Siemerink, Acting Assistant Engineer for the Pretoria District, was in charge of the entire construction process. Leo Geers and Paulus Hofman were two of the five Departmental draughtsmen on the project. New Dutch émigré Jan Schallies was appointed as project surveyor.[4] The large Dutch presence on the Union Buildings District Engineer's staff was mirrored in the contractors. Two of the three construction components were awarded to the firm of the Dutch-born Matthé Meischke, who had worked in the Transvaal before the War and was soon seen as 'one of the country's leading contractors'.[5] His team on the Union Buildings included his own nephew, Coenraad Meischke and father and son, both Jan de Jong.

1 Bakker, 2014.
2 Minnaar, 2000: 104; Ploeger, 1994: 90.
3 Greig, 1970: 190.
4 Union of South Africa, Public Works Department, 1912.
5 Editorial, 1911: 10.

Cape Town, keystones depicting animal heads incorporated into the main façade of the Cape Provincial Administration Building (now Western Cape Provincial Parliament), designed by Jan Schuurmans Stekhoven in 1937; photo 2020

Province

Under the new Union, the four colonies—Cape, Natal, Orange Free State and Transvaal—retained a large measure of administrative independence, each with its own administration. To house the offices of the ever-growing Cape Provincial Administration (CPA) a new building was constructed in Cape Town in 1939. The commission was awarded to Fred Glennie and Jan Schuurmans Stekhoven.

'Stek' emigrated to the Cape in 1919 and, like Glennie, worked in the practice of Baker, Kendall & Morris before starting on his own. For the CPA building, they designed a strict granite-clad façade, softened by the use of teak Cape sash-windows and enlivened by sculpted ornaments: a Stekhoven calling-card.[6]

Town

The establishment of local government took place at various stages in the different colonies. Infrastructure, including fire stations, water works and recreation facilities, needed to be constructed by newly established municipalities. In the Transvaal, municipal drawing offices were often staffed by former Dutch émigrés of ZAR DPW. Notable examples include Frans van der Ben, who was First Class Draftsman (city architect) in Pretoria by 1902, and Herman Luitingh who became City Engineer in Potchefstroom.[7] Much of their work may have been utilitarian and inconspicuous, but not less important for that.

With the growth of administrative tasks and increase in wealth, many cities built a first or new town hall, not only to house their staff but also to express their significance to the local communities. Inspiration was often sought in historical precedent to underline historic continuity and the relevance of municipal governance. Town halls were sometimes the subject of a design competition. In Graaff-Reinet, for instance, the design competition for the town hall was awarded to the Amsterdam-born architect Folkert Hesse. The result is an outspoken Dutch Renaissance Revival style, which is curiously at odds with its official name: 'Victoria Hall' (1911). Today all façades are whitewashed, disguising the original bandings of red brick and white accentuated layers.

6 Personal communication, Michael Stekhoven. 12 February 2019.

7 Rossouw, 2005: 64–71; Ploeger, 1994: 90; see also Chapter 7.

Other town halls were commissioned to local architects such as the one in Utrecht, designed by former ZAR DPW district supervisor, H Hellberg (1913). For the Paarl Town Hall, (1927–8) the newly appointed town engineer, Henry Reitz, collaborated with Wynand Louw. For its design he adopted the whitewashed C17 vocabulary of the VOC, possibly seen by the architects as appropriate for a town that has its origins in the days of the first Dutch settlers. Reitz was the son of the former president of the Orange Free State and his Dutch wife, Cornelia Mulder. The family lived in the Netherlands under self-imposed exile during the South African War. When they returned to South Africa in 1907, Henry remained to study architecture [*bouwkunde*] at the Delft Institute of Technology where he would have been introduced to the built legacy of the VOC. After his return to South Africa, Reitz was first appointed town engineer of Knysna, and then of Paarl. In 1931 he designed the Franschhoek Town Hall. Reitz was later appointed first Professor in the Department of Engineering at the University of Stellenbosch in 1942.[8]

8 Koch, 2019.

Stellenbosch, Town Hall, design proposals by Jaap Jongens dated January 1938, completed 1941

Graaff-Reinet, Victoria Hall (Town Hall) designed in 1911 by Folkert Hesse; photo 1946

Utrecht, Kwa-Zulu Natal, 1913 Town Hall designed by H Hellberg; photo 2010

Cape Town, Sea Point Fire Station, completed in 1927 to the design of Frederik Bongers; photo 2020

Paarl, Town Hall, designed by Town Engineer Henry Reitz and Wynand Louw, constructed 1927–28; photo 2020

The Stellenbosch Town Hall (1938–41), in turn, was designed by the office of Walgate & Elsworth when Dutch émigré Jaap Jongens worked there. Two versions for its design by Jongens present either a Neoclassical or a then contemporary styling, reminiscent of Dudok's 1931 Hilversum Town Hall. Like its neighbouring winelands towns, Stellenbosch looked to the past, selected and built the historicising proposal.

Occasionally, utility met representativity. The 1927 Sea Point Fire Station, Cape Town, was designed by Frederik Bongers, who worked as architect in the City Engineer's Department between 1926 and 1959. The landmark building, located on the axis at the termination of Main Road, has a stately semi-circular arcaded entrance, positioned on-axis with the main thoroughfare; its Italianate styling clearly aimed at creating a very civic building.

Education

After 1902, the four autonomous colonial provinces developed their own policies for education. Each enacted its own legislation, but a commonality was that their concern was limited to a section of the population, for the most part not taking responsibility for the education of Black children besides that of the few schools in the so-called 'locations', or dormitory towns. Mission schools and charitable organisations attempted to fill this lacuna. In 1948 the National Party came to power and soon enacted the 1953 Bantu Education Act, which enforced racial segregation in schools at a national level. This brought education for Black South Africans under government control, effectively formalising a two-tiered education system.

Transvaal

Following the South African War, the Governor, Alfred Milner, outlined three policies that in unison would realize South Africa as a 'white man's country' on the ground of the 'superior civilization', especially that of the British. 'Boers' were delegated to second-class citizens until anglicized, and Blacks to third-class citizens with no hope of enfranchisement.[9] Initially, public funds for education were reserved for English-medium schools serving white communities. Public works departments were responsible for the construction of public educational facilities at primary, secondary and tertiary level. To further aid in the anglicizing of the Transvaal Boers, Milner established a number of English-medium schools in Pretoria and Johannesburg and Potchefstroom.

In response, the *Algemene Kommissie tot behartiging van het Christelik Nasionale Onderwijs* [Christian National Education, CNO] organisation was established in Pretoria to develop private Protestant Dutch-language schools.[10] Protestant groupings in the Netherlands contributed financially to establishing private CNO schools in farmhouses, wagon sheds and the like. In Heidelberg, for instance, the first CNO Volksskool started in the basement of the local Nederduits Gereformeerde [Dutch Reformed, DRC] Church in 1903. Four years later a purpose-built primary school building was inaugurated, bank-rolled by local inhabitants.

In Pretoria, former Dutch émigré ZAR DPW architects Johannes Kraan and Jan Wijers designed the new flagship CNO school in 1904, on a plot in the then young suburb Sunnyside: the Oost-Eind School.[11] They applied the same clear climatic response of the ZAR DPW, based on well-conceived solar shading principles, coupled with an ingenious ventilation strategy. As an architectural assertion of the 'Dutch-ness' of the school, it also continued the Dutch Renaissance Revival aesthetic of the ZAR period.

The CNO movement was short-lived. The steady flow of funds from the Netherlands was drying up. When the 1907 Transvaal Education Act sanctioned subsidised education in any 'European' language, the then existing 115 CNO schools were incorporated into the state education system.[12] To replace the farmhouse and wagon shed classrooms, a schools construction project was initiated by the PWD in 1908. In larger towns schools were designed in a mannerist Edwardian classicism, often executed in hard-baked brick, with expressive sandstone quoining and restrained classical detailing.

Pretoria was then expanding fast. The city developed new neighbourhoods and these in turn required schools. In Pretoria, De Jong jr. was appointed Clerk of Works for the City Council of Pretoria in 1931. He was responsible for both town planning and the design of public schools in the 1940s. This implied professional support of race-based segregation in the planning and design of townships and educational facilities. One of the primary schools he designed at Atteridgeville, inaugurated in 1940, carries his name. The JJ de Jong School has two arched openings leading from the street to the three-sided courtyard, today covered over.[13]

A proximate neighbourhood of sub-economic subsidised housing for White residents, Danville, was also designed by De Jong. Similar to the Atteridgeville school, De Jong's Westerlig Primary School (c. 1947) has an open-sided courtyard, extended horizontal face brick façade, with local Iscor-manufactured steel-framed windows and plastered lintels, accentuated by face brick chimneys. Although the two school buildings are seemingly akin, these similarities did not translate to equal construction budgets, fittings and finishes, or more importantly operational provisioning or educational opportunities for scholars.

Continuously improving road and rail infrastructure in the countryside led to the centralising of schooling facilities, and town schools were enlarged, often with hostels for serving the White children of an entire rural district. Dutch émigrés John van de Werke, Anton Voorvelt and Jaap van Niftrik were among the many architects appointed by the Transvaal Education Department to design and supervise the construction of such new schools. As an example, Van Niftrik was tasked to design the Schweizer-Reneke Afrikaans-medium high school (1951–52), and succeeded in bringing a unique aesthetic to the school-hall in particular, despite the limitations of official design specifications.[14]

9 Cross, 1986: 3.
10 Bot, 1936: 71.
11 See Chapter 3.
12 Bot, 1936: 73.
13 See Chapter 8.
14 See Chapter 1.

Heidelberg, Gauteng, Volks Primary School, completed 1907; photo 2017

Maseru, Roma Campus (now National University of Lesotho), staff and student accommodation, designed by Edy Payens in 1954; photo soon after completion

At the tertiary level, the 1921 Agriculture Building for the fledgling Transvaal University College, today the University of Pretoria, was designed to serve students mainly from Afrikaans farming communities. Although the authorship is generally attributed to PWD architect James Dey, Everhardus de Lange, a Dutch émigré who entered the employ of the PWD after the First World War, also contributed to the design.[15] It is an amalgam of the Edwardian styling of the PWD schools and Cape Dutch Revival. Its monumental gable and sculpted frieze clearly refer to a historic Dutch connection and early European colonial agricultural practice in the county.

Some other buildings on the University of Pretoria campus also contain a touch of Dutch. Notably the first Botany (1940) and Chemistry (1942) buildings were designed by the office of Moerdyk & Watson architects when Van de Werke, who had arrived in Pretoria in 1935, was working there. These buildings exhibit a distinct Dutch aesthetic inspired by the work of Willem Dudok and the De Stijl movement in the Netherlands. Van de Werke also designed a new men's hostel at the University for the Hervormde Kerk [Reformed Church], the church of choice for Protestant Dutch emigrants to the country. Constructed in 1940, Huis Voortrekker soon earned its nickname 'Glaskas' [greenhouse] due to the stark Modernist curtain-wall façade. Van de Werke later designed many educational buildings including that for Pretoria Normal College (1955). His last educational project was for additions to the President High School, Johannesburg (1980).[16]

The 1953 the Bantu Education Act gave government control over all tertiary education curricula. As a consequence, Black South Africans students chose rather to attend the Catholic University College, founded in 1945 at the Roma Mission outside of Maseru in the British Protectorate of Basutoland, now Lesotho. Due to this sudden influx, more housing was needed. Edy Payens, a Catholic Dutch émigré architect living in Bloemfontein, was appointed to design a village of single storeyed bungalows, which were constructed from local sandstone blocks. The village, completed in 1958, still serves as student and staff accommodation of what has grown into the National University of Lesotho.

15 Keith, 1998: 95; Swart, 2020: 135; Ploeger, 1994: 55–56.

16 Project List, John van de Werke, Department of Architecture, University of Pretoria; see Chapters 1 and 10.

Pretoria, University of Pretoria, first Botany Building, completed in 1940; photo 2019

Pretoria, Huis Voortrekker, (now University of Pretoria Xayata Hostel), designed by John van de Werke in 1940; photo soon after completion

The Cape

Higher education was already established in the C19 at the Cape. The Cape government had long been subsiding education before its first education legislation was passed. This, the 1905 School Board Act, legislated school attendance for White children up to the age of 14 and set out procedures for the establishment of Coloured schools, but set no legal obligation for the latter's attendance.

Education building designs at the Cape also incorporated historical building styles to present an image of community, belonging and continuity. The versatile Dutch émigré architect, Mello Damstra, designed a striking double-storeyed complex of lecture halls, offices and laboratories for the new Faculty for Natural Sciences (1904) at Stellenbosch. Its striking central Neo-classical Cape Dutch Revival gable, flanked by two Baroque Cape Dutch Revival exemplars, may have been specifically tailored to resonate with the culture of the predominantly Afrikaans-speaking student population. This design may very well have been the first use of Cape Dutch Revival styling in

Stellenbosch, Stellenbosch University Faculty for Natural Sciences, designed by Mello Damstra in 1904; photo of building and architect soon after completion

Cape Town, Jan van Riebeeck Combined School, designed by Jan Schuurmans Stekhoven in 1928–29; as published in *Laerskool Jan van Riebeeck 50*, 1971

Cape Town, Jan van Riebeeck High School, designed by Lyon & Stekhoven in 1931, as published in *Ons drie eeue*, 1952

an institutional building in the country, with many more to follow.[17] To accommodate the growth in the number of scholars, the Bloemhof Meisiesskool [Girls' School] in Stellenbosch, established as a private school in 1875, constructed a new building in 1907. Designed by Hesse, its Dutch Renaissance Revival styling—originally with exposed deep-red brickwork and white Baroque scrolls and pilasters—was common for public schools in the Netherlands at the time, but like Hesse's Graaff-Reinet Town Hall, more in tune with the preceding century than its own.[18]

17 The building, altered and much extended, still serves as the Faculty of Natural Sciences of the University of Stellenbosch.

18 Since 1991 the renovated building today houses the Stellenbosch University Museum.

The School Board Act also established the Cape Schools Board (CSB). From the late 1920s onwards, the CSB embarked on a large school construction project throughout the province. Jan Schuurmans Stekhoven became the board's architect of choice for the western and northern Cape. His first school, the Jan van Riebeeck School (1927) initially housed both primary and secondary school pupils, but it was soon bursting at the seams. 'Stek' was now working in association with John Lyon, and their practice was commissioned to design a new high-school building. This school was constructed in 1931 in a gracious Cape Dutch Revival style. Like its older sibling, the double-storeyed building was built around a colonnaded courtyard. Its two identical, restrained gables—reminiscent of the gables of Great Constantia—face the city bowl and the ocean.[19]

19 The school building is now subsumed by bulky additions, its fine gables now lost, replicated by tacky imitations.

Stellenbosch, Bloemhof Meissiesskool (now Stellenbosch University Museum), designed by Folkert Hesse, 1907; photo 2020

Subsequently, the practice built more than 30 schools for the CSB, especially in the districts for White and Coloured communities. Built to CSB specifications, all of these schools have in common the limited pallet of materials: plastered brick walls, teak sash windows and half-shutters; pitched (often tiled) roofs. Decoration is limited to where it has most effect; many have their own distinctive Cape Dutch Revival gables marking the central entrances, like the Goudini High School at Rawsonville. All are finely proportioned. Many have courtyards. When the required building was small, it was designed to be able to grow around a future courtyard, sometimes with end-walls left toothed to accept future additions. The 1937 Porterville Primary School is a good example of a 'starter school'. Blind walls at the extremities of the back façade allow for additions outwards to create a courtyard school without needing to move a single window.

Stekhoven's practice, in which he was joined by Chris Wegerif in around 1950, continued to design schools after WW2. Wegerif designed the exceptionally well-proportioned and detailed Porterville High School (1957). It has a distinct Dudokian aesthetic and in the school hall the stage is framed in an angular concrete portal, characteristic of Wegerif's Anthroposophist leanings.

In the Eastern Cape, Siemerink was responsible for many schools for the CSB. Like Stekhoven, Siemerink's school plans were all bespoke and designed around courtyards, with a view to future extension. The 1928 Cummingham Primary School (now Quest School) in South End, Port Elizabeth, was built for the multi-racial community that at the time flourished here (until the 1948 Group Areas Act forced the segregation and brutal scattering of its community). Siemerink utilised the sloping site to great effect, raising the building on a near-monumental plinth. Schools were sized to the population they served, but the principles of climate and extendibility prevailed in his designs. Where double storeyed schools were constructed, like Dr Viljoen Primary School in Port Elizabeth (1931), he used the roof overhang to shade the upper floor windows and—similar to Stek's Jan van Riebeeck School of 1931—a curious but practical cantilevered canopy located over the lower floor windows. Siemerink & Brinkman also designed starter schools for small communities. The small two-roomed 1935 Hanover Road School with its teacher's house, constructed at a railway siding in the arrid Karoo, was designed with a hipped end on one extreme and a gable end on the other, so that it could easily be extended. Its main façade faces south-west so as to only receive direct sunlight in the late afternoon when the school would be empty.

Siemerink, or the CSB, seems to have attempted to relate school buildings to their cultural context through the choice of style: Palladian Neo-classicism in cosmopolitan English-speaking contexts, such as the Cummingham School; Cape Dutch-Revival for Afrikaner communities such as the 1939 Stulting primary school in Humansdorp. A constant in Siemerink's well-mannered designs is the attention given to the entrances into the school; always providing a central main entrance and two side entrances, the latter leading directly to the colonnaded courtyards.

Porterville, Porterville High School, designed by Schuurmans-Stekhoven & Wegerif in 1959; photo 2020

Port Elizabeth, Cummingham School (now Quest School), designed by Siemerink & Walker, 1928; photo 2020

Accommodating special needs

The education of children with special needs in South Africa was of necessity often taken up by private charitable initiative. The Louis Botha Memorial Home for Children was founded in Pretoria 1918 as a home for children orphaned by the Spanish Flu epidemic. Journalist Frans Engelenburg was instrumental in its creation. He may have proposed Frans Soff as an architect to design a new building for the orphanage. Soff, a Dutch émigré like Engelenburg, had designed Engelenburg's 1903 Cape-Dutch Revival home in Pretoria.[20] Constructed in 1923, Soff's design was for a reserved, sober, but graceful double-storeyed courtyard building with saddle roof and veranda (stoep) on both floors oriented to the east for morning sun.[21]

In 1933, the conservative Gereformeerde Kerk [Reformed Church] established its own orphanage in Pretoria, named after former ZAR President Kruger. The Frisian architect Pieter Dykstra, who emigrated to South Africa in 1927, was engaged for the project. The orphanage complex was planned to comprise a streamlined Art-Deco main building, flanked by Cape Dutch Revival pavilions for the various children's 'homes'. This combination of contemporary and historic idioms signalled the institution's modernity and its cultural affiliations. However, in the midst of a financial crisis, only a reduced version of the main building could be constructed.[22]

During the same crisis, the Jan Kriel Institute boarding school for children suffering from epilepsy was established in 1936 at Kuils River, outside Cape Town. Initiated by a DRC minister and his wife in memory of their son Jan who had died from this neurological disorder, the institute was initially housed in adapted farm buildings. A new bespoke complex was desperately needed. After the institute was officially adopted by the DRC and affiliated to the CSB, Andrews & Niegeman Architects was tasked with this challenging design assignment.

The overall layout of dispersed buildings designed by Niegeman is reminiscent of the Zonnestraal Sanatorium in Hilversum (1928-31 with staff buildings added later) by Jan Duiker. Niegeman most likely knew Duiker, as they had both been members of the CIAM-affiliated group 'de 8' in the Netherlands. Niegeman had already established his health-care credentials as an avant-gardist modernist architect for the Leeuwendal Maternity Home in Cape Town (1939) with its strong focus on hygiene. Like at Leeuwendal—and unusually for a church-aligned institute at this period of South Africa's history—Niegeman's Modernist design for the Jan Kriel Institute was minimalist and devoid of any historicism. All spaces

20 Rex, 1975: 241; see Chapter 1.

21 Ten years later two wings were added in a Cape Dutch Revival style by architect Charles Small. The building now serves as the Tshwane Regional Pharmacy.

22 This building is now used by the City Tshwane Electricity Division.

Pretoria, Louis Botha Children's Home (now Tshwane Regional Pharmacy), designed by Frans Soff in 1923; photo 2020

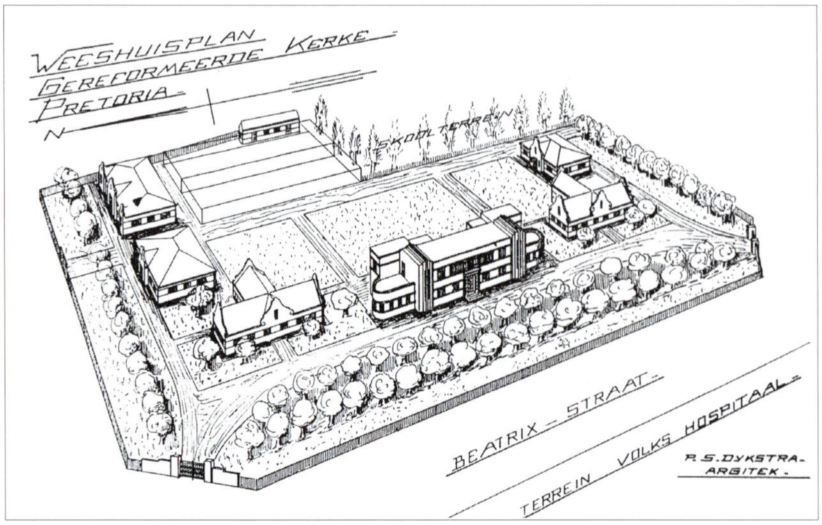

Pretoria, President Kruger Children's Home, bird's-eye perspective drawings, designed by Pieter Dykstra, as published in *Almanak vir die Gereformeerde Kerk in Suid-Afrika vir die jaar 1934*

were designed for optimal daylighting and ventilation as well as easy cleaning. Niegeman applied D-form concrete shell roofs that allowed a free span from exterior wall to exterior wall, leaving the interior free of structural elements. The complex was completed in stages: two girls' dormitories, a refectory and kitchen in 1947, followed by two dormitories for boys in 1949, a new school building and a staff-residence in 1952. The institute still functions today, its focus having broadened over time.

The international Camphill movement likewise provides education and life-long accommodation to a wide scope of children and adults with special needs. This approach is rooted in the international Anthroposophist movement initiated by the Austrian esoteric Rudolf Steiner and attempts to unite the rational with the spiritual in all human activities. Anthroposophy advances an expressionist 'organic' architecture with compositions based on the Golden Section and pentagon. As a key proponent of Anthroposophy in South Africa, Wegerif designed the Camphill Village on the Cape West Coast (1961–64). The hall, housing, dairy and a chapel were all designed with typical expressionist-organic features.[23] He also designed the Camphill Farm outside Hermanus in 1965 for the graduates of the related school and the first buildings of the Anthroposophist-aligned Waldorf School in Constantia, Cape Town (1967).

Healthcare

Whether public or private, health-care in C20 South Africa was provided along racially segregated lines. Like special needs education, community healthcare was often developed through charitable institutions, which, due to close cultural ties with the Netherlands, in cases reflected the 'pillarization' prevalent in Dutch society.

The Protestant Zuid-Afrikaansche Hospitaal (ZAH) was founded in 1904 in Pretoria, with six beds where patients could be cared for in their own language (Dutch) by *diaconessen*: unmarried Protestant nurses. The ZAH was affiliated with the Diaconessenhuis hospital in Utrecht, the Netherlands, even sending their aspirant nurses there for training.[24]

The ZAH was initially financially reliant on private donations from the Netherlands. By the 1920s it had also received subsidies from both province and municipality. Instead of sending trainees to Utrecht, the hospital itself wanted to train its own nurses. But to do so it legally required more than 40 beds. A new state-of-the-art hospital was envisaged. Dutch émigré architect Johan Burg (formerly of the NZASM and PWD) was appointed to design the new hospital building, in the 'oude Kaapsche bouwstijl' [old Cape style].

Burg's 1929 design was progressive for its time. It proposed a single-storey hospital that would be entered through a domed vestibule from the east, leading to a long east-west corridor. The rooms, located on the north of the corridor, would open onto a wide veranda onto which the patient's beds could be wheeled directly. The stoep would offer not only sweeping views of the valley, but more importantly fresh air and, in winter, healing sunlight to patients, according to the newest thinking in health-care. Two operating rooms were positioned on the cool south side of the corridor central to the length of the building.

As part of the design process, Burg's drawings were submitted to the scrutiny of the well-regarded Dutch architect Jan Hanrath, who at the time was completing the construction of the new Diaconessenhuis building in Utrecht. Hanrath was specifically asked to advise on the application of the *Kaapsche bouwstyl* to modern hospital design.[25] Hanrath forthwith suggested improvements to the design, made recommendations on the use of the most modern medical equipment, such as Philips electrical operating lamps, forwarded samples of Krommenie Linoleum and gathered information on FW Braat steel door and window frames. An extension to the hospital was put out to tender in 1935. By then it was not Burg, but Dykstra who was the project architect.[26]

Concurrently to the ZAH project, Burg designed a maternity home that would serve as a school for midwifery for the Moedersbond [Mothers Union]. The Moedersbond was created in 1918 by the Suid-Afrikaanse Vrouwevereeniging [South African Women Association] for the self-empowerment and healthcare of Afrikaner women. The three-storeyed maternity hospital, midwifery school and adjacent nurses' residence was

23 See also the interlude on Cross-continental careers.
24 Fraay-ten Bokkel Huinink, 1921: 38–39.
25 Hanrath Archive in Het Nieuwe Instituut, Rotterdam, HANR0149.
26 Marius, 1935: 2.

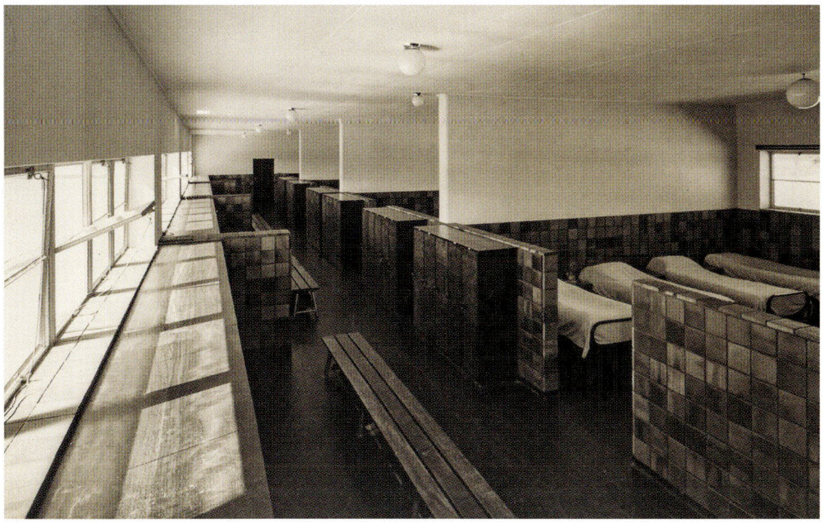

Cape Town, Kuils River, Jan Kriel Institute, interior of boys' dormitory, completed 1949, designed by Henk Niegeman; photo soon after completion

Pretoria, Moedersbond (now Lebone College of Emergency Care) completed 1931, designed by Johan Burg; photo 2014

Pretoria, Zuid-Afrikaansche Hospitaal, designed by Johan Burg in 1929; photo 2015

Port Elizabeth, Provincial Hospital, completed 1915, Public Works Department; photo 2020

completed in close proximity to the Pretoria General Hospital in 1931. Like Soffs' proximate children's home, the building faced east, with a wide central stoep on both floors, providing a safe private place for morning sunning of both mother and child. Its international Art-Deco styling presented the Moedersbond as a first-rate, progressive, even prestigious, institution.[27]

27 Today the building is used to train emergency response professionals.

Black communities were often denied proper care by either a discriminatory and negligent government, or through their remote locations. Rural healthcare was often incorporated into missionary endeavours. Payens was commissioned to design hospitals for Catholic missions, including the Seboche Mission Hospital (1956), in today's Lesotho. He prepared a pragmatic design, constructed with local sandstone under a simple gable roof marked by an ornamented wrought iron cross above the central entrance portico, as a reference to its religious denomination. Protestants were equally active in the healthcare-cum-missionary field. John van de Werke, for instance, designed a tuberculosis hospital for the DRC at Tshilidzini in the north of the Transvaal, now Limpopo, in 1961. This hospital was serviced by a contingent of Dutch doctors into the 1990s. Like Seboche, Tshilidzini still serves the population of its wide geographical area.

Segregation was always imposed where the South African government itself developed health-care facilities, even where facilities needed to be shared. Architects were obliged to defer to this status quo. In Port Elizabeth, Siemerink was appointed to design various additions to the Provincial Hospital (1915), the construction of which he had overseen while still a civil servant. These later additions included accommodation to facilitate segregation, including adding 'Coloured' servants' quarters (1930–31). Community initiatives for the care of the physically disabled were reserved according to race, especially when reliant on government support. The Port Elizabeth municipality, for instance, donated the land

Cape Town, Tygerberg Hospital, main building, completed 1976, designed by Henk Niegeman, Andrews & Niegeman; photo 2020

for the Walton Orthopaedic Home, created by the Cripple Care Fund. Siemerink & Brinkman were tasked with the design of the complex, which was completed 1947. Today it serves the administration for the Eastern Cape Provincial Health Services.

Andrews & Niegeman were awarded the design of a new large teaching hospital for the University of Stellenbosch in 1956. By now, the provisions of the Reservation of Separate Amenities Act (1953) legislated racial segregation of public facilities, effectively mandating better facilities for Whites. The architects and client insisted that all facilities of this, the Tygerberg Hospital (1956–76), would be identical on 'both' sides of the irrationally imposed racial divide. The consequence was a behemoth 18 000-bed facility, effectively a double-hospital. The only real difference between the two 'sides' lay in the number of beds provided: more in-patient wards were provided for 'Coloured' patients; all other facilities were identical.[28]

Niegeman took on the responsibility as lead designer and, in 1956, with representatives of the Provincial Administration, undertook a study trip to the USA, Canada, Britain and Europe to investigate international best practice. He personally designed the main hospital building up to the level of detail in the face brick façade and applied Wilhelm Ostwald's colour system for the finishing of walls and floors to create a harmonious interior.[29]

Cultural and sports facilities

The post-WW2 era heralded a new period of prosperity, and with it, construction of public facilities in towns and cities, mostly for use by White residents. In some cities Dutch emigrants took a lead in the municipal works departments. In Bloemfontein, for instance, the relatively unknown City Architect, JJ van Voorst, was responsible for the 1957 Municipal Library (now Adelaide Tambo Public Library).[30] The strongly modular façades carefully balanced the public nature of the building with thoughtful solar control, resulting in a refined, dynamic tectonic architecture.

28 Peters, 2018: 3; personal communication with Barney Shapiro, 13 February 2019.

29 Clarke & Kuipers, 2021; see also interlude on Cross-continental careers.

30 He registered as an architect in South Africa in 1946; Greig, 1971: 85.

Jaap Jongens entered into the employ of the City of Cape Town in 1940, remaining there until his pensioning.[31] As evidenced by the drawings preserved in his archive, Jongens was involved in a huge range of public projects. His many perspective drawings of the City's proposals for civic buildings on the reclaimed foreshore, while never executed, are both masterful and fascinating.[32] The Wynberg Public Library, built in 1958, exemplifies Jongens' attention to detail, his aesthetic drive as well as his constant evolution as a highly independent designer of note.

Jongens was also involved in the design of public recreation facilities, such as the Sea Point Promenade (1950s) as well as the Newlands Public Swimming Pool (1955, with R Nixon). Its large stand is covered by an impressive reinforced concrete cantilevered fold-plate roof carried on oblique columns. Jongens' Green Point Stadium (1956) shows a close kinship to Jan Wils' 1928 Amsterdam Olympic Stadium. Jongens might very well have watched the construction of the stadium while he was working in the Dutch capital before emigrating in 1936. In his design, Jongens translated the Olympic Stadium's monumentality, including its tall Marathon Tower designed to hold the Olympic Flame, into a restrained post-war aesthetic. After repeated alterations, little remains of the Jongens original today.

31 Jongens, 2010: 44.
32 See the interlude on this topic and Chapter 10.

Water security and supply constructions

When Jongens joined City Hall, Cape Town was expanding fast. A large new residential area, Q-Town (now referred to as Kewtown, Athlone), was being developed. Jongens was closely involved in the design of the urban layout, housing, a recreation centre, a large stadium/sports centre and even road infrastructure. The Athlone Waste Treatment Plant testing laboratory is one of his designs that was executed as originally planned. The building—constructed in a mix of rough baked bricks and covered by an expressive roof—presents a well-considered adaptation to local climate and material of an aesthetic that has its origin in the Dutch expressionist architecture of the 1920s.[33]

By 1950 the city counted approximately 720 000 people, and water security became a critical issue.[34] Under the direction of Chief Engineer, Solomon Morris, a new scheme was developed to bring water from the Wemmershoek Mountains. The project included constructing an earth-fill dam wall, a sluice-operated spillway, an inflow-outflow control station, a purification plant as well as a carbonation plant to aid the transport of the purified water through the 50km long pipeline to the Tygerberg Reservoir near the city. As indicated on the project drawings, Jongens designed all the buildings required. They show a kinship with then contemporary governmental architecture in the Netherlands. The sluice machine room takes as its precedent the 1938 Beatrix Sluice complex in the Lek Canal near Utrecht, designed by JP Josephus Jitta and LSP

33 Still in use by the City of Cape Town Scientific Services.
34 Morris, 1959.

Bloemfontein, Municipal Library (now Adelaide Tambo Public Library), completed 1957, design by City Architect JJ van Voorst; photo 2020

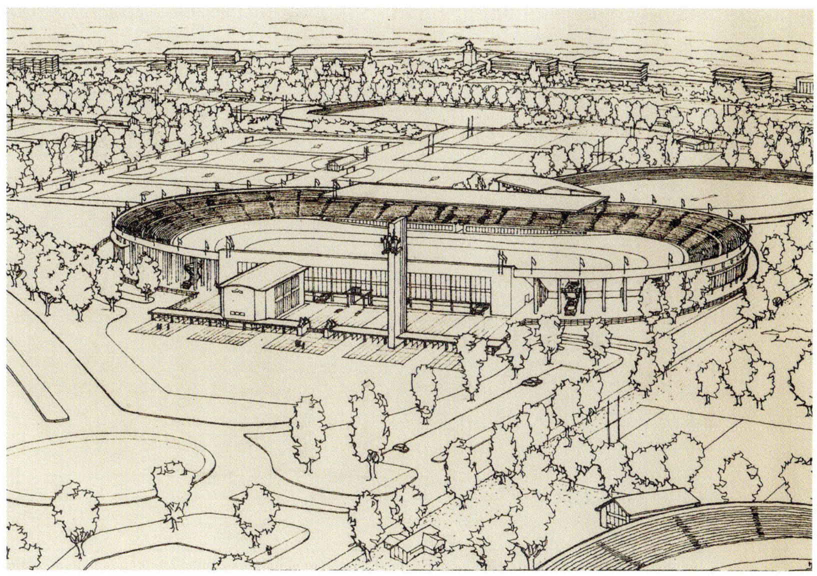

Cape Town, Green Point Stadium, bird's eye view, designed 1955 by Jaap Jongens

Amsterdam, Olympic Stadium, designed by Jan Wils, completed in 1928; photo 1930

Cape Town, Wynberg Library, façade drawing 1958, designed by Jaap Jongens

Scheffer. The double-storeyed main building of the purification- and carbonation plant, completed in 1957, is built of plain brick with D-shell vaulted concrete roof, set high on a plinth. The sweeping staircase leading up to the main entrance and the bas-relief city crest lends ita monumental stature. Although on a smaller scale, its architecture unmistakably echoes the Rotterdam Customs Office (1940–48), designed by the Dutch State Government architect at the time, Hayo Hoekstra.

Engendering Dutch community

Like other immigrant communities, the Dutch created their own networks in South Africa. When after WW2, a new wave of immigration swelled the ranks of the South African Dutch communities, existing social facilities could be improved and new facilities built. These efforts were supported, officially and financially, by the Dutch government, such as the refurbishing of the pre-existing Netherlands Club in Cape Town (1947–8) for which the interior, including all furniture, was designed by Jongens.

Bloemfontein's likewise large Dutch community constructed a multi-purpose building designed by the Dutch émigré architect Henk de Bie in 1958. Holland House included a hall, office and short stay apartments for new Dutch arrivals. These apartments were needed because government subsidised housing was reserved for South African citizens only. At the opening of the Holland House, the then Dutch Ambassador, Jan van den Berg, aware of potential animosity towards newcomers amongst the

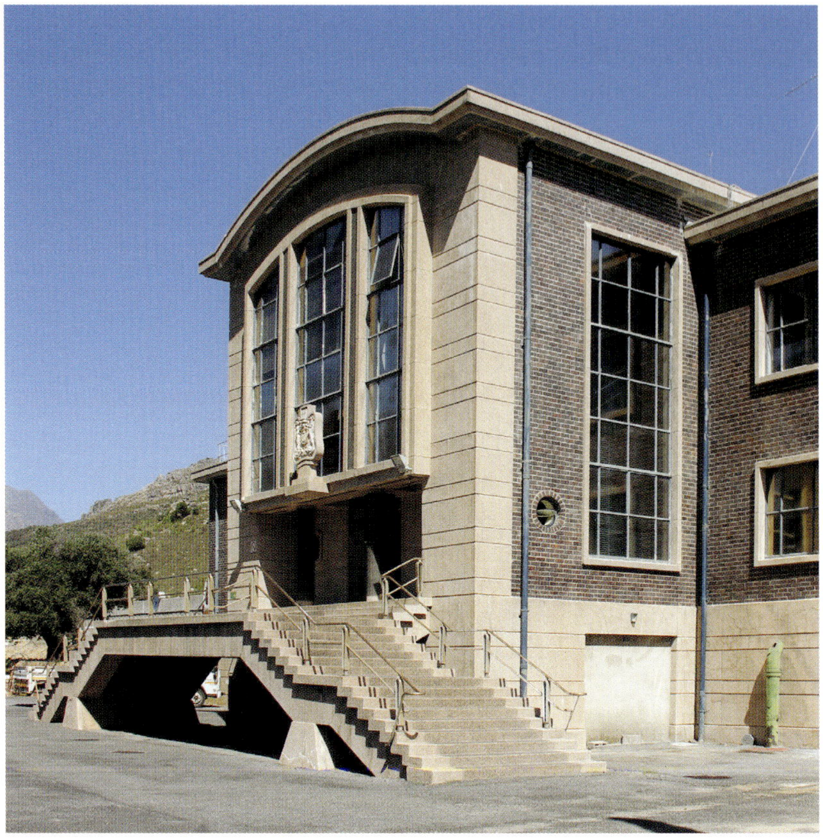

Wemmershoek, purification- and carbonation plant, designed by Jaap Jongens, 1957; photo 2019

Athlone, City of Cape Town Water Laboratory, designed 1947, Jaap Jongens; photo 2019

Wemmershoek, sluice machine room, designed by Jaap Jongens, 1957; photo 2019

Nieuwegein, Beatrix Sluice, completed 1938, designed by JP Josephus Jitta and LSP Scheffer; photo 1970

local population, cautioned that: 'a good Netherlands Society should not be a colony of strangers, but a part of the cultural life of the new homeland'.[35]

Adapting, adopting and accommodating

Civil service proved over the years to be a valuable means for Dutch émigré architects to become part of the architectural life of their adopted country. By serving in public works they became the vehicle for transferring architectural and technical knowledge to South Africa. But South Africa presented a continuously shifting force-field over the period of 1902-61. Public architecture could not escape serving as a vehicle for the expression of exclusion and separate identities. Public projects became an expression of ambitions of the client: a symbol of the presence of government, of national progress, of a link with history as ideological justification, as a resounding statement of modernity, or a combination of these.

At the same time, networks of association and patronage were crucial in the commissioning of architects aligned to causes of socio-cultural or religious groupings, all with their own cultural ambitions. This is an often-pragmatic heritage that has largely escaped attention. Yet these architects created long-lived institutions and public infrastructure that in numerous cases still accommodate government, provide facilities for education and health-care and, today, because of their careful and considered design, serve all South Africans.

35 Van Zinderen Bakker, 1959: 35.

Cape Town, Green Point Stadium designed by Jaap Jongens in 1955, bird's eye view

Bloemfontein, the Women's Memorial, designed by Frans Soff with sculptor Anton van Wouw in 1913; photo 1982

Commemoration and Celebration

Marieke Kuipers

From the inception of the Union of South Africa as a new nation, it has proved a great challenge to establish a kind of a collective or national identity amongst its diverse population. The concepts of both 'nation' and 'identity' were primarily political constructs of a white minority of English and Afrikaans speaking communities which was extended to European immigrants, even when they hardly shared the same memories and histories. Nonetheless, there were various endeavours initiated, albeit often contrived and full of ambivalences or controversies. Three examples of national commemoration and celebration may serve to illustrate the complexity of the South African past as well as the Dutch connections therein, in the design of three purposefully erected monuments and the immaterial heritage of great festivities and fairs at an international scale.

Bloemfontein, National Women's Monument

Just outside the capital of Orange Free State (OFS), the first public monument of the Union was inaugurated on 16 December 1913 by Tibbie Steyn, wife of the last OFS Republic's president. Together with the British peace activist Emily Hobhouse, they had advocated for the creation of a public place of commemoration to honour the thousands of Afrikaner women who, with their children, had suffered tremendously in the British concentration camps during the South African War, many losing their lives. Two Pretoria-based Dutch immigrants were commissioned to design this national *Vrouemonument*. The architect Frans Soff designed the solemn setting of an elevated circle surrounded by a protective ring of stone and marked by a 35 m high obelisk, while the sculptor Anton van Wouw made the central bronze figures of two grieving women and a starving child as well as the two friezes at the sides. Over 20 000 people attended this special inauguration that expressively aimed at reconciliation and peace.[1]

Later on, though, the site was appropriated for more male-oriented Afrikaner nationalist purposes, such as the commemoration of the *Great Trek* in 1938, which led to the building of the Voortrekker Monument at Pretoria (1949). In the recent decades of the current republic, the site has been partly transformed and repositioned as a cultural and spiritual meeting place for all the peoples of South Africa.[2]

Franschhoek, Huguenot Monument

The Huguenot Monument at Franschhoek [French corner] was inaugurated with great festivity in 1948. Ten years before, the Dutch émigré architect Jaap Jongens had won the preceding design competition.[3] After 250 years, the descendants of Huguenots wished to honour the cultural contributions made by their ancestors to South Africa since the first refugees had landed on the Cape, on their flight from France following their persecution after the Edict of Nantes

Bloemfontein, one of the bronze panels depicting displaced and dejected women and children; sculpted by Anton van Wouw in 1913; photo 2020

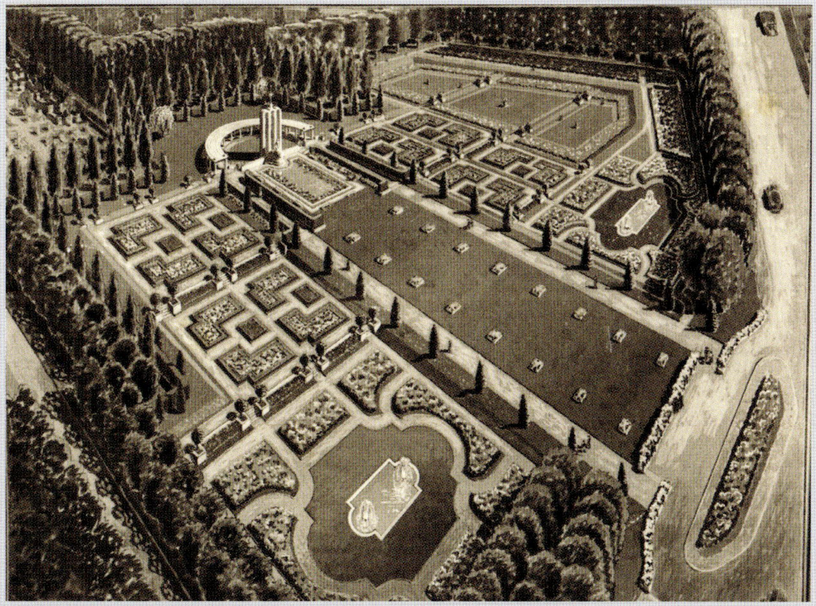

Franschhoek, the 1938 design by Jaap Jongens for the Huguenot Monument (garden layout not executed)

(1688) had forbidden their Calvinist practice. Being allowed to settle in, amongst other places, the Berg Rivier Valley, they brought their expertise in viticulture there, and disseminated it further afield. The design competition specified that the monument would express religious, historical and French characteristics and be suitable as an open meeting space. Jongens made various studies for his serene monument, on which the renowned South African sculptor Coert Steynberg also collaborated. The layout could well have been inspired by a similar combination of architecture and sculpture, the Van Heutsz monument in Amsterdam (1935, Gijsbert Friedhoff and Frits van Hall). Whereas the Dutch memorial has just one tall arch and a straight brickwork arcade, the Huguenot Monument consists of three arches, symbolizing the Holy Trinity, and a semi-circular arcade with Tuscan columns in the background. A feature shared by both memorials is the prominent placing of a female figure

1 Anon.1913. *Hollandsch Zuid-Afrika*, July: 1–6; Van Schoor, 1993.
2 Cloete, 1999; Labuschagne, 2014; Marschall, 2009: 234, 236–251; www.wmbr.org.za.
3 Coertzen, 2011.

Amsterdam, the Van Heutsz Monument and its setting shortly after the inauguration in 1935; designers: architect Gijsbert Friedhoff, sculptor Frits van Hall (renamed in 2004 as *Monument Indië-Nederland*)

Franschhoek, inauguration of the Huguenot Monument in 1948; designed by Jaap Jongens with sculptor Coert Steynberg

on a pedestal, with a reflecting pond in front. Both figures are symbolic personifications, and in Franschhoek it is related to freedom of faith and placed on top of a thoughtfully ornamented globe. According to the initial design, Jongens had opted for two nicely landscaped green spaces in the French garden style flanking the central green, but for economic reasons a more restrained public space was created, which still is in use for public commemoration and celebration.[4]

The Van Riebeecks

In 1952, the Tercentenary of Jan van Riebeeck's landing on the Cape (together with his wife and VOC fellows) was extensively celebrated in both South Africa and the Netherlands.[5] The well-orchestrated festivities of this commemorative year aimed at a new sense of connectedness between the two nations for both political, cultural and economic reasons, as well as a new unifying narrative of nation building, albeit only for the white South Africans. The race-based exclusion of the majority of the South African people in participating at an equal level in all activities raised criticism and resistance against the festival that inevitably served the political agenda of apartheid.[6]

Nevertheless, the re-enactment of the landing, for which the historic vessel *Drommedaris* was carefully replicated at full size, was a great public event, as were the related festival and the rides in–also replicated–carriages from various towns towards Cape Town.[7] The recently reclaimed land of the foreshore was temporarily used as the main location of the festival and fair.[8] Several Dutch-born architects had been active in the organisation and design of temporary buildings, exhibitions and signage – most prominently Jaap Jongens, who was at the time architect in City Hall. He was responsible for the design of the huge

Cape Town, re-enactment of the 1652 landing of Jan van Riebeeck with the specially replicated ship *Drommedaris* for the Tercentenary celebration, 1952

50 000 seat stadium and the arrangement of the circle of flags around the statue of the city founder, places that were carefully illuminated during the evening.[9]

The historic setting of the Culemborg Market square in the Netherlands was partly recreated in Cape Town as a picturesque décor for the fair. It showed a striking resemblance with Van Riebeeck's original home town in the Netherlands, when simultaneous festivities were held there and in other towns for his commemoration.

4 Jongens Collection, now in University of Cape Town Library Special Collections, Cape Town.
5 *Zuid-Afrika Maandblad* 1952, April (special); Anon. [1952]. The Festival in Pictures.
6 Rasool & Witz, 1992; Witz, 2003.
7 Rosenthal, 1952-53; Van Bank, 1996.
8 See also the interlude on Water and Concrete.
9 JC Jongens Collection, Cape Town; see also Chapter 4 and the interlude on Cross-continental Careers.

Cape Town, the replicated market square and town hall of Jan van Riebeeck's place of birth, Culemborg, in use as the Tercentenary Festival fair, 1952

The name 'Culemborg' was also adopted for the new railway's goods hall, that prior to this main function had been occupied by various stands of the Van Riebeeck festival fair. Its name was inscribed on the first foundation stone that was placed on the foreshore, to mark the beginning of new construction activities for the extended city bowl opposite Table Bay. Inside the nearby C17 Castle of Good Hope; two exhibitions were organised that displayed Dutch achievements over the centuries, one dedicated to the arts, the other to the recent works of civil engineering.

Culemborg, market square in use as the venue for a Van Riebeeck celebration in the Netherlands, 1952

Culture and trade went hand in hand in promoting the Netherlands abroad. In turn, the KLM airlines festively baptized a new aircraft of its gradually growing fleet after Jan van Riebeeck, for transatlantic flights alongside regular flights between Schiphol and South Africa. For this transformative event in modes of transport, a small procession was held with an ossewagen and a group of people in historic dresses, from the city of Amsterdam to the airport.[10]

10 Anon. 1952. *Het Parool*, 30 May: 1.

Amsterdam Schiphol Airport with historically costumed group and ox wagon to celebrate the naming of the new DC6B aircraft 'Jan van Riebeeck', equipped for transcontinental flights, 1952

Cape Town, historic photo of the main square during the Van Riebeeck Festival with pylons and other festive markers designed by Jaap Jongens, 1952

Cape Town, the statue of Maria de la Quellerie unveiled at its temporary location in the *Compagniestuin*, 1954

In the wake of these commemorations a bronze statue of Maria de la Quellerie, spouse of Van Riebeeck and herself of Huguenot extraction, was solemnly unveiled by prince Bernhard of the Netherlands in 1954 (since the Dutch queen Juliana did not wish to visit as long as the apartheid regime was in power).[11] The sculpture, made by the Dutchman Dirk Wolbers, was a gift from the Netherlands to South Africa, and it was intended to form a visual 'gate pair' with the 1899 memorial of her husband to mark the projected new Gateway to Africa.[12] As we know, the construction of the foreshore did not follow the initial planning and today the two statues are located on the square between the Heeregracht and Adderley Street, facing the city that grew out of their first settlement.

Johannesburg, 1957 Rand Show Netherlands Pavilion

The Rand Show was an annual consumer exhibition, held around Easter in the former Milner Park at Johannesburg since 1895. Originally directed mainly at agricultural production and technology, it later became a showcase for industries, including from foreign countries. The Netherlands was among the first in 1947 to celebrate its post-war revival and to reinforce its bonds with South Africa there.

Ten years later the Dutch government commissioned the émigré architect Jaap van Niftrik to design a new Dutch pavilion, replacing the previous one. This resulted in a surprising showcase of innovation and experimentation, attracting attention from a distance through its striking use of the orange map of the Netherlands besides the multi-curved façade and the colourful tulip beds in front.[13] The widely acclaimed building was inaugurated by the Dutch minister of Finance, Jelle Zijlstra.

Inside, 21 stands were created on the ground floor for various Dutch firms, and a sweeping spiral staircase led to the first floor, where another 8 stands were made, and an open space which could be converted into a cinema. As two major attractors for the public at large, DAF cars and a truck were displayed through a concrete arch towards the inner court, all cleverly illuminated by Philips lighting at night. In total, over 500 000 visitors were counted. With the knowledge that the show was just a temporary event, a specialised Dutch firm had provided demountable installations for exhibition and after this show they were to be used elsewhere in South Africa, Edinburgh and Brussels.[14] However innovative at the time of construction and despite serving for a few more years, the Dutch pavilion did not survive, the exhibition grounds becoming the West Campus of the Witwatersrand University.

11 Anon. 1954c. *Algemeen Handelsblad*, 6 Oct: 1; Van Ledden, 2005: 63.
12 Document in archival collection, Zuid Afrikahuis, Amsterdam.
13 See also Chapter 9.
14 Anon. 1957b. *De Maasbode*, 10 Jan: 6.

Johannesburg, Rand Easter Show with the Netherlands Pavilion in the background, 1957

Johannesburg, the Netherlands Pavilion on the Rand Easter Show under construction

Johannesburg, the Netherlands Pavilion at the Rand Easter Show by night, 1957; architect: Jaap van Niftrik, construction firm: Dura, 1957 (since demolished)

Beaufort-West, Rustdene, United Reformed Church, 'Die Ark', interior, designed by Arne Sikkel, 1967; photo 2020

5 Buildings for Communities of Faith

Nicholas Clarke

Introduction

South Africa embraces many religions and even amongst those of the Christian faith many denominations and movements coexist. Christian divides originating in the Netherlands persisted [and still persist] in South African society of Dutch descent. Increased emigration and Protestant missionary outreach from the Netherlands to South Africa from the late C19 until the mid C20 reinforced the historic links between the Protestant churches in the Netherlands and those in South Africa. Less-known is that an influx of Dutch Roman Catholics, coupled with a Dutch Catholic missionary endeavour, also saw buildings being constructed to the design of émigré compatriots for fledgeling communities of this faith. Dutch émigré architects made a fundamental contribution to the development of a uniquely South African church design tradition which sought to develop a pragmatic architecture that embedded the tenets of their faith in their local communities and building traditions.

Three Protestant sister churches

Those who travel South Africa's vast expanses will know that its towns are more often than not marked by church steeples or grain silos, others by minarets, these being more recent beacons in the landscape. But, more often than not, the tallest marker in the *platteland dorp* is a black brick-built steeple, capped by a rooster, being a *Nederduits Gereformeerde* Kerk [NGK, Dutch Reformed Church].

The three so-called Afrikaner Protestant *susterkerke* [sister churches] have been historically dominant in South Africa. All three were transplanted from the Netherlands and are closely aligned through a shared Calvinist Protestant theology. The NGK is the largest. Its roots go back to 1652 when the Dutch East India Company established an outpost at the Cape of Good Hope.

Following the British annexation of the Cape, a group of settlers decided to quit the Cape from around 1836, moving into the northern hinterland. As the NGK refused to minister to these *Voortrekkers,* they established the independent *Nederduits Hervormde Kerk van Afrika* [NHK] under the guidance of a Dutch missionary in 1837.[1] Twenty years later the NHK was sanctioned as the official church of the *Zuid-Afrikaansche Republiek* [ZAR, South African Republic], reinforcing the links between the African hinterland and the Netherlands.

The more progressive stance of the NHK led to the dissension of conservative *Boers*. They established the *Gereformeerde Kerk* [GK, Reformed Church] in Rustenburg in 1859, maintaining close contact with a similar dissident movement among Calvinists in the Netherlands. When the *Nederduits Gereformeerde Kerk* was formalised in 1886 in the Netherlands, it already had a counterpart in the GK in southern Africa.[2]

1 Hofmeyr, 2002: 95.
2 Van Gelderen, 1986: 8.

The three Afrikaner susterkerke have over time attempted in vain to reconcile their theological differences, which we will not dwell upon here.[3] That would be an ecumenical matter. For the purpose of our understanding of their church buildings it helps to know that they share a religious practice focused on the *preek* [sermon] and actively practice two sacraments, namely the *doop* [baptism] and *nagmaal* [communion]. Their churches are designed to focus on the spoken word, delivered by the *dominee* [reverend] often from a *preekstoel* [pulpit]. The preek is punctuated by communal singing, historically accompanied by an organ. The church building itself is not sanctified, but is rather seen as a vessel for the communion of the congregation.

A new Protestant church type

For settler communities a church building created permanence and a regular place of meeting and often resulted in the establishment of a new town. The current capital of South Africa, Pretoria, was started as *kerkplaas* [church place] in 1854, to which the name of its Church Square still refers.[4] And so too in 1908, a new church was built as the marker of a new town in the Hex River Valley in the Western Cape. The NGK Murray Church, a 'rather magnificent Gothic Revival edifice' was designed by Dutch architect Folkert Hesse, who settled in Cape Town in 1902 and was the author of many churches for the DRC in the Cape.[5] The Murray Church has a rectangular plan and its styling is articulated by simple buttresses and plaster mouldings, representative of the bourgeois ambitions of this outlying farming community. Despite its historicizing appearance, this church had an ingenious ventilation system, which combined air ducts built into the walls with steel framed hopper windows and a large roof-top extraction ventilator. Hesse also introduced a new spatial device by

3 Hofmeyr, 2002: 150–51.
4 Clarke & De Villiers, 2015: 69.
5 Fransen: 2004: 390–91.

De Doorns, former Dutch Reformed Church, 'Murray Church', now a farming supplies store, designed by Folkert Hesse, 1908; photo, 2020

sloping the floor downwards from the entrance to the pulpit, which gave all congregants a good view of the dominee. The centre of town, today De Doorns, developed closer to the railway station, where a new church was constructed in 1950. The old church today serves as an agricultural goods warehouse.

In fast-growing Pretoria, the NHK sold its church with the surrounding to the ZAR administration in 1896. Klaas van Rijsse made an initial design for a new building, but construction was delayed by the South African War.[6] The building was constructed under the guidance of by Dutch émigré architects, Johannes Kraan and Jan Wyers, who had both, like Van Rijsse, been formerly in the employ of the ZAR's Department of Public Works [DPW]. The Grootekerk (now Melodi Ya Tshwane United Reformed Church) was completed in 1906 and was at the time the largest construction project in the city and symbol of Afrikaner resurrection. While expressing the Dutch connections in the historicist aesthetic of the exterior, the interior is defined by technological and programmatic innovativeness.

Pretoria, Dutch Reformed Church, 'Grootekerk'/Melodi Ya Tshwane United Reformed Church, interior, designed by Kraan & Weijers with Klaas van Rijsse, 1902–6; photo 2014

From the outside, the church appears to be built following a traditional cruciform plan. Yet on entering the church, the visitor first encounters a corridor that runs around its perimeter. From this corridor one enters the main body of the church: a large theatre with semi-circular sloping auditorium focused on the pulpit. Its galleries likewise have semi-circular seating. The organ pipes were formerly located over the pulpit, a device which brought unity to word and song. The large church volume, uninterrupted by columns, is spanned by a system of timber trusses and steel tensile rods.

It is very likely that the architects of the church were following the prescripts for church design formulated by the Dutch preacher, statesman and Boer supporter, *Gereformeerde* [Reformed] theologian Abraham Kuyper. Many articles in 'his' Reformed journal *De Heraut* were circulated in South Africa and republished locally in the GK's own monthly *Die Kerkbode*.[7] Kuyper wrote widely on design principles for Reformed churches, his advice ranging from good ventilation and acoustics to the principles of good spatial design. Kuyper often referred to the spatial configuration of the Metropolitan Tabernacle—or Spurgeons Temple—in London (1861). This independent Reformed Baptist church was designed by William Pocock as a theatre in the round, with raked seating on the ground floor and two galleries arranged around the pulpit, all with a good line-of-sight to the preacher.

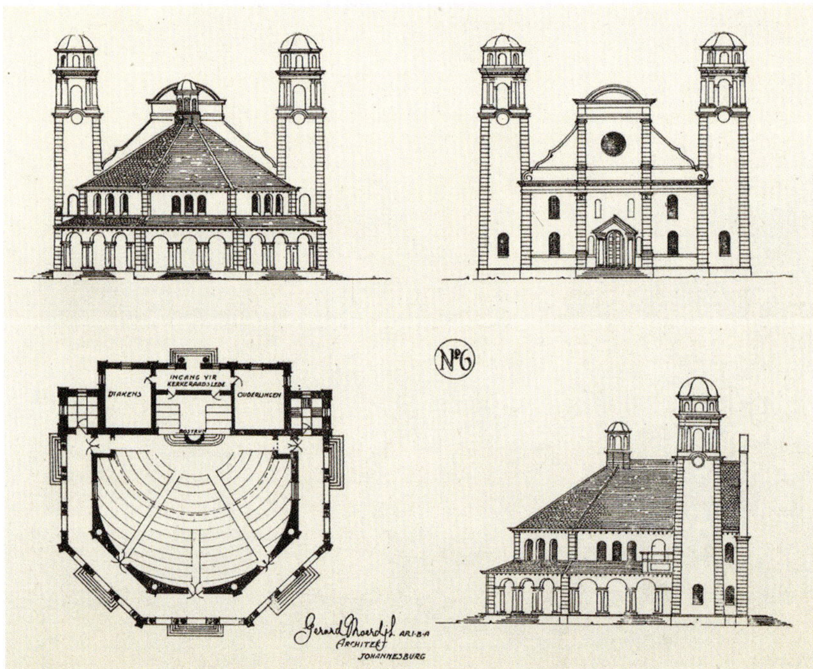

Design for a church for 1 000 congregants by Gerard Moerdyk, as published in his *Kerkgeboue vir SuidAfrika*, 1919

Kuyper took the view that, like oratory, poetry, music and architecture, so did the figurative arts such as sculpture and painting have a place in the Reformed Church: 'The Church is not in the least hostile to art for the reasons stated, but it has two natural requirements: firstly, that art should not dominate the Church, and secondly, that external beauty should not oppress internal beauty', which was Kuyper saying the aesthetics should not dominate the meaning.[8] Kuyper kept the matter of architectural style to be unimportant, but mentioned that 'Our good architects of old... were not mistaken to abandon the Gothic style, and felt drawn to the Renaissance style instead.'[9]

The Grootekerk's design in Dutch Renaissance Revival style adopted most of Kuyper's prescripts, specifically those that facilitated preaching to a large congregation in the days before sound amplification. The interior was, however, devoid of decoration. Figurative art in the church was anathema for the iconoclastic Protestants in South Africa.

The Grootekerk is the progenitor of the fan-shaped auditorium Protestant church type in South Africa. Its typological influence was all the greater because important later church designers, including Wynand Louw, Leendert Geers and Gerard Moerdijk (later Moerdyk) were all familiar with the church, not only through professional interest, but also personal experience. They all worked at the Public Works Department [PWD] in Pretoria during or soon after its construction and were all NGK members.

6 Fisher & Clarke, 2014: 202.
7 Vrieze, 1986: 60.
8 Kuyper, 1911: 77. Kuyper bundled his earlier articles for republication in 1911.
9 Kuyper, 1911: 10.

Louw spent a year in the PWD office in Pretoria in 1908.[10] A year later he adopted the fan-shaped plan for his first church, the Gothic Revival-styled NGK at Port Elizabeth (now Gqebera, 1909).[11]

Moerdijk's booklet *Kerkgeboue vir Suidafrika* [1919, Churches for South Africa] included among the 12 prototypes for churches of various sizes, a design for a church for 1 000 congregants with a 'full theatre plan' accessed by a circumferential corridor.[12] Although this plan is obviously reminiscent of the Grootekerk, Moerdijk claimed his design as an 'entirely new kind of church'.[13]

10 Roodt, 1981: 341.
11 Roodt, 1981: 341.
12 Moerdijk erroneously calls it a 'volle amfiteater vorm' [complete amphitheatre form]. Moerdijk, 1919: s.n.
13 Moerdijk, 1919: s.n. 'Dit is 'n heeltemal nuwe soort kerk'.

'Dudokian' influences

The Dutch Renaissance Revival aesthetic of the Grootekerk was however rather alien to most Afrikaners, especially those at the Cape. When designing a NGK for Swellendam (1911) Hesse, now joined in practice by his son François, was one of the earliest architects to move away from referencing historical European examples for Protestant church aesthetics, hesitantly introducing the Cape Dutch Revival as appropriate to a local Protestant community. Their Swellendam church is a somewhat erratic amalgam of a Baroque Cape Dutch Revival with Gothic Revival lancet windows and topped with a Dutch Renaissance Revival spire. The church's interior combined the fan-shaped auditorium with a cruciform plan, though having sight-lines still interrupted by internal columns.

The Cape Dutch Revival dominated Afrikaner Protestant church architecture during early C20, promoted by architects such as Louw and Moerdyk, both trained at the Architectural Association in London. Louw's 1921 NGK Swartruggens, which stands on a small hillock and is visible from afar, emphasized in the landscape the domination of Afrikaner Protestant communities through its use of the Cape Dutch idiom.

Swellendam, Dutch Reformed Church, designed by father-and-son Folkert & François Hesse, 1911; photo 2012

Swartruggens, Dutch Reformed Church, designed by Wynand Louw, 1921; photo 2015

Swartruggens, Reformed Church, designed by Pieter Dykstra, 1933–34; photo 2015

Johannesburg, Reformed Church Melville, designed by Pieter Dykstra, 1935; photo c1965

A decade later, another Cape Dutch Revival-styled church was built at Swartruggens (1933–34), now for the GK. The volumetric articulation of its somewhat expressionist tower indicates a different design tradition than its Palladian NGK counterpart. The architect was Dutch émigré Pieter Dijkstra (later Dykstra), who settled in Pretoria in 1927.[14] The son of an orthodox Reformed dominee with a fervent missionary zeal, Dykstra must have had an intimate knowledge of Kuyper's writing. He had already completed at least five Reformed churches in various stylistic idioms in the Netherlands and was probably already in contact with the GK in South Africa before emigrating. His first South African GK church was completed in Klerksdorp in the same year as his arrival.[15]

Dykstra was to remain a favourite architect for GK congregations, designing at least sixteen churches throughout his long career, including the new church for the GK congregation Johannesburg-Noord in Melville (1935).[16] Johannesburg was a melting pot of immigrants and Melville especially had a high concentration of new Dutch residents who had little affinity with the Cape Dutch Revival. Dykstra's church, an almost stark brick Romanesque Revival building devoid of extraneous decoration, was rather daringly minimalist for its time. The interior of the cruciform plan building was again theatre-shaped with a sloping floor. The pulpit with organ pipes placed above were designed as the only noteworthy point of interest. Any possible distraction from the sermon and communal song was avoided. Outside, the only extravagance was the tower with black slate covered spire, topped with a sword-like finial. This 'finger pointing towards heaven' was, according to Kuyper, a necessity, 'since we are dealing with church building in its own right, it should not be denied that every church, by its very nature, calls for a tower.'[17]

It was the architects Geers & Geers who freed Protestant church architecture from the shackles of revivalism. This practice was, as

14 Ploeger, 1994: 60.
15 Probably alterations to an existing building.
16 Harris, 2010: 104.
17 Kuyper, 1911: 10. 'Nu we den kerkbouw geheel op zichzelf behandelen, mag toch niet verzwegen worden, dat elke kerk uit haar aard om een toren roept.'

Villiers, Dutch Reformed Church, designed by Geers & Geers, 1940; photo 2015

Harrismith, Dutch Reformed Church Kerkenberg, designed by Geers & Geers, 1942; photo 2014

Johannesburg, tower of the *Nederduits Gereformeerde en Hervormde Kerk* Melville, designed by Geers & Geers, 1939–41; photo 2014

Clive Chipkin wrote, 'responsible for endless Dutch Reformed churches in Johannesburg suburbs and *platteland dorps*. These churches were distinguished by their carefully modulated rectangular or octagonal towers of golden-brown face brick supporting pyramidal steeples. Vertical recesses and openings in the towers, with narrow projecting slabs or dentils, looked to their prototype, Dudok's Raadhuis at Hilversum.'[18] Their early churches are crucial markers in the evolution of a home-grown church architecture, inspired by the secular 'Dudokian' vocabulary.

The practice, established in 1934, was a collaboration between father and son, Leendert and Geurt, the former a Dutch émigré architect; the latter worked in the Pretoria PWD office while studying architecture and then joined Moerdyk's office for a year during 1933. Their first church, the GK Benoni (inaugurated 1938, demolished 1991) had large expressionist lancet windows and a massive corner tower with black slate steeple.

Their subsequent second church, the NGK Melville (1939–41), however, avoided all historicising references.[19] While continuing the now-common use of the auditorium-in-crucifix floor plan, the facades and tower combined the 'Dudokian' geometrical abstraction with Art Deco details.

Geers & Geers' unabashed modernising aesthetic resonated with the aspirations of their Afrikaner clientele. Commission upon commission followed for congregations across the country, such as for the NGK Villiers (cornerstone 1940). The black slate spire soon evolved into a signature black brick-built spire, such as employed at the 1943 NGK Malvern (today Kensington) in Johannesburg, possibly due to maintenance and vulnerability of the slate to the Highveld elements – high storm winds and lightning strikes. In the interim, the 1942 NGK Kerkenberg, Harrismith avoided the slate spire. Here low-pitched roofs dominate in its careful articulation, creating a striking horizontal line offset against the sheer verticality of the expressive tower, topped by a small helm.

18 Chipkin, 1993: 112.

19 Van der Waal, 1987: 219.

Expressionist renewal

Interwar Dutch Expressionist architecture, particularly the churches of the Amsterdam School, inspired a new Protestant church type in South Africa after WWII. Several near-contemporary churches are emblematic for the transferral of the Expressionist movement to South Africa. Its early protagonists were Dykstra and Jaap Woudstra. Woudstra, like Dykstra, was a Dutch émigré architect and the son of a Reformed dominee. He entered into practice in 1951 with a grandson of a Dutch immigrant Reformed dominee and young University of Pretoria graduate, Johan de Ridder, who had worked in Dykstra's office (1944) prior to his studies.

Dykstra's GK Vereeniging (1951) and Pretoria-Noord (1955–6) and Woudstra & De Ridder's GK Pretoria-Brooklyn (1951), may have all sourced their external and internal form from such Dutch expressionist examples as Egbert Reitsma's Reformed Church Kollum and the Reformed Church, 'Noorderkerk', Nieuw Amsterdam by architect Willem van Straten (both 1925).[20] Here he employed the catenary-arch vaults in an expressive manner employed in combination with a fan-like plan and galleries as well as applied works of art. The same goes for the expressionist Reformed church buildings designed by architect Berend Boeyinga in Bergen and Haarlem-Noord (both 1927) with lofty vaulted centralised interiors and dominant roofs with a spire. Boeyinga was likewise the son of a Reformed dominee and had not only been in close contact with the Amsterdam School practitioners, but also studied and spread the 'Kuyperian' ideas on church buildings including the conditional acceptance of art.[21]

The Dykstra variants, based on the lancet arch, utilised the ground floor for raked seating; with additional seating in the galleries of three arms of the cruciform plan. Following the abstraction of Boeyinga's Bergen church, Woudstra & De Ridder's interpretation retain the catenary-arch, but its exterior is assertively modern. Its plan returned to an axially-oriented seating layout, much like the Bergen church but many of the Haarlem church's interior features, including an almost direct adoption of the design of the baptismal font, also found their way into the Brooklyn church.

20 Harris, 2010: 2015.

21 Falize, 1986: 77–80.

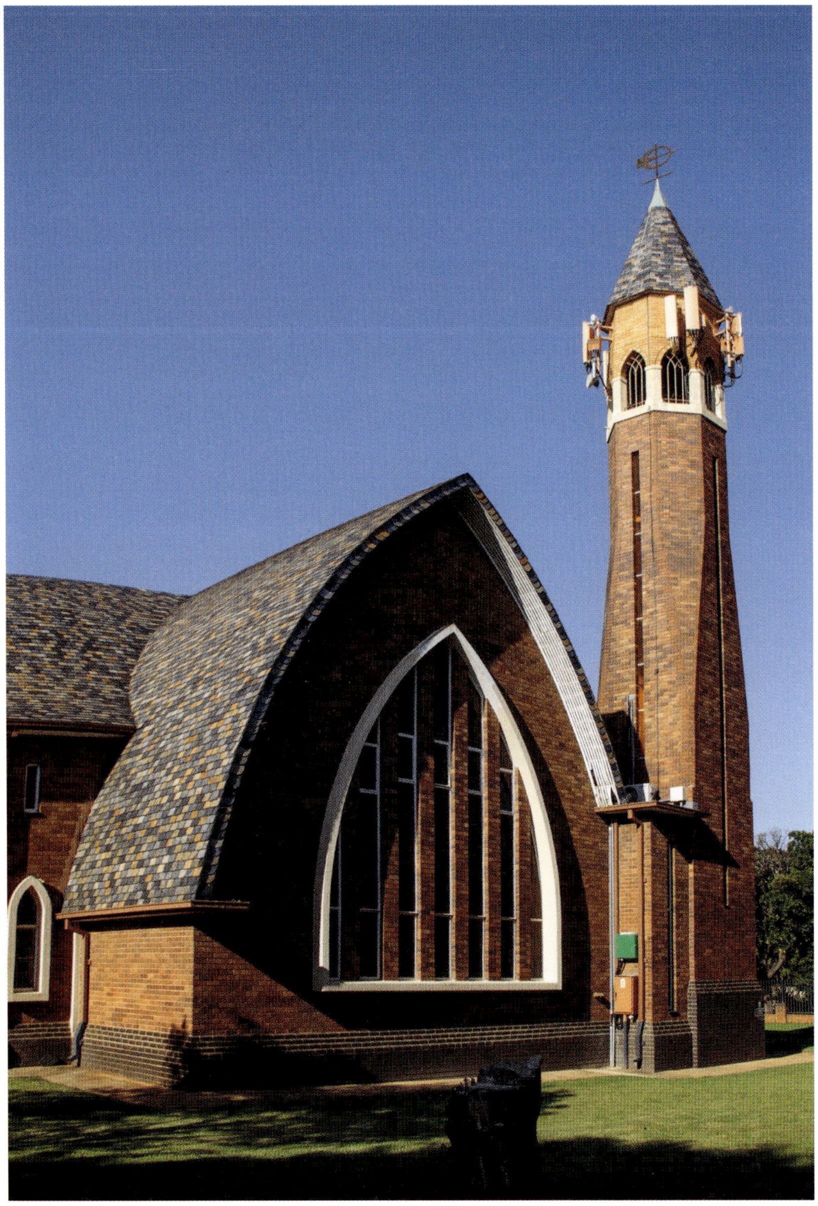

Pretoria, Reformed Church Pretoria-North, designed by Pieter Dykstra, 1956; photo 2020

Pretoria, Reformed Church Pretoria-North, interior, designed by Pieter Dykstra, 1956; photo 2020

Nieuw Amsterdam (Netherlands), Reformed Church, 'Noorderkerk', designed by W van Straten, 1925; photo 2012

Woudstra died shortly after the inauguration of the Pretoria-Brooklyn church in 1953. In his subsequent churches De Ridder abstracted the ideas contained in the Pretoria-Brooklyn church to the extreme: reducing it to a sculpted roof offset by a minimalist, but always striking tower. De Ridder saw the roof as a tent, the 'symbol of a church traversing the desert of this temporary dispensation en route to the eternal'.[22] The form however evoked other associations with the Protestant public with the bonnets (*kappies*) historically worn by Voortrekker women, hence the high roofed church type's nickname: *kappiekerk*. Its influence spread when prolific Afrikaner church architect J Anthonie Smith adopted the kappiekerk type and by the mid-1950s became its main champion at the Cape.[23]

Reconciling disparate streams

The influence of Geers & Geers' practice was pervasive in South African church building as, for example, the GK Kaapstad (1952) by Moerdyk & Watson and the NGK Gamka-Oos (1953) by Louw & Louw show. The Gamka-Oos church is a somewhat clumsy transitional form, amalgamating the steep dominant roofs introduced simultaneously by Dykstra and Woudstra & De Ridder with the Geers & Geers Dudokian aesthetic. The idiom was most prolifically spread by University of the Witwatersrand educated Hendrik Vermooten, a partner of the Geerses who established his own practice after Geurt Geers' untimely death in 1945.

After his son's death, Leendert entered into partnerships with long-standing employee of the firm, Dutch émigré Jan Koelewyn. After Jan Moors joined them, the firm was styled as Geers, Koelewyn & Moors. Both Koelewyn and Moors were graduates from the Rotterdam *Academie voor Beeldende Kunsten en Technische Wetenschappen* and relocated to South Africa in 1937. The practice continued to explore the possibilities of the Dudokian tradition, amalgamating it with the kappiekerk type. The GK Rustenburg (1959–60) presents a zenith in the consolidation of these vocabularies. Its abstracted tectonic articulation balances a steep slate roof floating above its face brick walls against its slender spire, which is carefully staged with horizontal banding in contrast with the vertical banding of the gable walls.

22 De Ridder, 1955, quoted in Le Roux, 2008: 41.
23 Le Roux, 2008: 24

Pretoria, Reformed Church Brooklyn, interior, designed by Woudstra & De Ridder, 1951; photo 2016

Beaufort-West, Dutch Reformed Church Gamka Oos, designed by Louw & Louw, 1953; photo 2020

Right: Rustenburg, Reformed Church, designed by Geers Koelewyn & Moors, 1959; photo 2015

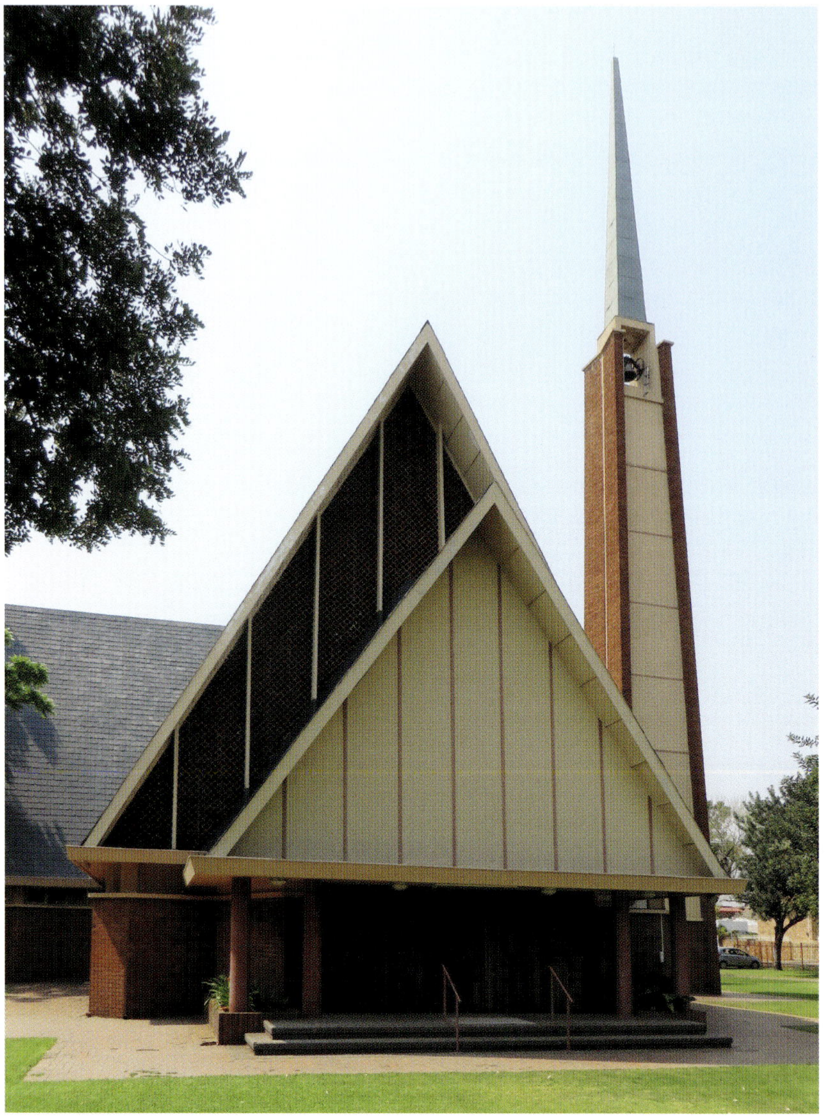

The kappiekerk, often moulded to Dudokian aesthetics, became 'iconic of the modern Afrikaner church building' and remained en-vogue for most of the C20.[24]

A Cape revolution

In the 1940s, when revivalist styles were still the norm for Afrikaner architects like Moerdyk and Louw and the heavy Geers & Geers Dudokian idiom was still making its entry, a young Dutch architect at the Cape, Henk Sikkel, was developing a decidedly modern church aesthetic. Sikkel, was a scion of a family of prominent Amsterdam-based Reformed dominees, all close associates of Kuyper. Sikkel emigrated to South Africa soon after graduating from technical college in 1935, registering as architect in 1939.[25] Rebelling against his family, he chose to join not the GK, but rather the NGK for which he was to design numerous churches. His earliest was for his own congregation, the NGK Pinelands, (1942), which he designed in a radically modern idiom. Devoid of any decoration, the building's beauty lies in its sweeping verticality, offset by a heavy face brick plinth. It reinterprets rather than copies tradition and in its materiality is regional in character. Its starkly minimalist interior is an expression of its construction and possibly also a consequence of war-time financial constraints. Sikkel's post-war NGK Sonnekus (1951) repeated the ascetic characteristics of the Pinelands church. This church was the calm before the storm that his NGK church at Ysterplaat (1959) would provoke.

The Ysterplaat congregation in Cape Town was led by a young dominee, Johan Heyns, who had been appointed a year after defending his doctoral degree at the Reformed-aligned Vrije Universiteit [Free University] in Amsterdam in 1953.[26] Heyns was a scholar and admirer of the writings of Kuyper, whose acceptance of figurative art was reaffirmed in the Netherlands by the 1954 Nederduits Hervormde Kerk report *Beginselen van kerkbouw*. Responding to the radically altered social conditions in the post-WW2 period, it concluded that the Protestant Church 'is heavily burdened with the guilt of banishing artists called by God from its walls and denying them the opportunity to participate in their own way among the congregation in glorifying God's honour and giving thanks for His grace. The congregations will have to get used to allowing the decorative and pictorial arts a place in the church and letting them fulfil a task there.'[27]

24 Liebenberg, 2014: 117.
25 Anon. 1935a. *De Tijd*, 12 Jul: 10; Anon. 1955. *Algemeen Handelsblad*, 12 Mar: 17.
26 Williams, 2006: 36.
27 Berghoef, 1954: 117.

Cape Town, Pinelands, Dutch Reformed Church, designed by Hendrik Sikkel, 1942; photo, 2019

Cape Town, Ysterplaat, Dutch Reformed Church, baptismal font and pulpit, designed by Hendrik Sikkel, 1959, carved wood pulpit panel by Swiss artist R Knöll; photo 2020

Many of the report's conclusions were immediately transferred to the South African context by Dutch Professor of Theology at the University of Pretoria, Adrianus van Selms. His 1954 publication *Beginsels van Protestantse Kerkbou* provided directives for Protestant church design in South Africa. Like Kuyper and the *Nederlands Hervormde Kerk Synode*, Van Selms supported the application of figurative art in Protestant church buildings, but noted that 'symbols which bear no relationship with the Holy Script and the Christian service are totally unacceptable.'[28] The South African Reformed susterkerke, however, maintained their near-total abhorrence of pictorial art in their 'Houses for the Word'.

Van Selms also called for a pragmatic design focused on the sacraments and the liturgical centre. Echoing Kuyper, Van Selms prescribed that the baptismal font should be a fixture in the church as a constant reminder of the purpose of the church building. When it came to the plan type, Van Selms, however, departed from Kuyper, preferring a rectilinear floor plan, as he thought that the centralised plan obfuscated the clarity of arrangement and use of the baptismal font and communion table.

Supported by Heyns, who knew Van Selms personally, Sikkel developed a design based on Van Selms' prescripts. The product was highly controversial and was soon reported in the local and the Dutch press as 'the most discussed church in South Africa'.[29] It was not the architectural design's rectangular plan or the exposed *beton brut* tower, but the inclusion of figurative stone and wood carving, a mosaic and a large expressive timber cross beside the pulpit, most of it by the Swiss émigré artist R Kröll, that caused distress. For instance, an artful figuration of fish and waves–not uncommon in Protestant churches in the Netherlands in the 1920s–was carved on the rough stele of Table Mountain sandstone that serves as baptismal font.[30] Heyns justified the carving as a symbol of early Christianity 'like the fish which can only live in the water, so the natural element for the Christian is the covenant of grace'.[31]

It took all of Heyns' oratory abilities to convince his flock that the church had been designed so that 'these symbols would speak to the congregation in an understandable language, yet would not distract in such a way as to detract from the preaching of the word'.[32] Still, iconoclast conservative Protestants were infuriated by the figurative

28 Van Selms, 1954: 7.

29 Anon. 1960a. *Die Huisgenoot*, 12 Aug: 18–9; Anon. 1961. *Trouw*, 29 Apr: 17.

30 Wattjes 1931, plates 199–200.

31 Heyns: 'zoals de vis slechts in het water kan leven, is het natuurlijke element voor de Christen het verbond der genade. Het is een symbool van de vroege Christenheid.' Anon. 1961. *Trouw*, 29 Apr: 17.

32 Heyns in *Trouw*, 29 April 1961: 17.

art, which they saw as an idolatry 'Roomse' (Roman Catholic) imposition. Van Selms was likewise wary of Roman Catholic influence. He was, for instance, in his *Beginsels* adamant that the communion table, while having a permanent presence in the liturgical space, should never be fixed in place and should always have legs lest it degenerate into an altar.[33] He also held the view that modern materials should not be rejected, because these reflected the function of the contemporary church building and traditional building materials were often more expensive.[34] Waste did not fit with Calvinist thrift.

The Ysterplaat church with its open bell tower of reinforced concrete, was the harbinger of change, based on the new guidelines that broke with the traditional architectural form as a carrier of Protestant identity.

A prime example of the radical move from traditional forms and materials is the NGK Harmonie, Pretoria (1961), designed by Dutch émigré architect John van de Werke. It served an evanescent congregation of mainly Afrikaans students from the nearby College of Education. These, after completing their education, disseminated the acceptance of non-traditional church architecture for Protestant churches with their spread across the country.

33 Van Selms, 1954: 45.
34 Van Selms, 1954: 75.

Catholic missionary expansions

There exists, amongst Afrikaners a time-long animosity to the Roman Catholic Church, that finds its origins in the C16 Reformation. Such was the local anti-Roman sentiment, that Catholic expansion at the Cape during the 1830s was one of the reasons for Protestant settlers to quit the Colony.[35]

Despite the overt resistance of the Protestant communities, partly supported by Dutch Reformed church communities in the Netherlands, the local Catholic presence grew apace during the C20. Framed as the *Roomse gevaar* [Roman danger], it unnerved the Protestant establishment not only because of their historical acrimony, but also because of what was believed as their divine right and calling to maintain and develop a South Africa of white Protestant superiority and control.

35 Denis, 1998: 90.

Pretoria, Dutch Reformed Church Harmonie, designed by John van de Werke, 1961; photo 2020

Surprisingly, the C20 Catholic influx was also largely a Dutch affair, driven especially by the Dutch Dominicans. Their female sisters were the first to arrive, founding Catholic schools and hospitals. In 1922, Dutch archbishop Bernard Gijlswijk was appointed as apostolic delegate, choosing Bloemfontein as his residence.[36] By 1924 he convened an ecclesiastic conference at Kimberley where he presented a strategy to spread the Catholic faith throughout the multicultural and multilingual country. All priests were to take compulsory courses in African languages, 'indigenous' sisters were to be recruited, chapels were to be constructed in small towns and seminaries were to be established specifically to produce Black priests.[37] These plans alarmed Protestants. In 1928 the NHK Synod officially recorded its opposition to governmental subsidies being granted to Roman Catholic schools, not in the least due to the success of the Catholics in the Free State, where numbers were steadily increasing, multiplying fourfold between 1924 and 1932.[38]

The already established German Spiritan mission in the Free State town Kroonstad was floundering under the weight of its own success. To assist them, Gijlswijk approached the Dutch Dominicans, who established themselves throughout the western part of that province in 1932. The increase of Free State converts was such that the Free State had to be divided into two vicariates in 1948, with its eastern seat in Bloemfontein. Dutch Dominican Gerard van Velsen, was appointed administrator of the eastern vicariate with its seat in Kroonstad. Van Velsen soon stole a march on the Protestant denominations when in 1948—the same year that the National Party first came to power—he convinced the Anglo American Corporation to sell land in the newly founded Free State gold mining town of Welkom. The Catholic Church here built various churches and schools and operated the mining hospital in the town.[39]

Van Velsen was elevated to bishop in 1950. He instituted an ambitious programme to convert Afrikaners to Catholicism, establishing the Katholieke Afrikanersentrum [Catholic Afrikaner Centre] in Kroonstad in 1952, which published an Afrikaans language monthly magazine 'Die Brug' [the bridge].[40] His plans for a Catholic Afrikaans boys' school in Kroonstad met with such resistance from the municipal council that it had to be shelved.[41]

For conservative Protestants, the threat of a 'Roomse indringing' [Catholic intrusion] was made palpable by the presence of a Catholic information stand at the 1952 Tercentennial Van Riebeeck Festival in Cape Town.[42] The stand subverted the Protestant 'claim' to the country by telling of how, long before the arrival Dutch Protestant settlers, Portuguese Catholic sailors had in 1501 constructed a chapel, dedicated to St Blaise and located in today's Mosselbay.[43] In addition, the number of Catholic Dutch emigrants to South Africa grew, from the 1930s onwards. They tended to flock together and established many new parishes in predominantly Afrikaner communities, like the Immaculate Conceptions Parish in Pretoria Gardens in 1958. To counter Dutch Catholic emigration, the DR Church synod in 1964 considered asking its counterpart in the Netherlands to advocate for Protestant emigration to the country.[44] The South African government and local authorities at the same time did their best to counter the Catholic care, education and faith mission.[45] The growing aversion to apartheid in the Netherlands, however, soon led to a sharp decrease of Dutch emigrants in the 1960s.

36 Denis, 1998: 153.
37 Denis, 1998: 115.
38 Anon. 1928. *Overijselsch Dagblad*, 14 Jun: 1; Denis, 1998: 161.
39 Denis, 1998: 167.
40 Denis, 1998: 179.
41 Denis: 1989: 181.
42 Denis, 1998: 173.
43 Anon. 1953a. *De Tijd*, 13 Feb: 2.

Catholic buildings

At least three Dutch émigré architects were active as designers of buildings for the Catholic Church: Anton Voorvelt, Edy Payens and Jan van Gemert. They emigrated independently during the late-1930s, mainly to escape the economic depression in the Netherlands, but their commissions for the Catholic Church in their new homeland only date to after WWII.

The large St John Vianney Seminary complex was built to the design of Voorvelt in the heart of Afrikanerdom, Pretoria between 1950 and 1952. Situated on a slope, the visual prominence of this stolid Catholic 'bulwark' is further emphasized by the crucifix-topped tower that rises

44 Anon. 1964. *De Volkskrant*, 13 Feb: 3.
45 Anon. 1960b. *Nieuwsblad van het Zuiden*, 19 Oct: 7.

Pretoria, Waterkloof, St John Vianney Seminary, designed by Anton Voorvelt, 1950; photo 2019

over the central entrance. The ensemble, laid out around two courtyards, contains an exceptionally fine chapel, which exhibits the same serenity as Voorvelt's 1937 Maria Church in Haarlem, the Netherlands.[46]

The Catholic ambitions for Kroonstad were even grander. The Dutch architect Cees van Moorsel, based in The Hague, was invited to design a new St Patrick's Cathedral for this vicariate on a plot of land on the town's main road, Reitz Street. His 1953 design presented a large austere Romanesque Revival complex consisting of an impressive cathedral with high tower, priests' accommodation and a small convent. The design, for unknown reasons, was never executed. The Bloemfontein vicariate was also fast expanding its presence and activities, especially in Black communities. The St Rose of Lima Church (1954), with associated St Mary's Primary School in the Bochabela neighbourhood of Bloemfontein is a good example. Its designer, Payens, was a devoted Catholic and pragmatic architect, who initially had settled in Kroonstad but soon relocated to the Free State's capital. St Rose of Lima is conventionally brick-built; its tower topped by a Rheinisch Helm, one of a very few in

46 See also the interlude on Cross-continental careers for Voorvelt.

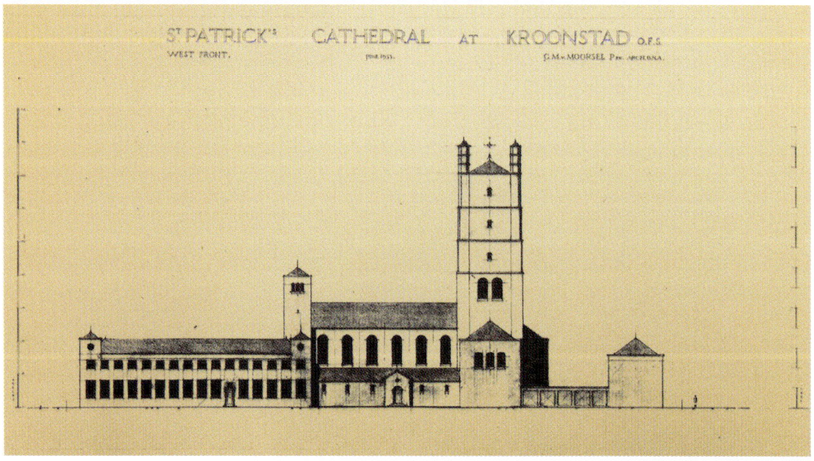

Design for a new Catholic Cathedral complex in Kroonstad by Cees van Moorsel, 1953 (not executed)

Pretoria, Waterkloof, St John Vianney Seminary, chapel, designed by Anton Voorvelt, 1950; photo 2019

Bloemfontein, St Rose of Lima Catholic Church, designed by Edy Payens, 1954; photo 2020

Maseru, Our Lady of Victories Catholic Cathedral, designed by Edy Payens, 1955; photo at inauguration, 1955

South Africa. It stands at the beginning of Payens' church-building career during which he sought to embed the traditionalist Church architecture preferred by his clients—mostly French and Dutch priests—into local African culture.

When Payens was commissioned to design a church for a new diocese of Maseru, Lesotho, the choice for the use of local sandstone was economic and contextual. Completed in 1955, this church was elevated to Our Lady of Victories Catholic Cathedral in 1961. The articulation of the cathedral's towers resonates strongly with the post-war architecture in the Netherlands, where precast geometric concrete elements were applied for graphic effect and cost reduction.

This same influence is visible in the small chapel designed by Voorvelt for the affluent eastern suburbs of Pretoria. The tower of his Pius X Catholic Church (1959) in Waterkloof, is constructed of such similar precast concrete blocks, framed in brickwork and an exposed concrete frame. A notable aspect of this chapel is that the focus is on the tower and western façade; the other façades of the body of the chapel are articulated only through structure and opening.

The focus on the main façade and neglect of all other elevations is even more pronounced in Voorvelt's St Mary of the Wayside Catholic Church (1959) in Maryvale, Johannesburg. Its most striking exterior feature is an enormous mosaic framed symmetrically by two identical towers. The artist was Italian émigré artist Armando Baldinelli, a good friend of Voorvelt and, like him a member of this congregation. Baldinelli also collaborated on the interior programme, and produced the mosaic, altar panel. Voorvelt's ennobling use of cheap materials, such as linoleum, pressed steel panels and concrete is as subtle as his delicate details for the lectern, communion rail and altar. This is the most expressive of the many churches, chapels, convent and school buildings and other buildings, including the Catholic Centre in Church Street, Johannesburg (1954), that Voorvelt designed for the Catholic Church.

His compatriot Van Gemert, also based in Johannesburg, was a close collaborator of bishop Van Velsen and responsible for numerous churches, especially for Black communities. After Van Gemert completed the new Saint Peter Claver Church (1958) in Seeisoville, Kroonstad, he and Van Velsen decided to commission a Black artist to provide the artistic programme. Artist Cecil Skotnes recommended his

Pretoria, Waterkloof, Pius X Catholic Church, designed by Anton Voorvelt, 1957; photo 2019

Johannesburg, Maryvale, St Mary of the Wayside Catholic Church, designed by Anton Voorvelt, 1959, façade mosaic by Armando Baldinelli; photo 2019

Johannesburg, Maryvale, St Mary of the Wayside Catholic Church, interior, designed by Anton Voorvelt, 1959, mosaic altarpiece by Armando Baldinelli; photo 2019

Pretoria, Loreto Convent School Chapel, interior, designed by Anton Voorvelt, c1961; photo 2020

Bethlehem, Catholic Cathedral of the Holy Ghost, designed by Edy Payens, 1959; photo c1960

student Sydney Kumalo to provide the sculpted Stations of the Cross and a ceiling painting. This commission launched Kumalo's career as an independent artist.[47]

Payens' Catholic Cathedral of the Holy Ghost, in Bethlehem (1960) was equally bold in its incorporation of art in architecture. For this then predominantly Afrikaner town it took its cue from the then-prevalent 'Dudokian' architecture but the main feature is a stylised relief of a white dove descending. This symbol of both the Holy Ghost and reconciliation was also a well-known symbol among Protestants and the choice to employ it here may have been a deliberate move to lower the threshold for the acceptance of Catholicism amongst the local Afrikaners. Despite Nationalist opposition, new Catholic schools were founded. Van Gemert designed Van Velsens abandoned Kroonstad boys' school project (c1956) while Voorvelt designed the St Benedict's College in Johannesburg (1957). Existing convent schools such as the Loreto Convent School in Pretoria also expanded. Its extensions bear all the hallmarks of Voorvelts' hand. The sublime interior of the school chapel (c1961) resonates strongly with Voorvelt's St John Vianney chapel, here articulated by lofty laminated timber lancet arches.

Payens' explorations of local building culture are most evident in his design for the Sacred Heart Cathedral in Bloemfontein (1962). The Cathedral was inaugurated as a multi-racial church and remained so throughout the years of apartheid. Set against a hill, the main façade with its sweeping stair offset against a campanile-like tower topped by a concrete crown dominates the approach. On entering the cathedral, the eye is drawn to a magnificent altarpiece set against a slate-covered wall, which Payens derived from local Sotho building practice. The mosaic altarpiece, which like all the other artwork in the cathedral was created by Sister Piëntia Selhorst, presents a crucifix set in a mandorla–the symbol of the junction of two worlds–but also reminiscent of traditional African hide shields.

47 Macdonald, 2016: 38.

Bloemfontein, Sacred Heart Catholic Cathedral, interior, designed by Edy Payens 1962, mosaic altarpiece by Sister Piëntia Selhorst; photo 2020

Eastern Free State or Lesotho, unknown church designed by Edy Payens, c1962; photo date unknown

Kroonstad, St Patrick's Catholic Cathedral, designed by Jan Willem van Gemert, 1965, with altarpiece by Cecil Skotnes; photo 2009

Payens designed numerous Catholic churches, chapels, schools and mission hospitals throughout the eastern Free State and Lesotho where these facilities provided vital services to impoverished and oppressed communities. He often had to deal with very limited means. The Assumpta church, Westminster (1962) is exemplary of his skills to create a worthy place of worship in a remote location.

Meanwhile, Van Velsen commissioned Van Gemert to provide a new design for the new cathedral in Kroonstad. The resulting St Patrick's Cathedral (1966) is an elegant low-slung cuboid space–a modernist receptacle for worshipers. Van Gemert collaborated closely with a team of progressive artists, Cecil Skotnes, Zoltan Borbereki, Eduardo Villa, Barbara Greig, Elizabeth Sebök and Fred Schimmel, to develop its artistic programme. Van Velsen purchased Maud Sumner's painting *The Green Christ* as a personal gift for the cathedral, which today houses one of the greatest ensembles of mid-C20 art in South Africa.

A truly South African church

A South African traveller will at some time pass through the Karoo town of Beaufort West on the main route between Gauteng and the Cape. Its skyline is dominated by the DR Church's white Gothic Revival spire, which was added to an existing church to the design of Dutch émigré architect Johannes Vixseboxse in 1919. But unless forewarned, one could easily miss the towerless *Die Ark* United Reformed Church (1962) in the Rustdene neighbourhood, designed by a then-recent graduate of the University of Cape Town, Arne Sikkel. Arne may have been given the commission through the intercession of his father, Henk, who had designed many churches for the NGK-aligned NG Kerk in Afrika.

The Ark is constructed of local stone, rough timber beams, and a ceiling of woven reed mats. This ceiling recalls the 'matjieshuis' dwellings of the Khoi ancestors of the community, in which usually bent laths, woven grass matting and rawhide covers are applied.

The Ark is, like the matjieshuis, a haven in the desert, a source of pride for the local community. It is a sublime culmination of the 'tent in the desert' type and the *kappiekerk* type at once while expressing the sincere search for a locally relevant church architecture for South Africa. This was one of Arne Sikkel's last South Africa projects. He soon emigrated to put his South Africa architectural skills to practice in the Netherlands.

Epilogue

In this chapter only some highlights of the vast number of churches designed by Dutch émigré architects in South Africa are explored. Various Dutch émigré architects made substantial contributions in the development of the C20 Protestant churches. They skilfully addressed both the programmatic assignment, which called for technical and spatial solutions to seat a large congregation while ensuring that the dominee could both be seen and heard clearly; and the stylistic design challenge: creating an aesthetic that was representative for the community that the church served. The contribution of the hitherto little known Catholic architects deserves, like their other émigré compatriots, further exploration. This heritage built for communities of faith presents not only a surprising large plurality in denominations, styles and types but also reveals the strong connections between the various communities in the Netherlands and their counterparts in South Africa.

Beaufort-West, Rustdene, United Reformed Church, 'Die Ark', designed by Arne Sikkel, 1967; photo 2020

Cape Town, panoramic overview in 1952
as drawn by Piet Worm, from his booklet
Die verhaal van Jan van Riebeeck

Pretoria, Netherlands Bank by Norman Eaton entrance doors in 2020

6 Building for Banking and Industry

Catherine Deacon & Marguerite Pienaar

Introduction

The Netherlands Bank of South Africa (NBZA), today Nedbank, has its associations with many C20 commercial and industrial buildings in South Africa. Its optimistic *spiering* [expansion] policy resulted in a property portfolio that exceeded those of many other South African banks at the time. The NBZA was also active in financing international trade and played an important role in supporting the exports of South African wool, hides, textiles and skins, and cut diamonds. The result of such investments soon materialized in new buildings, to which other Dutch industries also contributed. Various architects of Dutch origin conceived architectures of exchange and enterprise, and thus cultural transfers and other forms of transposition intertwine the architectural histories of South Africa and the Netherlands. This chapter will introduce a selection of works and present their place and contribution within the South African context as a shared Dutch heritage.

The Netherlands Bank of South Africa

In 1952 a children's book on Jan van Riebeeck was commissioned by the NBZA as a public relations outreach, celebrating the 300th anniversary of Dutch colonial settlement in South Africa. The simple narrative of the booklet, written in Afrikaans and illustrated by Dutch designer Piet Worm, however, features more than just bank buildings.[1] While not the original intention of the book, from a present-day perspective it can be seen as linking the bank's aspirations with the built environment as a thoroughly urban endeavour. The folded panorama of Cape Town, at its end, presents the city as a physical manifestation of the flow of money as an urban condition, with the many industrial and commercial visions expressed by buildings that 'reach for the sky'.

1 Worm, [1952].

Dutch origin

The Netherlands Bank was originally founded in 1888 as *Nederlandsche Bank en Credietvereeniging* (*NBCV*) in Amsterdam, which started its urban presence in South Africa as a modest building in Pretoria. The main purpose of the *NBCV* was, initially, to offer financial assistance to Dutch immigrants who wished to export goods.[2] In 1897 its second head office was opened, located prominently on Church Square, Pretoria, designed by Dutch émigré architect Wim de Zwaan in a mixed Dutch neo-Renaissance and *Art Nouveau* style.[3]

Following the end of the South African War, a deliberate change of its name to the *Nederlandsche Bank voor Zuid-Afrika* was made, so as to gain wider southern African support while helping rebuild the post-war economy.[4] A brief spurt of growth at that time resulted in their expanding to eight national agencies by the end of 1903, which included one strategically located in the harbour city of Cape Town in the Cape

2 Van der Merwe,1988.
3 Allen, 1971: 55-63; Bakker *et al.*, 2014: 201.
4 Van der Merwe, 1988: 9–15.

Pretoria, Church Square, second head office of the Nederlandsche Bank en Credietvereeniging (1897), designed by Wim de Zwaan; 2018

Colony and an important trade office in London in 1906. The subsequent policy of the bank then was to only open agencies in important trade, industrial and agricultural centres in support of its focus on international commerce. This aspect distinguished the NBZA from other local banks up until the late 1950s.[5]

Over subsequent decades the bank maintained a low profile, focusing on its international trade expertise whilst still being tightly controlled from Amsterdam. The ensuing economic boom following the First World War meant that South Africa enjoyed a good measure of prosperity from which the NBZA benefitted. Despite the worldwide depression from 1929 onwards, the bank was, by 1939, in a strong financial position. New buildings were constructed in Johannesburg, Pietersburg, Germiston, Bethlehem and a new *erf* was bought along Church Street, Pretoria for the construction of a new headquarters building.[6]

The outbreak of the Second World War had a substantial influence on the already cumbersome lines of communication between the Amsterdam Board of Directors and Pretoria. When the Netherlands was invaded by Nazi Germany on 10 May 1940, all communication with Amsterdam was severed. Yet the NBZA remained prosperous during the war years and reaped the benefits of a sharp rise in exports from South Africa including industrial diamonds, gold, textiles, hides, and wool. Under strict guidelines from the South African government and the watchful eye of the specially appointed local bank Controller, the Dutch émigré Jacobus Dommisse, the bank extended its trading activities considerably, positioned favourably in serving the war effort with its London branch.[7] In 1944 the first branch to open in an industrial area, in support of the local factories of the so-called 'rags industry', was located in Salt River, Cape Town.[8] By the end of the War in 1945 the NBZA had twenty-two agencies and thereafter between 1945 and 1951 an additional eighteen branches were opened in burgeoning industrial and commercial centres, including Salisbury (now Harare) and Bulawayo in Rhodesia (now Zimbabwe).[9]

Post-war evolution

After the War it became clear that the future of the NBZA lay in the formation of a full South African banking company, not only so as to secure working capital for its operations but also to win local trust. From within the bank pressure mounted for the severing of ties with Amsterdam so as to establish a stronger South African identity. Two influential characters, Johannes Keuning (at the time assistant chief agent) and local chief agent Jan Pieter Kakebeeke, though both Dutch-born, urged the establishment of NBZA as independent of its European counterpart so as to catch the 'kabeljou' [cod, in a figurative sense] for the South African industry and to enable further 'spiering' [extension] of the bank in South Africa.[10]

In 1948, notwithstanding the official formalizing of apartheid, Dutch émigré banker Bernard Holsboer accepted the position of assistant managing director of the NBZA in Pretoria under the condition that the bank would become a South African Company.[11] In 1951 the bank was finally registered in terms of the South African Companies Act and renamed the Netherlands Bank of South Africa Limited.[12] In that same year the bank opened its new headquarters in Pretoria, designed by a well-known local Modern Movement architect, Norman Eaton, who had, by that time, also designed several bank buildings for the then Landbank.[13]

A perspective drawing of this new headquarters building was included in Worm's children's booklet on Jan Van Riebeeck, linking it to the special relations between the Netherlands and the Union of South Africa.[14] While, from a current-day stance, one might consider this 300-year colonial history as contentious, it is impossible not to take into consideration the past political timeline as a backdrop to these events. Though upholding a political neutrality in public, the Bank was extremely critical of the apartheid regime. While not openly antagonistic towards the national government, their disdain for the political situation is attested to by several internal banking communications and annual reports.[15] An entirely neutral public face resulted in fewer Afrikaners doing business with them. During the entire period under discussion, the Bank refused to appoint anyone with Afrikaner ties to their staff. The NBZA was the first trade bank to open facilities for black citizens in 1957, providing a dedicated service counter in the Eaton-designed Pretoria branch.[16]

Since the bank focused on business, it excluded dealing with the funds of the man on the street. Instead, it diversified its services as a niche bank to include insurance, leasing, financing and merchant banking. By 1956 the bank had more funds in new buildings as part of its investment portfolio than most other South African banks at that time. By the early 1970s the bank had established approximately 120 branches in southern Africa, which concentrated their focus on commercial and industrial enterprises.[17]

Spiering and flexing

Since its inception, investing in property was an important policy directive of the Netherlands Bank. Besides extending its network of branches, the bank also practiced the act of flexing, both as a show of impressive power as well as for adapting to new circumstances. Their early banking offices claimed a central urban position in the major towns. It became essential that they be associated with prominent buildings of identifiable character which reflected their distinction as a niche bank.[18]

East Cape

In the eastern part of the then Cape Province, the first Netherlands Bank branch in Port Elizabeth, designed by the Dutch émigré architect Henk Siemerink, opened in 1926 to serve the prosperous wool industry. The polished rusticated granite base and symmetrical classical façade with a deep cornice of terracotta tiles became the blueprint for several

5 Van der Merwe, 1988: 183; also see Verhoef, G. 1987.
6 Van der Merwe, 1988: 163.
7 Van der Merwe, 1988: 167–80, 184, 221; Verhoef, 1987: 4.
8 Verhoef, 1987: 677.
9 Verhoef, 1987: 427.
10 Verhoef 1987: 2–23.
11 Verhoef 1987: 38.
12 Verhoef, 1987: 47.
13 See the original drawings in the Eaton Collection in the Architecture Archive of the University of Pretoria.
14 Worm, [1952]: rear side of the panorama folder.
15 Verhoef, 1987: 663–64.
16 Verhoef, 1987: 669.
17 Van der Merwe, 1988: 1–46; Verhoef, 1987: 1–90.
18 Verhoef, 1987: 498–99.

Port Elizabeth, the Main Street Branch of the Netherlands Bank, by Hendrik Siemerink, 1926, with plinth remodelled in c1955, by Siemerink & Brinkman (demolished)

East London, Netherlands Bank Building at the corner of Oxford and Union Street by Hendrik Siemerink, opened in 1927, as published in *Architecture in South Africa Vol 1*, 1933

Port Elizabeth, the 1936 North End branch of the Netherlands Bank located prominently along Govan Mbeki Avenue, designed by Gertruida Brinkman née Siemerink, as published in *Port Elizabeth: From a border garrison town to a modern commercial and industrial city*, 1966

bank buildings at that time. Siemerink, who relocated his practice into this bank building and was, by then, partnered with Hugh Walker, also designed the Netherlands Bank branch in East London (1927). This still extant building also reflects classical revivalist tenets. Built on a concrete foundation, with a plinth of King Williams Town blue mountain stone, the ground floor is faced with Queenstown free stone. All external doors, windows, and shutters are of teak. The floors are of reinforced concrete and the building is covered with a corrugated asbestos-fibre roof.[19] Its similarity with the much larger Union Buildings at Pretoria was no coincidence since Siemerink had played a key role on the construction site as the assistant engineer on behalf of the Public Works Department, before entering into private practice in Port Elizabeth.[20]

From the 1930s onwards the new NBSA buildings reflected styling associated with Art Deco and Streamline Moderne, as seen in its branch in Smith Street, Durban, by Chick & Bartholomew (1934).[21] Another stylistic inspiration at that time was the brick-faced 'Dudokian' architecture, named after the Hilversum-based architect Willem Dudok, for example, in the 1936 North End Netherlands Bank building in Port Elizabeth.[22] Intriguingly, this was designed by Siemerink's daughter, Gertruida Brinkman, only ten years after Henk had completed the Neo-classical Main Street branch.[23] Gertruida joined her father's practice in 1932 as one of the early formally qualified female architects in South Africa. She was responsible for the majority of the subsequent design work of the firm (Siemerink & Brinkman, with her husband, Jack Brinkman from 1935).[24] The corner of the NSBA building along what is now Govan Mbeki Drive is prominently articulated with a strong rectangular tower that lends it its severe character, reinforced by the choice of a darker face-brick.

Gauteng

Golden-brown face-bricks were often chosen as material for other bank branches of the time, having projecting ledges and other features showing Art Deco-influences. The newly formed partnership between James Stadler Burg and Clement Scarr Lodge produced the expressionist

19 Cumming-George, 1933: 134.
20 Interview with Bruce (son) and Bryan (grandson) Brinkman, Port Elizabeth, 2 November 2019.
21 Cumming-George,1934: 91; the building was demolished to make way for the Norman Eaton designed building.
22 Harradine,1994, 2002: 205.
23 Interview with the Brinkmans 2 November 2019.
24 Brinkman, s.a.: 20. The practice is still extant today, with both her son Bruce and grandson Bryan as partners.

Springs, the 1936 branch of the Netherlands Bank, designed by Burg & Lodge

Johannesburg, the 1938 Von Brandis Branch, designed by Geers & Geers

Springs branch of the Netherlands Bank in 1936 as their very first commission in private practice, in addition to the simplified design of the Benoni branch. They were soon to assist Burg's father, Johannes Rienk, an established Dutch-born and trained architect practicing in Pretoria.[25]

Johannesburg

In the mode of the Art Deco and 'Dudokian' language, the Von Brandis Branch in Johannesburg (1938) was designed by a Dutch émigré father-and-son partnership, Leendert Geers & Geurt Geers, characterized by its rectangular corner articulation, golden-brown face-brick, vertical recesses, and narrow projecting slabs. This firm was also engaged for the Hollandia House on the corner of what is now Helen Joseph Street and President Street (1939), where its Dutch connection was overtly expressed by the legend *'Nederlandsche Bank voor Zuid Afrika'* and the arms of Queen Wilhelmina of the Netherlands. Hollandia House was occupied for three decades by Geers & Geers, who also designed many Dutch Reformed churches across South Africa and the Netherlands Bank branch in Pietersburg (now Polokwane) in 1939.[26]

The story of the Netherlands Bank buildings on the corner of Fox and Simmonds Streets, Johannesburg, located in the financial district of the 'Golden City', reflects the changes in architecture through three stages. The façade of the first Netherlands Bank Building, (c1897), was used to catch the eye along Fox Street with intricate detailing, caryatids beneath the pediments, projecting cantilevers and wrought iron balustrading.[27] Yet it was demolished to make way for the second building, 1926, designed by Percy Rogers Cooke & Harold Wolseley Spicer to take up the prominent corner of Fox and Simmonds Streets. Within a classicist revival language, an attractive rounded corner entrance and pronounced horizontal articulation of the façade, the building expressed self-confidence.

Johannesburg, Hollandia House, 127 Helen Joseph Street, designed by Geers & Geers in 1939, as published in *Kunsgeskiedenis: Boukuns*, 1941 (since plastered and painted)

25 The firm became known as Burg, Lodge & Burg in 1941; see Bakker et al, 2014: 204.
26 Chipkin,1993: 112.
27 Stoloff. 1947; Van der Waal,1987: 65.

Left: Johannesburg, first Netherlands Bank Building, c1897, located at 82 Fox Street, Johannesburg (later demolished for the second branch)

Below: Johannesburg, second Netherlands Bank Building, 1926, designed by Cooke & Spicer on the corner of Fox and Simmonds Street, after face-lift of the 1950s (later demolished for the third bank on this place)

Right: Johannesburg, the 1962 new headquarters of the Netherlands Bank, Fox Street under construction, designed by Hellmut Stauch

Remarkably, the façade was simplified at a later date, (possibly during alterations in the mid-fifties) with the stripping of all embellishment to reflect a more restrained exterior.[28]

The second Netherlands Bank branch building was ultimately demolished to make way for the new headquarters, an ambitious Hellmut Stauch-designed building constructed in phases from 1962 to 1964 at the height of the influence of the Modern Movement in South Africa.[29] In stark contrast to its predecessors, the urban life and interior of the Bank integrate seamlessly on the ground-floor. The building is defined through stark rectangular massing, glass curtain walls, a large horizontal roof-plane beneath which are columns and vertical planes of marble and glass, along with Brazilian influences such as the roof garden and relief-work across vertical surfaces.[30] In complying with both the maximum urban height restrictions and floor area ratio, the new headquarters fully met the modernist urban merchant bank typology of the 1960s.

Translated typologies

A similar approach was adopted in part by the Dutch émigré architects Henk de Bie & Wim van Wijngaarden for the branch (1964) in Bloemfontein, capital of Orange Free State province.[31] Like many of its counterparts, it is positioned on a prominent corner, in this case opposite the main post office on Hoffman Square. The banking hall is uncommonly located on the first floor, reached directly by escalators encased in glass at the corner. The design begs comparison with the elegant 1954 Huf Building in Rotterdam, designed by Van den Broek & Bakema for a shoe store with a fully glazed ground floor as an invitation to enter the space. Considering that Van Wijngaarden was originally from Rotterdam and emigrated to South Africa in 1955, it is quite conceivable that the Huf commercial prototype was transferred to the bank building in Bloemfontein.[32] One might speculate as to whether De Bie & Van Wijngaarden did not feel that a translucent interface on the ground floor would be a security risk for the bank, and so placed the banking hall on the first-floor, conveniently reached with a fluid transition by way of an escalator. Like the Huf Building, the ground-floor is used for retail space, providing additional income for the bank, thereby merging the retail typology with the functional requirements of the bank.

28 Verhoef (1987: 430) mentions that the building was enlarged in 1956.
29 A&B [SA]. 1962a, Aug: 20–27.
30 Gerneke,1998: 214.

31 De Bie, 1965.
32 Peters & Raubenheimer, 2019: 39; Anon. 1954b, *Algemeen Handelsblad*, 26 Mar: 11.

Bloemfontein, the 1964 design for the Netherlands Bank Building, by De Bie & Van Wijngaarden

Rotterdam, the multifunctional Huf Building, opened in 1954, designed by Van den Broek & Bakema, as partially depicted on the cover of the Dutch journal *Forum* in 1957

Another curious prototype that was transferred from commercial architecture to the banking typology came from the American 'drive-up' format (pioneered in the 1930s). The very first convenient drive-through for the Netherlands Bank was opened in 1956 on the corner of Frederick and Anderson Streets, Johannesburg, with signage guiding customers to those lanes open for business.[33] Also, in the then Rhodesia's capital Salisbury a drive-up branch was built, with a glazed rounded corner and a slim concrete canopy in front of the counter.

While commercial cues started to establish a new glass 'type' of bank building, Dutch brick-focused influences can be found elsewhere, such as the 1962 branch located on the corner of Buitenkant and Albertus Streets, Cape Town. This was designed by the worldly Modern Movement architect Max Policansky, who had, amongst others, briefly worked in the offices of Henk Wijdeveld in 1934 in Amsterdam.[34] The bank building, with its earthy face brick, rounded corner, relatively traditional massing, flat roof with projecting eaves and concrete window box frames, is reminiscent both of the Amsterdam School, schools by Dudok and JJP Oud's streamlined housing in the Hook of Holland and Kiefhoek in Rotterdam.[35]

33 Verhoef, 1987: 430.

34 Van Graan, 2011: 133, 202.

35 Groenendijk & Vollaard, 2006: 174–76, 274–75, 282, 341, 486–87.

Salisbury/Harare, drive-through branch of the Netherlands Bank, opened in 1951; photo c1956

Pretoria headquarters

Interestingly, Oud had another, more explicit link with the NBZA, as he had completed a design for the 'Nederlandsche Bank voor Zuid Afrika te Pretoria'. The drawings are not dated, but the project title suggests that it was before the bank's renaming in 1951, possibly 1946.[36] Oud's cubistic design, rendered in brick, had a low plinth with projecting canopies over the sidewalks. The entire western façade was articulated in a flat, horizontal and, perhaps, derivative manner, with no street interface along the sidewalk along the entire western edge. The heavy massing of the main building is relieved by its articulation with the sky, which is achieved by a slender floating roof, with pronounced lettering along the parapet of the southern façade.

Considering that the *erf* [plot] in Pretoria was obtained in 1939 for the purpose of constructing a new headquarters for the bank's expanding operations, it is conceivable that a distinguished Dutch architect, Oud, was appointed by the Amsterdam Board to design the NBZA new flagship in South Africa.[37] Undoubtedly, the Nazi-invasion and occupation of the Netherlands (1940–45) halted the assignment. The then latent ambition for independence from Amsterdam came to fruition directly after the War. It is therefore plausible that the appointment of the well-known local architect Norman Eaton resulted from these machinations.[38]

In contrast to Oud's design, Eaton's rendition for the new bank building in Pretoria was of a richly crafted and elegantly proportioned building with a stronger vertical emphasis. Earth-coloured brick fins on a grid derived from standardized window sizes provide depth and animation to the façades along the prominent street fronts. The lower levels are articulated with rectangular piers clad in smooth, light travertine, so that the rest of the building above seems to float, defying gravity. Placed upon an outward-curving base at ground level through to recessed ground floor windows, a positive interface along all street edges is ensured. Initially the client did not approve of the proposed face-brick

36 The drawings are in the JJP Oud archive at Het Nieuwe Instituut, Rotterdam (OUDJ 110276379).

37 Van der Merwe, 1988: 163.

38 The first drawings from Eaton's practice, styled Meiring, Eaton & Louw Architects, date from March 1946 (Eaton Collection, Architecture Archive of the University of Pretoria).

Perspective drawing by Meiring Eaton & Naudé Architects of Norman Eaton's design for the new Netherlands Bank Building for Pretoria, 1946

Undated perspective drawing by JJP Oud for the *Nederlandse Bank voor Zuid Afrika* for Pretoria, probably made in 1946 (not executed)

finishes: 'we are tired of face-brick, there is too much of it in Holland... this is our headquarters, we must have something more impressive'.[39] Eaton evidently managed to convince them otherwise with specially manufactured narrow bricks rendering a weave-like texture for the entire upper envelope of the structure. The building was designed as a flexible container, in line with Dutch modernist tenets. Rich detailing and textures reference not only Dutch history but also, prominently, to African motifs, including bronze heraldic panels, Benin-figurehead door handles, crafted tiles, seating, and a public water fountain.[40]

Durban

Eaton also designed the 1960 branch in Durban, on the Kwazulu-Natal coastline, arguably his best work. His response to the subtropical environment was to peel away the skin of the building, so that it

Pretoria, the executed 1953 Netherlands Bank by Norman Eaton in 2020

Pretoria, 1953 Netherlands Bank by Norman Eaton interior, shortly after completion

becomes a layered façade. The woven screen wall previously seen in the Pretoria bank has again become a container of space. The screen wraps the cube at mezzanine level, where it is offset from the building so that it seems to float as a green, glazed cube above the urban podium. Although supported by travertine piers, spaces between the piers are glazed so that the ground floor banking hall appears completely open. African references are subtle, embedded in the weaving of the screen and the brick-carpet of the roof garden. The building is recessed from the street so that it generously returns public space to the city.

39 Harrop-Allin, 1975: 94

40 See also Chapter 10.

Pretoria, the bronze gates of the 1953 Netherlands Bank, designed by Norman Eaton

Durban, the 1960 Netherlands Bank Building, designed by Norman Eaton; photo 2014

Materialized investments

Many local Dutch industries held accounts with the NBZA from the early C20, with successful industries of notable Dutch emigrants, including the *Koedoe Apteek* in Pretoria, the *Holland Afrika Lijn* in Port Elizabeth, the South African Mining and General Investments company and the Nectar Tea and Coffee Company, to name but a few.[41] Some of the earliest ventures of the Bank, preluded by the financial optimism that started in 1908–09, was related to the Pretoria Iron Mines Ltd., established by the Dutch-born engineer Cornelis Delfos and developed to the Iron and Steel Industrial Corporation (Iscor) in 1928.[42] Ties were close—Dommisse served on the company's board for many years.[43]

Various industries burgeoned as a result of Netherlands Bank investment in early C20, such as the diamond industry and wool industry.[44] The Boere Saamwerk Beperk [Farmers' Cooperative] was one of the most important clients of the NBZA, to the extent that the bank opened the branches in Port Elizabeth and East London exclusively to serve the cooperatives in the 1920s.[45] The opening of the Worcester Netherlands Bank branch in 1929 was another strategic decision on the part of the NBZA to be centrally located to serve the emergent wine industry.[46] Another agency was built in Wellington in 1964 for the same reason, designed by Dutch émigré architect Jaap Jongens in the office of Chapman & Spoor.

By the end of the 1960s the nature of the bank's commercial offerings had shifted. By the 1970s the Netherlands Bank buildings had become the first of the modern-day brand with its conception of the large-scale commercial Nedbank Centre. Investments in property were transferred to shares in large-scale property development, as well as the financing of developments, which included amongst others the Foreshore, Roggebaai and the Motor Centrum, Eloff Street, Johannesburg, their investment potential often researched by the Bank's in-house urban economists.[47]

41 Van der Merwe, 1988: 48–55; Geljon, 2017: 524–26.
42 See (Van der Merwe 1988: 45-48) for a comprehensive list of industries linked to the Netherlands Bank until 1945; Geljon (2017: 524-526) lists several Dutch industries. Also see sahistory.org.za/old-pretoria-iron-mines-iscor-pretoria.
43 Ploeger, 1994: 60.
44 Van der Merwe, 1988: 172.
45 Van der Merwe, 1988: 186.
46 Van der Merwe, 1988: 187.
47 Verhoef, 1987: 502.

Dutch related architectures of industry

Dutch architectural influence and exchange in South Africa extended beyond the banking sector to architectural typologies serving the needs of commerce and an ever-industrializing environment. Industrial expansion and economic growth also coincided with the introduction of the International Style in the 1930s.[48] Dutch émigré architects also made their contribution and a selection of their significant industrial buildings will be examined here, including works by Siemerink and Niegeman.

Siemerink and partners

One of the most prolific practices to benefit from the rapidly industrializing context was that of Siemerink in Port Elizabeth. The city was strategically placed geographically on Algoa Bay to serve as an urban centre for the import and export of goods. Soon the architecture of production lines with long, low sheds started to define the city, which would have had an equally profound effect on modern life. The manufacture of motor cars, organized along conveyor belts, became the city's most important industry.

Siemerink's successive firms designed numerous warehouses, garages, as well as some of the major commercial and industrial projects. But one of his earliest projects was not industrial, the world-famous Snake Park and Aquarium (1919–25, demolished), rendered, as with their NBZA branch there, in an eclectic neo-classical language.[49] An early industrial work located further afield in Salt River, Cape Town, is the Wool Warehouse (1927) for the Boere Saamwerk Beperk (now converted to a church). This has clearly separated functions and originally had its own rail siding for off-loading the wool with conveyor belts. The (former) storage premises, constructed of reinforced concrete and steel, are covered by a saw-tooth roof. The Streamline Moderne styled office block at the front originally housed the manager's room, typists' room and general offices on the ground floor, and a board room, tea-room, buyers' room, and lavatory on the first.[50]

48 Jones, 1992: 5 and Duncan-Brown,1991: 77–78.
49 Harradine, 1994: 147.
50 Cumming-George, 1934: 79

Cape Town, Salt River, the 1927 Wool Warehouse for the Boere Saamwerk Beperk designed by Henk Siemerink, as published in *Architecture in South Africa Vol 2*, 1934

Directly linked to the car industry at Port Elizabeth is Siemerink & Walker's concrete building for the Ford Motor Car Company on York Road (1928).[51] Compared with its American precedent, the Highland Park Ford Plant in Detroit (1910) by Albert Kahn, it is somewhat restrained. This local rendition, with saw-toothed sheds over the assembly halls, is wrapped with offices and public interface, decorated with some Art Deco details in both the exterior and interior.

Their building for General Motors (SA) Ltd was the epitome of the 'decorated shed', resulting from revisions during the design process.[52] The initial design sketch presented a long, low horizontality of the factory building to the rear contrasted by the vertically articulated front portion in an eclectic style. However, in the final product (1928), the classical pediments and false columns had made way for a more Streamline Moderne aesthetic. Being two storeys high, it contained a large showroom, offices on the top floor and in the wings, a cafeteria.[53] The rear factory portion, vast in extent, consisted of reinforced concrete walls, pier and panel construction and was topped with a steel saw-toothed roof oriented south for optimal daylight, covered with corrugated asbestos-fibre roofing. The ambitious factory grounds were well conceived, and included pavilions, sports fields, a swimming pool and a test track for cars. The building is extant but has been significantly changed through the years.

51 Duncan-Brown, 1991: 92.
52 Coined by Venturi, Scott Brown & Izenour, 1972.
53 Duncan-Brown, 1991: 93.

Port Elizabeth, Ford Motor Company, designed by Siemerink & Walker in 1928, as published in *Architecture in South Africa Vol 1*, 1934

Port Elizabeth, part of a perspective sketch of the initial design for General Motors in North End, by Henk Siemerink in 1928

When Gertruida joined the practice in 1932, she had recently been brought into contact with the international Modern Movement ideas of her lecturer at Witwatersrand University, Rex Martienssen, and absorbed these in her designs.[54] The private house 'Ridgewood' for the managing director of the Ford Motor Car Company at the time, AH Stockelbach (1936), is a sterling example, being arguably the finest house in the International Style in Port Elizabeth, with its curved lines and flat roof showing influences from the work of Erich Mendelsohn and other European modernists.

Under the name Siemerink & Brinkman the firm made another notably advanced contribution to the urban industrial identity of Port Elizabeth with their factory for Mobbs Limited (completed in 1952). Located in the industrial precinct of North End, in close proximity to the North End Netherlands Bank, the factory manufactured children's footwear and women's clothing. The design of a double storeyed structure of reinforced concrete-framed construction with cavity brick walls, given its location on a sloped site, allowed for direct access at natural grade to each floor. The architectural response for even lighting onto a large uninterrupted factory floor to serve the manufacturing process was facilitated by a reinforced half-shell south-light roof.[55] It is still well-used today as a factory space and makes for a prominent landmark in its setting.

54 Interview with Bruce & Bryan Brinkman, Port Elizabeth, 2 November 2019
55 A&B [SA]. 1952, Jun: 38–41.

Niegeman and others

Contemporaneously, architectures of exchange were unfolding on the urban and industrial landscape of Cape Town, particularly in Salt River. In Main Road the modernist Judge Clothing Manufacturers, the first Rex Trueform factory, was completed in 1938, designed by Max Policansky and the Dutch modernist Henk Niegeman.[56] They had met before in Europe and Niegeman's wide experience was welcomed, emphasized by him placing his signature on the working drawings.[57] Prior to arriving in Cape Town, Niegeman had worked in Germany and, among other countries, been engaged in designing industrial and residential buildings in Russia

56 Nwati, 2007; Wolff, 2014: 16; see also the interlude on Cross-continental careers and Chapter 9.
57 UCT Library Special Collections, Cape Town.

Cape Town, Salt River, aerial view of the Bertish Clothing Factory (today House of Monatic), designed by Henk Niegeman, as published in the Dutch journal *Bouw* 1951

Port Elizabeth, Factory for Mobbs Limited, 1952, designed by Siemerink & Brinkman; photo 2020

Cape Town, Salt River, The Judge Clothing/Rex Trueform, designed by Henk Niegeman in Max Policansky's office, showing the post-1944 Andrews & Niegeman alterations; photo 2019

Cape Town, Salt River, the Rex Trueform ensemble, designed by Henk Niegeman, photo from the Dutch journal *Bouw* 1951

and California.[58] He entered into a partnership with his colleague at Policansky's office, Edward Douglas Andrews, in 1939 and it was later recalled that Niegeman's 'clarity in design, thought and meticulous attention to detail' had provided a strong foundation for the practice's approach to architectural concepts, to design development and to standards in construction.[59]

58 Van Graan 2011: 133–34.
59 A&B [SA]. 1990: Sep: 23.

The design for the clothing factory of M Bertish & Co (now House of Monatic), also in Main Road, may well have been the first commission for the newly founded practice, but the exact date is unclear.[60] The factory, in operation from 1951 and still extant, consists of two wings. The primary wing displays rhythmic glazing between structural columns contrasted with solid walls punctured by circular windows to indicate the cores of circulation. This wing culminates in a windowless street-facing façade, exhibiting the company branding and topped with a curved, floating roof. A secondary wing, far more utilitarian in appearance, meets the rear of this primary wing at a right angle, parallel with the road.

After six years, the Judge/Rex Trueform building was razed by fire, destroying most of its physical fabric. On account of Niegeman's previous engagements, his partnership with Andrews was commissioned to carry out the necessary changes and additions that followed after the fire-damage.[61] This began a sustained professional relationship between the client and the architect. The 1944 post-fire alterations were extensive. The saw-toothed roof pattern was extended right up to Main Road, accommodating an expansive manufacturing area which took up the entire first floor. Staff amenities, originally facing onto Main Road, were repositioned to the back of the building. Original openings were bricked up resulting in a solid street-facing façade.[62]

60 Van Graan 2011: 136-138, 177.
61 Anon. in Cape Times 1944, cited in Wolff, 2014: 29.
62 Wolff, 2014: 32.

Cape Town, Salt River, the 1939–40/48 Rex Trueform ensemble, designed by Henk Niegeman; photo 2016

Rex Trueform's expanding business required additional premises, resulting in the iconic factory across the road from the original, with Henk Niegeman as lead designer. This second factory was designed as a six-storey building of two contrasting structures at right angles, one solid brick, the other transparent glazing, meeting midway along the one façade at a circulation core. The shorter, glazed section was set back from the road with a lower administration building set between factory and roadside. Following general CIAM principles of function-based spatial separation in the disposition of buildings, their access and internal routing, here the layout also facilitated segregation of users based on a functional hierarchy and thus, in the South African context, on race. White staff members entered from Monrose Street, coloured people, working on the production floors, entered from the rear side.[63] Maximum penetration of natural daylight into factories during operating hours was a major requirement for clothing manufacture. The use of glass curtain walling for admitting light into the working spaces applied principles adopted by European modernists for factory buildings, as seen at the Van Nelle tobacco, coffee and tea factory at Rotterdam designed by Brinkman & Van der Vlugt (1928–31).[64]

Niegeman found an innovative solution to maximise daylighting whilst limiting the heat gain associated with large glazed surfaces. Here he employed various treatments of glazed facades using different orientations, including glass sunscreens and the newly invented system of heat-absorbing glass placed in a zig-zag pattern on the Main Road façade. Although a reinforced concrete column, beam and floor slab

Worcester, the 1946 Hextex Factory designed by Henk Niegeman, view from the water tower; photo 2020

method of construction was used throughout, longer spans and glazed walls contributed to the feeling of vast and limitless space in the uninterrupted factory section.[65]

The twin staircase located at the knuckle of the building gives some indication of the volume of workers that would have accessed the building daily. They represent the modernist aspiration for accommodating the needs of the user alongside technological

63 Pather, 2017.
64 Van Graan, 2011: 138; Kuipers, 2017.

65 Wolff, 2014: 44, 49.

Cape Town, Salt River, façade and outer staircase of the Rex Trueform ensemble, designed by Henk Niegeman; photo 2019

Muizenberg, former Shell Training Centre, today SA Naval College, designed by Henk Niegeman in the 1950s; photo 2020

advancements. The freestanding staircase is architecturally refined and has been described as being the 'signature of Niegeman'.[66] With the subsequent additions made in the 1960s much of the striking zig-zag façade was unfortunately demolished. The 1963 extension was built where offices for the Department of Native Affairs once stood.[67]

For a vast textile factory outside Cape Town Niegeman designed Hextex at Worcester, named after the nearby river Hex and opened in 1946. It consists of two series of low-slung, saw-tooth roofed factory buildings with a reinforced concrete structure along an open central axis (for fire prevention), dominated by the metal-clad water tower with the central office block at the front. The buildings are extant and serve their original purpose, namely the processing of sheep wool for garments and decoration.

In Plumstead, Cape Town, the premises of the Instrument Manufacturing Corporation were built to Niegeman's design, exhibiting a straightforward and functional modernism. The factory building won the bronze medal of the Cape Institute of Architects in 1963 while demonstrating that industrial efficiency and quality architectural expression are compatible.[68] The reinforced concrete construction and glazed façades accentuate the horizontality, alternated by the asymmetrical shed roofs. The building now houses municipal functions.

66 Interview with Tavill 2012, cited in: Wolff, 2014: 51.

67 Wolff, 2014: 75.

68 Greig, 1971:185.

Indirectly linked with industry is Niegeman's former Staff Training Center, built for the Shell oil company at Muizenberg near Cape Town (today in use as South African Naval Staff College).[69] The elongated structure is a high-calibre example of the practice's work, incorporating features of the International Style and reminiscent of the Dessau Bauhaus rhythm in the placing of the bedroom balconies. North-facing rooms share a common corridor along the south façade and a delicately glazed box envelopes the generous public stair to the west of the building. The solid eastern façade is punctured only by round portal windows alluding to the landings of the service stair within.

Niegeman's design skills and attention to detail can also be seen in an undated (and re-discovered) conceptual design for a Department Store building, presumably for Foschini in Cape Town. The board-mounted pencil sketch is beautifully of its time and represents the potential of an architecturally well-executed and elegant corner building to contribute to the urban environment.

Cape Town, Sea Point, perspective of the new Foschini Building, designed and drawn by Henk Niegeman

Conclusion

The power and longevity of the physical structures are striking, as reflected in our research. Similarly, the power of archival information confirms how architecture exists in different modes. Drawings from the archives communicate the *zeitgeist*. They also help to construct a historical thread when the physical manifestation is long gone or altered beyond recognition.

In compiling this chapter, the interconnectedness of banking, commerce and industry has become explicit in more ways than one. There is the obvious connection with the Netherlands Bank financing and supporting a selective commerce and industry, which found realization in built form. Likewise, industry dictated where new branches would open.

It was also the Bank's policy to only open branches in prominent locations, which resulted in the selection of conspicuous corner sites. Architects responded in different ways in their defining of corners, with a variety of urban corner typologies. The interconnectedness between banks and industry also played out in the stylistic and functional development of the type. While the chronology of banks traces the changes in architecture through various traditions, it increasingly borrowed from modes normally exclusively associated with commercial architecture, for instance, the banking hall making way for retail space or the drive-up fast-food typology transferred to the revered institutional typology. Streamline Moderne appeared most often in buildings related to transportation and movement but was readily adapted to the hallowed domain of banking and its public face.

The projects represented here illustrate the continuity of modernism, but also show how it transferred regionally, depending on contextual influences. The Dutch legacy also lies in the production of buildings that were at the forefront of modernism as mechanisms of progress. Such extraordinary responses of innovative modernist architecture and engineering came from the industry's need for large spaces and structural spans, along with the modernist concern with daylight. The Van Nelle-inspired idea of the factory as a well-honed brand identity ushered in the age of consumerist spectacle to the South African built environment. The dissemination of rational and flexible Dutch planning has further resulted in many extant buildings still being used for their original purpose. The spatial and formal legacy extends to durable finishes, as embodied in the work of Dudok, exhibiting characteristically good, sound, building methods. Ultimately the range of projects reinforces an urban identity and opens avenues for further discovery of the rich exchange between the Netherlands and South Africa.

69 A&B [SA]. 1957, Aug: 47–49.

GOODYEAR
CASTLE WINE & BRANDY CO LTD

M BERTISH & CO LTD

Cape Town, design for M Bertish & Co, by Andrews & Niegeman Architects

Pretoria, Erasmus Castle,
Frans Van der Ben, 1903;
photo 2020

7 The Picturesque and the Practical

Evolution of the Pretoria dwelling (1902–61)

Arthur Barker

Introduction

Some 9 000km south of Amsterdam lies South Africa's administrative capital, Pretoria. It was officially established in 1855, thereafter becoming the seat of the *Zuid-Afrikaansche Republiek* (ZAR) [South African Republic] (1852–1902). In its infancy, Pretoria was characterised by small, single-storey vernacular dwellings that had their Dutch architectural origins in the Cape region of South Africa.

From the late C19 onwards, new Dutch immigrant architects played an important role in the development of the regional architecture of the first Cape settlers and *Boers* [farmers], bringing with them recent and ornate picturesque influences. This approach provided a sense of familiarity for the new inhabitants who, in a new environment, had only their training and experience to rely on. A small band of immigrants took up positions with the *Nederlandsch Zuid-Afrikaansche Spoorwegmaatschappij* (NZASM, Dutch-South African Railways Company) or the ZAR's *Dienst Publieke Werken* (DPW, Department Public Works). A so-called Republican Style was established, founded on Dutch Neo-Renaissance architectural principles. It resulted in an aesthetic of spikes, air vents and wooden verandahs epitomised by Pretoria residences such as the 1898 *Mea Vota*, built for the NZASM engineers, Westenberg and Van der Made.[1]

In the early C20, after the South African War, another wave of Dutch immigrant architectural designers arrived who were, initially, more prone to picturesque expression in their architecture. In time, through the influences of place, prevailing culture and available technology, a more regionally appropriate and 'practical' architecture emerged. Politics and, at times, the perceived need to forge an *Afrikaner* identity, also played a role, while the development of a regional architecture was the result of adapting existing traditions, borrowing building practices and forging innovation over time.[2]

Through a traditive process, symmetry gave way to asymmetry, formality was tempered by practicality while low-scaled models replaced dominating forms. Attached verandahs became integrated *stoeps* and once compact plans were stretched to the limits of their sites. Additionally, cellular spaces morphed into continuous spatial configurations, while vernacular building methods were combined with newly available industrial materials.

In this chapter the evolution of the Pretoria dwelling is presented in the context of a localised regionalism that would, eventually, be characterized by traditional plan forms, rustic brick, low-pitched iron roofs, deep shaded eaves and verandahs, sun shy windows, landscape sensitivity and climatic responsiveness.[3]

1 Picton-Seymour, 1977: 301.
2 Labuschagne, 1998: 25.
3 Fisher, 1998: 125.

The Picturesque

The Picturesque has been defined, variously, as a literary and painterly English, or rather Western European, tradition (as a counter to Neoclassicism) where pictorial values, established between building and landscape, are heightened. The Picturesque is closely associated with Romanticism and the Arts and Crafts movement, through its relationship with untamed nature, the need for a simpler, less industrialised life and sense of nostalgia. In late C19 Dutch architecture, it was expressed through variants of American Stick and Swiss Chalet styles, mixed with local elements such as the Dutch *Jugendstil* which was analogous to the Belgian/French *Art Nouveau* movement, with its roots in the English and the German Arts and Crafts traditions. The Picturesque was the subject of a broader debate at the end of the C19 among Dutch architects centred on the key terms 'truth' or 'character', and closely associated with eclecticism, beauty and national revival.[4] The Picturesque was also used to distinguish Dutch national architecture from foreign monumental architecture, while reinforcing the increasing importance of the visual.[5] At the same time, well-illustrated books, journals and newspapers, such as the *Bouwkundig Weekblad* [Architectural Week Magazine] and *Architectura* (1893-1926), contributed to a broad dissemination of contemporary examples of Picturesque villas and *landhuizen* [country houses] built in newly developed residential areas for the privileged, for instance in the Gooi region, south east of Amsterdam.[6] Under the influence of romantic painters, the almost unadorned *Gooise landhuisstijl* [country house style] evolved, inspired by the organically-shaped thatched roofs of Dutch rural domestic architecture.

Variations of the Picturesque style were often used for the design of the weekend country villa, where new-found wealth and a desire for a 'rural life' could be expressed. The often eclectic style was typified by an aestheticisation of the everyday and expressed through irregular plans and fenestration, and imposing silhouettes.[7] Through transmigration and publication, these informants, together with those of the late C19 Dutch Republican Style, created a new eclectic local architecture in Pretoria around 1900. The architecture of Dutch villas found new expression in South Africa, where they were often used as a style for the design of residences for the *nouveau riche* in developing Pretoria suburbs, such as Brooklyn and Waterkloof and surrounding farms.

Picturesque beginnings: Frans van der Ben

The mansion Erasmus Castle (1903), originally named Bella Vista, was built on the Erasmuskloof farm south of Pretoria.[8] It represented a new stage in the development of a localised regional architecture through the incorporation of the typically curved forms of the a-historic *Jugendstil*

4 Van der Woud, 2017.
5 Van der Woud, 2017.
6 De Haan, 2016: 148, 159; Teeuwen, 2016: 10.
7 Grillner, 2008: 670; Collins, 1998: 43.
8 Rossouw, 2005: 72.

Drawing of Villa Gruno, designed by WJ Brandts, as published in the Dutch journal *Vademecum voor de Bouwvakken* 1890 (plate 20)

that became popular in Europe in the end of C19. Although historiography has it that American pattern books had served as a source of inspiration for the eclectic design, it reflects potential Dutch influences too, such as the unbuilt Villa Gruno.[9] Frans Van der Ben, whose name appeared on a certificate of completion, and who had previously worked with both Leslie Simmonds and the newly appointed City Engineers office from 1900, was responsible for the design of Erasmus Castle.

Van der Ben was born in 1860 in the Dutch naval town of Den Helder and was registered as a *machinist* [mechanical operator] before he immigrated to South Africa around 1895. He was also known as a good draughtsman and had, earlier, been associated with the design of the Park Keeper's Residence in Burgers' Park, Pretoria.[10] This iconic villa, adorned with towers, fretwork and pinnacle gables recalled examples in Dutch contemporary pattern books and architectural journals such as those published by the *Maatschappij voor de Bevordering der*

Pretoria, Brooklyn, House Neethling under construction with local labour, Italian builders and Dutch family, 1903

Bouwkunst [Society for the Advancement of Architecture]. In view of the available opportunities for training, practice and exchanges through publications and meetings in the Netherlands at the turn of the century, Dutch immigrant architects would have been armed with an array of precedents.

The Picturesque aesthetic of Erasmus Castle, situated on a hill with expansive views and large gardens, is an eclectic ensemble of Jugendstil, Neo-Gothic, Dutch Romanticism and elements of the existing local Dutch Republican style, such as the spiked gable. The design echoes Dutch *landhuizen* such as Constantijn Muysken's sketch proposal of 1894, for an English inspired villa with splayed cellular plan, spiked turrets and fretwork gable ends.

Small verandahs were often integrated into Dutch Gothic Revival *landhuizen* but the dominance and verticality of the main façade was retained. In Erasmus Castle, however, its verticality is tempered by the addition of an extensive verandah that provides protection from the sun and rain in summer while connecting adjoining spaces and providing external space for recreation.

Picturesque villas: Paulus Westmaas

In 1904, Paulus Westmaas, previously an Amsterdam-based contractor, designed a richly decorated villa, called Neethlinghuis, in the newly established suburb of Brooklyn. The client was an agricultural economist, JD Neethling, and the house was built by Anselmino, an Italian contractor.[11] The imposing formal presence of the original red face-brick villa, together with a well-manicured garden, created a typical Picturesque ensemble. The two symmetrical and angled bay-window towers are reminiscent of the villa (1876–81) that the Dutch architect Pierre Cuypers designed for the chief director of the RijksMuseum in Amsterdam.[12]

9 Picton-Seymour, 1977: 7; Walle, 1890.
10 Rossouw, 2005: 63.
11 Meiring, 1980: 93.
12 De Haan, 2016: 134.

Pretoria, Erasmus Castle with stoep, Frans Van der Ben, 1903; photo 2020

Pretoria, Brooklyn, House Neethling, designed by Paulus Westmaas; photo 2020

Pretoria, Brooklyn, Osbourne House, designed by Paulus Westmaas, 1904; photo 2020

In a similar manner to Van der Ben's design of Erasmus Castle, Westmaas tempered the verticality of Neethlinghuis through the addition of a covered, timber-framed and balustraded verandah (now altered) on three sides of the house. Other limited practical advances in the moderately dry, subtropical climate were environmental protection through an underfloor ventilation system, substantial brick walls and a timber louvre window in the main gable for roof ventilation.

The addition of extensive verandahs was a regional development, informed by the hot, wet summers but not, however, consistently applied. Westmaas' Osbourne House (1904) is a case in point where the original, timber-framed, three-sided verandah created a grand south street entrance while providing protection from the rain and not the sun. However, Westmaas dealt with overheating in the roof spaces through the careful placement of louvred dormers. The architecture of these elements and the slanted gables recall the Chalet Style slanted versions like that of the Florence Grove Villa (1887–88) in Baarn, Netherlands (by the architect Van Doornik) which, in turn, reflected the gable overhangs on some rural Dutch farm buildings.

Baarn, Prins Hendrikpark, Florence Grove House, designed by Willem van Doornik, 1887–88; photo 2020

Picturesque translations: Johannes Rienk Burg

The Leeuwarden-born architect, Johan Burg, arrived in Pretoria in 1895 in pursuit of a healthier climate and the promise of work with the NZASM. His search for an appropriate architecture in the ZAR, and later in the Union of South Africa, was not unlike Gerard Moerdijk and Norman Eaton's nationalistic design explorations. Around 1910, he designed a student residence in Duncan Street, Hatfield, consisting of six thatch-roofed *rondawels* [circular huts], five of which were connected by a

Pretoria, Brooklyn, house in Marais Street, Johan Burg, c1930s; photo in 2020

Pretoria, Hillcrest, Duncan Street, rondawel-houses, Johan Burg, 1910

symmetrically placed entrance and rectangular service block. Thereafter Burg undertook a number of Picturesque design explorations, expressing importance through silhouette, while satisfying wealthy tastes and a desire for a rural existence.

In the March 1919 issue of *Die Boerevrou*, an Afrikaans language women's magazine, Burg's design for a house for a wealthy farmer was published. The explanation and accompanying sketch expressed an Arts and Crafts approach to building that relied on locally available materials such as stone from the site and reeds for the thatch roof. The design was also an adaptation of the traditional H-shaped plan of the Cape Dutch farmhouse, but Burg accentuated the use of a generous *voorhuis* [foyer] where the men could gather, without disturbing the organisation of the homemaker's formal dining room.[13] The plan, with double doors between main living spaces, broke the traditional cellular layouts of the time, pre-empting Modern Movement functional and spatial influences.

However, it is Burg's 1930s double gabled designs in manicured garden settings that created his signature Picturesque style. The arrival of the Dutch in the Cape in the mid-1600s resulted in the formation of a number of subsequent inherited vernacular styles, influenced in the late 1880s by the Arts and Crafts approach of Herbert Baker that already had its roots in British and European vernacular traditions, particularly through its manifestation in England as the Dutch influenced 'Queen Anne Style'. The resulting 'Baker School' (often associated with the Cape Dutch Revival) synthesised the Cape Dutch into a Classical eclectic approach by adopting and transforming vernacular elements. Internal planning was a fusion of traditional centralised organisations and an Arts and Crafts organicism.[14]

Following the form of traditional side gables, used in H-shaped plans for Cape Dutch farmsteads, Burg developed the form of his double gabled houses for the NZASM with the aesthetic of the Cape Dutch. Frans Soff, another Dutch architect who immigrated to the ZAR in the early 1890s, designed the Engelenburg house (1903) in Arcadia.[15] This Cape Dutch Revival residence, with one (of two) elongated gables partially designed in the Flemish Style, could also have served as inspiration for Burg. Burg used the distinctive Cape Dutch Revival double gable in a number of houses for the builder Corbishly, as well as for Ellis in the suburbs of Waterkloof and Brooklyn in Pretoria, for Dutch and English clients and the legal fraternity.[16] This was probably initiated through Burg's association with the development of the Pretoria Country Club area for the South African Townships Company.

Although Burg's houses are Classical forms in their landscape, the addition of a covered, recessed, centrally placed verandah with Doric columns provides a more contextual and climatic grounding. The double doors leading from, and between, the front living spaces also provide greater internal spatial continuity and connectedness to the garden. Roof spaces are ventilated through gable-end vents while corrugated iron roofs are the order of the day.

13 Fisher & Le Roux, 1989: 3.

14 Barker, 2012: 36–37.

15 Allen, 1971: 39; Rex, 1975: 241; see also Chapter 1.

16 Pretorius, 2018.

Jugendstil inspiration: Hendrik (Henk) Horstmanshof

Henk Horstmanshof, from Alkmaar, only arrived in South Africa in 1921. He did not study architecture but trained as a carpenter and plasterer and was known as an enthusiastic contractor, developer and artist. He read voraciously about architecture and developed his own Picturesque design approach, heavily influenced by the brick details, chimneys and small-paned cottage windows of the *Jugendstil*, emulating the Lutyensesque versions of Dutch thatched roofed houses.[17] Many of his residences, particularly the Metro building in Pretoria West (now demolished) and a 1940s house in Uvongo, Natal, resemble the brick detailing, large roof overhangs, under eaves window and horizontal organic forms of Frank Lloyd Wright's residences. Horstmanshof travelled to the then Dutch East Indies (and Fiji) and it is possible that there he was exposed to the Arts and Crafts inspired architecture of Liem Bwan Tjie, who was born in Semarang into a Chinese family and educated at the Delft Institute of Technology, and had worked under Eduard Cuypers and Michel de Klerk, before returning to the Dutch East Indies in 1928.[18]

In 1924, evidently with the assistance of one labourer, Horstmanshof built his first house at the corner of Jorissen and Rivier streets, in Sunnyside.[19] It displayed many of the typological traits of the Arts and Crafts movement that were to become part of Pretoria's later regional style. A centrally located and deeply recessed verandah was framed by two symmetrical gable ends and teak bay windows. A rusticated stone base set against plastered and painted walls preceded later face-brick plinths, while large lead-lined windows heralded the advent of floor to ceiling industrial steel-framed versions of later years. Roofs were covered in teak timber shingles[20] with adequate roof overhangs and without gutters and downpipes.

In 1926, Horstmanshof built another speculative house in Farenden Street in Arcadia where he used his artistic abilities to paint uncoloured lead-lined glass, localising and economising the tradition of using stained glass windows found in many Dutch *landhuizen*.[21] In a less speculative 1929 house at 751 Park Street, Horstmanshof introduced high-level, teak-framed windows between ceiling and verandah roof, all under eaves protection, uniquely extending the connection between inside and outside while increasing light to the central living space. The shading of the recessed north-facing verandah is enhanced by additional recesses on either side of the entrance foyer. The stone plinth and plastered and painted wall combination are reminiscent of Dutch-Indonesian examples.

A year later, Hortsmanshof built his most renowned set of dwellings near the Union Buildings, aptly named *Trianon*, or more affectionately, Tiny Town. The complex was originally intended as an artist's commune.[22] The fourteen economically planned housing types, recently refurbished and slightly altered, are arranged around well-tended gardens with fountains, ponds and bridges.[23] In one semi-detached type, Horstmanshof provides a deeply recessed and generous entrance verandah, while continuing the use of his trademark large lead-lined windows and face-brick plinths.

17 De Haan, 2016: 195.
18 Personal email communication with A. Horstmanshof. 11 June 2020; Merkl, 2020; Den Dikken, 2002.
19 De Jong, 1991: 50.
20 Personal email communication with A. Horstmanshof. 11 June 2020.
21 De Jong, 1991: 50.
22 Personal email communication with A. Horstmanshof. 11 June 2020.
23 De Jong, 1991: 51.

In the 1940s, Horstmanshof designed a house in the Wolfaardt Estate (now Woodhill) to the east of Pretoria city centre, using his characteristic symmetrical layout with face-brick plinth and double gables adorned with drawings of bushveld scenes.[24] But the Arts and Crafts influences were by then downplayed, with limited rustication, the use of industrially manufactured steel framed windows and the exclusion of bay windows.

24 https://www.bronberger.co.za/index.php?option=com_content&view=article&id=1632:hendrik-sy-tyd-ver-vooruit-met-eerste-landgoed-ontwikkeling-&catid=50:toeka-se-dae&Itemid=76; Hortsmanshof, 2020

Pretoria, Sunnyside, 751 Park Street, designed by Hendrik Horstmanshof, 1929; photo 2020

Pretoria, Eastcliff, house in Tiny Town, designed by Hendrik Horstmanshof, 1930; photo 2020

Pretoria, lead lined windows in the Arts and Crafts style in Osbourne House (right), Hortsmanshof's 751 Park Street, Sunnyside house (above left) and Van de Werke's House De Haas in Brooklyn (above right); photos 2016 and 2020

Landhuizen: Johannes (John) van de Werke

A predilection for the Picturesque amongst immigrant architects continued unabated. Johannes Van de Werke arrived in South Africa in 1935 following a largely construction-oriented architectural education in his hometown of Utrecht. The architecture of his initial dwellings, such as the undated House De Moor, recall Dutch versions of the Modern Movement, but also resonate with the early work of Norman Eaton in his 1933 House Boyes in Brooklyn.[25]

Van de Werke's 1939 House Du Pont, also in Brooklyn, resembles some of his student work completed in the vein of the Modern Movement and closely follows the flat roof and circular window forms of the Dutch architect Sybold van Ravesteyn's own house (1933) at 112 Prins Hendrik Avenue in Utrecht.[26] Even though Van de Werke cleverly resorts to using extensive overhangs on his Modernist flat roofs, like other local architects of the time he realised that these types of solutions would not deal with heavy summer downpours. However, the introduction of a practical face-brick plinth tempers the orthodoxy of the modernist architecture and provides some contextual associations.

Van de Werke then reverted to using the Picturesque Dutch *Gooise landhuizen* style, characterised by organic plans, large roofs, dormer windows and building materials employed as close to their natural state

25 Cumming George, 1934: 62.
26 De Rouw, 2014: 192–95.

Utrecht, own house, designed by Sybold van Ravesteyn in 1932

Pretoria, House De Moor, designed by John van de Werke in the late 1930s

Pretoria, Brooklyn, House Du Pont, designed by John van de Werke in the 1930s (now demolished)

as possible. Van de Werke would have been familiar with these building typologies as many were published, for instance in the 1916 publication *Het Moderne Landhuis in Nederland* [The Modern Country Villa in the Netherlands] compiled by Leliman and Sluyterman.[27] The external aesthetic and form of Van de Werke's Picturesque interpretations of the *landhuizen* were complemented with more contemporary interiors, possibly influenced by the Dutch magazine *Het Landhuis* [The Country Villa]. The February 1935 issue depicts a brick hearth and fireplace surround, timber mantelpiece and plastered chimney that closely resemble those used by Van de Werke in houses such as De la Hunt (1940) and another extant, but undated, example in Alexander Street, Hillcrest.[28]

Van de Werke's predilection for roofscapes was probably initiated in his student days, when extensive typological studies and detailed technical explorations were undertaken. His use of *landhuis* as a precedent also paralleled that of the Pretoria architect Norman Eaton's early regionalist forays, particularly his Arts and Crafts inspired, timber framed and thatched roofed House Anderson (1939).

27 De Haan, 2016: 185.
28 https://resolver.kb.nl/resolve?urn=dts:553004:mpeg21:pdf.

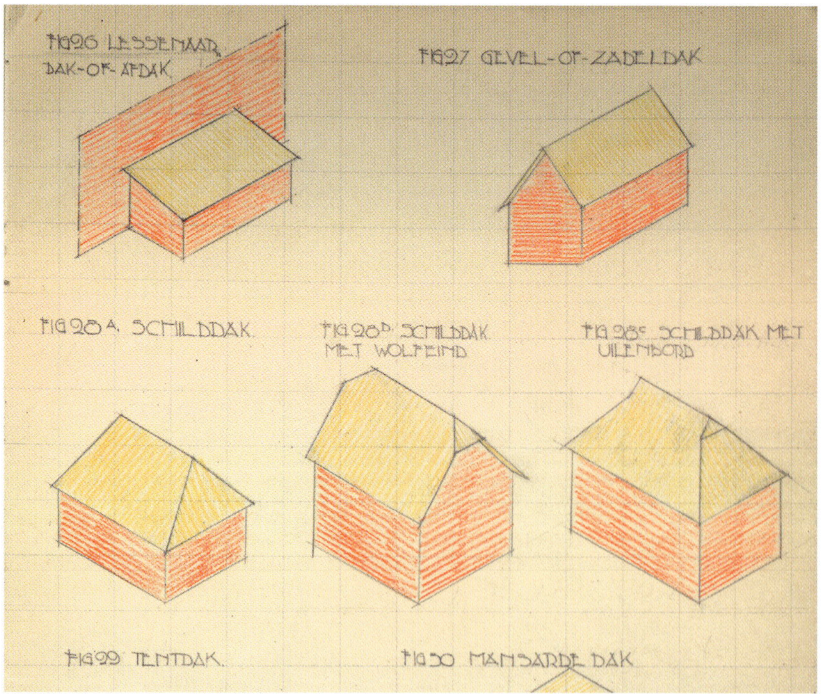

Utrecht, detail of student project of Dutch roof types by John van de Werke, 1927

Hilversum, House Bool included in the cover of JP Fokker's monograph *Het Eigen Huis*, 1931

House De la Hunt in Olivier Street, Brooklyn, is Van de Werke's earliest recorded *landhuis* style dwelling, complete with eyebrow dormer windows, shallow face-bricks in a Norwegian bond, tall, *landhuis*-inspired tapered face-brick chimneys, timber siding, and rooms partially located in the roof space. The architecture recalls Dutch precedents such as house JL Bool (1930) in Bachlaan Hilversum by Smits and Van der Linde, featured on the cover of JP Fokker's monograph.[29] The *landhuizen* were precedents that Van de Werke often returned to throughout his 44-year long career, as late as 1970 with, for example, a proposal for House Goldstein in Garstfontein and House Grové in Lynwood, built in 1974. The lead-lined windows of House De la Hunt reflect a Horstmanshof-like Arts and Crafts design approach. Materials, such as iroko floors, doors and windows, red cedar shingles and a yellow face-brick from the Primrose Brick Company were chosen for their natural qualities.

In House De la Hunt, Van de Werke provides a covered verandah to the living room and an outdoor sleeping balcony (now enclosed) to the first floor bedroom above, recognising the need for shelter from the elements and an outdoor lifestyle appropriate for the Pretoria climate. The rusticated base, constructed with black facings from the Witwatersrand Brick and Tile Company, is not only a memory of earlier local stone precedents in Pretoria, but is also a practical device that provides a denser brickwork to limit water penetration.

The undated House Harrison is a less organic ensemble of the *Jugendstil*, Frank Lloyd Wright's Prairie-style architecture and Dutch *landhuizen*. The house is a compact north-east facing home, shaded through an extensive, but less organically shaped roof with low hanging eaves and a covered verandah. Over time, the well-manicured garden has completed

29 Fokker, 1931.

Pretoria, Brooklyn, House De la Hunt, designed by John van de Werke, 1940; photo in 2020

Pretoria, Colbyn, House Harrison, designed by John van de Werke in the 1940s; photo 2020

the Picturesque approach, tempered by the orthogonal roof and integrated dormers of the first-floor bedrooms. Van de Werke tempers a symmetrical formality in the layout of House Harrison by creating a recessed southeast facing entrance and extending the living spaces outwards under roof cover through a partially integrated verandah (now enclosed). Internal planning is still organised in a cellular manner but the emerging trend of double internal and external doors signifies greater spatial continuity and hints at the architectural changes that were to come. Van de Werke also recognises the need for appropriate solar orientation and locates all service spaces to the south west and living and sleeping spaces to the north east. Through these, and later architectural innovations, the foundation for a more regionally appropriate architecture began to be laid.

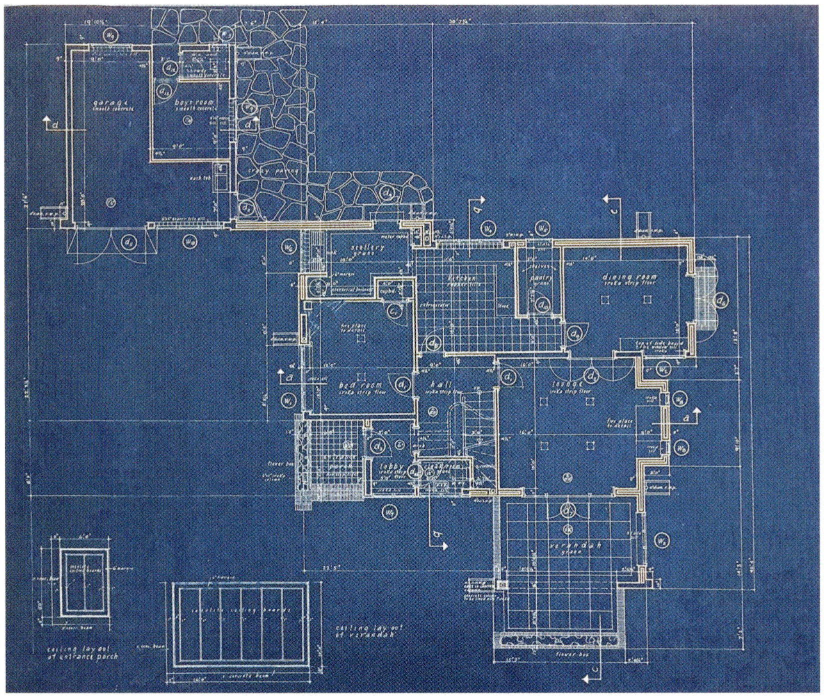

Pretoria, Colbyn, House Harrison, blueprint of the plan by John van de Werke, 1940s

The practical

The antecedents of changes in building form, climatic orientation, planning and materials that began to be seen in Pretoria after WW2 were not only influenced by international architectural developments, but also had their origins closer to home, particularly through the development of local architectural 'vernaculars'. The Picturesque approach was still influential in these post-war decades, more so in planning than aesthetic, through its relational, organic type of spatial composition, but the 'practical' architecture that followed was focussed on climatic suitability, new ways of living and the fusion of natural with industrialised building materials.[30]

In 1855, the typology of the vernacular *hartebeeshuisie*, developed in the Cape, was adopted in early Pretoria.[31] The burgeoning settlement was dotted with dwellings constructed of double-pitched thatch roofs, roughly plastered white walls and simple gabled ends or hipped roofs.[32] Later, the availability of corrugated iron for use on lower roof pitches fostered a verandah architecture or *burgelike woning* [civic house] to deal with the hot, wet summers.[33] These additions to thatch roofed dwellings were commonly seen in buildings such as those depicted with Arnold Borel and a South African family by a Swiss Protestant missionary organisation around 1900.[34]

30 Grillner, 2008: 673.
31 Moerdijk, n.d.
32 Cleghorne, 1922; Rodd, 1989.
33 Moerdijk, n.d.
34 Image from the *DM-échange et mission archive*, archived in the digital depositary of the University of South Carolina.

The establishment of the NZASM led to the importation and assimilation of a number of Dutch architects, including the Amsterdam-born architect Wim de Zwaan, who immigrated to South Africa in 1888. The NZASM designs had a profound effect on the subsequent work of De Zwaan and Burg and were an important driver for the establishment of a 'practical' and Pretoria-based regional architecture. The design of Burg's domestic dwellings was mainly informed by his development of NZASM typologies such as semi-detached units with double gables and corner

Pretoria, house with a thatched roof with missionary Arnold Borel and African family in front, c1900

Pretoria, Erasmuskloof, relocated historic house originally built in the 1880s; photo 2020

verandahs, while De Zwaan produced compact, climatically suitable buildings with ventilated pyramid-shaped roofs, generous overhangs, and timber shutters for windows.

During, and after, the second decade of the C20 an earnest search for a more contextually and culturally responsive architecture in South Africa began. Despite also working in the idiom, Gerard Moerdijk pleaded for the assimilation of traditional architecture with contemporary requirements, arguing that the Cape Dutch style was not suitable for either the climate or the more sober atmosphere of the Transvaal.[35] Newer Dutch architectural influences were, however, prominently featured. The 1938 *Star Newspaper Ideal Homes* newspaper competition highlighted the architectural eclecticism of the times, with Arts and Crafts homes (not unlike Van de Werke's dormer roof examples) juxtaposed with Horstmanshof-like ensembles and Alan Fair's attempt at recreating the modernist form of Oud's workers' houses at Hoek van Holland through an interpretation of its flat roof, ribbon window, concrete eaves and circular window forms.

35 Moerdijk. n.d.

In the late 1930s and early 1940s, the building industry in the Union of South Africa was 'archaic', as there was little mechanization on site, very few building components were being locally produced, and the small labour force was biased towards a craft building approach.[36] Coupled with wartime shortages of materials, this prompted a move towards an architecture that synthesised the use of simpler and more widely available materials and technologies with modern needs. The publication of Le Corbusier's house *le Sextant* at Les Mathes, France, in the March 1938 issue of the *South African Architectural Record,* highlighted how the application of natural materials could be formed through a Modernist aesthetic.

NZASM inspirations: Johannes Rienk Burg

While Burg was employed with the NZASM (1895–1903), he designed a number of station buildings on the Pretoria-Komatipoort (Eastern) Line, as well as type houses (A, B and C) used by the employees of the company.[37] These simple, symmetrical, and compact houses were often designed as semi-detached buildings.

Burg's first private residence (c1912) (one of only about twelve houses in the area at the time), was built at 181 Duxbury Street in Hillcrest.[38] It includes some of the aspects of NZASM designs, such as a stone and

36 Herbert, 1975: 234.
37 Ploeger, 1989: 32.
38 Pretorius, 2018.

Pretoria, Hillcrest, Duxbury Street, first own house, designed by Johan Burg in around 1912; photo 2020

Pretoria, Hillcrest, Lunnon Street, second own house, designed by Johan Burg in the 1920s; photo 2020

brick plinth, but the simplicity of the design and construction, possibly due to limited funds, demonstrates a number of appropriate climatic design principles for Pretoria. There are large roof overhangs to the north, a generous recessed entry verandah and large, well shaded windows with small panes.

Burg's sensitivity to context was not only founded in his NZASM designs but also in his understanding of the particularities of site. Around 1904, he designed a small group of buildings for a parsonage in Burger Street, Pretoria North. The simple elongated buildings, with locally sourced stone for the walls, included slate floors and were strategically placed amongst the trees, with appropriate northerly orientation for the living areas.

Burg's more luxurious home in Lunnon Road (c1910s) is a development of his type B NZASM house.[39] The main gable and associated fretwork mimic the aesthetic of Burg's type plans for semi-detached dwellings. The usual deeply shaded corner verandahs, present on the entrance façade of NZASM designs, are extended along the eastern and western edges and defined by concrete columns rather than the usual timber construction. A further development of the NZASM typology is the bay window and the introduction of dormer and gable ventilation openings.

39 Van Schouwenburg, 2020.

NZASM and the Indo-East: Wilhelm (Wim) de Zwaan

De Zwaan, born in Amsterdam, arrived in Johannesburg in 1889 after his architectural education in the Netherlands and apprenticeship to the Amsterdam City Architect.[40] In 1890, he moved to Pretoria and worked for the DPW for several years.

The origins of De Zwaan's signature pyramid-shaped roof dwellings can be described as international and local. These roof forms, as well as Dutch gables or gablets, were commonplace in agricultural architecture, such as in the *Stolpboerderijen* [Bell farms] in the northern parts of the Netherlands. Similarly, the Indo-European hybrid villa, with its pyramid-shaped roof with extensive verandah and large wall openings, was ideal for the hot, humid climate of the Dutch East Indies and its simple form was probably regarded as appropriate for the semi-humid conditions in the east of the ZAR. De Zwaan may have been responsible for (or possibly influenced by) the corrugated-iron clad prefabricated pyramid roof and verandah houses erected for stationmaster's quarters, on the NZASM Eastern Line at line. The existence of conical thatched roof *rondawel* dwellings, such as that constructed for the district engineer (KM 16) at Komatipoort on the Eastern Line in 1893, may also have influenced De Zwaan's pyramid roof forms.

40 Ploeger, 1994: 59.

Pretoria, Brooklyn, 421 Milner Street, speculative house for SA Mining and Finance Co., designed by Wim de Zwaan in the 1910s; photo 2020

When De Zwaan settled in the newly established mining town of Johannesburg in 1889 he was employed as an architectural assistant. Architecture at the time was characterised by prefabricated corrugated iron clad and roofed buildings with characteristic chimneys, roof ventilators, interspersed with pyramid roof forms.[41]

De Zwaan's early private work, in association with Van Dyk, closely followed the Republican style but the additions of verandahs and roof ventilators set the scene for a more 'practical' architecture. The 1890 house in Main Street, Pretoria, designed for Christiaan Joubert, the head of mining for the ZAR, included a central gable with detailed fretwork, but was offset with a roof ventilator and front covered verandah.[42] The extensions to Sammy Marks House (c1898) outside Pretoria are also attributed to De Zwaan, through his association with Van Dyk. They echo the formal and climatic nuances of their earlier work but are founded on the elongated form of the original 1882 dwelling.[43] Around 1899, De Zwaan completed a house for Alois Hugo Nellmapius in Doornkloof, Irene, south of the city centre of Pretoria. It had dormer vents of varying shape in the roof, large, shuttered windows and doors, and detailed fretwork on the balustrades and supports to the wide columned *stoeps* [verandahs]. De Zwaan's late C19 houses with extensive *stoeps*, for the Lorentz and Van Boeschoten families at Zwartkops, were less ostentatious but climatically suitable for the Highveld climate.

From around 1904, De Zwaan designed houses in twos for the South African Township & Mining Company in the area between the Pretoria Country Club, and Main, Premier and Lawley streets in the suburb of Waterkloof, Pretoria. This township was, at the time, associated with the Afrikaner elite, as many high-ranking government officials built their homes there. The houses were designed according to a functional model that required three bedrooms, living and dining rooms and an outside toilet. The dwellings were constructed with corrugated iron clad pyramid-shaped roofs, wooden windows (often bay windows), shutters and recessed corner *stoeps*, recalling the NZASM plans for semi-detached dwellings.

De Zwaan's Waterkloof dwellings are compact buildings and, consequently, some have not survived the ravages of time and physical expansion. All that remains of an example in Milner Street is the tell-tale roof ventilator and, now concrete tiled pyramid-shaped roof. Current changes at a post-modernised house in Albert Street have revealed the nature of pressed-metal ceilings, Oregon pine roof trusses and a unique roof lantern that still provides light to the centrally located passages.

Another house in Milner Street, Waterkloof, with limited alterations, includes Burg-like, but less elongated, double gables, and a *stoep* with Neoclassical columns. Further up the road, sensitive extensions have been added to the original dwelling that still highlight the pyramid-shaped roof, ventilator and recessed *stoep* with a circular enclosing balustrade wall. In Julius Jeppe Street, Waterkloof, the architecture of another home is almost intact. Wooden shutters provide shading to the symmetrically placed windows that flank a partially recessed and well-shaded entrance *stoep*.

41 Munro, 2015a.
42 Swanepoel, 2008.
43 Munro, 2015.

Practicalities: Van de Werke's post-war houses

During and after WW2, the building industry was severely restricted, with little investment being made in that sector. No new buildings are recorded in Van de Werke's ledger between 1942 and 1947. Although the Picturesque *landhuis,* through dominant roof forms, always remained a feature of his *oeuvre*, the impact of a depleted economy, limited resources, and the recognition of an architecture more suited to place, climate, and prevailing tastes, caused his post-war outputs to move away from these arrangements. Similarly, the political upheavals of the 1940s, reactions to the failings of the orthodoxy of the Modern Movement, further influenced Van de Werke's design approaches.

In 1950, Van de Werke, together with the Pretoria-based architect Lockwood Hall, designed compact and efficient subsidised worker's housing in Proclamation Hill for the National Housing and Planning Commission (NHPC), epitomizing the 'practical' for another class than that of his usual clients. The north facing units with corner *stoeps* (providing summer shading) and clear distinction between served and servant zones, preempted Van de Werke's designs for his later linear plan layouts for wealthier clients.

Pretoria, Eastwood, stair in House Sturdy, designed by John van de Werke, 1955; photo 2020

Pretoria, Centurion, Clubview, House Arnold, designed by John van de Werke, 1951; photo 2020

In the 1950s, Van de Werke designed a number of efficiently planned T-shaped houses, including those for Arnold in Clubview and Coetzee in Waterkloof, both in 1951, Sturdy in Arcadia in 1955 and Falcke in Brooklyn in 1956. Van de Werke's new typology took account of climatic orientation as well as the smaller sites that became available. Garages and the ubiquitous servants' quarters were placed in a separate wing to the southern edge of the site, with the kitchen and guest toilet acting as bridge to the living areas.

Van de Werke's skill with inventive planning instilled new spatial efficiencies, such as using part of the roof space over the main living areas for bedrooms and bathrooms, ensuring that on narrower sites north orientation would still be possible. Roof overhangs provide adequate shading and Van de Werke introduces tapered gable walls to tie the roof to the site. He also develops another of his signature design elements, the organically-shaped staircase that seamlessly joins ground and first floors, creating an Arts and Crafts and Modernist synergy. By now, industrial materials are the order of the day, Van de Werke resorting to a combination of timber cladding and steel framed windows with an 'apricot Tuscan' tiled roof finish in House Sturdy.

By 1955, Van de Werke started to experiment with smaller, linear plan layouts, adopting regional design trends in line with other Pretoria architects such as Eaton, Robert Cole Bowen and Helmutt Stauch. North orientation and efficient plan layouts had become the norm, while new ways of living necessitated increased internal spatial connections and protected outdoor living. For instance, House Van Reenen (1955) in Vryheid, Natal, included a linear plan layout, with separate served and service zones, and a rectangular dormer window in the vein of Stauch. The typical Van de Werke tapered face-brick chimney was, however, still present.

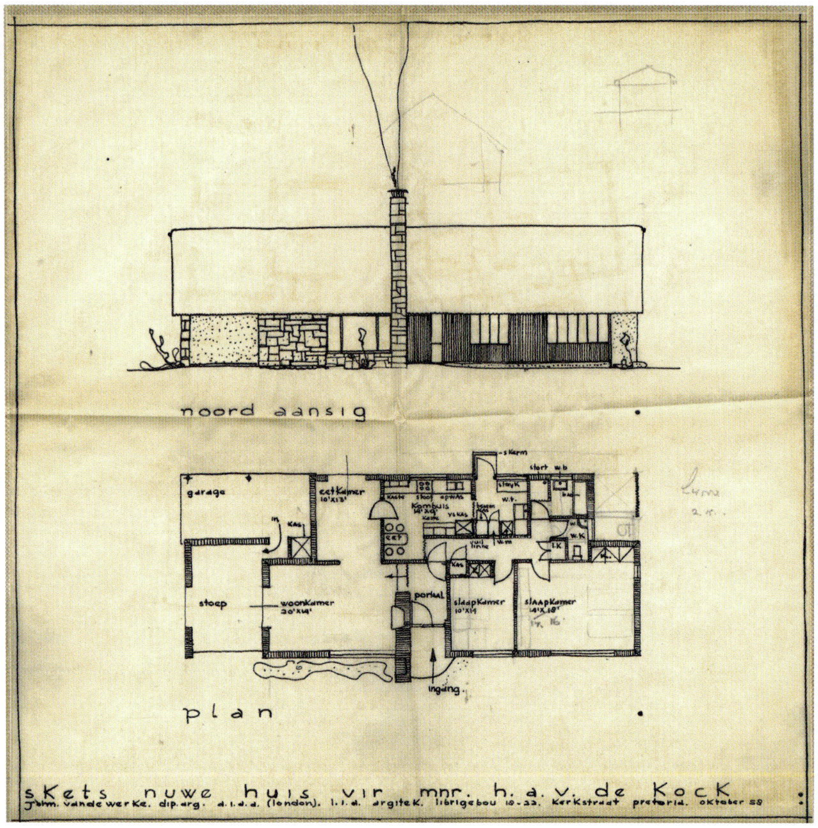

Pretoria Waterkloof, Pretoria, House De Kock, sketch plan by John van de Werke, 1958

Van de Werke further developed these simple climatic and spatial design principles in suburban houses in Muckleneuk for Poole (1955), for Ackerman in Hillcrest (1957, now demolished) and in Sandfontein Works for Kirkness (1960). In the 1958 Waterkloof Ridge house for HAV de Kock, Van de Werke organises all services and dining room on the southern edge of the residence, with two bedrooms, the entrance, and the living room adequately shaded by the roof overhang on the north. The now rectilinear, timber shingle-covered roof is still a dominant design element, in this case without habitable spaces integrated into it, but its low-slung nature connects the house to its site and creates cover for a large integrated *stoep*. Van de Werke's hallmark tapered chimney is shifted to an internal location, not only to heat the spaces but also, in a Modern Movement fashion, to provide a screen wall to the living room that extends outwards past the entry foyer. Living spaces are directly connected to one another without doors, although the kitchen is still a separate space. Van de Werke alters his unique tapered gable wall to a vertical variation, still framing the edge of the building and grounding the roof to the site. Stone walls and timber cladding provide contextual allegiances, while white painted brickwork, the economic building flavour of the times, and small-paned steel framed windows, provide a combined Arts and Crafts and modernist aesthetic.

Conclusion

The Picturesque beginnings of Dutch architecture in Pretoria in the early 1900s, influenced by the aesthetic of Dutch Gothic Revival, Swiss Chalet, American Stick Style, *Jugendstil,* Dutch and American pattern books and Dutch *landhuizen*, slowly evolved into a more 'practical', spatially efficient, and climatically suitable architecture. The concomitant influences of local architectural traditions such as *voortrekker* vernacular dwellings, NZASM infrastructure, Republican style buildings, reactions to the orthodoxy of the Modern Movement and the effects of WW2, assisted in forging a Pretoria regional architecture that continues to stand the test of time.

The influence and the contributions of Dutch immigrant architects to the regional domestic architecture in Pretoria stretched far beyond the town, and beyond the post-WW2 period. Images of submissions for the 1957 Ideal Homes and 1959 Virginia House newspaper competitions popularised the regional approaches that were expressed through recessed, north-facing shaded *stoeps*, face-brick plinths, linear organisations, large roof overhangs and floor to ceiling windows.

Photographs of Van de Werke's houses were used as promotional material by the South Africa State Information Office, and also in publications by the city of Pretoria celebrating its centenary.[44] Van de Werke's House De la Hunt, extolling the virtues of light-coloured face-brick and warm timber, was shown in a 1960s publication geared towards homemakers.[45] The February 1969 issue of the journal *Perspective* also depicted front and rear views of this house, marking its late commercial appeal. When the architectural directions of the 1960s were summed up, reference was made to typical features that could be associated with Pretoria regionalism—clerestory windows, single pitch roofs, reductions in and honest use of materials, rusticity and simplicity of space.[46]

The enduring legacy of an important, and largely unrecognised, Dutch influence on domestic architecture dots the suburbs east of the city centre of Pretoria. Many current homeowners proudly care for their unique dwellings that continue to function, with some alteration, to the demands of C21 living. These extant dwellings are a testament to the education, experience, fortitude and creativity of a small band of Dutch architects who, far from home, sought a new life and career. A unique, and practical, Pretoria regional architecture was forged through the influence of Dutch precedent, an inherited vernacular and the exigencies of place and technology.

44 Stark: 1955.
45 Lotter, c1963: 74–75.
46 Teeger, 1965: 7.

Pretoria, Waterkloof, House De Kock, designed by John van de Werke, 1958; photo 2020

Cape Town, Hadjira 'Haya' Isaacs, assisting in the kitchen of the Vallie family, 1996

The Kitchen – Heart of the Home

Esther de Haan

The kitchen is the most eloquent room in the home. It speaks of cooking and service, tradition and technology, urban and rural environments, gender and class. Living conditions, both climatically and socially, when compared to the Netherlands, are essentially different in South Africa. Whereas new concerns such as hygiene, efficiency and comfort gained great priority between 1900 and 1960 for the layout and equipment of Dutch kitchens, some South African kitchens were made suitable for the separate roles of the mistresses and their domestic helpers, particularly in the larger houses of white families. Many kitchens, however, were located in small houses or apartments. For these often 'servantless homes', as in Europe, the same modern trends were actively promoted among the housewives.

Considered, in the main, as a private space, the kitchen has been seldom depicted by its owners and users. The kitchen is (from the male's perspective) no place for representation but a place for work and unobserved private daily life. Three examples, spread over time, type and region, will provide us with an illustration of the merging of Dutch and local kitchen concepts as the heart of the South African home.

Ideas for *Afrikaner* kitchens in Transvaal

The South African War had reduced a large segment of the Afrikaner, or Boer, population, particularly in the former Transvaal and Orange Free State, to poverty. A generation later, Afrikaner intelligentia initiated efforts to uplift their compatriots through popular media, like *Die Boerevrou*. This monthly magazine, established in 1919, was the first journal to inform Afrikaner women in their own language about contemporary developments in architecture and housekeeping.[47]
The Dutch immigrant architect Johan Burg published a concept for a *plaashuis*, a vernacular farmhouse for an Afrikaner family. It had the relatively spacious kitchen [*kombuis*] at the rear, accessible from the small *stoep* and the central corridor, that facilitates separate circulation for men and women from the broad front *stoep*. The L-shaped corridor is further connected with a pantry, dining room and *voorhuis*, as well as with two bedrooms and a bathroom (meant to be the housewife's pride).[48]

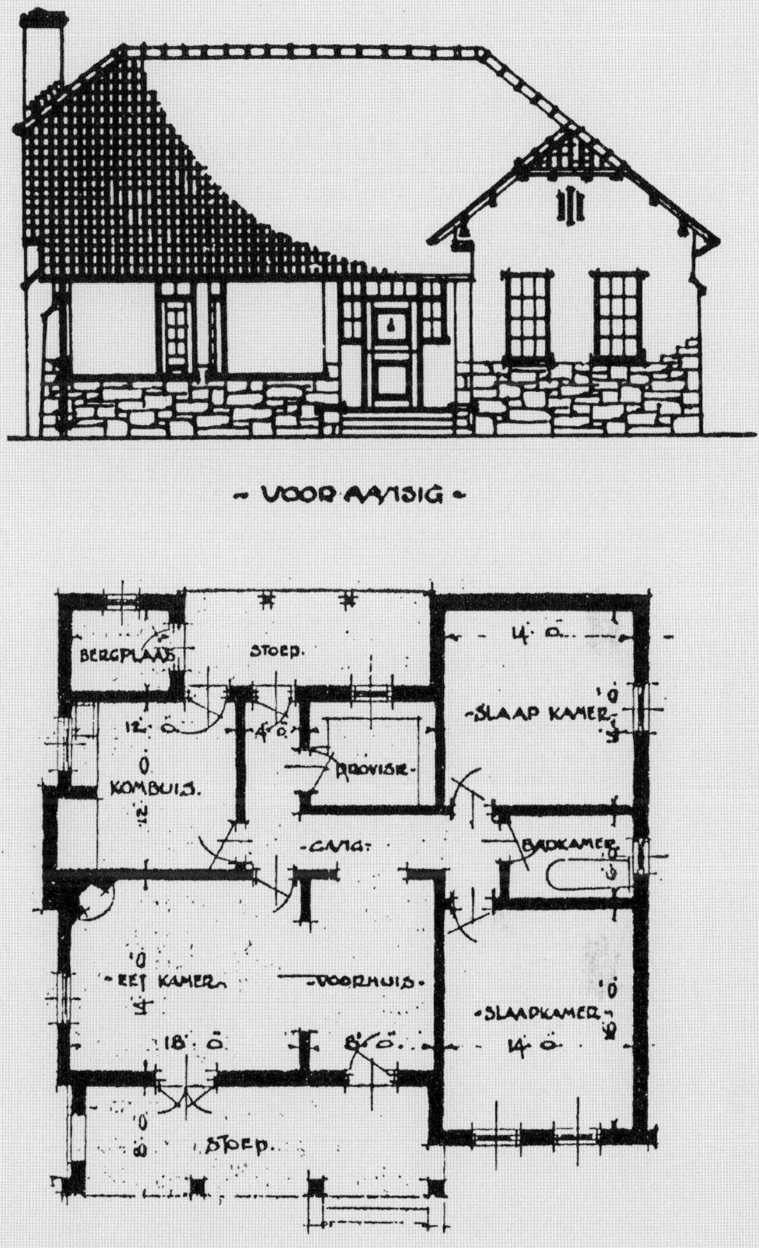

Front and floorplan of Burg's Afrikaner farmhouse, as published in *Die Boerevrou*, 1920

Other issues contained practical guidelines, such as efficient walking lines, a properly placed stove, kitchen table and cupboards, sufficient light sources and fresh air, easy-to-clean floors and wall covering.[49]

From the 1920 Ideal Home Exhibition, organized by the *Daily Mail* in London, the exhibited *back to back stove* was presented to the Afrikaans reader as an ultramodern device: a closed heater made of iron, running on coal, and filled with cold water from the outside pump. Placed in the connecting wall between kitchen and living room, the heater could serve as a stove to cook in the kitchen as well as a heat source in the living room.[50]

The Transvaal housewife was instructed how to make her own kitchen table and other furniture, including a self-improvised refrigerator.[51] Suggestions were also provided to make the kitchen pretty; it was, after all, the place where "the heaviest and most important work of the house" was done.[52] When around 1930 electric kitchen equipment became available in the cities, such machinery was not within the reach of everyone because wages were low for most people and/or the size of the kitchen was too small to accommodate them.[53] Due to the global economic crisis, the army of domestic helpers steadily grew, but

47 Van Rensburg, 2012; Le Roux, 1989.
48 Burg, January 1920, in: Fisher, Le Roux 1989, 2–3.
49 Van Duijn, August 1920, in: Fisher, Le Roux, 1989, 48–49.
50 Fouché, October and November 1923, in: Fisher, Le Roux, 1989, 53–58.

51 Rees, October 1924, in: Fisher, Le Roux 1989, 108–109.
52 Anon. 1926, Aug., in: Fisher, Le Roux 1989, 100–101.
53 Van der Waal, 1987: 229.

The back-to-back stove in the dining room, published in *Die Boerevrou*, 1920

publication of *Die Boerevrou* had to cease. Other women's magazines pictured modern, pleasant kitchens, fashionable work-dresses and time saving kitchen equipment that should uplift the status of the white household servant.[54] The fundamentally unequal and racist treatment of black servants, however, remained unchanged.[55]

A minimum kitchen in Atteridgeville, Pretoria

The Atteridgeville settlement was initiated by the Pretorian government in 1939 and, formally, aimed to improve the living conditions of black people who were forced to move from the centre of Pretoria. The first 980 simple brick, single story houses were designed by Dutch-born architect JJ de Jong, at the time Clerk of Works for the Pretoria City Council.[56] These houses had one to four bedrooms, electric lights in all spaces and an indoors toilet and bathroom. The combined kitchen-living room was furnished with the essentials the government deemed necessary to educate the residents in European cooking and dining culture: a Dover nr. 7 coal stove, a kitchen table, two benches or chairs and a kitchen cupboard.[57] However, they were already familiar with European kitchen

54 Anon. 1931b. *Die Huisgenoot*, 21 Aug: 63 and 67.
55 Jansen, 2015.
56 See Chapter 8.
57 Coertze, 1969: 20.

Atteridgeville, living-cooking area in one of Jan de Jong's 'model township' houses, with the Dover number 7 coal stove under the chimney, 1950s

Atteridgeville, open shelved cupboard displaying pottery and porcelain in one of Jan de Jong's 'model' houses, 1950s

culture since many had been employed in service in white households for generations. Most families did not choose to implement the imposed European traditions in their own household and kept their traditional ways of cooking and dining. Often food was prepared outside on the veranda. Particularly in summer, the use of the coal stove in the kitchen raised indoor temperatures to unbearable levels. In winter, when cooking was done inside, many households persisted in using a coal-fired barrel for preparing food and heating. The incorporated kitchen table and chairs were not always used daily by all families; some families sat on benches when gathering and dining. Richer families, though, invested in more comfortable furniture and suchlike. Finally, the open shelved kitchen cupboard for pottery and porcelain was a success: the material display of one's (modest) wealth, deeply rooted in European culture, was widely adopted among the residents of Atteridgeville.[58]

58 Coertze, 1969: 138-147.

Linking kitchen and dinner space in a modernist bungalow, Hout Bay

The widely traveled Dutch-born architect Henk Niegeman settled in Cape Town in 1936 and started a joint practice with ED Andrews three years later.[59] In around 1943 he built a modernist house for 'two people and three dogs', overlooking Hout Bay with an overhanging curved roof. It was called 'Alma Ata' after the hometown of his Russian wife. The open-plan bungalow required, according to Niegeman, only a few spaces, including a kitchen to cook in connected with a space to eat.[60] Such a spacious cooking-dining area became popular with middle-class families in the Netherlands in the 1950s, as domestic helpers disappeared and modern kitchen equipment for ventilation became available.[61] Yet they were also promoted in such popular media like *Die Huisgenoot* or *The Lantern,* and in various fairs in South Africa.

Although the dining space is merged only with the lounge, the kitchen is still separated by a wall; Niegeman designed several solutions to connect the kitchen and dining space. A circular hatch in the wall above the dining table served for passing dishes from the adjacent kitchen, and through a small glazed peephole in the same wall, "the lady of the house was able to see the switches of the stove and the taps above the sink when sitting at the dining table".[62] The access to the kitchen was like a stable door and "enabled the housewife to take part in any conversation going on in the lounge and for the guests to hear the milk boiling over".[63]

59 See also the interlude on Cross-continental Careers.
60 Andrews & Niegeman, 1944.
61 Oldenziel & Bouw, 1998; Stempels, 1958.
62 Andrews & Niegeman, 1944, 277.
63 Andrews & Niegeman, 1944: 278.

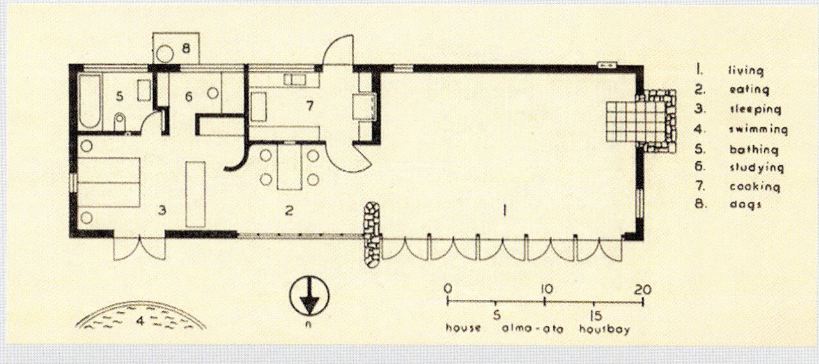

Hout Bay, floorplan of Henk Niegeman's bungalow 'Alma Ata', illustrating the linked kitchen and dining area (no 2 and 7), as published in *SAAR*, 1944

Hout Bay, living room in Henk Niegeman's house 'Alma Ata', view towards the dining area, with a glimpse of the glass table and the stable door to the kitchen, 1940s, as published in *SAAR*, 1944

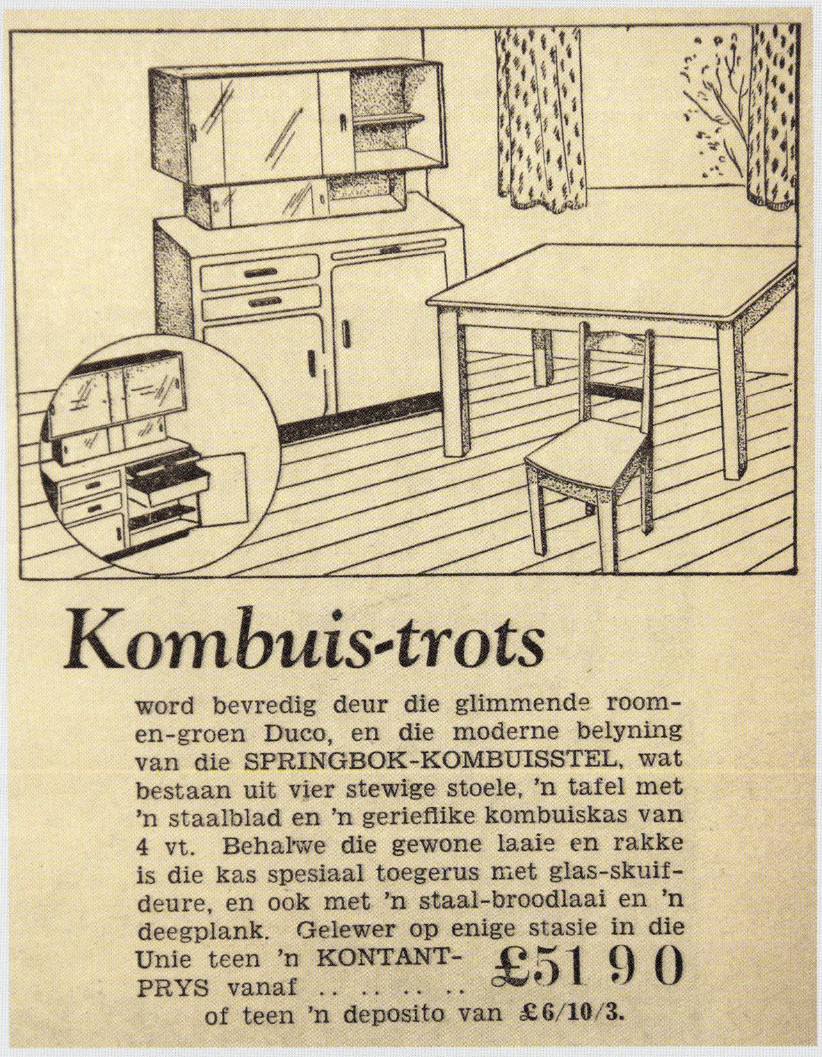

Advertisement for Springbok kitchen equipment, meant to evoke 'kitchen-pride', as published in *Die Huisgenoot*, 1946

Combined, yet separated working room and kitchen, as presented on a fair for a modern compact home and published in *Die Huisgenoot*, 1946

Johannesburg, 'modern' kitchen in an unknown middle class family house designed by Jaap van Niftrik, approximately late 1950s

Niegeman furnished the dining and kitchen space with a dining table made of glass that cantilevered from the kitchen wall. For the kitchen space he designed cupboards in light and dark indigenous limbawood, and chose red quarry tiles for the kitchen floor, being decorative, cool, and easy to clean.

Evolution

Once the prefabricated equipment was introduced in various sizes, materials, forms and finishings to the kitchen market, customers were steadily encouraged to purchase a new set of cupboards, sink and other such furnishings, appealing to their 'kitchen-pride'. Whereas many kitchens were primarily used as the female workspace of the household, some were large enough to also accommodate an 'eating corner' for the family. In contrast, the small urban apartments only had compact standardized kitchens and were partly combined with the living room, like in similar examples in Europe.

Over time, almost all kitchens have been modernized by means of new furnishings and equipment.[64] Consequently, authentic kitchens of the first six decades of C20 have become very rare for whatever category of class. An exceptional example of a 'personalized' kitchen is the one in House Smal in Pretoria, designed by John van de Werke in the early 1970s. This show-kitchen honours not only the Dutch connections in the 'Delft' tiles, but also the virtues of one's own home. Daily life in 'the heart of the home' has become comfortable for many in South Africa, but such comfort has often remained out of reach for many more who still work in other families' homes.[65]

64 Scott, 1964: 59–65.

65 Jansen, 2015: 285–312.

Pretoria, personalized counter of the kitchen annex area in House Smal, decorated with 'Delft blue' tiles with the old Dutch motto 'one's own fireplace is worth gold'; photo 2018

Atteridgeville, view into the backyards of the houses at Moroe Street and beyond, 1940

8 Model Township Atteridgeville

Mathebe Aphane and Kees Somer

Introduction
Various Dutch-born architects were active in urban planning and public housing in South Africa in the mid C20, deriving their inspiration in this field from their home country. These contributions were often made in the service of local authorities or national bodies. For example, John van de Werke (together with GH Lockwood Hall), during WW2, designed housing for the National Housing and Planning Commission (NHPC), and Willem van Beijma worked for the NHPC on the designs for a 'Non-European' (NE 51) series of standardised housing types in 1951.[1] In Pretoria, another Dutch-born architect, Jan Jacob de Jong, as architect at the City Council (1931–45) and City Architect (1945–55), was responsible for the planning and design of the new settlements of Atteridgeville and Danville, and possibly also Proclamation Hill. Atteridgeville was built from the late 1930s onwards under his leadership, as a 'model township' for the 'urban native'.[2]

However, the origins of Atteridgeville cannot be dissociated from the socio-political developments in South Africa and the housing policy of Pretoria in the first half of C20, including severe conditions of racial segregation. In this respect, it was similar to other townships built under the 1920 Housing Act to substantially improve the living conditions of the black population, like Langa near Cape Town (a 'respectable' township), Lamontville south of Durban ('a model village') and McNamee Township in Port Elizabeth ('a garden village').[3] With this as its background, the development, urban characteristics, amenities and housing types in Atteridgeville will be discussed. The chapter concludes with an evaluation of 'old' Atteridgeville as a 'model' settlement—'model' in the sense of being worthy of emulation—based on testimonies from past and present residents.

Pretoria - segregated city
In the late C19 in the Transvaal, the mining of gold and diamonds in South Africa had led to rapid urbanisation and an unprecedented housing shortage. Workers came from the rural areas as well as other colonies of the British Empire. While more black people increasingly arrived at the urban areas, the Kruger government of the *Zuid-Afrikaansche Republiek* (ZAR) established 'non-white' locations near the city centres to prevent their settling in the 'white areas'. Due to the mixed influx, white officials fearfully wrote to the authorities about the 'promiscuous herding of Indians, Malays, whites and black people who lived in friendly terms'.[4]

After the South African War, both black and Afrikaner people migrated in their droves from the rural areas to the big cities, in an attempt to escape poverty. The 1913 Land Act of the Union of South Africa allocated only 7.5% of the land to 75% of the population. However, the city centres and the most fertile parts were reserved for the white inhabitants. This

1 See also Chapter 10.
2 City Council of Pretoria, 1943.
3 Maylam, 1995: 30.
4 Bonner & Segal, 1999: 12.

Atteridgeville, overview of the model township in its pioneer phase, about 1940

led to forced removals of the black population and the degradation of their living conditions.[5] The workers came to live in temporary mining camps of corrugated iron, 'shanty towns' or 'slums', which often became permanent. The government used two factors as an excuse to put urbanism and housing in place to gain control over the black urban population that lived around the cities: the threat of new epidemics and the formation of the first black trade unions.[6]

The black residents were seen as too militant and politicised for the government to permit them to live in such close proximity to the whites in the urban areas. Since labour was still needed for the cities the national government decided to establish 'townships' or 'locations' at the peripheries of cities for the housing of black citizens.

In 1923 the Native (Urban Areas) Act No. 20 was promulgated 'to provide for the improved conditions of residence for natives in or near urban areas and better administration of native affairs in such areas' and intended to 'deal' with the prevalence of black people in urban areas. It conferred the responsibility for housing on local authorities, though without providing clear guidance. In 1925, after the black population

5 Vestbro, 2012: 1.
6 Vestbro, 2012: 2.

challenged the forced removals and failure to provide alternative accommodation through litigation, the courts declared the action of the government invalid. The subsequent 1934 Slums Act, however, enabled the government to forcibly remove black people from the 'slums' without any prospects of court action.[7] In the 1930s, under the responsibility of local municipal authorities, thousands of houses were built as part of public housing programmes. The central government granted loans and had to approve the schemes. There were two categories: economic housing, providing rental and owner-occupied houses that were affordable for people of a certain income, and sub-economic housing, with rents that did not cover all costs. By the end of the 1930s, some 130 000 people had been rehoused in these state housing programmes.[8] Within this framework, a 'New Native Location' was established near Pretoria, which would become nationally known as 'Model Township' Atteridgeville. The planning of Atteridgeville was, since the founding of Pretoria in 1855, the first attempt at providing black housing on a large scale.

There is strong evidence that black Africans had already settled near the Apies River before colonisation, albeit not in formal settlements. The earliest black district developed in 1867 on the grounds of the Berlin missionary post and became Schoolplaats in 1875.[9] West of this area, the ZAR government developed a 'location' for black people called Marabastad in 1888. During the South African War many black people came to Pretoria. The authorities were overwhelmed by this rural-urban migration and could not immediately solve the resulting housing crisis. After 1902 the provision of black housing was placed under the Health Department of the City Council of Pretoria (CCP). New townships were developed: Lady Selborne (1905), Eastwood (1905) and Bantule (1912). Hove's Ground, an existing squatter camp, was taken over by the CCP in 1922. Under the guise of clearing the 'slums', 'non-white' people were removed from those locations close to the city centre and segregated according to race. For example, Marabastad's residents, 'an amalgamation of Africans, Asians, and Coloured people', had to be rehoused into separate townships where each group would live in isolation.[10]

During the 1930s the African population of Pretoria exceeded 35 000. The South African Iron and Steel Corporation (ISCOR), which commenced operations in 1934, needed labour, but adequate shelter became scarce.[11] The 1936 Natives Trust and Land Act caused even more blacks to be evicted from rural land. To relocate the residents of overpopulated Marabastad, a new location was designated in 1936, west of central Pretoria, to be developed as a 'model' township.

Atteridgeville 1936–2020

The 'model' siting of the township was proposed by Patricia Atteridge, who was a Member of Parliament and chairperson of the City Council's Committee for Non-European Affairs: 'A certain piece of land approximately 1,000 acres [about 400 Ha] in extent, lying eight miles [10 km] west of Church Square, City of Pretoria, and bounded on all sides by Pretoria Townlands.'[12] It would have sewage, water and electricity and consist of 3 000 dwellings, playing fields, offices, schools, churches, a hospital, a community centre, a railway, two houses for white officers,

7 Bonner & Segal, 1999: 15.
8 Miescher, 2015: 267.
9 Coertze, 1969: 1–13.
10 Moseneke, 2016: 30.
11 City Council of Pretoria, 1999: 1.
12 Coertze, 1969: 10.

People moving from Marabastad to Atteridgeville, around 1940

Atteridgeville, houses ready for roofing, Moroe Street looking west, 1939

Atteridgeville, view of Sehloho and Temba streets looking south, July 1940

Atteridgeville, first occupants of Moroe Street 19 and 21, May 1940

Atteridgeville, semi-detached house with later added furniture in concrete, c1950

Atteridgeville, official opening of the model township on 5 August 1940, with lady Patricia Atteridge in the centre and HG Lawrence, Minister of the Interior and Public Health (left)

but was to be separated from the white suburbs by the municipal plantation, the police dog training centre and the industrial complex of ISCOR. The general plan was approved in 1937 and De Jong was entrusted with coordinating its implementation. The sub-economic houses were constructed in two phases: 980 in 1939-42, and 552 in 1945-50. On 26 May 1940 the first residents moved into 'the new native location'. The new settlement was originally intended to be called 'Motsemogolo' (large township). Yet it was named after Patricia Atteridge, who endeavoured to improve the living conditions of black people in Marabastad and was nicknamed both Mmabatho (mother of the people) and Mmadisopo (the soup mother) because she alleviated poverty by starting a soup kitchen for the children. Atteridgeville was officially opened by the Minister of the Interior and of Public Health, HG Lawrence on 5 August 1940.

After the National Party had come to power in 1948, the construction of Atteridgeville was temporarily halted, while the planned relocation of residents from other areas around Pretoria had not yet been completed. The population density in Marabastad increased from 14 people per house in 1943 to 19 in 1946. Atteridgeville's population also grew during this period. The increasing number of squatter communities around Pretoria forced the government to draw up a regional plan for developing other townships. Atteridgeville was also extended to the south and west. Part of this development was the creation of Saulsville in 1953, originally a suburb for whites only, which also provided for hostel accommodation for single people. The remaining black residents of Marabastad and those of Bantule and Hove's Ground were moved to Saulsville, as were the residents of the squatter area Mooiplaas who were evicted under the 1950 Group Areas Act. The three relocation schemes—old Atteridgeville, new Atteridgeville and Saulsville—were merged into Atteridgeville/ Saulsville, numbering over 10 000 family homes by the late 1950s.

Aerial view of Atteridgeville in the 1940s

Construction in Atteridgeville again came to a virtual standstill in the 1960s and 1970s because the government decided that housing provided for blacks be limited to designated 'homelands'.[13] In 1983 Atteridgeville was given municipal status and a year later the first Council election was held. Today it has an official population of 65 000, but with the ever-growing informal settlements on the western side it is probably threefold that number. What De Jong's contribution was to the 'old' Atteridgeville–or 'Oustad'–will be discussed in the following paragraphs.

Urban layout as a co-production

Due to a perceived lack of experienced planners in South Africa, the necessary expertise was sought overseas. Municipalities thus frequently attracted experienced foreign professionals for their urban planning activities. In early C20 South Africa, the British planning system served as an example for the development of planning procedures and practices. Provincial planning ordinances were largely based on British town and country planning acts. Thus, for carrying out civic surveys they followed the methods of Patrick Geddes and Patrick Abercrombie, and many urban designs were clearly influenced by the Garden City concept of Ebenezer Howard and Raymond Unwin.[14]

13 Mashabela, 1988: 26.
14 Muller, 1995: 14.

In 1932, the Witwatersrand Joint Town Planning Committee (WJTPC) was formed to implement the principle of regional planning in this part of the Transvaal, following the example of initiatives in Europe and the United States.[15] In 1934 the WJTPC engaged the British firm Adams, Thompson & Fry as consultants. As representative, the experienced engineer and surveyor Francis Longstreth Thompson came to South Africa for a few months a year as 'regional planner' for the municipalities of the Witwatersrand and Pretoria. From 1935 the office in Johannesburg had the British urban planner PJ Bowling as a permanent representative, who lent his own style to the WJTPC. Instead of developing 'joint' activities for the whole area, he alternately made provisional town planning schemes for each municipality. He did this in close cooperation with the officials and town planning consultants of the constituent municipalities, going through all the details together. Adams, Thompson & Fry's contract with the WJTPC ended in April 1939. Bowling remained on as a consultant until he was called up as a war reservist in mid-1940.[16]

15 Mabin, 1993: 50.
16 Mabin, 1993: 52.

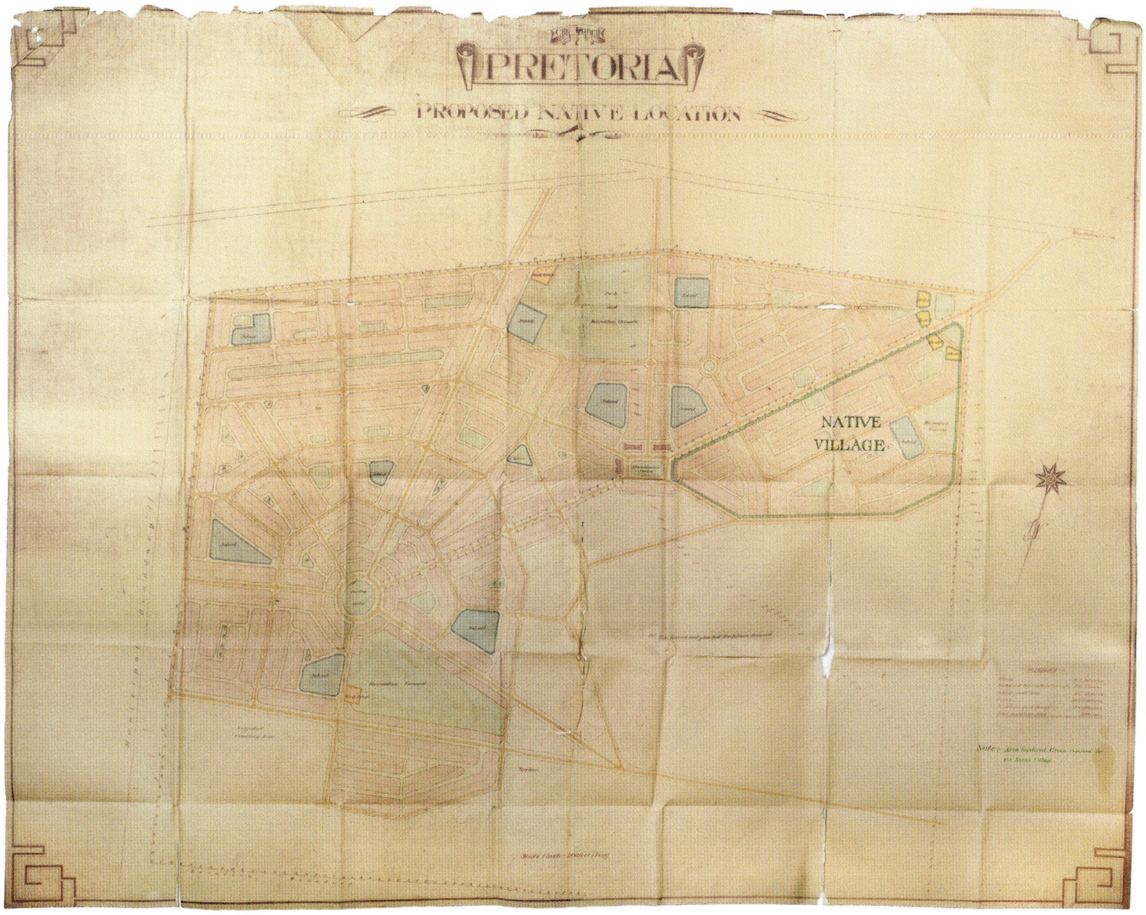

Plan by the City Council for Atteridgeville with the Native Village located northeast, c1939

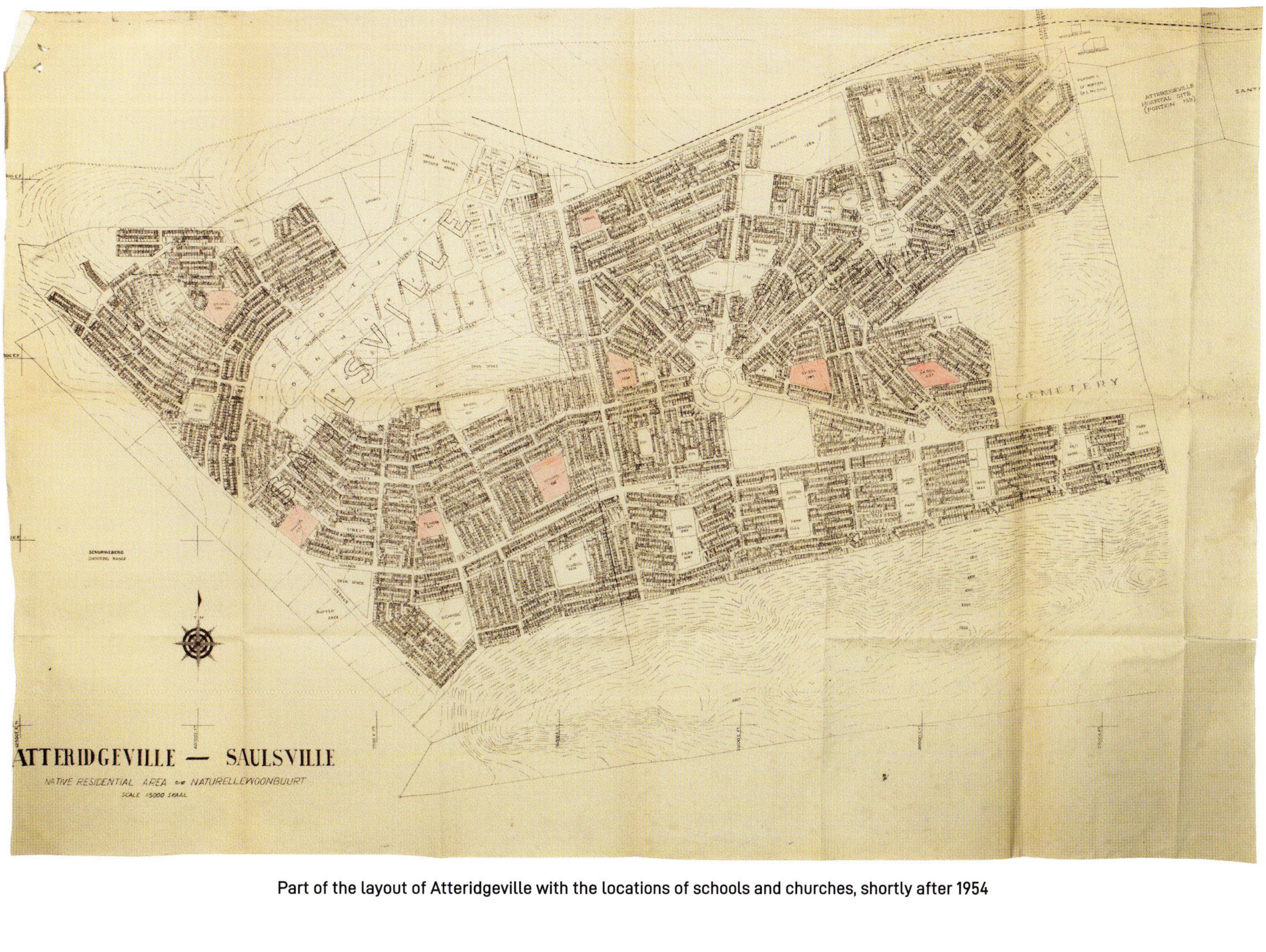

Part of the layout of Atteridgeville with the locations of schools and churches, shortly after 1954

It is, therefore, not surprising that the plan drawing of Atteridgeville is signed off by 'Adams, Thompson and Fry Regional Town Planning Consultants'. In practice, the design must have been made by Bowling in close collaboration with De Jong, who is considered responsible for the planning and execution of Atteridgeville. The plan of the new settlement was based on a simple geometrical pattern adapted to the contours of the site. The centre was placed on an elevated plain overlooking the rest of the township. A straight main road joined Church Street West, now known as Dr WF Nkomo Street, providing direct access to the city via Seeiso Street, lined with jacaranda trees which characterise the streets in Pretoria. We see a clear hierarchy of through and local roads and elements that derive from the repertoire of garden suburbs worldwide, such as circular and rectangular squares with fanning radial streets. Because of this variety in urban design, combined with several detached and semi-detached houses, the design for Atteridgeville, like that of most other townships, was very different to the modernist plan for a Native Township made in the same period by architecture students at the University of Witwatersrand under the sway of the so-called Transvaal Group, a loose association of progressive architects around Rex Martienssen.[17] Both townships were supposed to house 20 000 inhabitants. Whereas the latter, with its large-scale apartment buildings, was imbued with the visionary ideas of Le Corbusier, Atteridgeville's design in the main resembled those of white neighbourhoods developed simultaneously in Pretoria.[18] It is very likely that these also came from the Bowling-De Jong duo.

17 Japha, 1998: 424–25.
18 Stals, 1998: 93.

The carefully designed urban structure and the high level of public amenities, achieved in a productive collaboration, was favourably mentioned by DM Calderwood in his thesis *Native Housing in South Africa* (1953). In this, the implementation of the Nationalist government's post-war township building at minimised cost, was addressed.[19] Calderwood became Head of the Architectural Division of the National Building Research Institute (NBRI), part of the Council for Scientific and Industrial Research (CSIR) formed in 1945. The NBRI's task was to research the provision of low-cost urban housing. In his retrospective introduction Calderwood stated that Pretoria had realized 'a very good Native Township at Atteridgeville'.[20]

'Many up-to-date amenities'

According to its 1943 article 'Atteridgeville – A model Native township near Pretoria', the CCP wanted 'to improve the circumstances of its Native community by the elimination of slums and the provision of respectable residential areas, together with many up-to-date amenities for educational, social and hygienic advancement'.[21] At the time of construction, however, there were no guidelines as to the number of amenities to be provided for the density of inhabitants in black residential areas. The regulations for white neighbourhoods thus served as guidelines adapted to these specific circumstances. For example, fewer shops were planned than prescribed, as it was assumed that most residents would do their shopping in the city.[22]

19 Haarhoff, 2010: 5.
20 Calderwood, 1953: 3.
21 City Council of Pretoria, 1943: 159.
22 Coertze, 1969: 14.

Atteridgeville, Polyclinic, probably designed by Jan de Jong, 1947

The 1943 explanation of the plan by the CCP provides insight into the ambitions of De Jong and his associates. The urban structure has generous open areas and recreational fields and its roadways were to be macadamised. At that time, three schools had been built (including the JJ de Jong Primary School) and more would follow. In addition, the plan provided for municipal administration offices, a clinic, a police station, some dozen churches, a building for the detention of juvenile delinquents and a centre for the teaching of home crafts, which would be incorporated in a large unit comprising a creche, a nursery school and a domestic science centre. For practical reasons, shops would be clustered in shopping or trading centres. Such centralisation was unusual in townships. In Atteridgeville, traders had a similar situation in terms of location, and the trade would be controlled to allow for fair competition. Up until then a number of houses were being used as shops. For economic reasons their architectural character was not given prominence. 'The dignity of the shopping centre, however, will be enhanced by the municipal administration offices, the police station and a clinic which is to be slightly more elaborately designed', was the explanation.[23]

By the end of 1951, the CCP construction programme was completed, but the provisioning of amenities was only carried out in part. In addition to the 1532 houses, Atteridgeville had nine churches, an administration office, four parks, a large sports field, four primary schools and one

23 City Council of Pretoria, 1943: 160.

Atteridgeville, one of the scattered blocks of shops in 2018

Atteridgeville, nameplate of the JJ de Jong Primary School; photo 2019

Atteridgeville, the JJ de Jong Primary School, designed by Jan de Jong in c1950; photo 2019

Atteridgeville, church of the Swiss Mission in 2018

secondary school, an outpatient clinic, a soup kitchen for school children, and a cemetery. Nineteen of the fifty-eight streets were asphalted and had bicycle paths.[24] A year later, a post office followed, but due to lack of funds it was not until 1955 that the first shops were located in different buildings scattered throughout the district. The planned rail and train station that connected Atteridgeville with Pretoria CBD was only opened in 1958. The lack of financial resources also hindered the necessary maintenance, upgrade and extension of these facilities.[25] This was all the more problematic because the population density of 'old' Atteridgeville had increased considerably over the years. 'Backyard living' had almost doubled the number of inhabitants and, in many places, hidden from view the clarity of structure and carefully designed houses on relatively large plots of land.[26]

Housing types by JJ de Jong

There is a clear distinction between the various dwellings that De Jong designed for the first two phases of 'old Atteridgeville', that we will hereafter refer to as Oustad, and the standard 'type' houses built in the extension of the late 1950s. In 1938, prior to the township's construction, several experimental houses were built using a variety of materials: cast blocks from cinder and cement concrete as well as others of fired bricks. Based on these results it was decided that semi-detached (duet) houses would be built for economic reasons, constructed of brick for durability and provided with steel windows and indoor sanitary services.[27] In practice, however, detached houses were also built, on a deep plot of over twelve by twenty-four meters, fenced with diamond-mesh wire. The inhabitants received two fruit trees to start a garden. The first phase consisted of 143 two-roomed and 588 three-roomed duet houses, and 175 three-roomed, 67 four-roomed and seven five-roomed houses. The outer and inner walls of the houses and the chimneys were made of brick, and the floors of ash concrete. The roofs consisted of corrugated iron, fixed to the walls with metal purlins, but some experimented with cement roofing due to the scarcity of iron. The wooden exterior doors were horizontally subdivided (stable doors); interior doors were omitted. The construction was executed by private construction companies appointed following a tender procedure, using only white workers. This was based on an existing agreement between the CCP and the Pretoria Master Builders Association, according to which skilled construction work was reserved for whites.[28]

After the first phase was completed in 1942, the tender for the rest of the township was started only two years later. However, due to a low response to the call for a tender, the City Engineer decided to purchase all necessary materials, however scarce, and make these available to two approved firms for building the houses at a fixed rate. This second phase was for 164 two-roomed and 176 three-roomed duet houses, and 167 three-roomed and 45 five-roomed houses. No information is available regarding these quantities, nor about the specific layout for which De Jong was primarily responsible. We do know that the seven

24 Coertze, 1969: 42–43.
25 Stals, 1998: 95.
26 Stals, 1998: 80.
27 Coertze, 1969: 13.
28 Coertze, 1969: 19–20.

five-roomed houses in the first phase were experimental, with a view to their suitability as sub-economic housing for whites to be provided by the CCP elsewhere in the city. The two-roomed duet houses elicited criticism because they could only accommodate small families without possibilities for expansion. The demand for housing for larger families led to the considerable increase in the number of five-roomed houses in the second phase.[29]

29 Coertze, 1969: 20.

Compared to other townships at the time, the houses in Atteridgeville showed some remarkable elements. The houses were connected to the electricity network and all rooms had a light bulb fitting. All houses had a covered *stoep*. This transitional space between outside and inside had a granolith floor and gave direct access to the living room through the front door. In addition, the sanitary facilities had been integrated into the design. The first houses had a toilet and shower in a room at the rear of the house, which was also accessible from the outside and

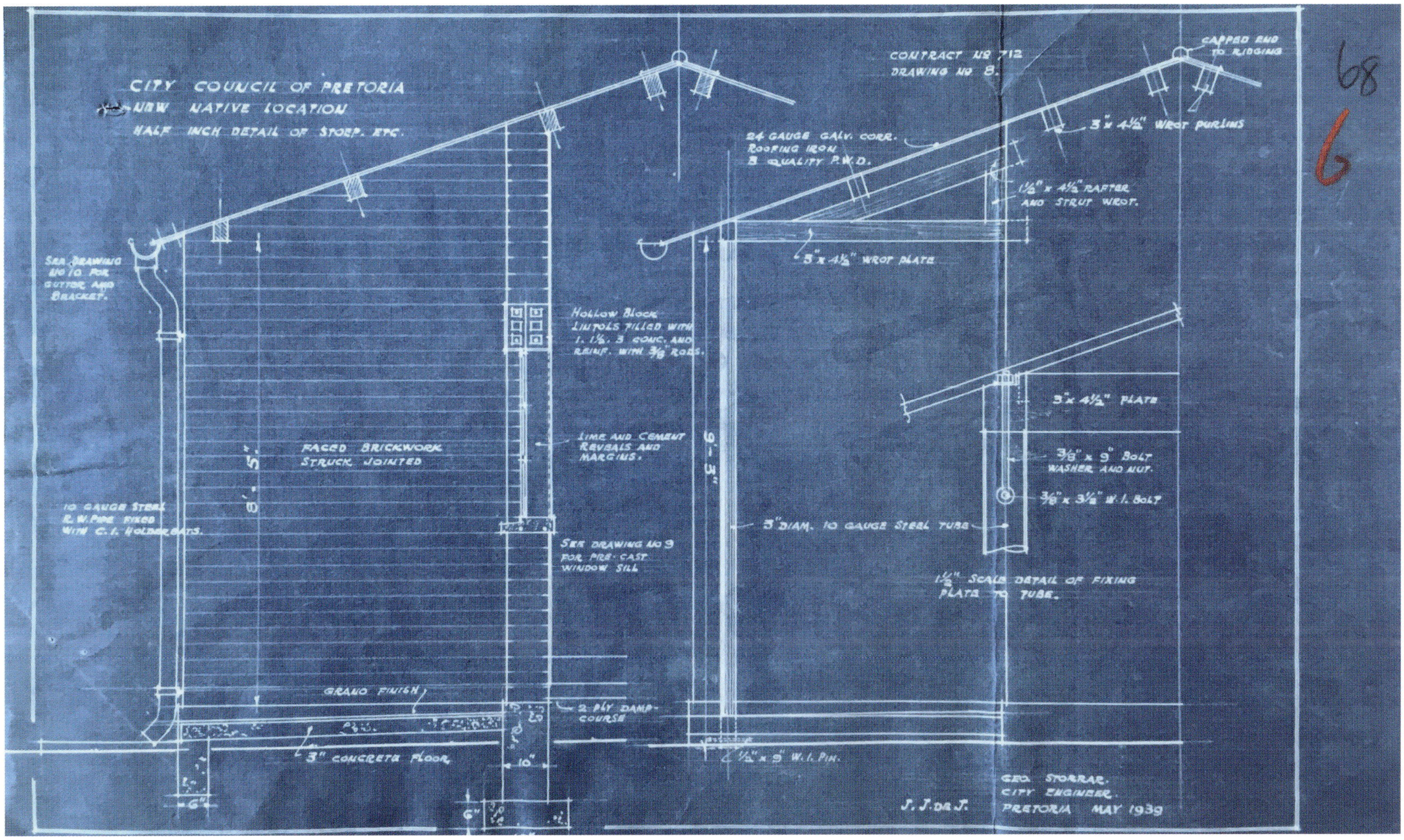

Atteridgeville, blueprint indicating technical details and materials for the sub-economic houses with stoep designed by Jan de Jong, May 1939

Atteridgeville, one of the first houses occupied in 1939

Atteridgeville, a furnished living room and kitchen of the first construction phase, in the 1940s

Atteridgeville, a furnished bedroom in the 1940s

in most cases had been extended. In the second phase this space was completely incorporated into the house and the shower was swapped for a bathtub made of concrete. These were also provided with a relatively large storage space, which was accessible from both inside and outside. It is possible that the integration of the sanitary facilities was made at the expense of the kitchen; the living room also functioned as such, being equipped with a coal stove for cooking and heating in the winter. This was not ideal, given the pollution the stove caused. Only the five-room house of the second phase had a separate kitchen and living room. Most living rooms gave direct access to the bedrooms. Only in some types of the second phase was an attempt made to increase privacy through transitional spaces. Another difference was that the height of the interior walls was not extended to the roof in the first phase, but was in the second phase.

A 'Native Village'

In addition to sub-economic housing, economic housing was initially planned for Atteridgeville. The future residents were supposed to have been given an opportunity to build their own houses according to the so-called 'Bloemfontein system'. This referred to the 'hygienic Native township' Batho, developed in Bloemfontein in 1918, which was held as the ideal of a 'location' which served for the relocated residents from Waaihoek. A loan from the municipal government enabled them to build and own their houses in Batho.[30] In Pretoria the CCP was prepared to make a similar arrangement. In the first plan a 'Village Section' was reserved for this provision, in the northwest area of the township. Later this 'Native Village' was extended to the east. However, despite great interest in house ownership in Marabastad, the plan had to be postponed due to lack of funds.[31] The Central Housing Board (CHB) of the Department of Health, established in 1920 to control the housing activities and loans of municipalities, would not allow economic houses to be built in Atteridgeville until three-quarters of the sub-economic housing were completed.[32]

30 Du Bruyn & Oelofse, 2019: 63.
31 Coertze, 1969: 15.

In October 1940, according to municipal correspondence, 414 houses, each inhabited by an average of three families were counted in Marabastad; 250 families had already been moved to Atteridgeville, with twelve to fourteen families moving every day. In Atteridgeville, 519 sub-economic houses had been completed and another 200 were almost finished. About 200 Marabastad inhabitants, who already had their own house, wanted to live in an economic house: ministers, school teachers, traders and the like.[33] A small number of them were deemed able, under the supervision of the City Engineer, to build their own houses. However, the majority would be satisfied with a four-room house of the existing sub-economic type, albeit with the additional installation of ceilings and interior doors. The CCP intended to build this type in mass production and to sell it to the newcomers, but the CHB refused despite repeated pleas from homeowners in Marabastad and Hove's Ground.[34] The planning of new Atteridgeville offered new opportunities for adopting the Bloemfontein system in 1954. In the new part another 'Native Village' was projected with 372 plots for self-construction economic housing. When in 1956 only 34 of these houses were executed, the CCP decided to build on the remaining plots itself and offer these houses for sale.[35]

Standardisation: the NE 51/6

In 1951, the National Housing and Planning Commission (NHPC, which in 1944 had replaced the Central Housing Board), the Native Affairs Department and the aforementioned NBRI had jointly drawn up 'Minimum Standards of Housing Accommodation for Non-Europeans'. These were the result of four years of research in which around 150 specialists had participated. The minimum standards were then concretised in standard type plans that were referred to as 'NE' (Non-European) '51' (the year of creation, 1951) and the number of the variant.

32 Town Clerk of Pretoria, 1940.
33 Letter of the Town Clerk of Pretoria to the Secretary of the Central Housing Board d.d. 16-10-1940; SANA, Folder Native Affairs Department, File No. 81/313 (H)(5).
34 Letter of the Manager of the Native and Asiatic Administration Department CCP to the Secretary for Native Affairs d.d. 23-10-1940; SANA, Folder Native Affairs Department, File No. 81/313 (H)(5).
35 Coertze, 1969: 51.

Atteridgeville, NE 51/6 standard type house in 2020

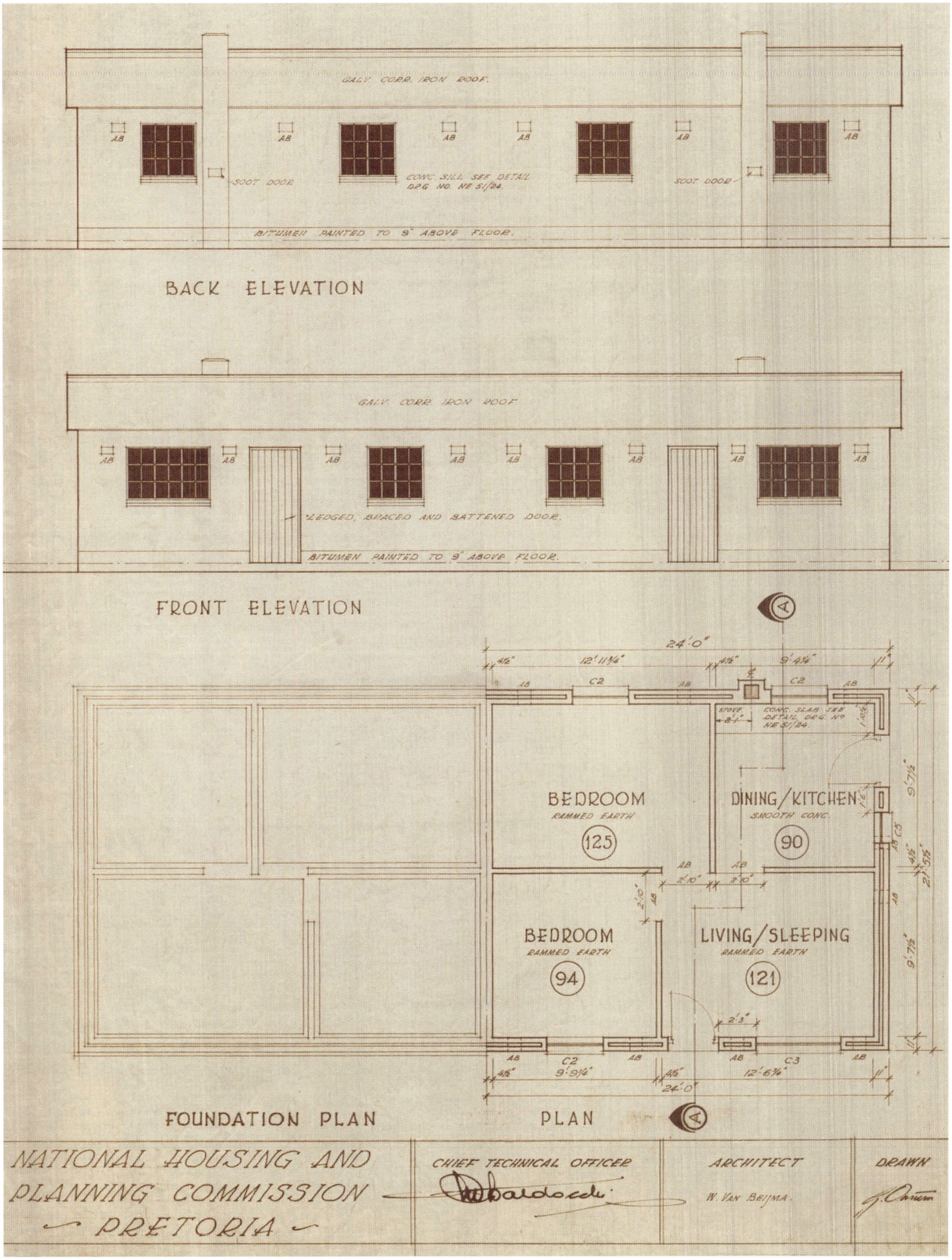

Elevations and plan of the NE 51/7 standard type house by Willem van Beijma for the National Housing and Planning Commission, 16 October 1951

Atteridgeville, experimental house with concrete roof, built around 1955; photo 2018

The main ones were the NE 51/6 and NE 51/9 three-room houses of which the last one had indoor sanitary facilities. In fact, these were four-room houses, because they counted three rooms and a dining room/kitchen. The standard type plans were developed with a notable Dutch input. The NE 51/9 is based on a CHB design for sub-economic housing for Europeans dating from 1939, modified in 1948 by Willem van Beijma as Chief Architect at the Directorate of Housing of the NHPC into a three-room house for Non-Europeans.[36] In 1951, Van Beijma elaborated several semi-detached variants of the NE 51/6 (NE 51/7 and NE 51/8) and the NE 51/9 (NE 51/10 and NE 51/11).[37]

After the 'Minimum Standards of Housing Accommodation for Non-Europeans' and the NE 51 series were published this model was avidly followed. In order to obtain state loans municipalities needed their housing plans approved by the National Housing Commission, but NE 51 housing schemes were approved 'without further enquiry'.[38] As a result, tens of thousands of such standard homes were built throughout the country, often in a frightening pattern of linearity and monotony. In Atteridgeville the standard four-room house of type NE 51/6 prevailed. Arguments for this choice were its favourable dimensions, the housing needs of future residents from Bantule and Hove's Ground and the fact that experience had been gained in Vlakfontein (later Mamelodi) to the east of the town, which allowed production to be maximised.[39] Economics also played an important role. The sub-economic housing in Atteridgeville resulted in losses for the municipality, and it was partly for this reason that it was decided to switch to economic housing.[40] Because the tenants had to be able to bear the costs, the most economical of the standard dwellings, the NE 51/6, was chosen. This made a clear distinction between the mix of housing types designed by De Jong for the CCP–from two to five-room houses, duet and detached in 'old Atteridgeville' (predating 1950)–and the uniform NE 51/6 houses of the NHPC after 1951. These houses also differed in terms of layout and facilities.

In his *Native housing in South Africa*, Calderwood considered De Jong's three-room house in Atteridgeville an improvement in layout compared to houses in Orlando, near Johannesburg, although he would have preferred to leave the stoep out in favour of a separate kitchen.[41] He attached greater value to the four-roomed house designed in 1946 in Sharpe Native Township, near Vereeniging, later Sharpeville: 'an admirable plan ... which demanded only a small adjustment in window arrangement to make it an attractive housing unit'.[42] This house shows a striking resemblance to the housing types of the CHB and Van Beijma that led to the NE 51/9, and can therefore be added to this range of plans. Whereas the NE 51/6 houses in new Atteridgeville had a separate kitchen/dining room, in contrast to most of the older De Jong houses, there were two major drawbacks. Firstly, the stoep was omitted from the NE 51 homes in keeping with Calderwood's preference, although this element was greatly appreciated by the vast majority of residents.[43]

36 Le Roux, 2019: 11.
37 Drawings available in WIReDSPACE: https://hdl.handle.net/10539/11081.
38 Le Roux, 2019: 4, note 6.
39 Coertze, 1969: 51.
40 Coertze, 1969: 35.
41 Calderwood, 1953: 19.
42 Calderwood, 1953: 20.
43 Stals, 1998: 28.

Secondly, the sanitary facilities were not provided internally. The differences between the 'old' and 'new' Atteridgeville houses illustrate the watershed that the apartheid regime in 1948 had created. Still without the binding standards of the NDRI, the CCP and De Jong had pulled out all the stops to provide the new residents of Atteridgeville with the best possible housing under the new political dispensation, sustaining the idea of a Model Native Township.

Interactions between spaces and people

The forced removal of peoples from their homes would have long-lasting and devastating effects on any human being. However, the new inhabitants of Atteridgeville had no choice but to make the best of their lot. The local authority, in an attempt to quell unrest, purveyed the idea that to reside in the new township would be better than living in the slums of Marabastad. De Jong and Bowling designed the model township within the tight framework of segregation laws and a minimal budget. Their plan offered a new form of urban development in black townships and the new location indeed offered some sort of a step up for most.

In 1943, four years after the construction of Atteridgeville had started, the CCP claimed that the new district would be a success: "everywhere the houses are surrounded by well laid out gardens and much other evidence that the people living there are happy and contented".[44] Based on interviews with residents and personal memories of this chapter's co-author Mathebe Aphane, the residents of 'Oustad' did not like the two-roomed semi-detached houses, but overall they were happy that their streets were not as dusty and muddy as those in Marabastad. The narrow width of the minor streets was welcomed as it offered passive surveillance and a sense of a close-knit community. This is evidenced in the way people tended their yards and pavements in front of their houses. They planted lawns on the street-facing side, started front gardens and grew vegetables in their backyards.

44 City Council of Pretoria, 1943: 159.

Atteridgeville, three-room house from the first phase of construction (1939–42); photo 2020

When the prospective residents of Atteridgeville were told of their imminent relocation, they did not trust the government to have their interests at heart, though their basic needs were very modest: space for cooking, eating, sleeping, bathing and recreation. If these basic needs were met, residents were arguably going to be satisfied. In the houses designed by De Jong, where there was no ambiguity in the designation of spaces, the question 'how is this supposed to function?' never arose.[45] The new residents of Oustad started modifying their houses as early as the mid-1940s. Upgrading and modifying the internal spaces to suit family needs and lifestyles was common. The floor plans for the houses only varied slightly, which offered very little manoeuvre for modifications. As a result, most houses ended up looking similar when extended. The only differences concerned the render on the walls, the elaborate doors or the size of the windows.

Once their economic situation improved, most residents used the storeroom space as a place for a fridge and an electric cooking stove. The built-in coal stove was then used for space-heating in the cold winter months. In later years additional kitchen space was created by breaking and extending the outer wall of the storeroom. The door of the store would be reused. The living/kitchen space was used as a dining room, working/homework and living area. Sometimes it turned into a makeshift bedroom for the children. This space also underwent modifications, with bigger windows and the coal stove being replaced by a fireplace. The bedrooms were small and did not offer much space for the storage of clothing. Most residents would therefore store their children's clothes under the bed and the parent's clothes in a wardrobe in the bedroom. The second bedroom would be for the children or for visiting guests. Such overnight family visits were a way for most black families to keep a bond with relatives. When there were visitors, the children had to give up their beds and sleep in the kitchen or on thin foldable mattresses on the floor. The major modifications that happened in these spaces was that people would replace the windows and extend the main bedroom. The bathroom had a concrete bath, but the most common modification in this space was that residents changed the concrete baths for propriety bathtubs and relocated the concrete ones outside for laundry.

The stoep, whose worth Calderwood had called into question, was well liked by the community. It is the one space that gave the people some pride. It was polished and shined daily and only important visitors were allowed to enter the house across the stoep; others were expected to go around the back of the house and use the back door to enter. The stoep served as an extended outside room which was used for various activities: entertaining visitors, taking family portraits, talking to neighbours, listening to the radio, playing jazz or reading. Some of the households used the stoep as a makeshift shebeen, a subculture which defined the life in most townships insofar as recreation was concerned. For the families who could afford it, the stoep was enclosed and the wall dividing it from the kitchen would be demolished to create a bigger living space. Then a new stoep was built adjacent to the living room, as a transitional space into the house. Saturday mornings were spent for 'spring cleaning' and gardening. While all this was happening, the children would be playing on the streets or the nearby 'park'. These green spaces were designed to be within view of the houses.

45 Linstra, 2016: 6.

Atteridgeville, three-room house from the second phase of construction (1945–50); photo 2020

Atteridgeville, extended type house; photo 2020

Atteridgeville, current streetscape dominated by parked cars; photo 2020

A well-connected community

The educational, religious, health, sports and infrastructural facilities in (old) Atteridgeville were beneficial for the residents. Atteridgeville had, within walking distance, creches/kindergartens, primary schools, and high schools which attracted scholars from other townships around Pretoria; even churches were used as classrooms during the week. De Jong designed the schools to have coal stoves inside which made teaching and learning more congenial. Generally, Sunday mornings and Thursday afternoons were reserved for Christian rituals. For most Christian denominations the Sunday morning ritual involved cooking a big lunch for the family before going to church, although the design of Oustad, with its thirty churches, was considered excessive by a number of residents.

Every block had a 'park', a green patch where children in the area could play in plain sight of the adults. The big municipal parks were much used during the festive seasons for the celebration of important South African holidays. Atteridgeville has tennis courts, softball, bowling, soccer, athletics and rugby grounds. The 'Superstadium' was used for athletics competitions amongst schools as well as for small and larger soccer matches on Saturday and Sunday afternoons. Community halls were used for performing arts, dancing and movies. Community meetings and local political meetings and campaigns were hosted at the local community halls.

An outpatient clinic offered primary health and antenatal care to the residents. They also ran a successful TB (tuberculosis) clinic. Any family member who contracted tuberculosis had all his or her cohabiting family members put on a preventive health programme and given a monthly supply of milk and medication. In the 1970s a tertiary academic hospital was built on the eastern side of Atteridgeville, which meant that the sick did not have to go all the way into the city. Most people from Atteridgeville and surrounding townships trained as nurses in Kalafong Hospital. Atteridgeville had two railway stations, Kalafong and Atteridgeville stations. Municipal buses ran through the main artery through the township and privately-owned taxis were available. This ensured quick and easy access to places of work. The panorama painted by the local artist Titus Matiyane clearly illustrates all connections.

The underpinning reason for the creation of townships was segregation, and to move black people out of the cities, but close enough to the white areas for them to be able to provide labour for white people. The main aim was to divide and conquer black communities in order to reduce the risks of mobilization against the apartheid regime. Ironically, Oustad was designed so well that instead of quieting the voices of the residents and leaving them despondent, the township dwellers formed a well-connected community of residents who looked after each other for the advancement of all; no person in the community was to be left behind, everyone was to advance.

The main lesson to be drawn from the planning of Atteridgeville is that governments cannot solve housing problems by (mass) producing houses without considering the basic necessities that support the daily lives of the residents. The important question is whether the existing matchbox housing still serves a contemporary way of living. History shows that when governments roll out houses in the middle of nowhere, for example the NE 51 types or after 1994 the Reconstruction and Development Program (RDP) houses, without amenities, people resist them for very good reasons. This leads to poor living conditions and sprawl. The design of any township should be based on ethical values. This will result in a sustainable solution to the country's housing issues. As an ex-resident of Atteridgeville, Mathebe Aphane can vouch that the living conditions in Oustad were much better than in most townships across South Africa at the time and better than the subsequent expansions of the 1960s and later of this Model Native Township.

Atteridgeville, informal street trade, photo 2018

Atteridgeville, part of the panorama by local artist Titus Matiyane, c2007

BIDGEVILLE

Johannesburg, Brixton, tower of the Dutch Reformed Church building designed by Geers & Geers, 1938–40; photo 2017

9 Technological Trajectories from North to South

Michael Louw

The influences of immigrant Dutch-born architects, contractors, suppliers and educators who practiced in the Union of South Africa can still be noticed today. The overseas transference and translation of the technological trends of C20 Netherlands, however divergent, to southern Africa was further influenced by differences in climate, the availability of skill and labour or the lack thereof, available materials and socio-political circumstances.[1] This chapter explores the technological trajectories and their tangible results along themes of adaptation, daylighting, efficiency, labour, urgency, industrialisation, and innovation, and it concludes with the immaterial legacies.

Technological trends in the Netherlands

In the Netherlands, early C20 architectural production and its related technologies clearly exhibit tensions between modernity and tradition. By tradition, most buildings were constructed of load-bearing brick walls and wooden beams, which demanded skilled labour. Then, newly introduced building methods using steel frames or reinforced concrete for larger building types, such as offices, department stores and factories, called for different approaches to design, education and organisation of the construction practice, apart from aesthetic preferences. While late C19 architecture manifested a great variety of historicist styles, the C20 architects often sought structural expression and a 'fair use', not imitating, of materials, particularly those which were considered modern at the time.

In the rational Stock Exchange building by Hendrik Berlage in Amsterdam (1903), the varied use of materials was applied in accordance with their constructive function. The (precious) stonework is carefully positioned where the loads are the greatest (or where there are prominent features) while brickwork is used for the general wall construction, also in the interior. The structure and materials of the building, from its external façades to its internally exposed metal roof trusses and its barrel-vaulted floors, are at no point hidden from view.[2] However, Berlage was also enamoured with the decorative qualities of a-historic ornaments and strove to create a *Gesamtkunstwerk* of applied arts and furniture, which would pave the way for two divergent directions.

The proponents of the Amsterdam School used elaborately crafted expressionist brickwork, sometimes in conjunction with newer technologies, as Joan van der Mey, Piet Kramer and Michel de Klerk demonstrated in the *Scheepvaarthuis* in Amsterdam (1913), in collaboration with the practice of the Van Gendt brothers who designed the reinforced concrete frame that is clearly visible in the hall. The functionalist trend of the *Nieuwe Bouwen*, or Modern Movement, was advanced by the introduction of the self-supporting (reinforced concrete) frame, which in the C20 was considered as 'the most important architectural occurrence of the present century. It liberated the building from the 'straitjacket' which until then had been needed to hold the building up.'[3]

Structural expression was developed further by the modernists, in particular by Jan Duiker, who had studied in Delft and had 'a thorough, historically enlightened education, firmly founded on a knowledge of

1 Law, 2015: 117–20.

2 Van Dijk, 1992: 14; Molema et al., 1996: 16.

3 Molema et al., 1996: 25.

Amsterdam, Stock Exchange designed by Hendrik Berlage, 1903; view of the multi-coloured barrel-vaulted ceiling; photo 2019

Amsterdam, Scheepvaarthuis, designed by Joan van der Mey, Piet Kramer, Michel de Klerk and Van Gendt brothers, 1913; view of the hall; photo 1977

Hilversum, former Zonnestraal Sanatorium, main building after restoration; architects: Duiker & Bijvoet, 1931; photo 2007

Amsterdam, National Aviation Laboratory; architects: Van Tijen & Maaskant; postcard, 1947

modern technology...'[4] His and others' ideas were eventually 'radicalised into an argument for an industrialised building system'.[5] Duiker's Nirwana Flat in the Hague (1929), the Open Air School in Amsterdam (1930) and the Zonnestraal Sanatorium in Hilversum (1931) all make use of concrete frames and large areas of steel-framed glass.[6] The emphasis on technology is key and is described as 'the product of profound knowledge, technical know-how, spatial invention, and something more: the determination to acknowledge a new-found sincerity in design as the result of a global rethinking of the building – its function, typology and method of construction.'[7]

The body of work that was produced during the 1930s to 1950s in South Africa by various Dutch-trained practitioners exemplifies the *Nieuwe Bouwen* approach that aimed to redress what Dutch modernist architect Han van Loghem called 'the enormous backwardness of technique in the building world'; after mentioning the disadvantages of materials like brick and wood, he argued for a 'dynamic architecture, which has overcome the conception of gravity and which in place of this gives a poised play of forces which the new materials iron and reinforced concrete make possible, whilst transparent building elements cause the heaviness to the feeling to disappear'.[8] During and after WW2, another movement arose which was open to hybridisation between tradition and modernity, called the 'Shake Hands Movement' or as Willem van Tijen termed it, a 'marriage of brick and concrete', exemplified by his and Hugh Maaskant's National Aviation Laboratory in Amsterdam (1941).[9]

The conflicting positions of those who were in support of functionalism, industrialisation, mass-production and new materials and those who advocated a return to traditional forms, materials and craftsmanship in the Netherlands, are also reflected in works produced by immigrant practitioners in the Union of South Africa.

Adaptations of craft and material hybrids in South Africa

Dutch contractors, like Matthé Meischke, who immigrated to the then Transvaal Republic in 1889, were known for the high quality of their building work, which often incorporated traditional stonework and framed concrete construction. He completed numerous prestigious commissions, like the post offices in Rissik Street, Braamfontein, Fordsburg and Jeppe in Johannesburg (all 1898). Despite Meischke's

Johannesburg, central section of the Town Hall; construction executed by Matthé Meischke; photo 2018

4 Molema et al., 1996: 20.
5 Van Dijk, 1992: 22.
6 Groenendijk & Vollaard, 1992: 88, 89, 132, 133, 198.
7 Casciato, 1996: 7.
8 Van Loghem, 1932: 61.
9 Van Dijk, 1992: 22.

Cape Town, Provincial Building, designed by JZ Schuurmans Stekhoven & FM Glennie in 1939; carved stone façade with concrete barrel vaults visible beyond; photo 2020

Cape Town, Provincial Building, designed by JZ Schuurmans Stekhoven & FM Glennie in 1939; concrete barrel vaults under construction, 1939; in *The South African Architect*, 1940

involvement on the side of the Boers in the South African War, he not only built the Johannesburg City Hall (1910–15) but was also awarded most of the building work for the two wings of the Union Buildings (1913) in Pretoria, to the design of Herbert Baker.[10] The Union Buildings were constructed out of locally available and traditional materials like timber from Zimbabwe, tiles from Vereeniging and locally quarried granite, light-coloured sandstone and red sandstone, in combination with industrial materials like concrete and imported glass prisms to reflect light into the basement.[11] Extensive use was also made of brickwork (estimated at 14 million bricks) for the internal office walls.[12]

As a result of economic or structural necessity, a hybridised approach of innovative technology and traditional materials was often applied in South Africa. The Provincial Administration Building by Jan Zeger Schuurmans Stekhoven in collaboration with Frederick McIntosh Glennie in Cape Town (1939) employed a reinforced concrete frame and concrete barrel vaults spanning over Keerom Street, in combination with brickwork and finely carved stonework on the street facades.[13] Teak sash windows and doors were combined with 'a modern type of anti-slam door closer', while natural lighting and ventilation were augmented by the provision of electrical convection heating and artificial lighting.[14] The Dutch-born architect Jaap Jongens, who arrived in South Africa in 1936, similarly used a hybrid combination of materials for his well-known Huguenot Monument in Franschhoek (inaugurated 1948).[15] Seemingly

10 See also Chapter 4.

11 Fisher, 2004: 38–47.
12 www.thepresidency.gov.za/content/union-buildings.
13 Anon. 1939, The South African Architect, June: 94.
14 SAAB. 1944, Nov: 41.
15 The monument itself was completed in 1944 under supervision of Charles Percival Walgate; the central sculpture is made by the South African artist Coert Steynberg; Pienaar, 1948; see also the interlude on Commemoration and celebration.

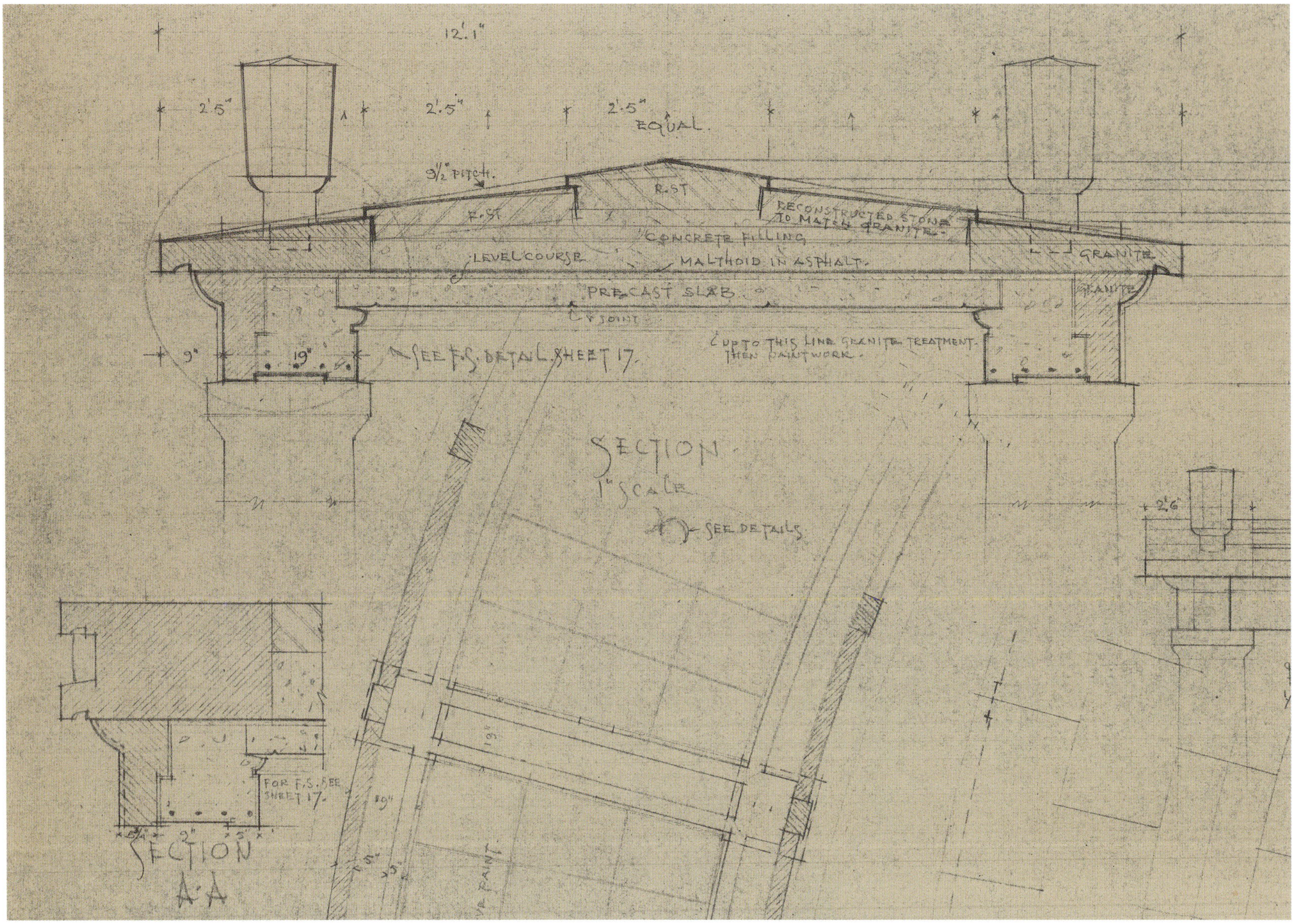

Franschhoek, Huguenot Monument, architectural design by Jaap Jongens, drawing showing the combination of modern and traditional materials, 1944

Franschhoek, Huguenot Monument, architectural design by Jaap Jongens, 1944; intricately carved granite blocks at the base of the sculpture; photo 2019

Franschhoek, Huguenot Monument, architectural design by Jaap Jongens, 1944; curved colonnade executed in Paarl granite, reconstituted stone and concrete; photo 2019

Franschhoek district, Wemmershoek Dam control station, designed by Jaap Jongens in 1957; the entrance staircase showing the combination of modern and traditional materials; photo 2019

Cape Town, section of the Tygerberg Hospital with diaper pattern; architects: Andrews & Niegeman, 1945–76; photo 2018

constructed entirely out of stone, it was made of Paarl granite in combination with reconstituted stone and reinforced concrete. He also employed a similar material palette at the Wemmershoek Dam control station and outside water purification plant (1957).

The extensive use of clay brick construction, often in conjunction with reinforced concrete, is applied in most churches designed by Geers & Geers, widely spread in South Africa. In Tygerberg Hospital (1976), the largest in the West Cape, designed by Andrews & Niegeman, the uncommon use of face brick is emphasized by the decorative brick technique known as diapering, where bricks of different colours or levels of protrusion are arranged in repeated patterns.[16] The choice of brickwork, though combined with complex tree-shaped concrete columns and concrete shell-roofs for the laundry and parking structures, was primarily made to reduce the need for maintenance.[17]

Concerns regarding maintenance, cost, and construction time, coupled with the increased availability of industrially manufactured materials, led many practitioners to use modern materials to imitate traditional materials, especially for interior finishes.

Traditional patterns of encaustic tiles, often found in the foyers of public buildings, were later imitated through vinyl or linoleum floor tiles, such as those manufactured by the Dutch firm Nederlandsche Linoleumfabriek Krommenie. The Dutch émigré architect Anton Voorvelt used linoleum to emulate marble and a green profiled metal ceiling to save costs in the Catholic churches Our Lady of the Wayside in Maryvale, Johannesburg (1954) and Pius X in Waterkloof, Pretoria (1957). Walls were made of a mix of concrete and brickwork (including diapering). The integration of modern and traditional materials here was seamless and the junctions were meticulously detailed.

Attention to detail is also evident in the drawings of Jongens and Niegeman. When describing Henk Niegeman, his successor, Barney Shapiro, remarked that 'Henk spent a lot of time looking at detail. It was just in his training, I suppose'.[18] This detailed-oriented training was in most cases supplemented with an acute awareness of climatic design.

16 Peters, 2018: 9.
17 Niegeman as cited by Peters, 2018: 9.

18 Personal interview with Bernard Shapiro, Tokai, 28 May 2019.

Cape Town, Rex Trueform Factory, designed by Andrews & Niegeman in 1948; the triangular south-facing windows in the courtyard; photo 2019

Daylighting

Sufficient access to sunshine and fresh air was topical in the Netherlands in the struggle against tuberculosis in the early C20. This is reflected in the designs of modernist Jan Duiker, who also sought to economise structure and develop efficient responses to hygienic, comfortable conditions in his transparent architecture, like in the *Openluchtschool* [Open Air School] in Amsterdam and Zonnestraal Sanatorium in Hilversum.[19] Ensuring that workspaces had good daylighting and fresh air was an important ambition for improving working conditions. For this purpose, the Van Nelle Factory in Rotterdam (1931) was designed as a shallow daylight factory by Brinkman & Van der Vlugt, with concrete mushroom floors and curtain walls of glass and steel.[20] These concerns are also manifested in a number of factories in South Africa, such as the Rex Trueform Factory in Salt River, Cape Town, by Andrews & Niegeman (1948). The garment manufacturer claimed that the wellbeing of its workers was the company's primary concern when it noted how the building's design would respond to this ambition:

'Wider use of glass is the newest thing in modern building methods and in [sic] the new factory walls facing north and south will be entirely of that material. Free-hanging sun screens with heat-absorbing glass will protect the north windows and prevent direct sun heat entering the factory. The south wall, which gets the afternoon sun, is being constructed of triangular windows. The part of the triangle which faces the sun will be of heat absorbing glass, too.'[21]

Writing in 1951 about the obvious climatological differences between the Netherlands and his new homeland, Delft-trained immigrant architect Henk de Bie specifically noted the large amount of sunlight, large diurnal temperature variations, and the lower annual rainfall in South Africa: 'The sun is friend and foe. During the winter one will try to get as much sun as possible, but in the summer it can burn mercilessly and it should be kept far away.'[22] He mentioned the advantages of Le Corbusier's *brise soleil* for larger buildings and the benefits of roof overhangs of 900-1200mm, using photos of the Rex Trueform factory as an illustration.[23]

A similar experiment to the Rex Trueform zig-zag windows (albeit horizontal in this case to allow for continuous workbenches along the street facing façades) was undertaken by Chapman & Spoor for a vehicle workshop in Cape Town (1960). Hessel Spoor, also Delft-trained, was acutely aware of climate and the firm specialised in sophisticated building skins designed as a response to climate. The façade at the

19 Van Dijk, 1992: 24; Van Heuvel, 1992: 10.
20 Van Dijk, 1992: 24; Groenendijk & Vollaard, 1992: 230.
21 Rex Trueform, 1947: 10, 25; Wolff, 2017.
22 De Bie, 1951: 60.
23 See also Chapter 6.

Bloemfontein, glazing arrangement in Henk de Bie's own house; *Architect and Builder* November 1963

Stanley Porter Building, designed with Jaap Jongens, consisted of aluminium frames that accommodated blue vitreous enamel panels, and panes of reflective and obscure glass.[24] Their slightly older Here Sewentien Building in Cape Town (1956, likewise with Jongens) made use of fixed vertical louvres below horizontal shading elements at transom level on all the upper floors (enabling the cleaning of the aluminium-framed windows), and retractable external aluminium louvres to protect the shop fronts at ground level when needed.[25] The exposed fanlights above the horizontal louvres were fitted with special Northlite glazing to allow for even light distribution.

Several Dutch practitioners with solar awareness experimented with different glazing combinations and shading devices, like Stekhoven, who (then with Glennie) used cross-reeded glass, non-actinic glass to reduce solar penetration, wired-cast and polished plate glass, and acid-etched glass in the Provincial Building in Cape Town.[26] In his own house in Bloemfontein (1963), De Bie planned for all bedrooms and living areas

24 A&B. 1960b, Nov: 2–9; Rennie, 1978: 61. The building is still extant in Buitengracht Street, but the zig-zag windows have been removed.
25 Three floors of the building in Long Street were occupied by the 'Klub Here Sewentien' that aimed to promote Afrikaans interests, A&B. 1956a, July: 33; Rennie, 1978: 143; the aluminium louvres have been removed.
26 SAAB. 1944, Nov: 43.

Cape Town, Rex Trueform Factory, designed by Andrews & Niegeman in 1948; southwest-facing facade showing the expressive use of structure, glazing and vertical shading fins; photo 2019

to have a northern aspect: the glazing arrangement allows winter sun to penetrate the living spaces and the summer sun is kept out.[27] The house's multi-layered roof construction of Q Deck steel sheets, overlaid with 50mm thick fibre-cement boards, covered with a lightly reinforced cement screed and waterproofed with three layers of Ruberoid roofing was an innovative attempt at a thermally efficient composite roof construction.[28] Two years later, De Bie used glazed balconies at the Ember el Mar building (1965) in conjunction with glass sliding doors to mitigate the large diurnal temperature variations in Bloemfontein.[29]

Some architects also experimented with modern materials such as Perspex and fibreglass, for example, at the *Nederduitsch Hervormde* Church in Cape Town (1960). The church, designed pro-bono for the local Dutch community by Jaap Jongens for Chapman & Spoor, was built on a cramped corner of Hatfield and Dunkley Streets, but has since been demolished. It had a zig-zag roof carried by complicated steel trusses covered with Perspex sheets to admit natural light from above. The daylight was reflected off angled boards lined with aluminium foil, and onto a suspended ceiling over the interior, creating a glowing interior.[30] In Johannesburg, Jaap van Niftrik's 1957 Netherlands Pavilion at the Rand Easter Show was an eye-catching experiment, for which he made use of green tinted corrugated fibreglass to create the curved façade of the main exhibition foyer (a world first use of corrugated fibreglass sheeting in a façade according to reporting at the time).[31] An internal steel framework with a light planter box that ran the length of the façade supported the fibre glass sheets, formed into curved fins. These fins, compared in published texts to an insect's scales, admitted natural daylight while enabling the building's façade to become a glowing beacon at night. Small ventilation slits allowed for natural airflow, while concealed internal lighting, designed and installed by Dutch lighting firm Philips, was also applied. The building was erected by the Dutch firm Dura Construction Company in only three and a half months, but it no longer exists.[32]

27 Peters, 2019: 41.
28 De Bie, 1963: 17.
29 Peters, 2019: 43.

30 A&B. 1960, Feb: 55; the church has been demolished.
31 Anon. 1957b. Construction in southern Africa, Apr: 47;
32 Anon. 1957b. Construction in southern Africa, Apr: 47–49; A&B. 1957, Jun: 39; see also the interlude on Celebration and commemoration in this book.

Cape Town, Nederduitsch Hervormde Church, designed by Jaap Jongens (at Chapman & Spoor) in 1959; section showing the use of Perspex sheets to reflect daylight into the building via angled boards covered with aluminium foil; in *Architect and Builder*, 1960

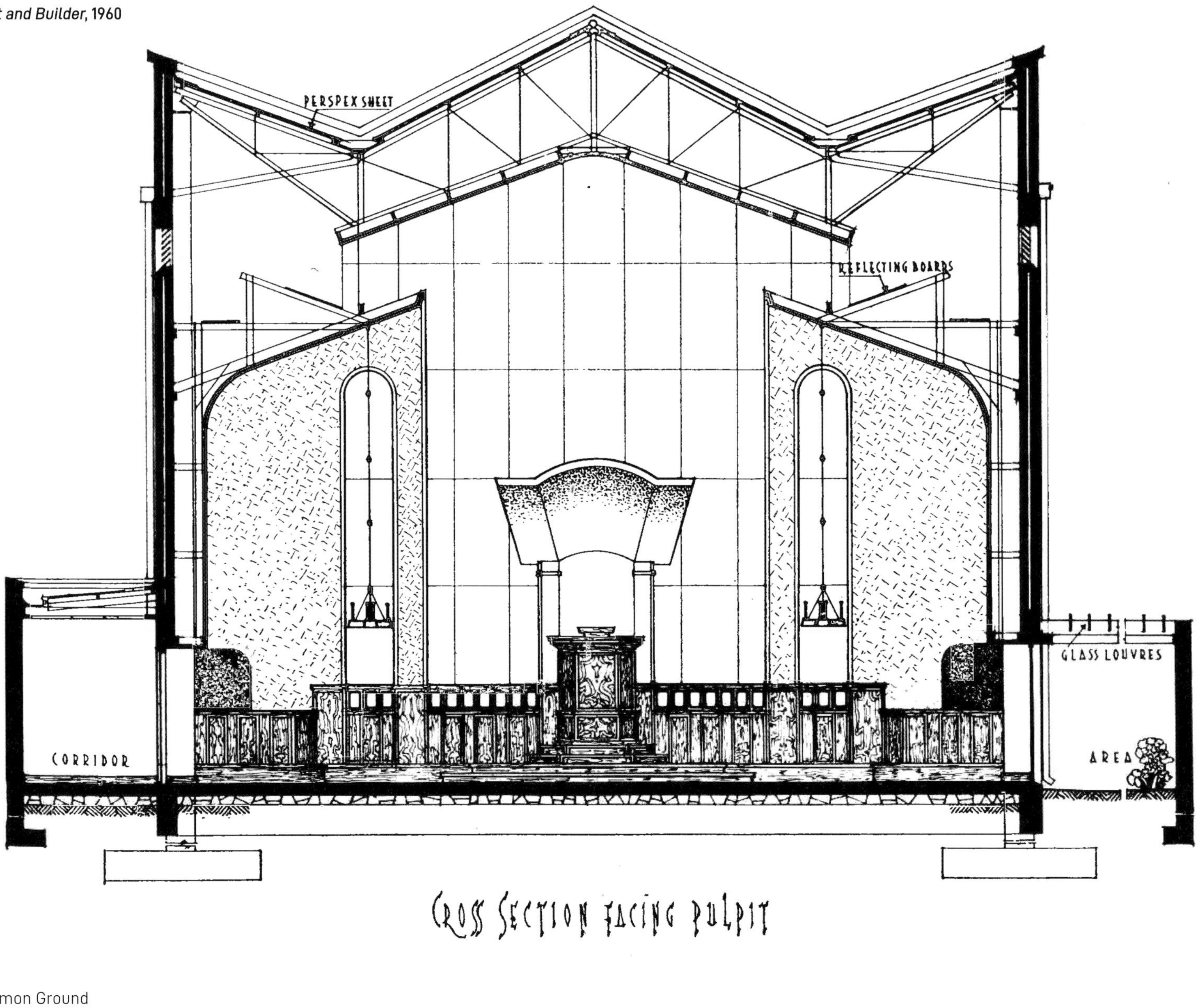

Johannesburg, Netherlands Pavilion at the Rand Easter Show, designed by Jaap van Niftrik in 1957; luminescent fibre glass facade

Efficiency and labour

The factory building was well-suited to the functionalist approach of adherents to the *Nieuwe Bouwen*. The need for productive efficiencies, large uninterrupted spaces, evenly distributed natural daylighting, and the use of new materials were all opportunities for experimentation and expression. They often resulted in expressive structural forms that seem to 'overcome the conception of gravity', as Van Loghem put it, but they also illustrate the desired modernity of new technology and materials.

A good example of structural expression using steel are the 1960 factory buildings in Epping for Cape Steel, a subsidiary of De Vries Robbé from the Netherlands, by Chapman & Spoor, with Spoor and Jongens as design architects.[33] The administration block's externalised rectangular section steel portal frames advertised the company's products, while Vierendeel girders that span twenty metres over the drawing office allowed for clerestory windows uninterrupted by diagonal bracing.[34]

Half-shell concrete roofs were especially popular among Dutch-born practitioners for their long spans as well as the opportunities they offer for daylighting. The factory for Mobbs in Port Elizabeth (1952) by Gertruida Brinkman was constructed in only seven months using a double storey reinforced concrete frame that supports long-span half-shell roofs.[35] Natural daylight is admitted through southeast-facing clerestory windows that were fitted with sand-blasted prismatic glass, which, when reflected from the white distempered curved roof forms, facilitated an 'entire lack of shadows'.[36]

Émigré architect Henk Niegeman, co-founder of Andrews & Niegeman, also made regular use of half-shell construction and D-form concrete roofs; for instance, the factory for Arderne Scott Timbers in Epping, Cape Town has both (with boarding that was covered with malthoid and aluminium paint).[37] Niegeman, a member of the avantgardist *De 8* in Amsterdam, was very familiar with the *Nieuwe Bouwen* principles and explored new materials and construction systems wherever possible, as is evident in the well-known Rex Trueform Factory and in the M Bertish

33 This company had already opened a factory in Cape Town for the Cape Steel Construction Company Ltd. in 1938 in partnership with the Bouw- en Montagebedrijf N.V. of Rotterdam and the Netherlands Bank of South Africa, De Vries Robbé-Nieuws, No. 1, Wednesday 14 December 1938: 1.

34 Some of the factory buildings are still extant on Gunners Circle, but the administration block seems to have been subsumed or replaced by a larger building, See A&B. 1966, Mar: 9–14.

35 This was a manufacturer of women's clothing and children's footwear. The building, in Cowlin Centre, Kensington, is currently being used by Fox and Swan Sweets.

36 A&B. 1952, Jun: 41.

37 A&B, 1952, Nov: 32–35.

Cape Town, Cape Steel administration block and drawing office, designed by Chapman & Spoor (with Jaap Jongens) in 1960; externally exposed steel portal frames on the complex's administration block advertising its products; photo: Charles Field, in *Architect and Builder*, 1966

Cape Town, Cape Steel administration block and drawing office, designed by Chapman & Spoor (with Jaap Jongens) in 1960; interior view with vierendeel trusses and clerestory windows; photo: Charles Field, in *Architect and Builder*, 1966

Building (now House of Monatic) in Salt River, Cape Town, and the PJ Olivier School in Grahamstown.[38] The practice designed an innovative folded concrete roof structure for the Instrument Manufacturing Company (IMC) offices and factory in Plumstead (now in use as Plumstead municipal offices).[39] The roof spans more than 24 metres and, according to consulting engineer CF Templer, it was the longest spanning concrete shell roof of its type in the world at that time (1963).[40] The roof structure was pre-stressed and vibrated in situ using pan vibrators, and there was no structural connection between the shell triplets which allowed for uninterrupted clerestory windows. In a similar fashion, the Dutch immigrant architect Jaap van Niftrik employed these structural forms for the (Total) Glen Road Service Station in Bloemfontein,[41] as did Jongens for the pump house of the Newlands Municipal Swimming Pool, whilst working at the Architectural Branch of the City Engineer's Department of Cape Town.[42]

Speaking of the advantages of folded roof structures, Templer lists these as 'low cost, long span, fire-resistant roof structures of aesthetic quality' and he argues that they allow for 'structural efficiency so necessary in these times of steadily rising building cost'.[43]

Unfortunately, the flexibility and efficiencies that the functionalist-inspired concrete roof construction systems provided in terms of productive flows, also enabled the efficient separation of the flow of people according to status, class or gender. In South Africa this was also extended to race during Apartheid, as shown in Rex Trueform, the Mobbs factory and others.[44] In addition to this, the separation of labour according to race was, and to some extent still is blatantly evident,

38 A&B, 1990, Sep: 22.
39 This building won an Institute Medal in 1963, A&B. 1990, Sep: 23.
40 A&B. 1962, July: 26.
41 SAAR. 1961, Sep-Oct: 20. This building is still extant but altered.
42 A&B. 1962, May: 14–20.
43 Templer, C.F., 1962: 26.
44 Wolff, 2017; A&B. 1952, Jun: 41.

Cape Town, factory for M. Bertish & Co. (now House of Monatic), designed by Andrews & Niegeman in 1939, with D-form concrete roof; photo 2019

where practitioners were almost exclusively of European descent. The building trades showed similar racial divisions; menial and undesirable tasks were mostly reserved for Blacks. These divisions tended to become even more pronounced during times of urgency, and the racial inequality also extended to other aspects of construction. During a strike in 1919 it became apparent that White workers were protected by unions and received payment despite striking, while Black workers fell outside of the unions and were summarily dismissed.[45]

45 Law, 2015: 118.

Port Elizabeth, Mobbs Factory (now used by Fox and Swan Sweets), designed by Siemerink & Brinkman in 1952; half-shell concrete construction; photo 2020

Cape Town, Plumstead, interior view of the former Instrument Manufacturing Company offices and factory in Plumstead (now Plumstead Municipality) designed by Andrews & Niegeman in 1962; photo 2020

Cape Town, pump house of the Newlands Public Swimming Pool, designed by Jaap Jongens in the City of Cape Town Chief Engineer's Department, 1955; photo 2015

Payment differences were similarly race-based, consolidated by the Industrial Conciliation Act (passed in April 1924) and 'justified' on the basis that higher living standards were required by White labourers than those of their Black equivalents. These agreements were politically motivated and sprang from deeply rooted racial attitudes which were the unquestioned norm.[46]

46 Law, 2015: 120; Hartdegen & Terblanche, 2007: 82.

Urgency and industrialisation

During the early part of the C20, mass-housing delivery had become an urgent priority in the Netherlands due to the massive urbanisation and growth of the population. Architects were forced to experiment with new building methods shortly after WW1, when traditional building materials were scarce. This led to various housing experiments in precasting and lightweight concrete, such as Amsterdam's 'Concrete Village'.[47] At the time, however, there was still a strong resistance to the necessary level of standardisation. Only after the huge devastation of WW2 were more Dutch decision-makers and architects, other than just the modernists, inclined to apply concrete systems for mass-housing developments consisting of upwards of a hundred units.

Experiments of this kind eventually found their way to South Africa, where housing delivery is still a national priority to this day. The Central Housing Board of the Department of Public Health in Pretoria developed standardised designs for low-cost housing. These were, regrettably,

47 'Betondorp'. Kuipers, 1987.

Amsterdam, concrete houses of the Bron System in 'Concrete Village', designed by Dick Greiner, shortly after completion in 1925

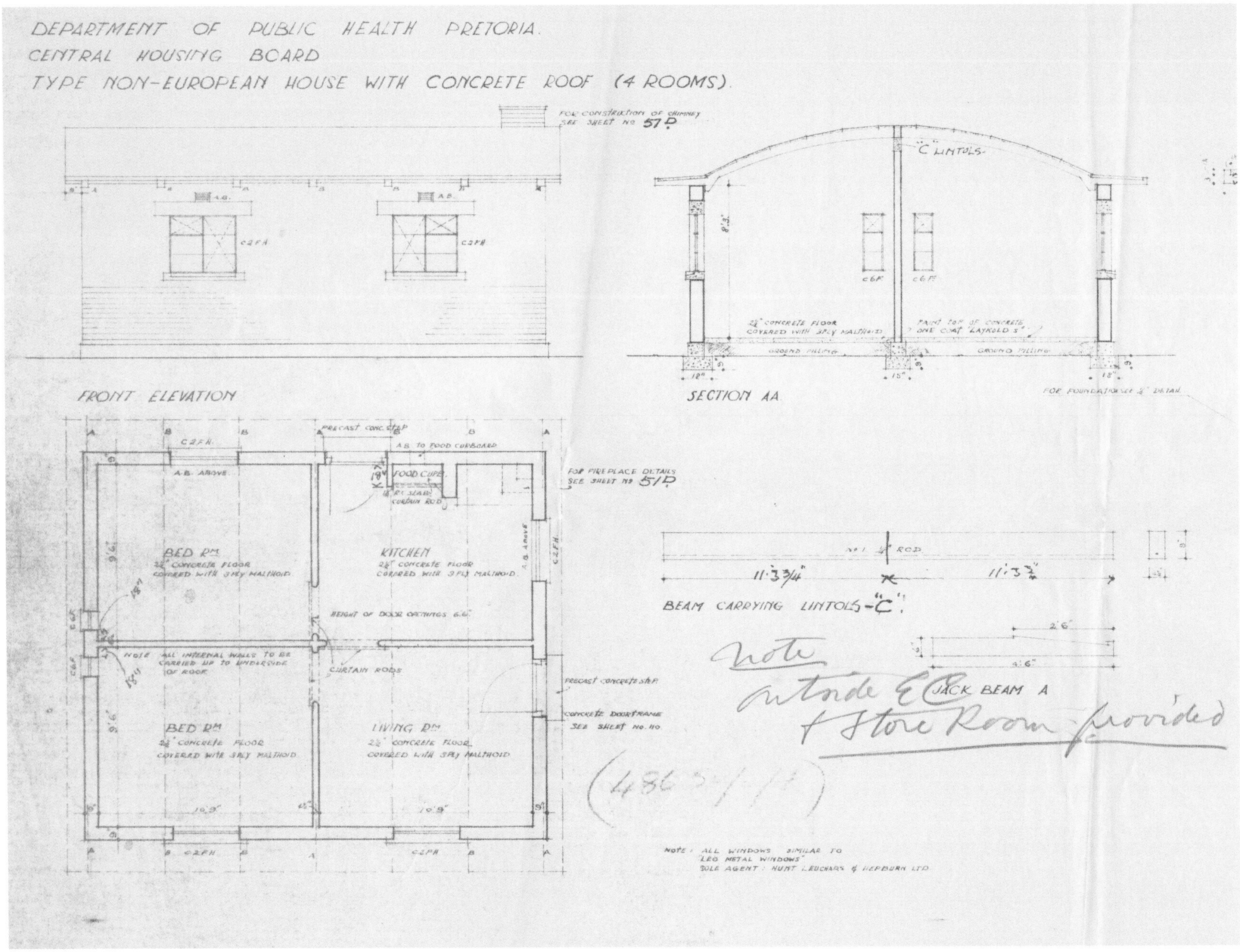

Pretoria, drawing for the 'Type non-European house with concrete roof (4 rooms)' by the Central Housing Board of the Department of Public Health, 1942

often associated with the implementation of racial segregation and forced removals to new settlements. For instance, the first houses in Atteridgeville, designed by the Dutch-born architect JJ de Jong, were built from 1939 onwards in barrel-vaulted and double-pitched formation with concrete, in an attempt to provide a roof covering with better thermal qualities than the ubiquitous corrugated metal sheet. While corrugated sheeting was used from the beginning, some houses were built with concrete roofs due to the shortage of metal during WW2. The drawings for the 'Type non-European house with concrete roof (4 rooms)' of 1942 and the 'Three room house for non-Europeans' (drawn by Pieter Dijkstra) in 1943 show house designs that make use of standard 230mm brick walls and robust roof constructions that consist of reinforced concrete beams with 38mm thick precast concrete slabs laid between them, which are all waterproofed.[48]

After the war, corrugated sheeting became the material of choice again, but at Danville, a subsidised sub-economic suburb for Whites developed by the City of Pretoria, more experiments were undertaken. Under De Jong's supervision and in collaboration with the National Housing and Planning Commission, a housing experiment was constructed which included concrete Creteweld system houses as well as *existenzminimum* dwellings designed by Dutch émigré architect Willem van Beijma in the National Building Research Institute.[49] Nine 'experimental' houses using concrete roofs were also built at Atteridgeville by the National Building Research Institute during the 1950s.

48 The drawings are in the University of Pretoria's Cleland Collections; it is uncertain if Dijkstra's designs were executed. See also chapter 8 of this book on the Model township Atteridgeville.

49 National Archives of South Africa, TAB, GEM/H5/37/2 (93).

Cape Town, lightweight concrete blocks of the Welschen system by Dura Construction used for Rottingdean Court in 1952; *Architect and Builder*, August 1953

There often was (and still is) a clear difference between the quality and specification of construction systems for housing wealthy (predominantly White) people and the provision of mass-housing for poorer (predominantly Black) people based on what Templer refers to as the 'corrugated iron on gum poles' school of design'.[50]

Innovative concrete techniques were also used for accommodation in more affluent areas, like Rottingdean Court (1952, now Crownebay) in Camps Bay, Cape Town. This apartment building was built by Dura Construction using the Welschen system, which made use of primary and tertiary beams cast in-situ combined with secondary beams and slabs that were precast on vibrating tables. Welschen system walls were either made of in-situ cast concrete, 63.5mm thick ash-concrete, or lightweight concrete blocks cast on site. The project description claims that the advantage of this construction system is that, in the main, it calls for unskilled labour, and can be economical if used on a large scale for housing projects.[51]

While speed, economy and labour were often the main considerations for using prefabrication in concrete housing, urgency was sometimes necessitated by other factors, such as expropriation of property by the state. This was the case with the wine producer Sedgwicks in Cape Town. The winery needed new premises with minimal disruption to its operations, large uninterrupted floor areas and a structure that required no maintenance. These were built in Epping to the design of Andrews & Niegeman, with future expansion in mind.[52] The administration block has four in-situ concrete frames with a sandblasted finish that support precast, prestressed concrete beams and precast floor slabs. The former winery building and the maintenance workshop have cruciform concrete columns cast in situ that support precast, pre-stressed beams and purlins; wall panels were also precast. All the precast units were designed and assembled to be reusable.[53]

Further innovations

Building on previous innovations, some Dutch-born practitioners, like Hendrik Sikkel, continued to develop shell structures and pre-casting techniques. While in partnership with JE Egan (Egan & Sikkel), he designed the first hyperbolic paraboloid concrete roof in South Africa for the new factory of the Reckitt & Colman Group in the Epping Industrial Estate.[54] Sixteen hyperbolic paraboloids were cast with a shell thickness of only 64mm. This type of construction, that was almost simultaneously applied in the filter building of a drinking water company near Rotterdam, was more economical than using D shell roofs. The forms are almost entirely in compression (which reduces the chances of cracking) and provide less of an opportunity for dripping condensation, the roof covering is simplified, and rainwater is collected at a central point. This system was widely adopted in Epping, Cape Town, where several large industrial buildings of a similar design are still extant.

50 Templer, 1962: 26.

51 A&B. 1953, Aug: 56–58.

52 These buildings, bounded by Bofors Circle, Dacres and Eliot Avenues, currently house the company CTP Cartons and Labels.

53 A&B. 1970, Mar: 14–19.

54 A&B. 1962, Oct: 10.

Cape Town, Epping Winery (now CTP Cartons and Labels), designed by Andrews & Niegeman in 1970; contrasting sandblasted in-situ frames and smooth precast prestressed beams of the administration block; aluminium louvre system; photo 2020

Sikkel & Partners, with Dutch émigré architect Barend Knuppe as supervising architect, developed a composite roof construction for the Natal Plywood and Chipboard Factory in Pietermaritzburg (c1966–67). This consisted of precast, prestressed, hyperbolic paraboloid concrete shells of 18m length and approximately 2,5 metres diameter, which could efficiently convey water and dust off the roof. The clear spans of 5 metres between them were spanned by curved galvanised Inverted Box Rib (IBR) sheets to form a series of barrel vaults. The calculations for these wind resistant shells were done by computer in Germany.[55]

55 A&B. 1967, Mar: 2; today the building is Willowood Park.

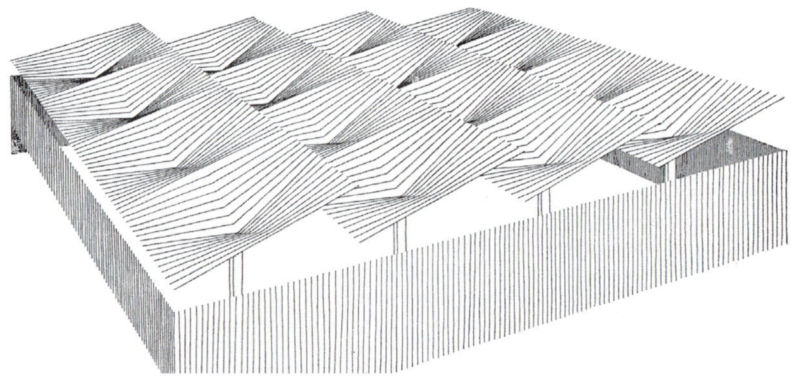

Cape Town, Reckitt and Colman Factory; diagrammatic sketch of the hyperbolic paraboloid roof; drawing by Egan & Sikkel as published in *Architect and Builder*, 1962

The client was a partnership between Plywoods and Bruynzeel, two wood factories with Dutch roots. Director Kees Bruynzeel was not averse to experimentation and he commissioned an innovative timber house for himself and his family in Welgelegen, Stellenbosch. It was entrusted to architects Bijl, Green & Todeschini in association with Munnik, Visser & Black and completed in 1962.[56] The design was conceptualised around a hyperbolic paraboloid timber roof that consisted of three layers of tongue-and-groove South African pine boards on non-structural timber joists that were only used as formwork and for fixing the yellowwood ceilings; the first floor's timber frames (which accommodate double-glazed windows) fit into plastic-lined sockets in the roof to allow it to move independently during high winds.[57]

Other Dutch practitioners who experimented with timber construction include Frans te Water (House Georgeu, Clifton), Knuppe (own house, Pietermaritzburg) and Henk Niegeman (House Thögersen, Tokai).[58]

Legacies

The successors of well-known Dutch practitioners often took over their practices and built on previously established know-how. Barney Shapiro, for instance, who worked for Andrews & Niegeman, particularly on the Tygerberg Hospital, became a hospital specialist and eventually President of the International Federation of Hospital Engineering after closing the practice in 1999.[59] The descendants of Dutch architects often followed the same career path as their ancestors, like Bryan and Bruce Brinkman (descendants of father and daughter Hendrik Siemerink and Gertruida Brinkman) who are still practicing as B4 architects in Port Elizabeth, as well as Nicoline Jongens (granddaughter of Jaap Jongens), who is an architectural designer in the Cape. Other descendants often chose slightly different but related career paths, like Adrian Jongens (father of Nicoline) who is one of the foremost acoustic specialists in Cape Town, or Michael Stekhoven (son of JZ Schuurmans Stekhoven) who is the director of one of the leading paint manufacturers in South Africa, Duram.

56 Munnik, Visser & Black oversaw the final construction stages after Bijl, Green & Todeschini dissolved in 1961 due to financial difficulties after the Sharpeville massacre; Bijl, 2012.
57 A&B. 1963, Nov: 3.
58 A&B. 1953, Dec: 56–60; A&B. 1954, May: 44–47; A&B. 1966, Feb: 14–19.
59 Personal interview with Bernard Shapiro, Tokai, 28 May 2019.

Berenplaat, interior view of the filter building of the Rotterdam drinking water factory with hyperbolic paraboloid concrete roof construction, designed by Wim Quist; photo 1965

Cape Town, Epping Factory (used by First Factory Shops), interior view of the hyperbolic paraboloid roofs as pioneered by Egan & Sikkel in South Africa; photo 2020

Building contractors like Meischke played a prominent role in the construction industry. He was the President of the Master Builders Association (MBA) South Africa from 1909-1910.[60] Builder Jan de Jong (not the architect), who immigrated in 1938 and worked with his sons, became President of the MBA Pretoria in 1971 and was responsible for several landmark buildings in Pretoria.[61] Another builder in Pretoria, Jerry Han Spaans, who arrived in 1952, built a number of embassies, houses and commercial buildings. His son Jerian Spaans owns the construction company Spaansbou CC, while his daughter Anita Spaans works as a Quantity Surveyor, both in the Southern Cape.[62] Jan van der Sluys, who immigrated to South Africa in 1948 with his family, was one of the founding members of the MBA Boland in Paarl in 1948.[63] His descendants are still involved in the construction and development industry, and their companies, Van der Sluys Projects and Van der Sluys Strukture, are associated with a number of notable projects in the Western Cape.[64] They were among the first construction companies in South Africa to implement a broad-based profit-sharing scheme for all its employees, which eventually also led to the establishment of a worker's trust.[65] The aforementioned are only exemplary and it is certainly not a definitive list.

The Dura Construction Company (which became part of Grinaker-LTA in the 1980s) was another Dutch concern whose technological expertise, particularly in concrete, has been passed on through the years.[66] Dura Piling, established in 1953, became known as Dura Soletanche Bachy in 2003. In 2007 the Vinci group in turn acquired Soletanche Bachy, and by 2009, Soletanche was combined with Freyssinet (well-known for its advanced use of concrete construction) into the Soletanche-Freyssinet holding group.[67]

Dutch brickmakers Rosema & Klaver started their company in 1941, after a preceding cooperation as contractors at Pretoria since 1936.[68] The current Rosema Group manufactures clay bricks as an affiliate of Corobrick under the name of Era Bricks.[69] The firm Scheltema, founded by Cornelius Scheltema in 1931 in Cape Town, initially importing Dutch

60 Hartdegen & Terblanche, 2007: 17.
61 De Jong, 2020.
62 Spaans, 2020.
63 Upplu Chain Network, n.d. Van der Sluys Strukture. [Online] Available: https://www.scnet.co.za/Company.aspx?SMMEID=88533; Hartdegen & Terblanche, 2007: 107.
64 In 2010, the company's name was changed into Isipani Construction, https://www.isipani.co.za/our-heritage.
65 This was done in 1993 through Interdependence and Transformation in South Africa, ITISA.
66 Aveng Grinaker-LTA., Undated. History. [Online] Available: http://www.grinaker-lta.com/about-us/history.
67 Dura Soletanche Bachy. [n.d.]. *About us*. [Online] Available: https://www.durasb.co.za/index.php?id=2&main=_main&/About%20Us/#top.
68 Ploeger, 1994: 79, 109.
69 https://www.claybrick.org.za/news/making-history-29-march-1963; http://www.rosema.co.za.

clay roofing tiles, worked on prominent projects like Groote Schuur, the President's residence, the Supreme Court and, more recently, the original Victoria and Alfred Waterfront and Cape Town International Convention Centre.[70] PG Bison, one of South Africa's largest wood-based panel manufacturers, can be traced back to the firm Bruynzeel Products and to Kees Bruynzeel, who had been director of the Bruynzeel Doors factory at Zaandam but moved to South Africa in 1956 and established the Bruply Doors company in Stellenbosch.

In architectural education, technological trajectories are strongly felt. For instance, Frans te Water lectured at the University of Cape Town (1960–70), where Jan Nauta taught Theory of Structures. Henk Kaal lectured at the University of Pretoria and worked at the then South African Bureau of Standards (SABS) before joining the National Building Research Institute (NBRI) at the Council for Scientific and Industrial Research (CSIR). However, Hans Wegelin has arguably had the most widespread influence in terms of architectural technology education in South Africa. He taught Design and Building Science at the University of Pretoria (1970–2005). His technology and detailing column in the South African Institute of Architects' official journal *Architecture SA*, known as *Argiknepe* or *Architrix* (1991–2004), was very popular. Wegelin's building information retrieval system (1987) was developed into the TOBi database, the first such system in South Africa that could be operated on a personal computer, and is still in use today.[71] His books about construction and specification are today valuable references for practitioners.[72]

70 Scheltema Roofing, *Ceilings, Partitioning: History*. [Online] Available: http://www.scheltema.co.za/about/history.

71 TOBi, *Trefwoordestelsel vir die Ontsluiting van Boukundige inligting* / Keyword System for the Retrieval of Architecture and Building Science Information.

72 Wegelin, 2009/2017; Wegelin, 1990/1992/1994/1998; see also Chapter 11.

Pietermaritzburg, Natal Plywood and Chipboard Factory; architects Sikkel & Partners; precast hyperbolic paraboloid shell being hoisted into position; photo in *Architect and Builder*, 1967

Stellenbosch, House Bruynzeel (now House 'Stormvogel'), designed by Aart Bijl and others, 1962; the hyperbolic paraboloid timber roof and one of its two concrete supports; photo 2018

Conclusion

The technological influences of Dutch-born architects, contractors, suppliers and educators are still visible today. As with most other things in South Africa, architectural technology was intertwined with the economy and politics: the exploitation of resources and labour, inequality in terms of education and the allocation of work, and an unequal distribution of technological advancements in most cases, were all a regrettable part of its development. The positives, however, are an enduring legacy of innovation, experimentation, and, often, contextual and climatic responsiveness.

Cape Town, the Foreshore with newly constructed Duncan Dock; photo c1945

Water and Concrete

The Table Bay Harbour and Cape Town Foreshore project

Roger Fisher

The largest tangible residue of shared Dutch C20 heritage in South Africa is Cape Town's Foreshore and its related Duncan Dock and Sturrock Graving Dock. These projects, commenced in 1935, included what was possibly the most ambitious land reclamation undertaken in any city in the world at that time. The harbour scheme was envisaged to better protect and provide larger moorings for the ever-increasing sized vessels that visited there. In creating the harbour there was opportunity for extending the available land to build the infrastructure required for the developing industry and commerce of Cape Town. At the time of its completion (1945), the Foreshore added just under some 200ha of land to Cape Town City, artificially created in Table Bay. Today the actual evidence of this civil engineering achievement is underfoot or submerged beneath the ocean, hence aesthetically unremarkable, but the ever-extending built fabric and busy maritime activity is much in evidence.

Over the preceding century there had been various extensions made to the Cape shoreline and schemes put forward for the enlargement of Table Bay Harbour. But by the mid 1930s there was the requisite political will to promote and finance the project. On 15 May 1935 the then Prime Minister, General JBM Hertzog, officially inaugurated the dredging operations. Within two years it was decided to go ahead with a comprehensive scheme involving the construction of a deep-water quay from the existing south arm of the Victoria Basin right across the City front to Woodstock Beach. The contract for the dredging and land reclamation, signed on 9 December 1937, was awarded to the Dutch firm, *Hollandsche Aannemings Maatschappij* (HAM).[1] In charge of the operations was the Delft trained civil engineer Constantijn van Kretschmar van Veen (son of the former director of the NZASM, Jacob Adriaan Van Kretschmar van Veen), who, prior to this, had been engaged in large harbour constructions in the Dutch East Indies (Surabaya) and at Walvis Bay (SWA, now Namibia) before settling in Cape Town from 1938 until 1946, although he had visited in 1937 to acquaint himself with the prospects of the harbour project.

War loomed in Europe, and so it was with some relief that the Dutch firm, L Smit & Co, towed out a flotilla of approximately 35 Dutch vessels, which included a rock breaker, specialised dredgers, tugs, as well as cranes from the Netherlands, to Cape Town in South Africa. These were employed in the difficult task of damming the open sea, dredging the basin, and reclaiming the foreshore.[2] In HAM's employ were 60 Dutch workers and about six times as many South Africans—black, white and 'coloured' (as they were then racially classified)—approximately in equal numbers.

Cape Town, aerial view of Table Bay Harbour extension under construction by the HAM in 1939

Cape Town, aerial view of the Foreshore extension, Table Bay Harbour with Duncan Dock and Sturrock Graving Dock in 1946

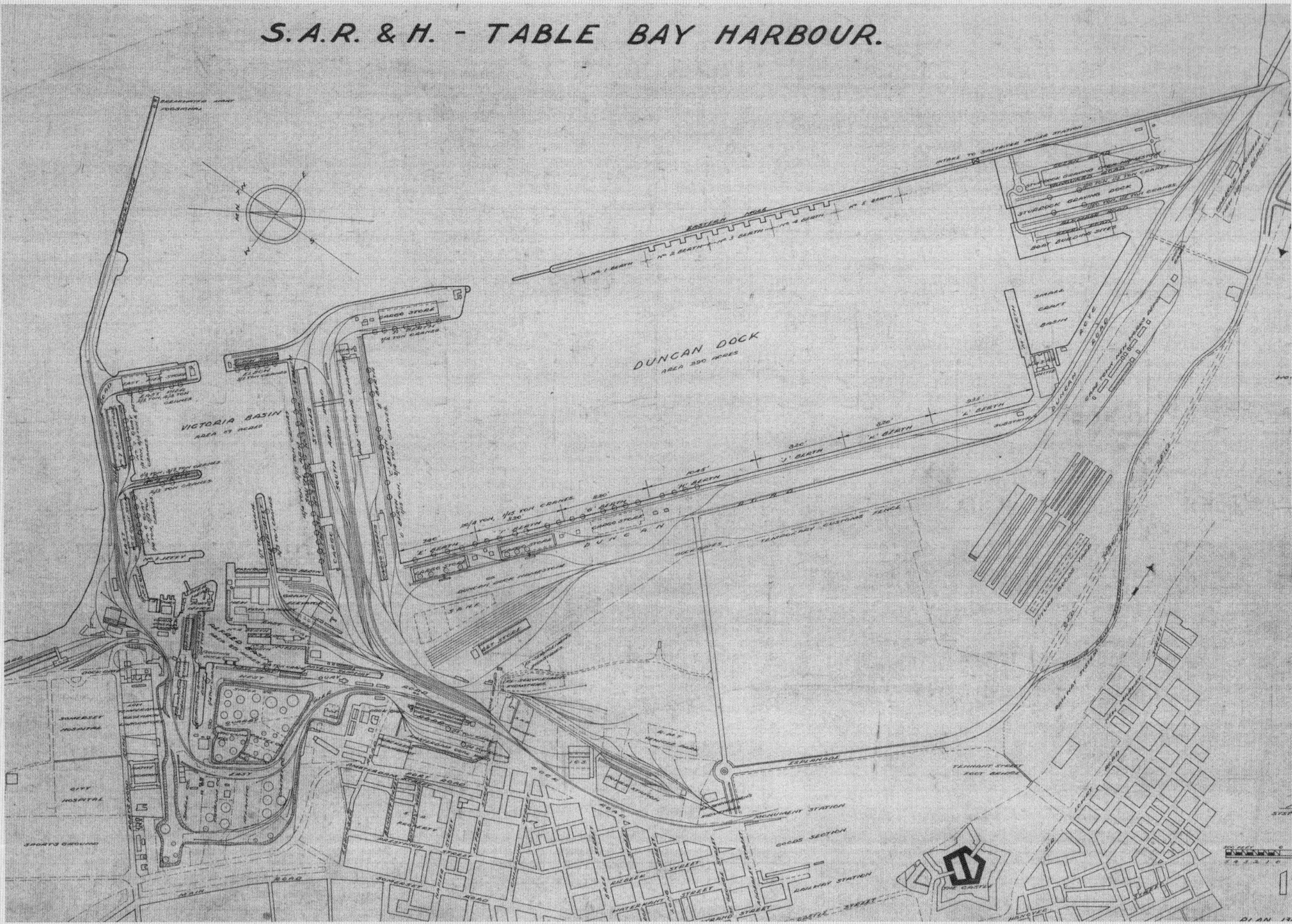

Cape Town, 1949 plan for the Foreshore with the Duncan Dock, produced by the South African Railways and Harbours

Cape Town, the Italian salvage ship 'Arpione' at work hoisting up obstacles from the bottom of Table Bay, 1937

Cape Town, historic publicity photo of a bucket dredger of the HAM operating under Dutch flag in Table Bay during the deepening of the harbour basin in the late 1930s as published in *Dredge, Drain, Reclaim*, 1955

Cape Town, bird's eye view of the Table Bay extension works under construction by the HAM; drawing by B Black, 1938–39

Robben Island, the former Murray's Harbour, originally constructed as landing place for guns to protect the radar installations located there, c1940; now port of arrival for visitors to the World Heritage Site

From time to time the dredging was hindered, or equipment damaged, by submerged shipwrecks or metal fragments, such as cannons and cannon balls, all lying on the ocean floor as jetsam from the wreckage wrought by the disastrous gales for which the Cape of Storms was named, as well as other historic maritime disasters. These needed to be found and salvaged before construction could progress.

The new basin, measuring 600 by 1800m, was merged with its forebear through the removal of the old breakwater. It was named Duncan Dock for the then Governor General. The outbreak of WW2 added a sense of urgency to the endeavour, and in that time the new basin was put into partial use. The date for contractual completion was extended to 31 July 1945, not only for logistical but also for strategic reasons. During these war years the company also built the Murray's Bay Harbour on Robben Island, a strategic endeavour for the radar station located there, at that time a top-secret military innovation.

South Africa's engagement in the war effort necessitated a dry dock for which the HAM was also contracted. The Sturrock Graving Dock

Cape Town, view from the entrance of the nearly completed construction of the Sturrock Graving Dock in Table Bay Harbour, c1940

Cape Town, aerial view of the Sturrock Dock in Table Bay Harbour with the frigate Good Hope entering, at its opening on 18 September, 1945

Cape Town, aerial view of the new foreshore and railway station in 1966

Cape Town, view of a rock breaker in action for the extension of the Table Bay Harbour, as published in the Dutch journal *Tijdschrift voor Economische Geografie*, 1940

(1940), named for the then Minister of Railways and Harbours, required enormous volumes of concrete for its construction. The HAM mastery of concrete technology had been greatly advanced by the associated Dutch civil engineers, who had already constructed large dry docks at the harbours of Amsterdam and Rotterdam and, at that time, enlarged the Noordzeekanaal locks in the Netherlands for providing access to ocean-going steamers.

Landward of the new basin, an area of 194ha was reclaimed for industrial and commercial development. The material for this massive landfill operation comprised, for the main part, sand, mud, and broken rock dredged from the newly excavated basin and pumped to the shore. In addition, the scheme entailed the depositing of clean and selected building rubble from around Cape Town, as well as municipal waste. The foreshore area of Cape Town was, however, still submerged until the 1940s, its laying dry for purposes of construction following in stages thereafter.

While the addition of a vast tract of land and a new world-class harbour offered opportunity, there was at the time of its commissioning no clarity nor consensus as to an over-arching vision for incorporating the newly created dockland precinct into the cityscape of Cape Town. As most arrivals to the country were then still by sea and, in particular, through Cape Town as the port of entry to South Africa, a grand Gateway to Africa was envisaged, and foundations even provided, but the project was never completed.

The complexities of government and municipal liaison created their own logistical confusions in the planning for the realisation of such a vast project. But they all reached agreement in the national effort to celebrate the tercentenary of the landing of Jan van Riebeeck as the Van Riebeeck Festival of 1952 (today seen as symbolically legitimising the then white colonial hegemony).[3] The first facilities to be built were the SA Railways and Harbours warehouses which initially served as the Festival exhibition venue. After the Festival they were turned to their intended purpose. The first buildings to be erected thereafter were the Culemborg Railways complex, named after the Dutch town of Van Riebeeck's birth, of which a recreated market street had formed part of the Festival exhibit.

Cape Town, the 'Gateway to Africa', designed for the head of Heerengracht Street in the harbour precinct; perspective of the 'Q-scheme' by the Chief Housing Architect's Branch of the City of Cape Town, 1941 (project not executed)

Today, the Foreshore houses amongst other notable civic and civil facilities, the Civic Centre, the Artscape Theatre, the Cape Town International Convention Centre and a range of hotels and office buildings. The upgrading of the Waterfront and Foreshore into a vast industrial, commercial, residential and shipping frontage is still being developed. It has dramatically changed the character of the City harbour precinct, obliterated many historical landmarks and features, and transformed the relationship that the early Dutch colony of the Kaap de Goede Hoop–with its *Casteel* and *grachte*–once had with the sea, yet it has created the character of the City of Cape Town as we know it today.

1 The South African subsidiary was named the Hollandse Aanneming Maatskappy.
2 Van Maanen, 1940: 216, 219.
3 See also the interlude on Commemoration and Celebration.

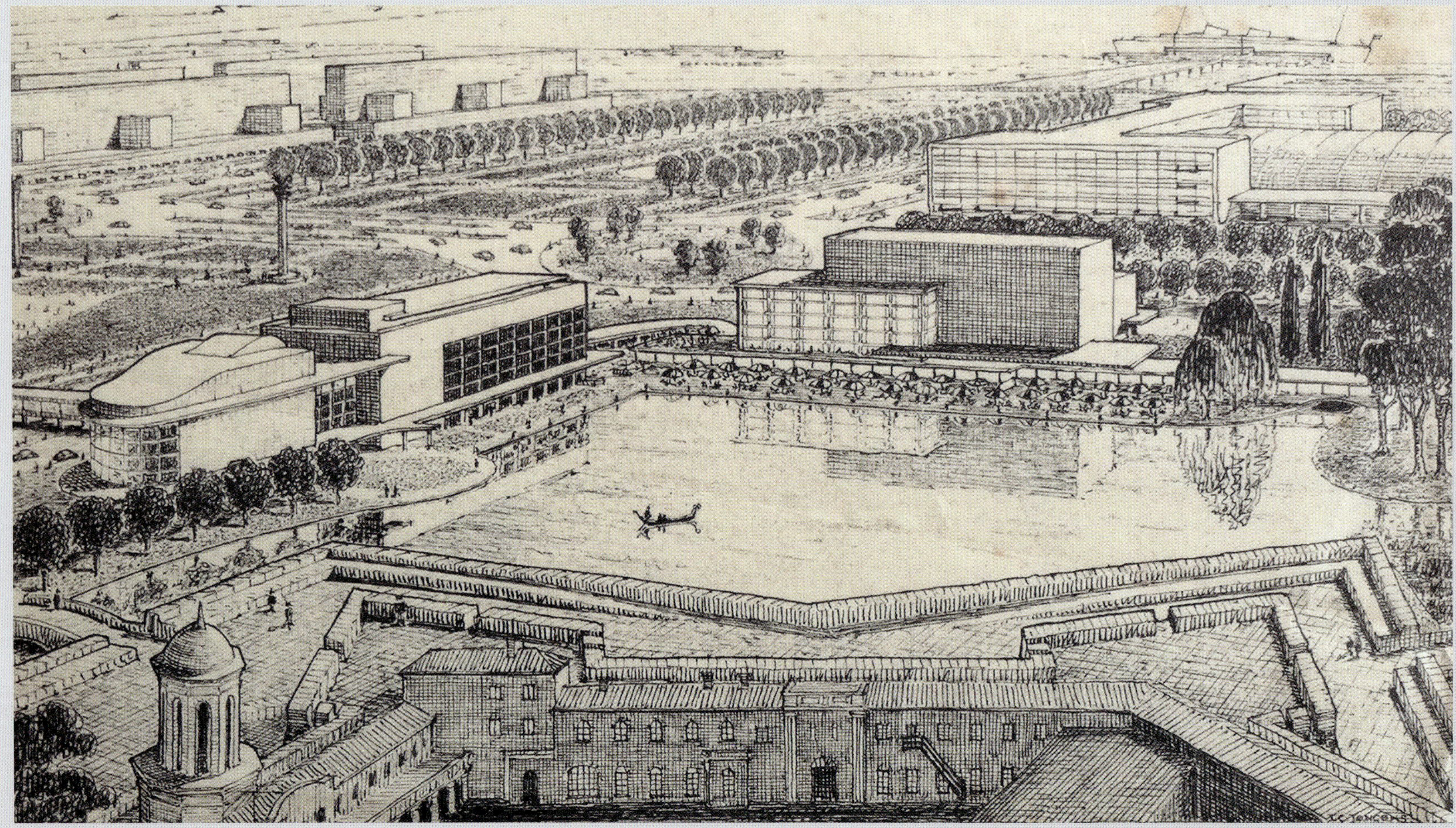

Cape Town, design for a civic centre to be built on the Foreshore, as drawn by the Dutch-born City Hall architect, Jaap Jongens, in the 1940s (not executed)

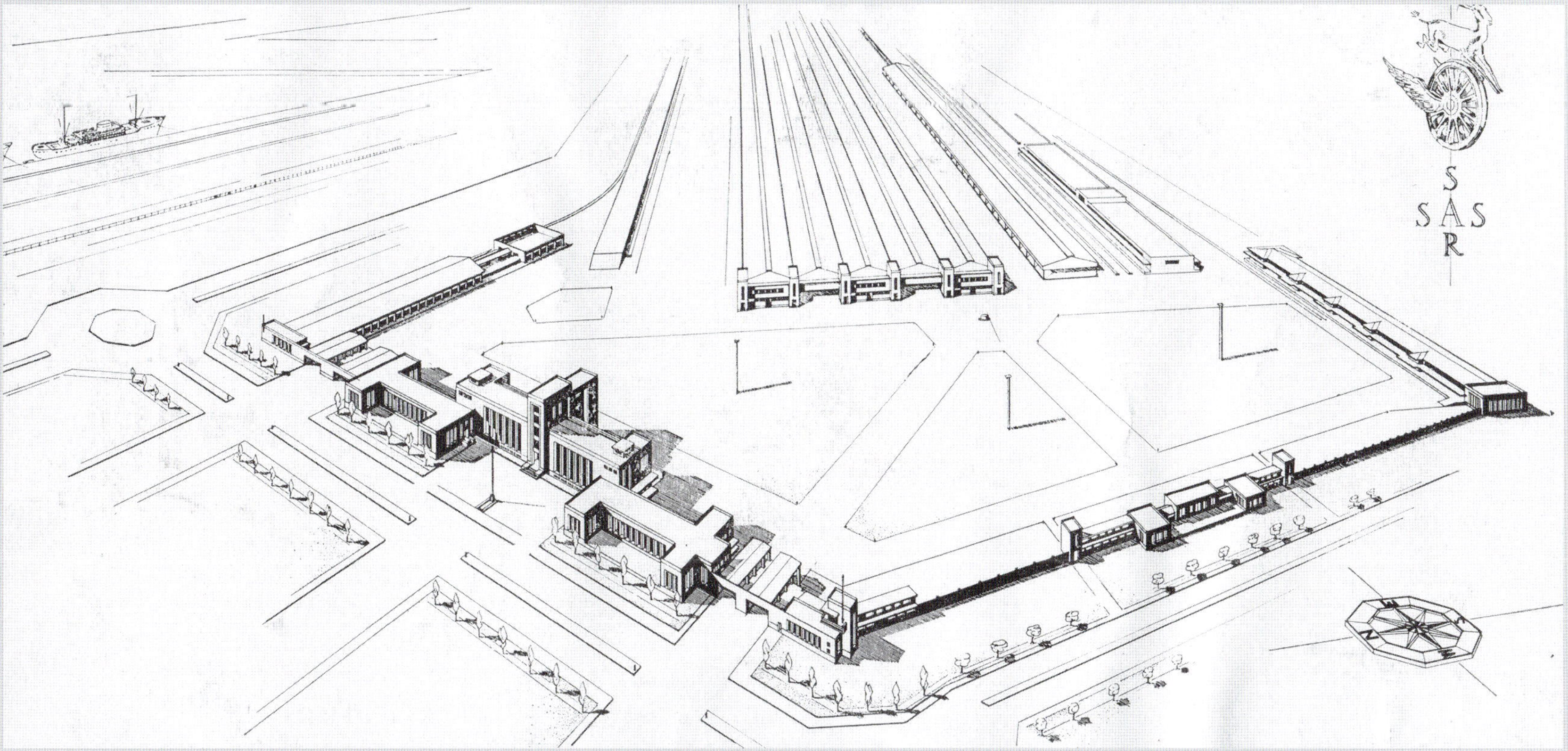

Cape Town, bird's eye overview of the planned 'Culemborg' railways precinct for the Foreshore, drawn by B Mansergh, as published in the journal *Architect and Builder*, 1953

Cape Town, view over the Foreshore and Harbour today

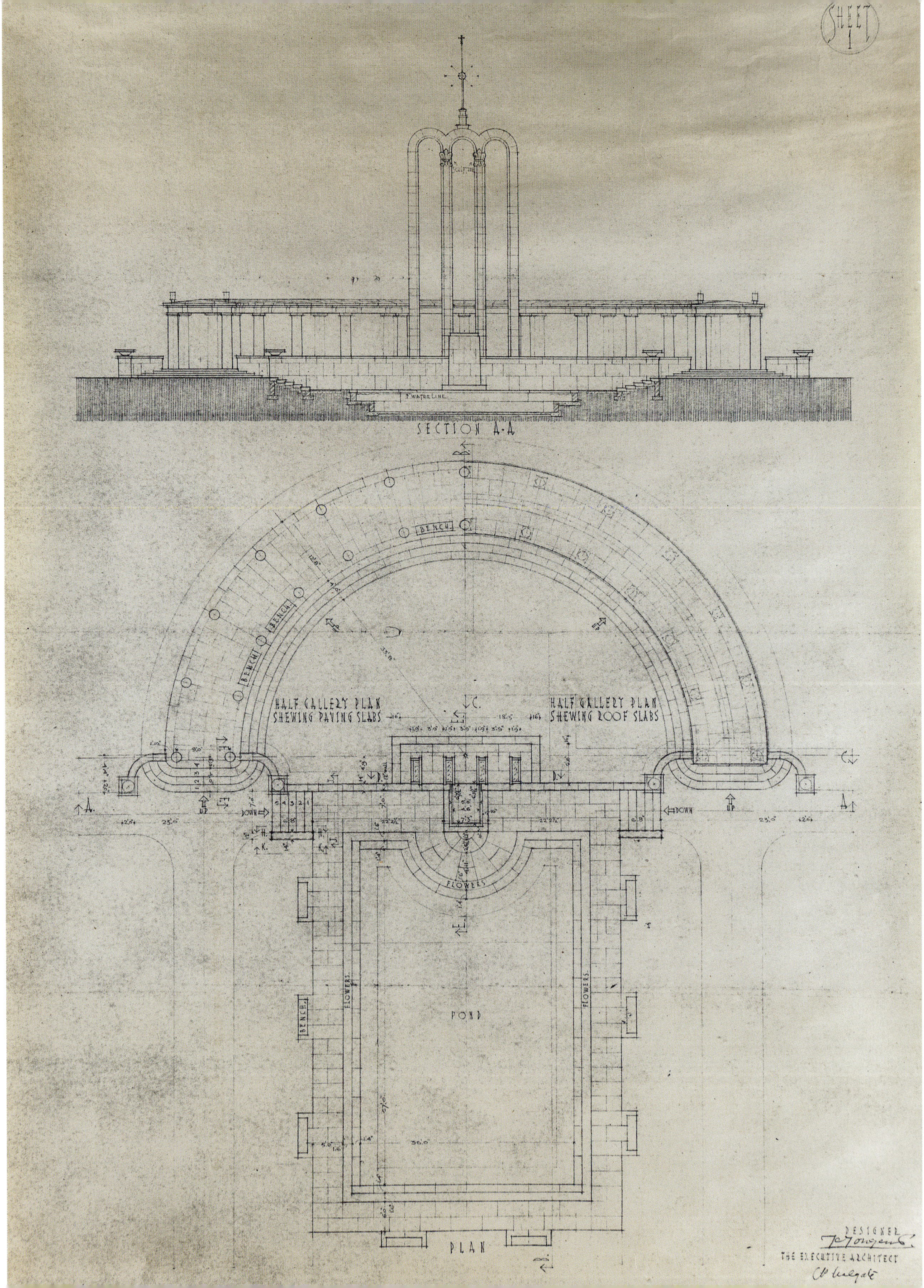

Franschhoek, Huguenot Monument, working drawing by Jaap Jongens, December 1940

10 The 'Tectonic' Archives

Shared heritage in architectural collections

Johan Swart

Introduction

The architectural history of South Africa is associated with an incredible diversity of cultural interactions and a varying stream of international exchanges. This has, over time, shaped the local production of architecture and the character of our spatial environments. A unique case study in this regard is the shared history of C20 developments where the agency of Dutch immigrants and the impact of intercontinental relationships played out within the South African context. These are narrowly related to the rise of the Machine Age, new technologies and new forms of architectural expression that emphasise the tectonic qualities of materials and surfaces. This chapter is an introduction to the resultant 'paper' legacies found in archival collections and will discuss the archive as a significant component of shared architectural heritage.

Buildings, archives and shared histories

Within the realm of architectural history, buildings and archives can be seen as two sides of the same coin. On the one hand, there are the constructed objects, buildings and urban spaces that shaped our physical environment, on the other hand the documents that directed their development, recorded aspects of their existence or retain evidence of their cultural context. The archive can be defined as a collection of documents, as the space where these documents are preserved or as a concept that describes continuously evolving networks of evidence as well as their academic interpretations. Architectural historians often utilise the archive for the interpretation of spatial environments and the description of buildings as historical artefacts. The archive itself is presented here as a domain for scholarly research and the archival items as historical artefacts in their own right.

The types of archival records are numerous and the collections within which they are grouped vary from small sets of biographical records to organised collections of practice drawings or thematically grouped sets of cultural historical documents. Drawings, specifications and correspondence give us insights into the practice of architecture, while sketchbooks, diaries and artworks can reveal the chronology, character and design thinking of the architect. Letters, certificates and scrapbooks talk about social histories, while photographs, reports and catalogues provide descriptions of historical episodes and available materials. Each item from the archive and each of the collections of which they form a part have a unique story to tell. They offer evidence that might aid our understanding of the history of the architectural profession and the associated personalities of the built environment. These items are also tangible artefacts with material reality, created through labour and utilised physically within the communication of architectural practice.

The concept of shared heritage, as evidence of the ties between nations and cultures like South Africa and the Netherlands which are based on a mutual past, is a helpful lens through which we can view the interconnected inheritance that surrounds us.[1] This can be applied equally to a variety of focus areas, such as spatial design, museum collections or cultural practices. Archives are especially important places of shared heritage, containing physical artefacts of shared provenance as well as information with the potential for illuminating other forms of shared heritage. Consider, for example, the story of global exchange told by records of the Dutch East India Company that can be found in archives as far afield as Amsterdam, Cape Town and Colombo.[2]

Histories of colonialism, globalisation and collaboration that relate to the notion of shared heritage have long been the subject of investigation for architectural historians. Hybridity and cultural exchange are embedded and evidenced in the drawings and other records safeguarded within architectural archives. Consider for example the drawings of Le Corbusier for the development of Chandigarh, now held at the Canadian Centre for Architecture (CCA), or the drawings by renowned British architect Sir Edwin Lutyens of the Johannesburg Art Gallery now held at the University of the Witwatersrand (WITS). These intercontinental linkages can be found in collections across a global network of architectural archives, museums and institutions.

Themes of shared heritage in South African architecture have often been explored in local scholarship, and records of this shared heritage are to be found in local archives. Examples related to Dutch influences include the historic legacy of Cape Dutch architecture, reflected in the archives of Geoffrey Eastcott Pearse, who created measured drawings of these buildings for his seminal publication *Eighteenth Century Architecture in*

1 See also discussion in Chapter 1.

2 The Archives of the Dutch East India Company are listed on the UNESCO Memory of the World Register. See https://en.unesco.org/programme/mow.

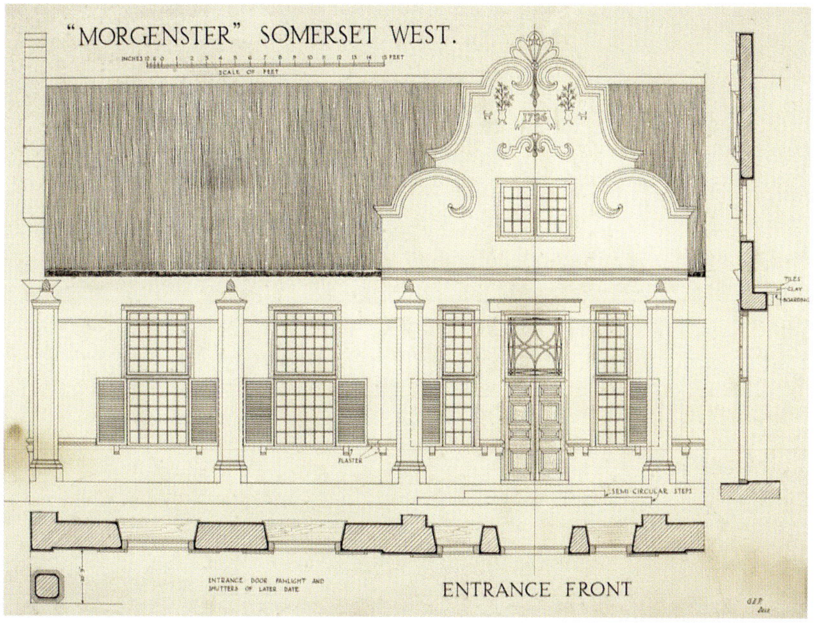

Somerset West, Cape Dutch house 'Morgenster', undated measuring drawing by Geoffrey Eastcott Pearse

Johannesburg, Post and Telegraph Office designed by Sytze Wierda, 1895, blueprint of the main façade

Frontispiece design of a memorial book on the occasion of the festive opening of the Delagoa Bay Railroad by Hendrik Berlage, 1895, photographed in 2018

South Africa.[3] Then there is the late C19 legacy of Dutch architects in the Zuid Afrikaansche Republiek (ZAR), reflected in drawings held at various local archives and recently researched for the Eclectic ZA Wilhelmiens project.[4] A drawing from the National Archives of South Africa shows a design by Sytze Wopkes Wierda for the Johannesburg Post Office (1897). Archives in the Netherlands also house items relating to the exchanges of this era. One such example from the collections of Het Nieuwe Instituut (HNI) at Rotterdam relates to the history of the Nederlandsche Zuid-Afrikaansche Spoorweg-Maatschappij (NZASM).[5] The well-known Dutch architect Hendrik Berlage produced page layout drawings for a memorial book that was published in 1895, on the occasion of the opening of the NZASM Delagoa Bay railway line.

The Tectonic archives

The current project, initiated under the heading Tectonic ZA Wilhelmiens, builds on previous shared heritage research, including *Eclectic ZA Wilhelmiens* and *Footsteps along the Tracks*.[6] This research is primarily directed at identifying and recording the legacy of Dutch architects and organisations in the South African context from 1902–61. Of the more than 70 architects identified for the project thus far, many are unknown to the architectural fraternity, very little has been published on their work and not one of the immigrant architects within this group has a monograph, survey, exhibition or academic study dedicated to their oeuvre. Yet the archival research and fieldwork has discovered among these architects a diversity of buildings that are of general cultural significance, often of exceptional architectural quality and, as the related fieldwork shows, mostly still in ongoing service of society.

3 Pearse, 1957.

4 Bakker et al., 2014.

5 Previously known as the Nederlands Architectuurinstituut (NAi).

6 Bakker et al., 2014; Clarke & Fisher, 2016; these and related South African-Dutch shared heritage projects are in the Department of Architecture, University of Pretoria, funded by the Royal Netherlands Embassy and the Netherlands Cultural Heritage Agency.

Architectural historians conduct archival research, along with other processes of knowledge gathering, such as oral history, literature reviews and fieldwork. The role that archives play within the research process is crucial, and the field of architectural history can scarcely progress without access to archival collections. Both the identification of shared heritage, as well as its academic description, often relies heavily on archival sources as well as on the archival projects and curatorial processes that are required to sustain the archives as a critical and trustworthy knowledge resource.

Within the Tectonic ZA Wilhelmiens project, researchers and archivists have uncovered valuable and insightful records from a number of established archives, while a number of entirely new collections have also been discovered along the way.

Dispersed archival records in public archives in the Netherlands, partly available online, provide cross-border background information on the architects of interest, while drawing collections in the South African context, such as those at the Architecture Archives of the University of Pretoria (AAUP), illustrate the contributions of various architects and practices.[7] Information that provides general context can often be found in state and regional archives, while there are those that relate to the specific interests of institutions, such as that of the Netherlands Bank of South Africa, or defined geographical areas, such as that of the Johannesburg Heritage Foundation. A fragmented distribution of valuable records also resides with local authorities, property owners, architectural practices, professional associations, individual researchers, or amateur collectors, extending the archival project beyond the boundaries of formally recognised archives.

From a research perspective, this vast archival landscape enables the interrogation of specific themes, the narration of historical trajectories and the construction of biographies, critiques and surveys. The archives are not static entities. They evolve in synergy with and in response to

7 Barker et al., 2016.

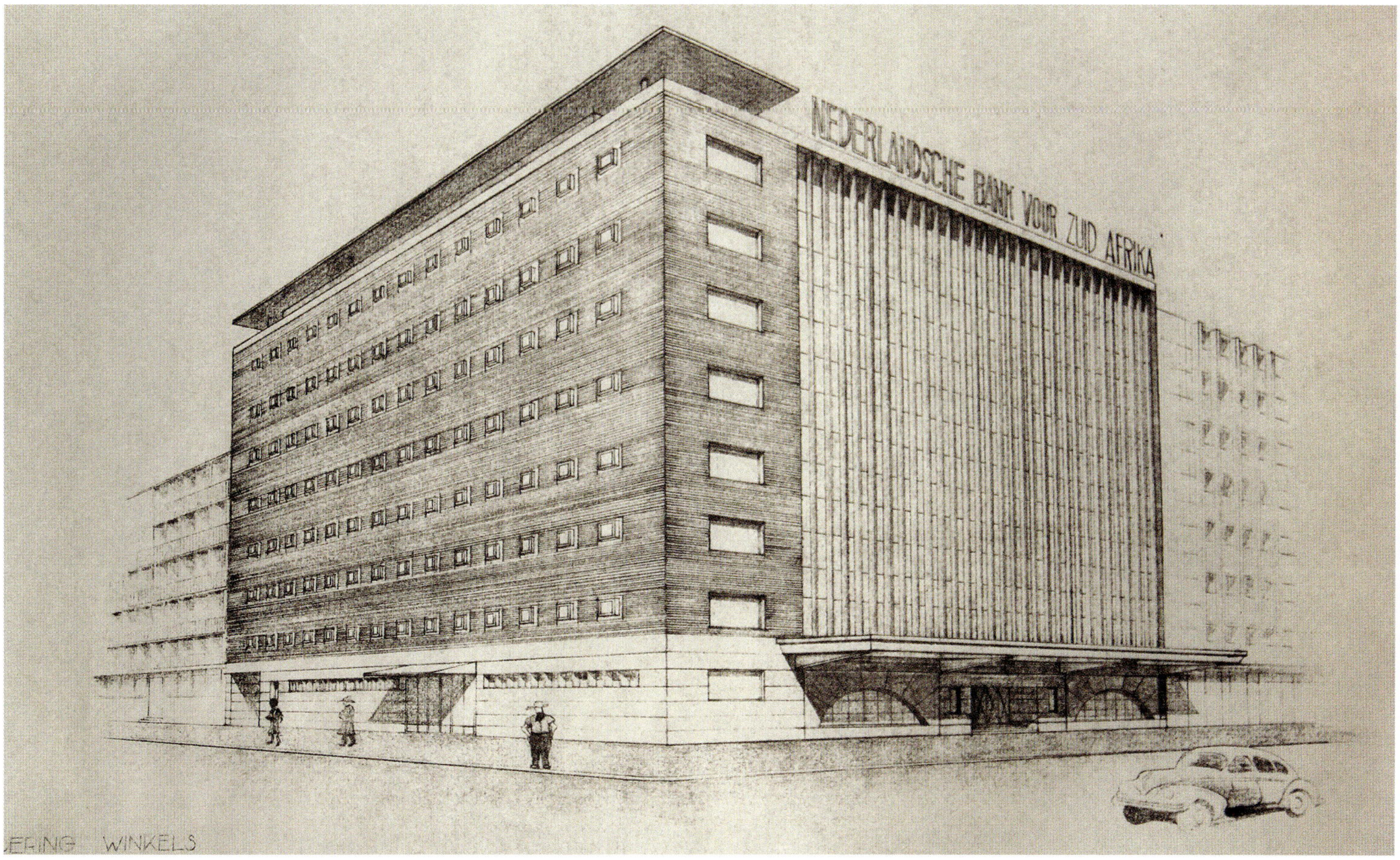

Pretoria, Netherlands Bank Building, perspective of a design proposal with shops by JJP Oud, 1946

Pretoria, Netherlands Bank Building, perspective drawing by Att Meiring research activities. Collaborative efforts between researchers and curators lead to implementing measures for the additional cataloguing and safeguarding of existing collections while engagement with the owners of newly discovered material can lead to the recording of metadata and the transfer of material from private hands to publicly accessible collections.[8] The existing collection of John van de Werke, for example, has been augmented with new material discovered by the Tectonic ZA Wilhelmiens researchers. New collections have also been made available for the first time, with the families of architects such as Damstra, Jongens, Van Niftrik and Payens, sharing collections with project researchers.

Within collaborative projects, the display or circulation of archival records can facilitate verification of knowledge and the discussion of emerging themes, while carefully planned research can aid in the creation of new information platforms such as online repositories and architectural databases.[9] As a whole, the networks of information within the realm of architectural history are often based in the archives and further developed through scholarly partnerships.

Through a series of discussions, the reader will be provided with a view of the archives from behind the scenes, showcasing drawings and other archival highlights from a variety of collections. The discussion of the following case-studies focuses on specific sets of documents that are selected and presented from a curator's perspective. Each set reveals a part of the broader historical narrative applicable to the theme of shared heritage of the Tectonic ZA Wilhelmiens project, but each set also introduces particular archival themes and insights. The archival context and content of each set is described and the lessons to be learnt from their interpretation highlighted. The majority of the sets of documents from these case studies are selected from the collections of the Architecture Archives of the University of Pretoria, along with items from related archives and newly discovered private collections.

International connections, Eaton and Oud

Two archives, one in Rotterdam and one in Pretoria, house the collections of significant Modern Movement architects in their respective countries. Common historical themes resonate between these archives across continents, but, as we will discover, they also contain drawings that relate the history of a specific shared heritage project at Pretoria, commissioned by The Netherlands Bank of South Africa.

The archive of well-known Dutch architect, JJP Oud, is preserved in the Collection of Het Nieuwe Instituut (HNI) in Rotterdam, formerly the Netherlands Architecture Institute, that also safeguards the collections of other prominent Dutch architects such as Berlage, Rietveld and Hertzberger.[10]

The archive of the South African architect, Norman Eaton, can be found in the Architecture Archives of the University of Pretoria (AAUP), an archive unit situated within an academic context and also responsible for the collections of other C20 South African architects such as Gordon McIntosh, Hellmut Stauch and John Fassler.

Oud and Eaton each played a leading role in the development of the Modern Movement in their respective countries. Their collections are main features at HNI and AAUP and represent their extensive careers and contributions through a variety of archival content including drawings, photographs, and personal papers. These collections are well known to the architectural fraternity and have enabled a range of scholars to discuss and disseminate these oeuvres through the publication of articles, dissertations, and monographs.[11]

One of Eaton's most significant and widely discussed projects was the Netherlands Bank Building, completed in Pretoria in 1953.[12] A set of drawings in the AAUP illustrates the development of Eaton's proposal and includes plans, sketches, technical details and perspective drawings. Less well known is the fact that Eaton was not the first architect commissioned to this project, as an earlier proposal had been made in the Netherlands by Oud. This evidence lies hidden at HNI where there is a limited set of drawings for the Pretoria project by Oud, dated 1946.

Although reference to Oud's involvement in this project has been briefly alluded to in earlier publications, such as an exhibition catalogue dating from 1981, the Oud drawings have not been displayed, digitised, or published until now.[13] This (re-)discovery, made during this 'Tectonic' project, allows for a critical comparison of the designs of both Eaton and Oud, thereby uncovering new aspects of the bank's inter-continental architectural patronage.

The two sets of drawings reflect the institutional narrative of the project, with the commission being handed over from Oud to Eaton in line with the Netherlands Bank's then strategy of localising their South African endeavour. The perspective drawings by Oud and Eaton show similarities in the treatment of architectural elements (for example plinth, brickwork, fenestration & roof canopies) and can be related to characteristics in the oeuvres of both architects. However, as we will see in the next section, unique aspects of Eaton's design emerge in his development of detailed components, invariably inspired by Eaton's interest in African motifs.

Archival evidence of African motifs

Apart from the drawings related to the Pretoria Netherlands Bank Building, the Eaton Collection at AAUP also contains general notes, sketches, diaries and travel records of this Pretoria born architect. This enables us to delve into the sources of inspiration that might have informed Eaton's designs. The noted 'African quality' of Eaton's work, and in particular his remarkably detailed design for the Netherlands Bank Building, can be traced back to sketches in his diaries.[14]

8 The Van de Werke Collection at AAUP was processed as part of the Tectonic ZA Wilhelmiens project. Drawings were unfolded and repackaged according to international best practice.

9 Archival discoveries were shared within the international project team using cloud data servers and presented to the public through exhibitions and lectures. New entries are being added to academic repositories such as UPSpace as well as online databases such as Artefacts.co.za and SAHRIS.

10 Bouman et al., 2012.

11 Examples include Pienaar, 2013 and Taverne et al., 2001.

12 Harrop-Allin, 1975: 90.

13 Oud et al., 1981.

14 Harrop-Allin, 1975: 96; Pienaar, 2018: 41.

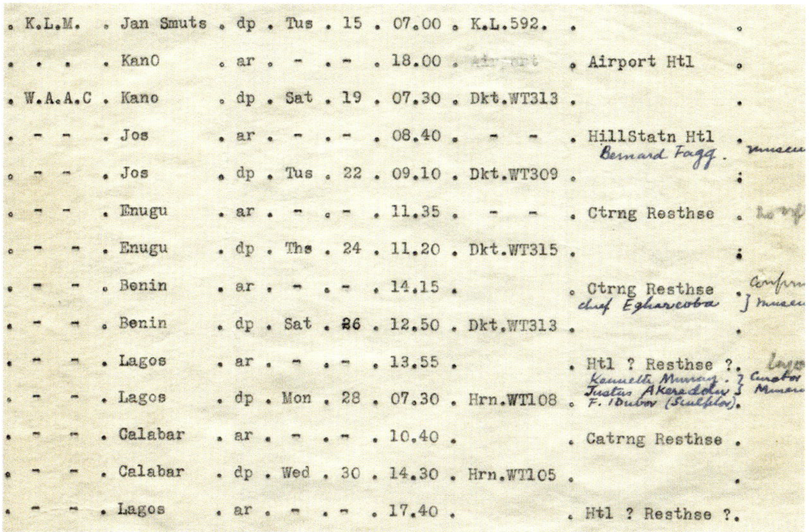

K.L.M.	Jan Smuts	dp	Tus	15	07.00	K.L.592.	
. . .	KanO	ar	-	-	18.00		Airport Htl
W.A.A.C	Kano	dp	Sat	19	07.30	Dkt.WT313	
- -	Jos	ar	-	-	08.40	- -	HillStatn Htl Bernard Fagg.
- -	Jos	dp	Tus	22	09.10	Dkt.WT309	
- -	Enugu	ar	-	-	11.35	- -	Ctrng Resthse
- -	Enugu	dp	Ths	24	11.20	Dkt.WT315	
- -	Benin	ar	-	-	14.15		Ctrng Resthse
- -	Benin	dp	Sat	26	12.50	Dkt.WT313	
- -	Lagos	ar	-	-	13.55		Htl ? Resthse ?
- -	Lagos	dp	Mon	28	07.30	Hrn.WT108	
- -	Calabar	ar	-	-	10.40		Catrng Resthse
- -	Calabar	dp	Wed	30	14.30	Hrn.WT105	
- -	Lagos	ar	-	-	17.40		Htl ? Resthse ?

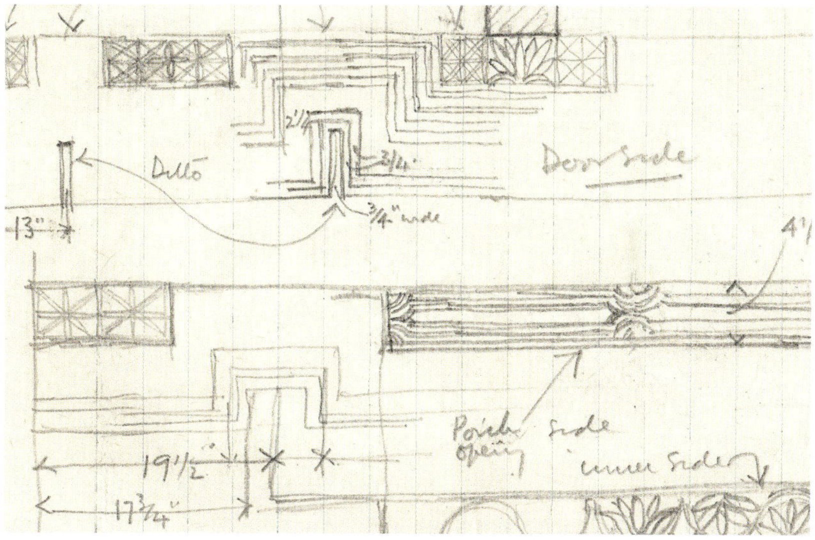

(top left and right) Pretoria, Netherlands Bank Building, main entrance, detail drawings, 1953; (bottom left) notes from a travel itinerary, 1955; (bottom right) detail sketches from the East Africa travel diary, 1950; all by Norman Eaton

Travel diaries contain sketches that record Eaton's interest in architectural details such as reed screens, seen in Uganda in 1943, or relief work from a 1950 visit to East-Africa. The translation of these observations into design details for the Netherlands Bank Building can be seen in the relief details on the custom designed seating and the fluted patterns of ceramic tile wall cladding.

Eaton produced custom drawings for a variety of elements and ornamentation. Of special interest is the placement of African inspired motifs, which introduces continental references from beyond the borders of South Africa into the discussions on shared heritage. Eaton's personal quest for an architecture sympathetic with its African context aligns with the efforts at that time of the Bank to establish a stronger South African identity.

An illustrative example is the design of the bank's main street entrance, which shows the introduction of Benin inspired figures as door handles. Eaton's broader interest in African culture and his search for African inspiration and motifs is well illustrated through his travel history, and specific places of interest, such as Benin, are recorded in a travel itinerary of 1955, along with other West-African places such as Kano, Calabar and Lagos.

The designs also include the juxtaposition of European references related to the corporate identity of the bank with the African motifs suggested by Eaton. This can be seen in drawings for the heraldic bronze panels over the main entrance. The final design of the panels was influenced by the well-known artist Alexis Preller, a friend of Eaton with a similar fascination for African forms.[15] Eaton produced scale 1:1 detail drawings of the panels which illustrated motifs such as the African inspired bird and an abstracted version of the Dutch coat of arms.

Biographical collections of Damstra, Van Niftrik and Jongens

While the archive of Norman Eaton is well preserved and utilised at AAUP, a number of previously unknown archives have been discovered in the course of recent shared heritage research. The collections of relatively unknown architects of Dutch descent such as Mello Damstra, Jaap van Niftrik and Jaap Jongens have been preserved by their families. This will allow researchers to write these architects into the narrative of South African architectural history.

15 Harrop-Allin, 1975: 90.

Pretoria, Netherlands Bank Building, open bronze panels over the entrance door, drawing at full scale by Norman Eaton, 1953

The previously unknown collection of primarily personal documents and photographs related to Damstra has been generously shared with researchers by his grandson Larramie Damstra. Such biographical information gives a unique insight into the life and career of the architect. Original documents, like Damstra's birth certificate (1873, Leeuwarderadeel), evidence the officially recorded moments of his life. Other documents tell us of his emigration to South Africa as well as a sojourn to the United States of America around the time of the South African War. Additional material has been collected or copied from a network of related archives by Larramie, thus expanding the collection over time. This includes, for instance, phone registries found in the Cape Town Library, family information from the Department of Home Affairs, and photographs from the Watson-Lockley collection at Stellenbosch University.

Original photographs showcase completed projects by Damstra, including his own houses. A photograph showing the architect and his wife sitting in the garden of their Palermo House reveals a family moment from nearly a century ago. But the information in this photograph also has contemporary and practical relevance; the current owner of the Palermo House has used the photo as reference for the excavation and reconstruction of the original garden walls and fountain.

While none of Van Niftrik's practice drawings remain, the family has kept his memory alive by preserving photographs, sketchbooks and other personal papers. These have been shared with researchers by his daughter Colette. A preserved letterhead from his practice indicates that Van Niftrik received an interior design qualification in Amsterdam, gained his architectural academic credentials from the University of the Witwatersrand and set up his practice in Johannesburg.

Other items in the collection relate to episodes in the life of Van Niftrik, and interpretation of them relies on the tacit knowledge of the family, being familiar with such personal events. Colette identifies her father in a photograph taken in war-torn Europe during his time in service of the Princess Irene Brigade. A sketch from a sketchbook depicts her mother seated on a chair designed and built by Van Niftrik himself. Another photograph captures Van Niftrik sitting outside their family home, attentively working on a mosaic panel, not in view, which he made and donated to a local school.[16]

The vast collection of Jongens contains biographical items as well as dozens of practice drawings and sketches.[17] All of this has been carefully organised and catalogued by his son Adrian and daughter-in-law Sharon.

16 The mosaic panel was the emblem of either Hyde Park High School or Bryanston Primary School.

17 The Jongens Collection has since been transferred to the University of Cape Town Library Special Collections.

PROVINCIE FRIESLAND. GEMEENTE LEEUWARDEN.

BURGERLIJKE STAND.

UITTREKSEL uit een REGISTER van Geboorten der gemeente LEEUWARDEN.

No. 759.

In het jaar een duizend acht honderd drie en zeventig, den elfden November, is alhier geboren: Melle Gerardus, zoon van Douwe Damstra en zyne huisvrouw Cornelia Catharina Meeuwis, beiden alhier

Birth certificate of Melle Gerard Damstra born on 11 November 1873, extract from the Leeuwarden Birth Register dated 27 January 1892

J.J. VAN NIFTRIK M.I.A. ARCHITECT (DIPL.) RAND
ARCHITECTE d' INTÉRIEUR AMSTERDAM
Phone 835-3068
P.O. Box 444
JOHANNESBURG
Liberal House
56 Marshall Street

Letterhead from the practice of Jaap van Niftrik at Johannesburg

Cape Town, Mello Damstra and his wife Julia seated in the lower garden of House Palermo, private photo

Cape Town, House Palermo, lower garden after reconstruction to the original; photo 2019

Photograph showing Jaap van Niftrik (standing in uniform) in service of the Princess Irene Brigade in Europe during WW2

Cape Town, proposed entrance to the 'Holland section' of the 'Liberty Cavalcade', sketch by Jaap Jongens, 1943

Drawing by Jaap van Niftrik of his wife while reading, page from a personal sketch book

Historical photograph of a model of the proposed Huguenot Monument at Franschhoek by Jaap Jongens

Cape Town, poster design for a fundraising concert for the benefit of the Netherlands in distress, by Jaap Jongens, 1944

A single drawing signed by De Jong and dated 1943 was recently found in the collections of AAUP. This sparked a search for more information about this elusive character that yielded proof of his Dutch origins, as well as fragments of information found in the National Archives of South Africa indicating De Jong's association with the urban layout of Atteridgeville, Danville and Proclamation Hill (all in the City of Tshwane), as well as the design of related public infrastructure and school buildings.[18] De Jong's drawing was discovered in the John Cleland Collection at AAUP as part of a set of drawings associated with the work of the Central Housing Board (CHB). Cleland served as advisor to the CHB which operated within the Department of Public Health from 1927 to 1943 and provided advice to various city councils regarding the development of low-cost housing.[19]

De Jong's signature on the drawing, along with the heading 'City Council of Pretoria, New Native Location at Atteridgeville' places De Jong within the politics of South African urban planning in the mid C20. This brings the development of Atteridgeville as a model township in line with national housing discussions at the dawn of the apartheid era. The title of De Jong's drawing is 'Type C Detached Dwelling', which conforms to the commonly expected nomenclature of scientifically grounded housing programmes of the time. This also suggests that the design was part of a broader series of type housing under development.

Various drawings give us different perspectives on the architect's career and are illustrative of the great diversity of projects in which Jongens was engaged.

A portfolio of Jongens's student work has been preserved and the drawings show early signs of design talent. Beautifully composed competition drawings highlight his ambitions as a young practitioner in the Netherlands around 1930. Of the numerous drawings related to projects in the South African context, some illustrate an ongoing connection to his country of birth. During WW2 Jongens produced a design for the Holland's Section of the Liberty Cavalcade in Cape Town and the layout for a poster which advertised a concert in aid of a war relief fund for the Netherlands.

Another aspect of shared heritage can also be seen in his 1940 design competition entry for the Huguenot Memorial in Franschhoek, a project that commemorates the influence in the Cape Colony of protestant immigrants of mainly French descent. A photograph showing an architectural model of the memorial and a beautiful set of design drawings produced by Jongens are preserved in the collection.

Housing history and the search for JJ de Jong

Unlike architects such as the aforementioned Damstra, Van Niftrik and Jongens, no archival collections have been found related specifically to Jan de Jong, who was the City Architect of Pretoria and played a role in that city's mid-C20 urban development. Apart from his birth and early address registration in Amsterdam, very little trace of him could be found in other archives and no information was forthcoming through family or community connections.

18 The following folders at the National Archives of South Africa hold information related to projects of Jan de Jong: NTS_5498_87-313-H2H9 (Atteridgeville Housing); NTS_5649_87-313-I (Atteridgeville Schools and Churches); GEM_540_H5-37-2 (Danville) and GEM_539_H5-27-2_93 (Proclamation Hill); see also Chapter 8.
19 Le Roux, 2019: 9.

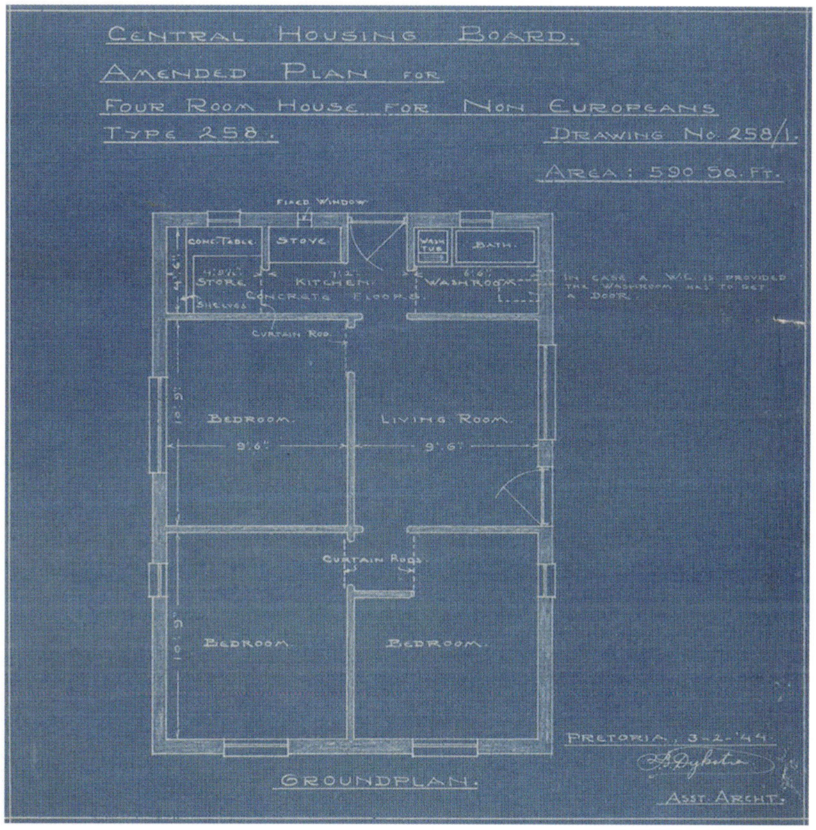

Pretoria, Drawing No. 258/1 for an amended plan for a 'four-room house for Non- Europeans, Type 288' by assistant architect Pieter Dykstra for the Central Housing Board, 3 February 1944

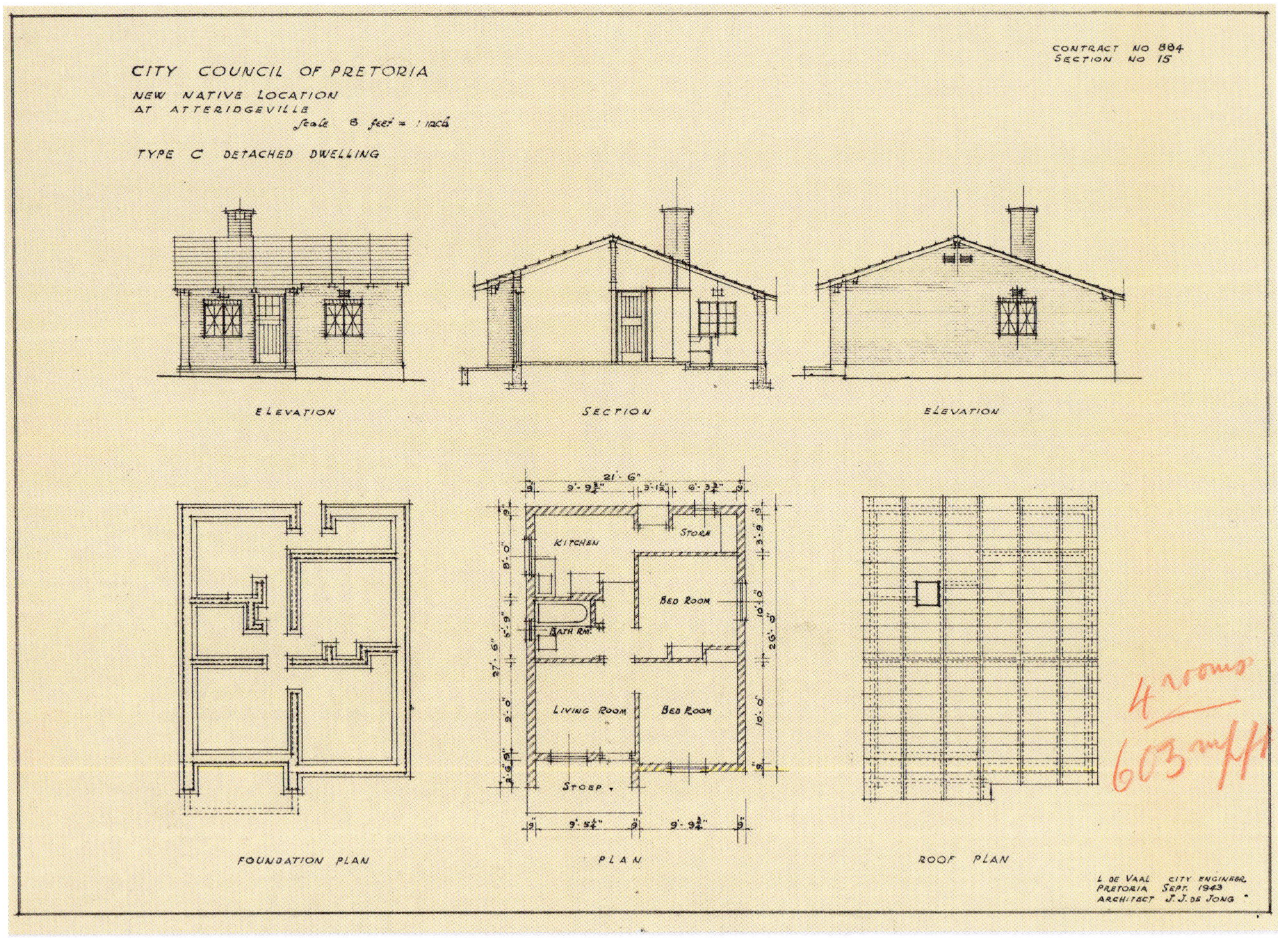

Pretoria, Type C Detached Dwelling design for the new native location Atteridgeville by City Hall architect Jan de Jong, September 1943

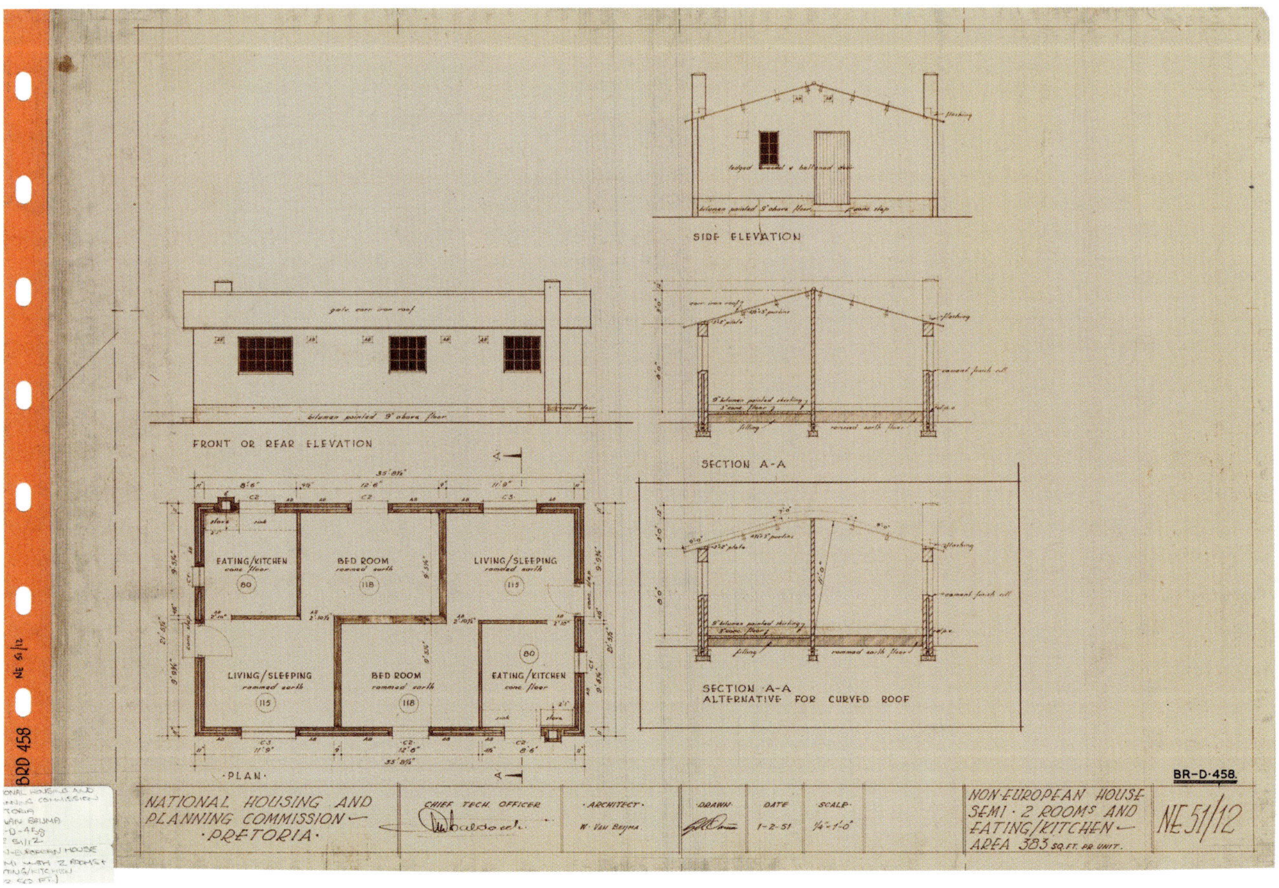

Pretoria, Design for a semi-detached 'Non-European House' with '2 Rooms and Eating/Kitchen - NE51/12' by architect Willem van Beijma for the National Planning Commission, 1 February 1951

Similar drawings by Pieter Dijkstra have been found within the CHB set in the Cleland Collection, while low-cost housing unit designs authored by the architect Willem van Beijma are kept in the archives of the Department of Architecture at the University of the Witwatersrand.[20] Van Beijma's drawing dated 1951 is titled 'NE 51/12', part of a well-known series of designs developed by the National Housing and Planning Commission.

The detailed scholarly research of the preserved archival material is of critical importance within the ongoing discourse of colonial legacies in South African urban environments. These collections can still yield new insights that range in scale from that of the history of urban planning through to the detail scale of technical specifications and layout design.

Beyond the identification of signatures on drawings, the backgrounds and contributions of practitioners of Dutch descent such as De Jong, Dykstra and Van Beijma will require further research. These architects, as well as architects of a variety of other nationalities, were employed in city councils and planning commissions during a critical period in South Africa's urban development and, as yet, their impact is not well understood.

20 See online collections on the WiredSpace platform.

Extracts from a photo album of completed houses designed by John van de Werke: (top left) house for Mrs MM de la Hunt, lounge interior; (top right) house for Mrs M de Moor; (bottom left) house for Mr HJ van den Heever; (bottom right) house for Mrs J Harrison

John van de Werke's portfolio of houses

While research projects often bring together pieces of archival information from various collections around a common theme, certain collections enable an in-depth discussion of the career of a particular architect and a comprehensive understanding of their design oeuvre. The Van de Werke Collection at AAUP contains sets of drawings from more than a hundred projects by John van de Werke, who was born and educated in Utrecht, the Netherlands. Many of the collected designs are for free-standing family houses in the eastern suburbs of Pretoria, such as Muckleneuk, Brooklyn, Waterkloof and Lynnwood, a geographical area where many other well-known South African architects also developed seminal projects.

With information such as dates, locations and clients often indicated on the drawings themselves, the collection can be seen as a database of the architect's output that allows researchers to generate timelines and map these works. With layout plans for almost all of the projects consistently available across the collection, researchers are also able to describe the work within typological or stylistic categories, amongst other possibilities. Photographs from portfolio albums within the collection illustrate the diversity of Van de Werke's work as well as the development of his work in response to the changing paradigms within which he practiced.

While the inventory of Van de Werke's collection might be utilised as a project survey, within this archive an original project list was also found indicating that there were additional projects beyond those for which indexed files and drawings are available. Researchers initiated

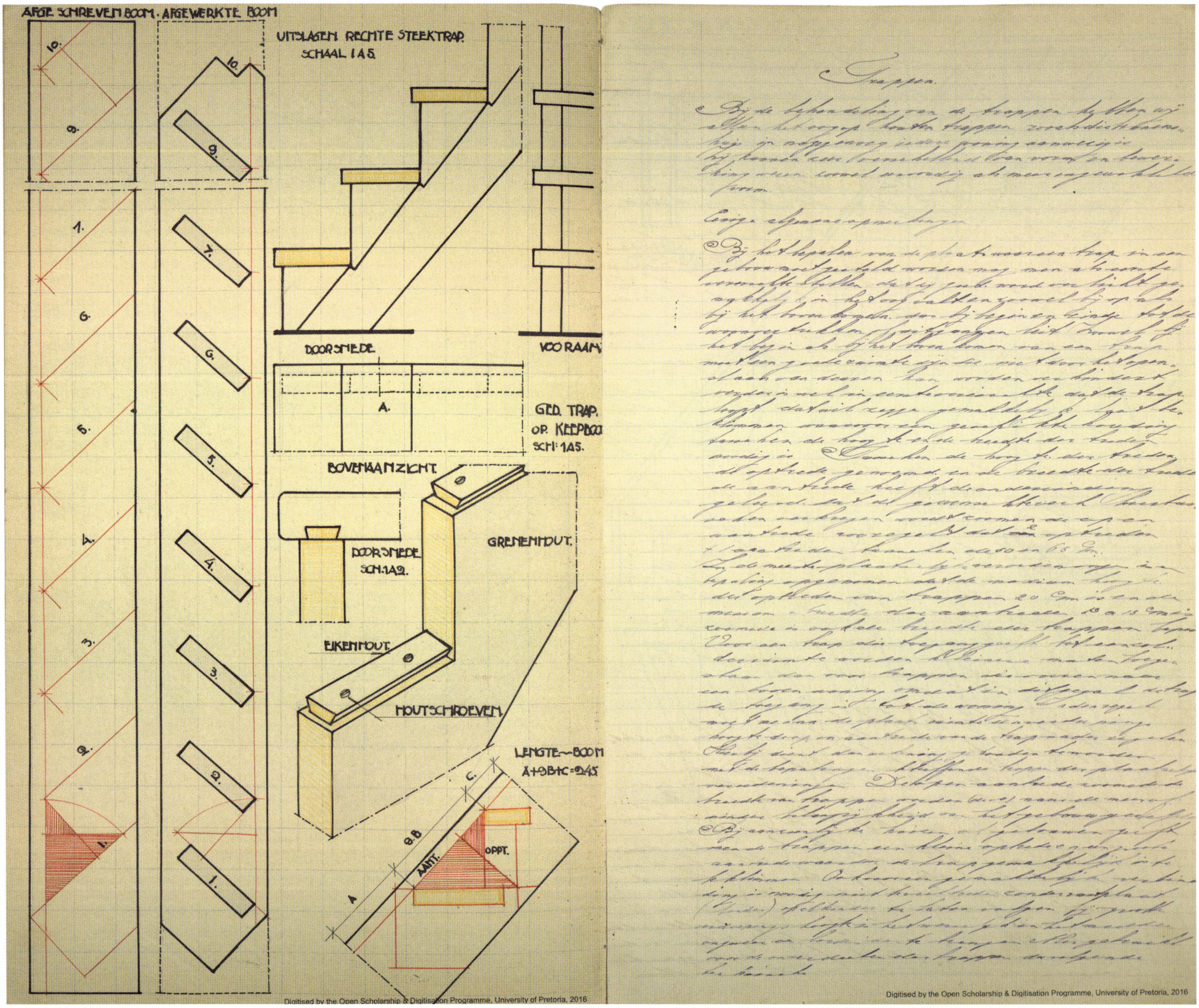

Page from John van de Werke's Utrecht MTS study cahier on construction elements, including a straight stair, 1917

Pretoria, House Harrison, original elevation drawings by John van de Werke and photo 2020

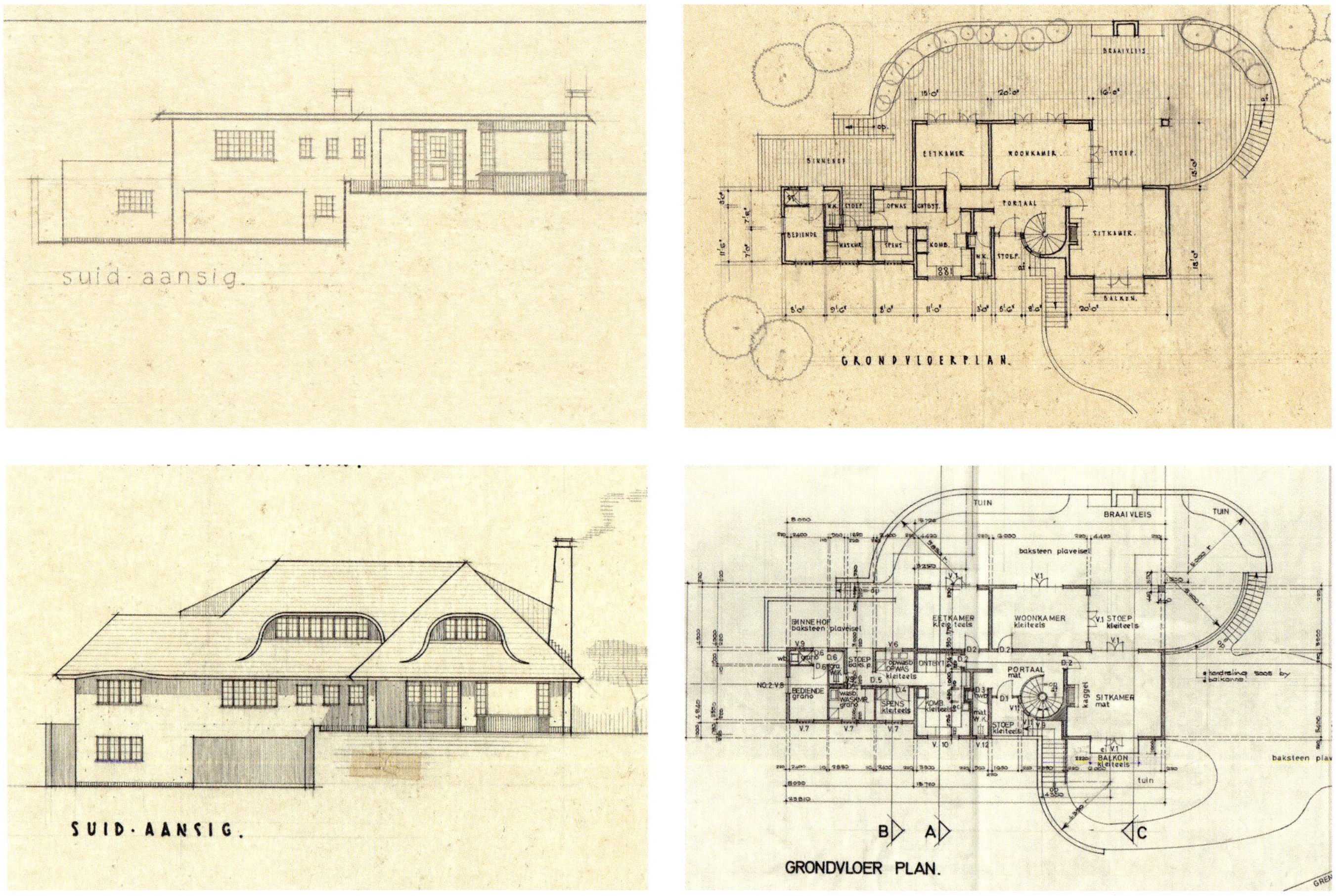

Pretoria, House Botha (top left) design proposal with flat concrete roof; (bottom left) design proposal with additional storey and high pitch roof; House Grové (top right), ground floor plan with dimensions in imperial units and (bottom right) ground floor plan with plumbing layout and dimensions in metric units; all by John van de Werke

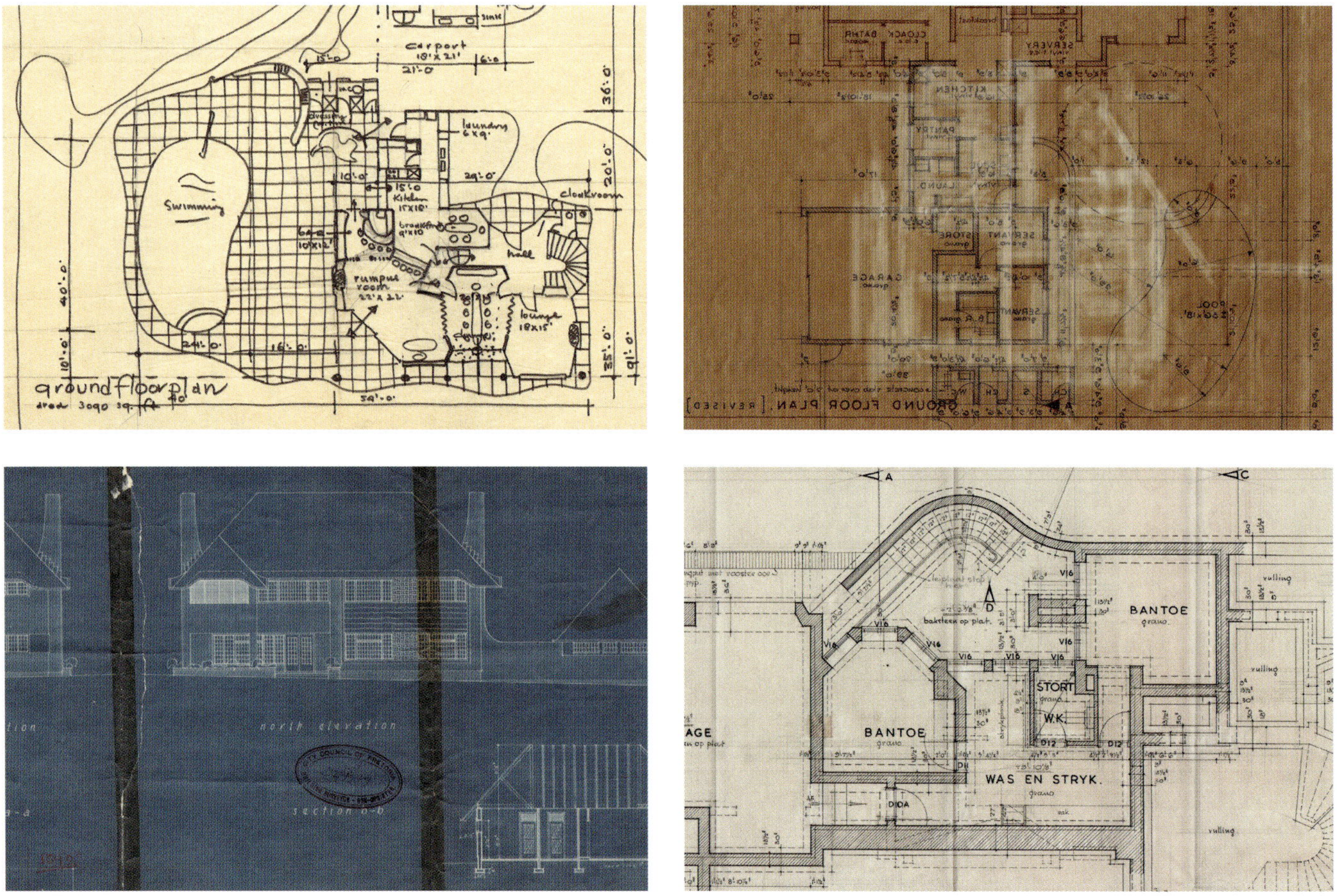

Pretoria, (top left) House Goldstein, ground floor plan; (top right) House Cohen, ground floor plan; (bottom left) House de la Hunt, north elevation; (bottom right) House Smal, basement plan; all by John van de Werke

a process of verification where the index and project list were cross-referenced, followed by fieldwork where the sites of Van de Werke's projects were located, documented in situ and information was fed back into an updated project list.[21] Additional documentation is often found in the possession of current owners or occupants of his houses and such discoveries can be added to the existing collection along with oral histories that might be recorded in the process.[22] This contributes to the evolution of the archives over time, and establishes relationships between the academic environment and the communities that reside in local neighbourhoods.

Except for House De la Hunt, little has been published or known of the work of John van de Werke, but the process of engagement with his archives now enables novel insights to emerge. Supplementing archival interpretations with fieldwork further enables us to understand both the post-occupancy experience of residents and how the buildings and neighbourhoods have changed since the original completion of projects.

Layered drawings and layers of history

From an understanding of the Van de Werke collection as a large data-set providing an overview of the architect's oeuvre, we move towards the interpretation of specific drawings sets, individual drawings or even portions of a single drawing within this rich collection for more nuanced details and interpretations.

The set of drawings for House Botha contains drawings of two elevations illustrating how Van de Werke conceived of two versions of the same design. The first version shows a lower flat-roofed house while the second version shows the same house with a steeply pitched roof containing an additional storey. Related technical drawings of House Botha show that it would have been possible for the first version to be constructed, occupied and then later extended into the proposed second version.

Drawings of House Grové illustrate typical layers of technical information produced within an architectural practice. The first drawing is a relatively simple layout plan specified in imperial units (yards, inches), while the second drawing of the same layout plan contains additional information such as plumbing specifications and flooring materials, and shows the same dimensions specified in metric units. The making of these drawings most likely coincides with the period of South Africa's switching to the metric system around 1970, where it was legislated that all dimensions be presented in metric units.

Specific markings on drawings can reveal additional details of architectural projects, and of the historical context in which they were developed. Annotations on the layout plan for House Smal indicate specific rooms in the lower level that were allocated to 'Bantoe' residents, who were likely employed as domestic helpers in the house.[23] An official stamp of the 'City Council of Pretoria' proves the successful completion of formal application and approval processes for House De la Hunt. Markings on a plan for House Cohen inform, unintentionally, how a drawing was modified to show a slightly altered layout by erasing lines and adding new lines on the same sheet of paper.

21 This process was led by Prof Arthur Barker with the assistance of the AAUP team.
22 Drawings for House Coetzee were collected from the original owner.
23 Bantoe (Afrikaans) or Bantu (English) is a linguistic term that was commonly used in the apartheid era to refer broadly to South Africa's Black population.

The layers of information within a set of drawings is diverse and sometimes almost hidden. A series of drawings can illustrate different layers of a project while the various layers of information on a single drawing can be uncovered and decoded. Each project represented in an architectural archive has its unique narrative that offers us glimpses into the processes of architectural production from concept to construction.

The language of Modern Movement projects

Drawings can be seen as the product of specific project dynamics or of the style and preferences of the designer. However, architectural representations often also conform to the styles and conventions of their time. The manner in which architects visualise and communicate often reflect prevailing paradigms. The Modern Movement brings with it specific types of architectural projects, such as flat-roofed dwellings, mass housing, concrete-framed structures, industrial precincts, high-rise buildings and civic projects on an urban scale. These often go hand in hand with drawing types that convey the architectural and ideological intentions of modernity.

Alongside the work of pioneering South African proponents of the Modern Movement, numerous architects of Dutch descent and of Dutch education contributed to its further development in their adopted countries. The contemporary and international spirit of mid-twentieth century interior design is captured in a photograph of the KLM international booking office conceived by Jaap van Niftrik.[24] The work of Jaap Jongens, especially his designs within the City Engineers Department of the Cape Town City Council, captures the ambitious scale and monumental simplicity inherent in the urban renewal schemes of the Modern project.[25] His perspective renderings for the Cape Town Foreshore redevelopment project are illustrative of this theme. While some drawings by Jaap Jongens, such as the Huguenot Memorial, combine a simplified classical language with aspects of modern

24 This photograph was featured in the Architect and Builder journal of October 1958 along with other contemporary designs for airline booking offices.
25 These designs included projects such as the Newlands Swimming Pool and Wemmershoek Dam buildings; see also Chapter 4.

Historical photograph of KLM Booking Offices, showing the interior as designed by Jaap van Niftrik in or before 1958, unknown place

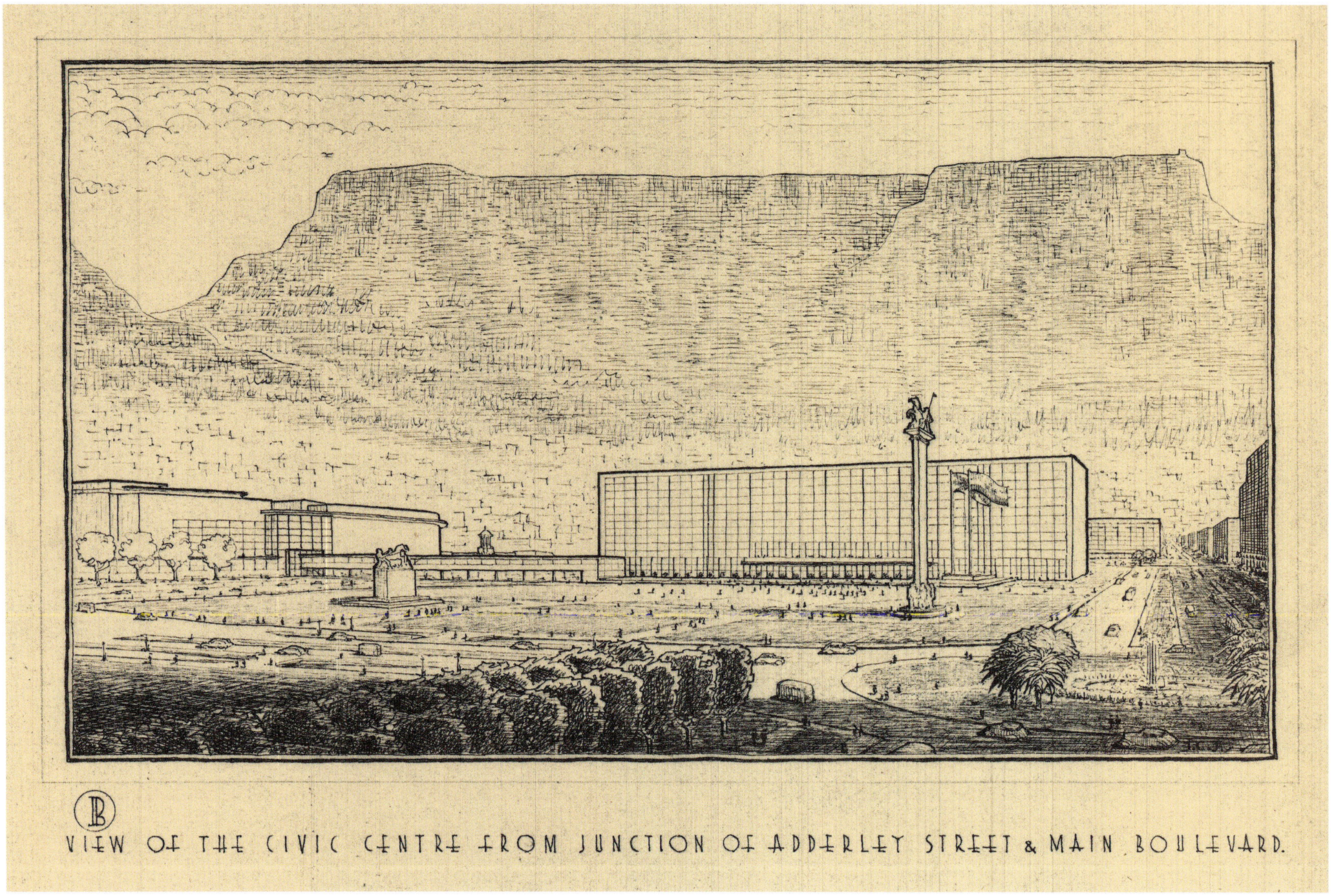

Cape Town, proposed Civic Centre seen from the junction of Adderley Street and Main Boulevard, perspective drawing by Jaap Jongens, 1943

construction, the axonometric drawing for the Cape Steel Construction Company is overtly modern in its representational technique as well as the materials and modularity that it represents.

Another architect well known for the design of industrial buildings is HTO Niegeman, who has been described along with his associate, ED Andrews, as 'pioneer modernist architects'.[26] The firm Andrews & Niegeman was responsible for the well-known Rex Trueform factory, the drawings of which have been described in recent scholarly publications.[27] Selected drawings by Henk Niegeman have been preserved by Barney Shapiro, a senior partner at the firm in its later years. An elevation drawing for a flat roofed dwelling is drawn with simple lines and abstraction elements typical of Modern Movement representation. There is also a more elaborate perspective rendering for the offices of M Bertish & Co presented in an architectural language that refers to the streamlined nautical designs that inspired many architects of the era.

Shapiro also relates how the tutelage of Henk Niegeman influenced his own approach to architectural technology and detail drawings. The technical development drawings for the PJ Olivier Preparatory School in Grahamstown, drawn by Shapiro in the office of Andrews & Niegeman, shows a systematic description of details related to the curtain-walling of a concrete-frame building. This drawing can be seen as an embedded record of the processes of knowledge transfer that are ongoing within an architectural practice.

26 Wolff, 2014: i.
27 Wolff, 2014.

Discussion

The sets of artefacts introduced in this chapter showcase the range of unique scenarios found within the archives and the potential for their interpretation across a variety of scholarly themes. Proposal drawings for the Netherlands Bank Building in Pretoria connect architects across continents and bear witness to the history of architectural patronage. Norman Eaton's sketches and details speak of an architect's quest for inspiration and the potential for the architectural integration of a variety of cultural references. The archival records of architects such as Damstra, Van Niftrik and Jongens provide access to nuanced and personal architectural histories, but also show how these are interwoven with the broader patterns of sociocultural history.

Remnants of planning documentation capture both the technical details and the urban ambitions of segregationist housing programmes, while leaving us with questions about the role of specific architects such as de Jong, Dijkstra, and Van Beijma. The drawing collection of John van de Werke can be read as a survey of a complete design oeuvre while the

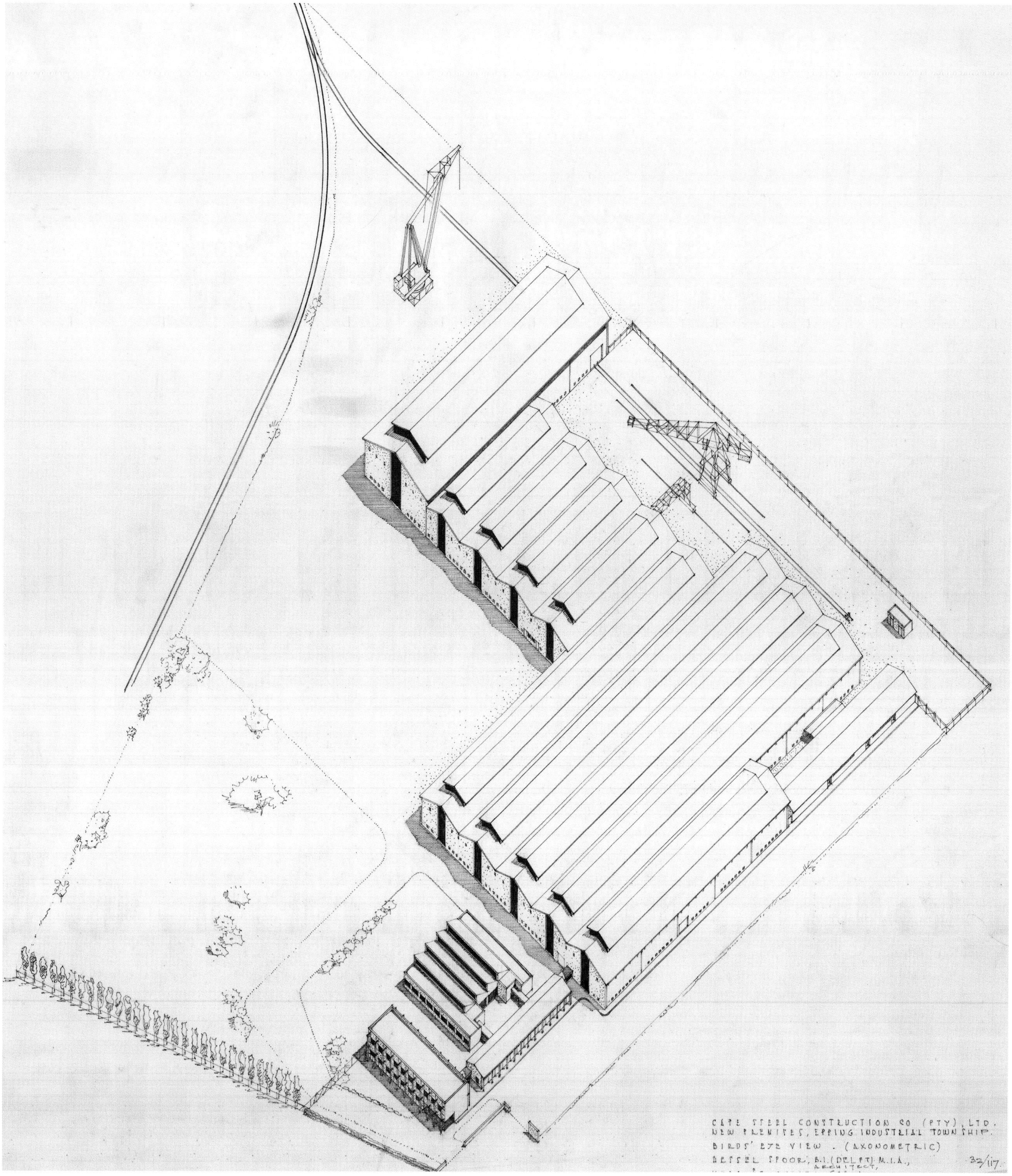

Cape Town, Epping, design for Cape Steel Construction Co premises, axonometric projection drawing by Jaap Jongens, 1943

layers of penmanship on specific drawings becomes evidence of practice processes and historical anomalies. Finally, as seen in the architectural visualisations of Modern Movement architects such as Niegeman, drawings can mirror the spirit and ambition of their time and transmit these ideals to future generations.

The variety of people, places and processes implicated in making, using and keeping architectural documents also means that the archives do not express a singular definition of shared heritage, but also its variety in form and format. The examples are all different: a South African architect producing drawings for a Dutch client; a Dutch document preserved in a South African collection; a fundraising proposal that represent moments of cross-cultural solidarity; a design that commemorates broader cultural exchanges; historical records of interest to both Dutch and South African researchers on low-cost housing; a South African drawing that recalls Dutch building traditions or a Dutch architectural education manifesting in South African practice.

A variety of sub-themes for the understanding of 'shared heritage' is likely still to be discovered or explored within the archives and the collections that have been discussed here from a perspective of 'Dutch-South African shared heritage' which, of course, can also be further researched through other lenses.

For these conversations to continue, the physical preservation of the archives also requires attention. Archives require custodians, collections require conservation strategies, curators require institutional support and archival projects require collaboration. The success of archival endeavours in the architectural realm is also dependent on recognition and support from the academy as well as its fraternity and the profession. Only a fraction of architectural collections in the South African context are preserved and accessible in archives, but these have already greatly enriched our understanding of local architectural history and our interpretation of architectural heritage, shared or otherwise.

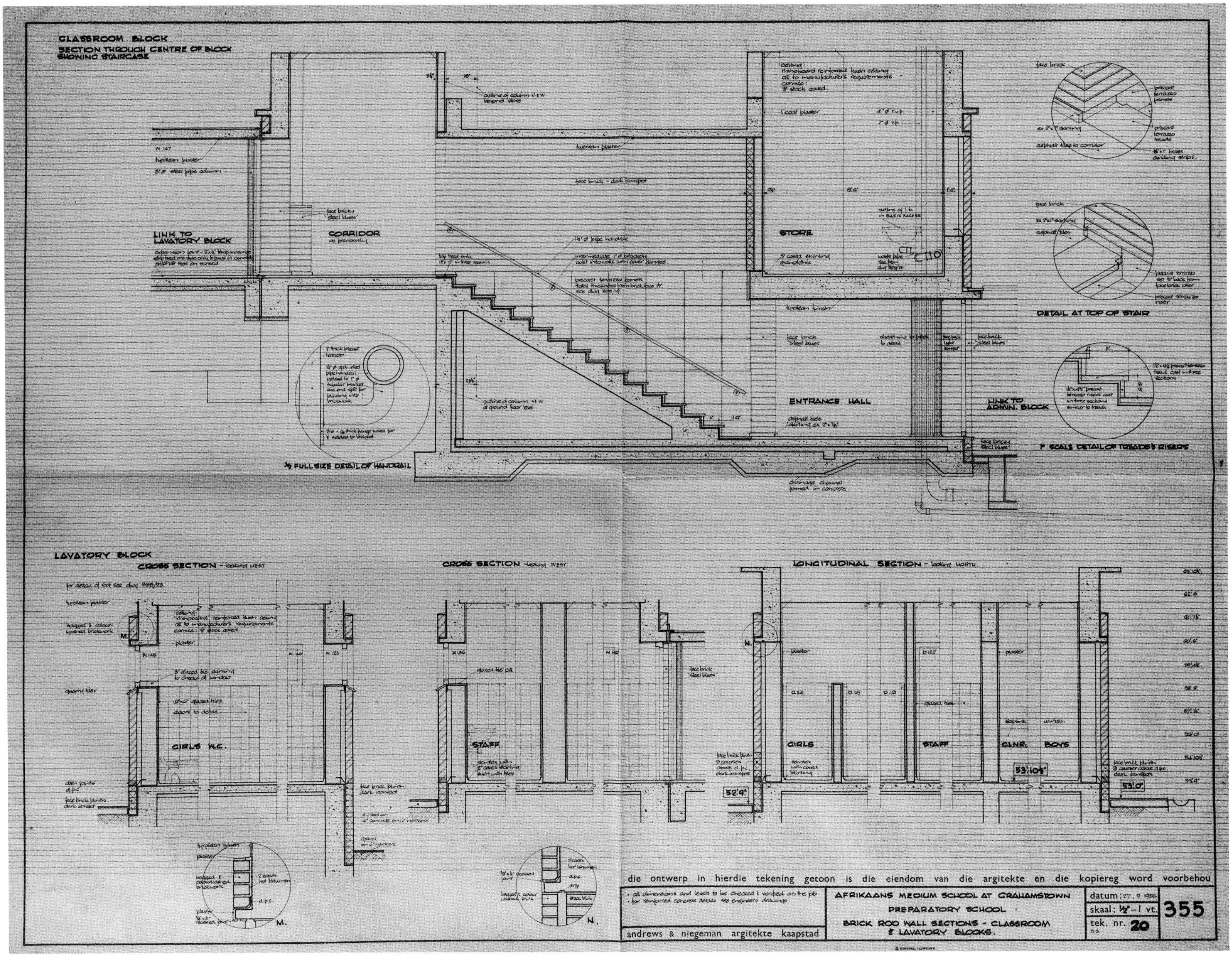

Grahamstown, detail construction drawings for the PJ Olivier Preparatory School by Barney Shapiro in the office of Andrews & Niegeman, 17 September 1955

Unknown place, design for a flat-roofed single storey house, elevation drawing by Henk Niegeman

Furthermore, it is a simultaneously uplifting and daunting thought that, as we speak, architectural practices continue to produce diverse sets of design documentation that will be collected by archivists in the years to come and interpreted by researchers as evidence of architecture as an ongoing and shared cultural process.

Many records that could have formed part of the 'Tectonic' archives have been lost or remain hidden. But through means of care or by virtue of luck, significant collections also remain preserved to be enjoyed, deciphered or debated. As the 'Tectonic' archives continue to be unlocked and extended, our interpretation of shared architectural heritage between the Netherlands and South Africa will evolve to further broaden our historical perspectives.

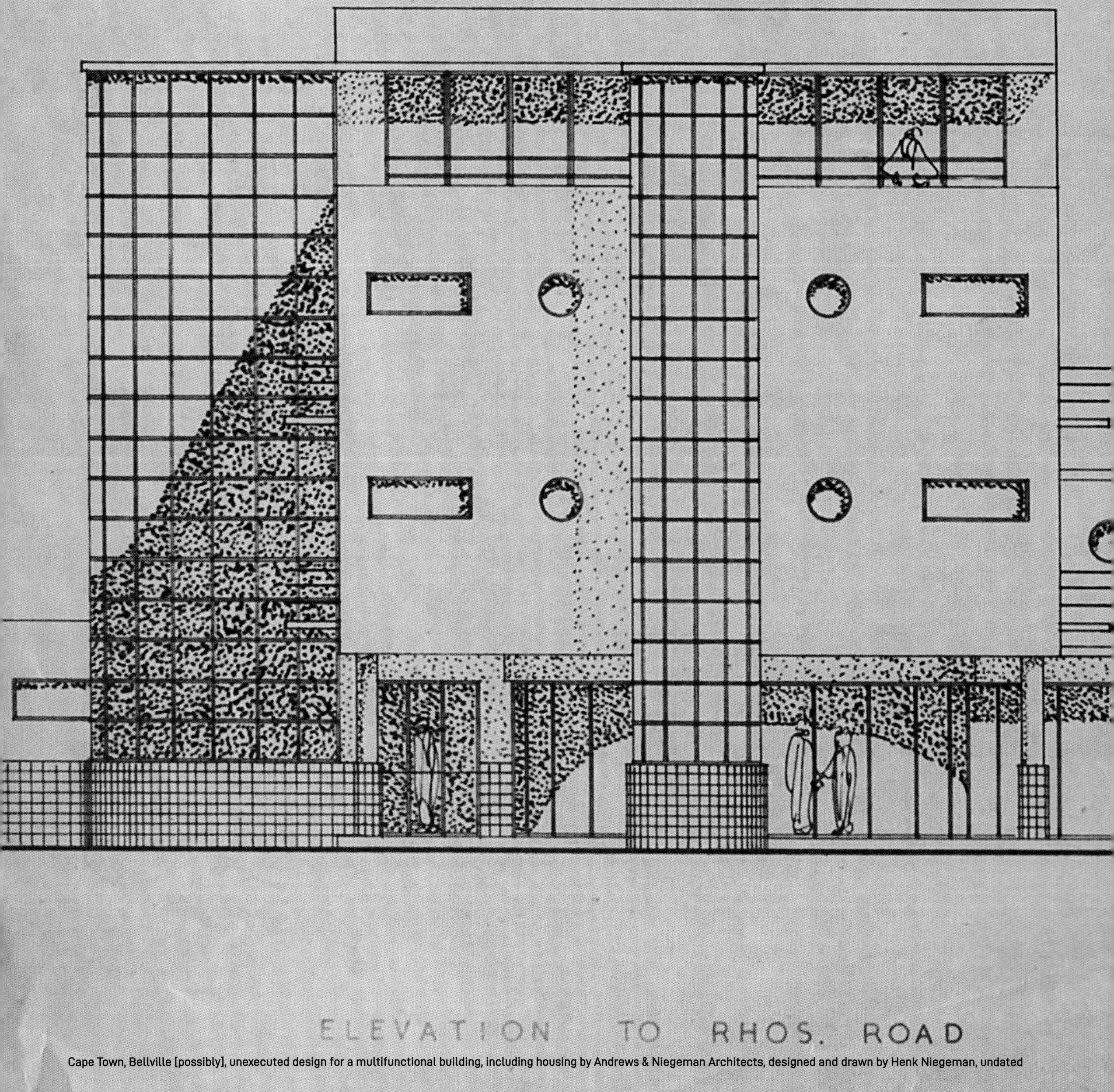

Cape Town, Bellville [possibly], unexecuted design for a multifunctional building, including housing by Andrews & Niegeman Architects, designed and drawn by Henk Niegeman, undated

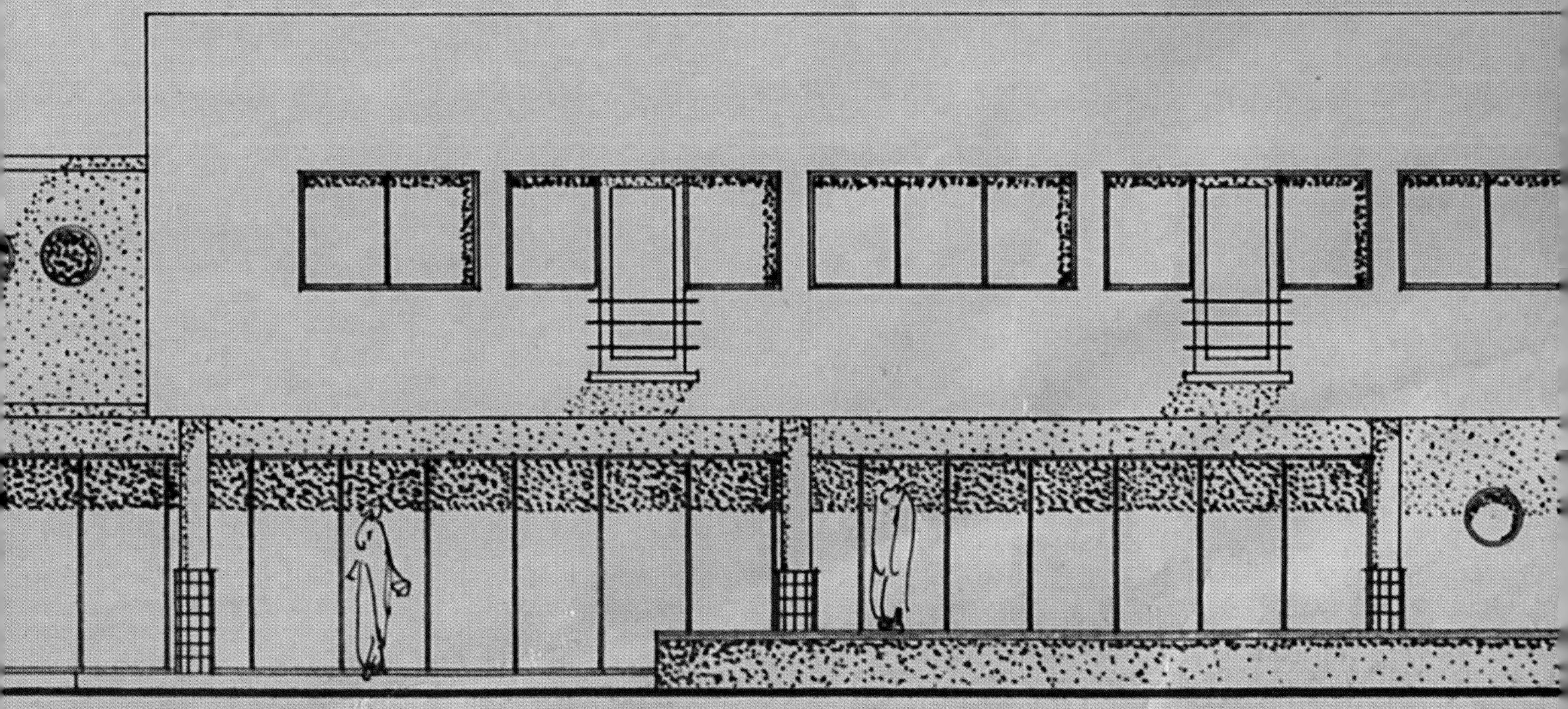

Pretoria, interior of the NGK Wapadrand, designed by Gerrit Brink; photo 2020

11 Constructing Stories

Oral histories of Gerrit Brink and Hans Wegelin

Mary Lange and Roger Fisher

Architects aspire to create expansive, even impressive, tangible legacies. A broad database, available online, includes the biographies of identified Dutch immigrant architects who had practices in South Africa during 1902–61. A variety of their works were published in journals or general books on South African architecture. Yet, the oral stories of their struggle to adapt to a different country, climate and society than that which they came from adds new insights to the history and the cross-continental exchanges of the built environment of South Africa. In this essay two Dutch immigrants, Gerrit Brink (born 1936) and Hans Wegelin (born 1940), serve as case studies for such an oral history. They are both Pretoria architects who studied and practised architecture in South Africa.

Two qualitative case studies are far from being ideal for drawing generalised conclusions. However, the findings recorded here were largely affirmed by their correlation to Barbara Henkes' examination of 'the migratory movement from the Netherlands to South Africa and the associated migration policies in both countries over the years 1910 to 1961'.[1] In conducting structured interviews and transcriptions, oral history opens fields for consideration in the recording of well-educated and literate professionals. It also acts as a counterpoint to adjudge theories and practices concerning non-literate people, or persons of language groups that have no orthography, as applied in other studies by the authors.[2]

1 Henkes, 2016: 642.

2 Lange et al., 2013. Available at: https://issuu.com/coolcapital/docs/engraved_landscape_biesje_poort_many_voices; Lange et al., 2014.

Intangible and tangible stories

In South Africa, up until 1999, heritage legislation (and subsequently its agencies, researchers and practitioners) followed the western preference for the preservation, conservation and elevation of their country's tangible heritage. In consequence, intangible heritage such as dance, music, ritual and oral narratives have been side-lined. However, it is the intangible that gives the tangible meaning: 'material culture ... is a physical residue of past intangible heritage, of past actions, event, beliefs, and their social and cultural contexts'.[3] So as to address the disparity in the recording of intangible heritage in South Africa as compared to that of the tangible, its government passed the 1999 National Heritage Resources Act (25), that defined and highlighted the importance of its intangible heritage.[4] In 2016 the South African Department of Environmental Affairs published the cultural heritage survey guidelines and assessment tools for protected areas in South Africa. Therein they defined Intangible Cultural Heritage or 'ICH' as including 'practices, representations, knowledge' and 'skills' with 'cultural practices' including 'orality, language, beliefs and customs'.[5]

This definition echoes much of the Dutch definition of cultural heritage in the new *Erfgoedwet* [heritage act, valid since 1 July 2016]. A difference is that the Dutch act includes the terms 'values' and 'traditions' and

3 Morris, 2014: vii.

4 Available at http://www.dac.gov.za/sites/default/files/Legislations%20Files/a25-99.pdf.

5 July 2016: 4; 14, available at https://www.environment.gov.za/sites/default/files/legislations/culturalheritagesurveyguidelines_protectedareas2016_0.pdf.

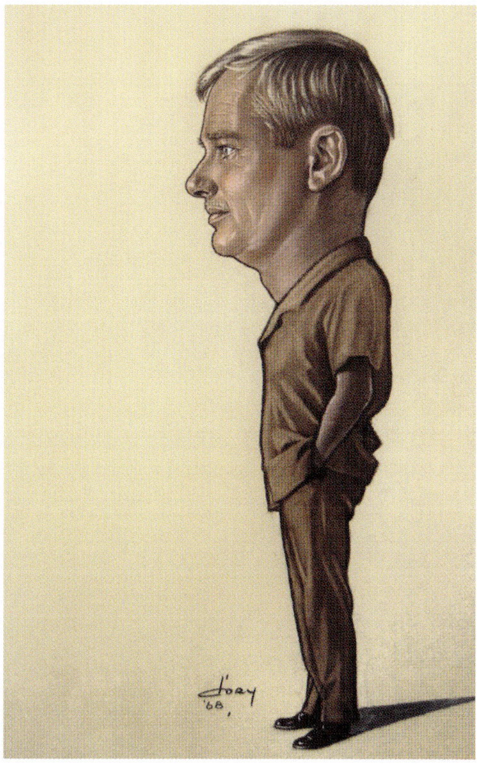

Hans Wegelin, cartoonesque portrait by d'Ory (original), also published in the journal *Architect and Builder*, 1968

Hans Wegelin in his living room in Pretoria; photo 2020

does not include the term 'orality'.[6] The Dutch act does, however, add nuances to the understanding of cultural heritage as having 'tangible and intangible resources', that despite offering 'a frame of reference' are nevertheless not static but 'continuously evolving':
'cultural heritage: tangible and intangible resources inherited from the past, created in the course of time by people or arising from the interaction between man and the environment that people, irrespective of the ownership thereof, identify as a reflection and expression of continuously evolving values, beliefs, knowledge and traditions, and that offer a frame of reference to them and to future generations.' (section 1.1)

The UNESCO 2003 Convention for the Safeguarding of the Intangible Cultural Heritage refers to the intangible as 'living heritage'. It also promotes 'language' as 'the principal vehicle through which living heritage is kept alive'.[7] In South Africa, the government originally introduced legislation to make provision for the heritage of people with a strong oral tradition and for those who did not have a formalised orthography, though having rich oral recall. Such an example of the recording and application of these oral traditions can be seen in the narratives of Khoisan and Nguni descendants of the Water Snake that have assisted in the interpretation of rock engravings.[8]

Moving theory into praxis

The recording of someone's story may appear to be as easy as pressing a record button. However, to be ethical, thorough and accurate such researchers apply a particular methodology. In the field of Visual Anthropology, an ethnographic style of data collection is the main concern. Visual anthropology is a discipline 'where three-dimensional objects or else images on paper or on film ... are being interpreted and understood'.[9] One of the three areas of visual anthropology is the 'symbolic use of space, architecture, and the built environment'.[10] Ethnographic research, in its standard practice, includes observation of participants over a long time, which includes conducting open interviews. The records of these engagements are then interpreted, and the data transcribed. In the case of architecture, the ethnographic participant is more often the user/viewer of architecture, but in the case of this research, the participants, here both architects, are also the creators of the built environment.[11]

The field of Cultural Studies includes a focus not only on the identity of the interviewee but also on general identity and power issues in society. Both fields have influenced the approach of this essay. This required developing a rapport with the interviewees while recording and transcribing the interviews conducted. The authors have also kept the focus of the data analysis on determining, inter alia, the identity and power relationships of each of the interviewed architects.

Hans Wegelin and Gerrit Brink are (now retired) architects with expansive tangible legacies. They are both from well-established architectural firms that have left their mark nationally on the South African built environment. The legacy of Hans Wegelin extends beyond his buildings to his numerous architectural journal articles and his revision of South African Public Works standard building specifications.[12] Although written biographies are digitally available on both of these architects, their oral interviews, for the most, have added valuable context and content that has hitherto not been recorded.

The authors are familiar with the environment where the participants live and have practiced. Both authors have lived in Pretoria for approximately thirty years each and co-author Roger Fisher has an in-depth knowledge of post-war architecture. The recording of the research included 'establishing rapport', note-taking and photographs, a requisite in establishing familiarity and a rapport with whoever's oral heritage is to be recorded.[13] It is, otherwise, very difficult to conduct a meaningful biographical interview if the researcher goes in unprepared. A rapport was thus established with both Gerrit Brink and Hans Wegelin before the interviews, which was sustained beyond the time of the interviews by way of contemporary communication channels such as WhatsApp, telephone calls and emails.

6 Available at https://english.inspectie-oe.nl/publications/publication/2016/9/14/heritage-act.
7 Available at https://ich.unesco.org/.
8 Hoff, 1997; Lange, 2011; Morris, 2010.
9 Hockins, 2014: 436.
10 Ruby, 1989: 9–10.
11 For example, Pavlides & Cranz, 2011.

12 Wegelin, 2010; see also Chapter 9.
13 Geertz, 1973: 313.

Gerrit Brink pointing at one of his design drawings in the Pierneef Church, Pretoria; photo 2019

In accordance with the requirements of the University of Pretoria, the authors followed a thorough process of ethical clearance that an ethics committee granted before the interviews. This process requires that researchers must provide evidence of informed consent forms that are to be signed by the participants before and after the interview. This document confirms that the participant is aware of why they are being interviewed and what the envisaged outcome of the interview will be. The informed consent form also includes the participant's agreement to whatever instruments may be used to capture their story, for example, a voice recorder and note-taking. Although a recorder may be intrusive and may affect the interviewee's response, current digital technology allows for recorders that are small yet still record high-quality sound, without the interviewer placing the microphone in front of the interviewee's mouth.[14] In this way, these interviews took place in a natural conversational setting with the recorder placed unobtrusively on a table or bench.

The Wegelin interview took place at the Wegelins' home and the Brink interviews took place at two churches that Gerrit had designed. Both participants chose to be interviewed in Afrikaans. Co-author Mary Lange transcribed the interviews and returned them to the participants so that they could check that the transcription was factual and that they remained in agreement that what they had said in the interview could be made public. Wegelin and Brink corrected, adjusted and added to the transcriptions before they returned them. They also both offered photographs of some of their designs and a curriculum vitae. This part of the process not only entrenches the trust that the participant has in the researcher/s, but also adds to the credibility of the research data.

The data collected were analysed with the use of a flexible comparative thematic analysis. This means that some themes were identified before and others during the analysis and that the themes from the participants were then compared. The interpretation of this thematic analysis and the other data collected, as well as textual evidence already available about the participants, results in a 'thick description' writing-up of the research.[15]

What follows is a construction based on relevant themes and conclusions that were identified before and during the analysis of their oral interviews. The construction partly collects factual bio-data and their contexts, and reflects on themes of cultural practice and tacit knowledge.[16] The latter in architecture 'is most often acquired through practice (being shown how) and involves knowing/recognizing the difference (connoisseurship) between something well-done and something done poorly or just average'.[17]

Born in the Netherlands

The Netherlands was politically neutral during the first four decades of C20, but was invaded by the German army in May 1940 and subsequently submitted to two parallel administrative systems during the next five years, with increasing pressure from the Nazis on the Dutch population.[18] Gerrit Brink was born four years before this difficult period, in 1936, in Apeldoorn, where Queen Wilhelmina had her residency in Paleis Het Loo at the time. He was one of ten children in a Dutch Reformed family. Gerrit's father was one of many Dutch citizens who arrived in 1942 that had been in forced labour. 'My pa het gewerk aan die 'bunkers' in Zeeland wat eintlik in opdrag van die Duitsers was om Engeland te kan bombardier' [My father worked on the bunkers in Zeeland that were built under the orders of the Germans so that they could bomb England]. Hans Wegelin's birth preceded the invasion by a few months as he was born in March 1940. Hans' father had to hide from the Germans and Hans lost his mother when he was three years old, in January 1944, because she suffered from a stomach ailment and received inadequate health care at that time.

After WW2 the relationship between the Netherlands and South Africa, in terms of emigration, was complex.[19] Part of that complexity was that the Netherlands government needed to rebuild the devastated country. However, the South African government, despite the shortage of skilled labour in their countries of origin, encouraged immigrants from European descent. This was done to counter the rise of black nationalism. However, several categories of European emigrants, including those Dutch people who had been Nazi sympathisers, were not considered.

Gerrit's grandfather was a farmer but he highlights that his father, Gerrit Martinus Brink, became a carpenter, and as he was one of ten children and as the ninth child, he did not stand a chance of inheriting a piece of the farm. Gerrit's remarks in this regard emphasise the difference in the size of farms in the Netherlands and those in South Africa, and consequently the greater opportunities the latter offered: 'daar was nie die moontlikheid in Holland om die plaas in tien te deel nie.' [in Holland there was not a possibility of dividing a farm into ten]. The Netherlands government would have needed Gerrit's father, as a carpenter, for the rebuilding of the country after the war. He would have fallen into the 'could be missed' rather than the 'not missed' category of potential emigrants before 1946.[20]

Hans Wegelin's father Arthur was a professional violinist in the Utrecht City Orchestra. The orchestra was founded in 1894 and had its home base in the Tivoli society on the Lepelenburg.[21] Utrecht was one of the areas that suffered in the 'Hunger Winter' of 1944–45, when more than three thousand children were evacuated and tens of thousands of people died in the Netherlands.[22] Hans recalls how he was also 'evacuated': 'Our "dienstmeisje" took me on the back of her bicycle through the night and snow to friends on the Veluwe. Apparently, I was known to be content with bread and water'. This famine resulted in the eating of foraged wild plants and tulip bulbs, sugar beets and potato skins while soup kitchen food is remembered as 'making people sick'.[23] Under these circumstances, Hans' father must have battled to cope with two young children on his own. Shortly after the War, he decided to start a new life elsewhere and found through family ties an affordable way to travel to South Africa, on the whaler 'Willem Barentsz'.[24]

14 Rapley, 2004.
15 Geertz, 1973.
16 All quotes cited verbatim in this text derive from the interviews from 31 October 2019.
17 Curry, 2017: 81.
18 See Chapter 2.

19 Henkes, 2016; see also Chapter 3.
20 Henkes, 2016: 650–51.
21 After the war, the venue was left mostly dilapidated and the orchestra changed its name into Utrecht Symphonic Orchestra (Isserlis, 2009: 336).
22 De Zwarte, 2016; Hamilton, 2003.
23 Vorstenbosch et al., 2017: n.p.
24 Grové, n.d.

The Dutch whaler 'Willem Barentsz' on which the Wegelins travelled to South Africa; photo 1950

Drawn to South Africa

Hans Wegelin's paternal uncle and aunt were already settled in South Africa by 1947 when his father decided to emigrate from the Netherlands to Cape Town. His uncle, also Hans, was a cellist in the Cape Town City Orchestra for many years. Musicians from western Europe, from before WW1, had introduced to Cape Town 'a new population with an interest in [classical] music'. During WW2 there was a great shortage of players in the orchestra because of 'deaths or enlistment' and because 'no players could be imported', thereby presenting opportunities for musicians after the War.[25]

It was family from the Netherlands, already settled in South Africa, who also influenced Gerrit Brink's father to emigrate to South Africa on 27 July 1953, arriving on the 16 August in Pretoria. Gerrit's uncle Willem had already settled in Pretoria in 1936 and visited the Brinks in Apeldoorn in 1952. This was the same year that the Defiance Campaign was launched by the African National Congress and by opponents of the more stringent application of the Nationalist Party's apartheid legislation.[26] Willem's description of South Africa must have been attractive, as it persuaded Gerrit's father to emigrate: 'Nou die rede waarom hy geëmigreer het, was dat hulle gesien het dat daar nie 'n toekoms was vir die kinders, en dat Holland nie vir hulle rooskleurig gelyk het nie. Inteendeel het dit eintlik baie rooskleurig geword.' [The reason why he emigrated was that they did not see a future for their children in Holland as it did not appear to have a rosy future. In actual fact, it did become rosy.].

Dutch networks

In South Africa, the Wegelins and the Brinks arrived with very few belongings. They were helped to get onto their feet financially and cope emotionally in a foreign country by the strong communal networks that Dutch immigrants had created. These networks went beyond their immediate families to cultural and craft groups and clubs.[27]

Hans Wegelin's father met his second wife, Wytske Zoetelief Tromp, in Cape Town at a social occasion held at the Dutch embassy. This was after one of his concert performances at the Cape Town City Hall: 'en daar is toe die ambassadeur se vrou se suster. Sy was nog 'n oujongnooi. En die tweetjies het toe ontmoet' [and there was the ambassador's sister-in-law. She was a spinster. And that is how the two met].

25 Gollom, 2000: 2, 96.
26 Advance, 1952.
27 See also Chapter 3.

Hans Wegelin and Lucette Greeff on their wedding day, 1965

Dutch immigrants such as the Wegelins and the Brinks also survived because of their admirable work ethic. In order to make a living Hans Wegelin's father bought a motorbike: 'en met sy viool op sy rug ry hy by die dorpies en gee les' [with his violin on his back he rode to the towns to give lessons]. A network of Dutch-speaking women in Cape Town looked after Hans and his sister during this time. One of these women's daughters, Lucette Greeff, would later become Hans' wife.

Gerrit Brink was seventeen years old when he emigrated from the Netherlands to South Africa with his parents and his three siblings. Before this, he had followed in his father's footsteps and after primary school he attended an *ambachtsschool* [vocational school] in Apeldoorn. He studied carpentry and in two years passed with honours at the age of sixteen. When Gerrit arrived in Pretoria he was keen to work at an architects' firm. He visited thirteen firms, but he only spoke Dutch, and not one of the firms wanted to employ him. Through a friendship he had made in Pretoria, he heard that at the Pretoria Department of Public Works there was work similar to that which he had done at the City Building Department in Apeldoorn. So, he gained employment there for a year. In that same year (1952) Gerrit applied to study part-time (in the evenings) at the Department of Architecture of the University of Pretoria, and there too one had to be able to speak Afrikaans.

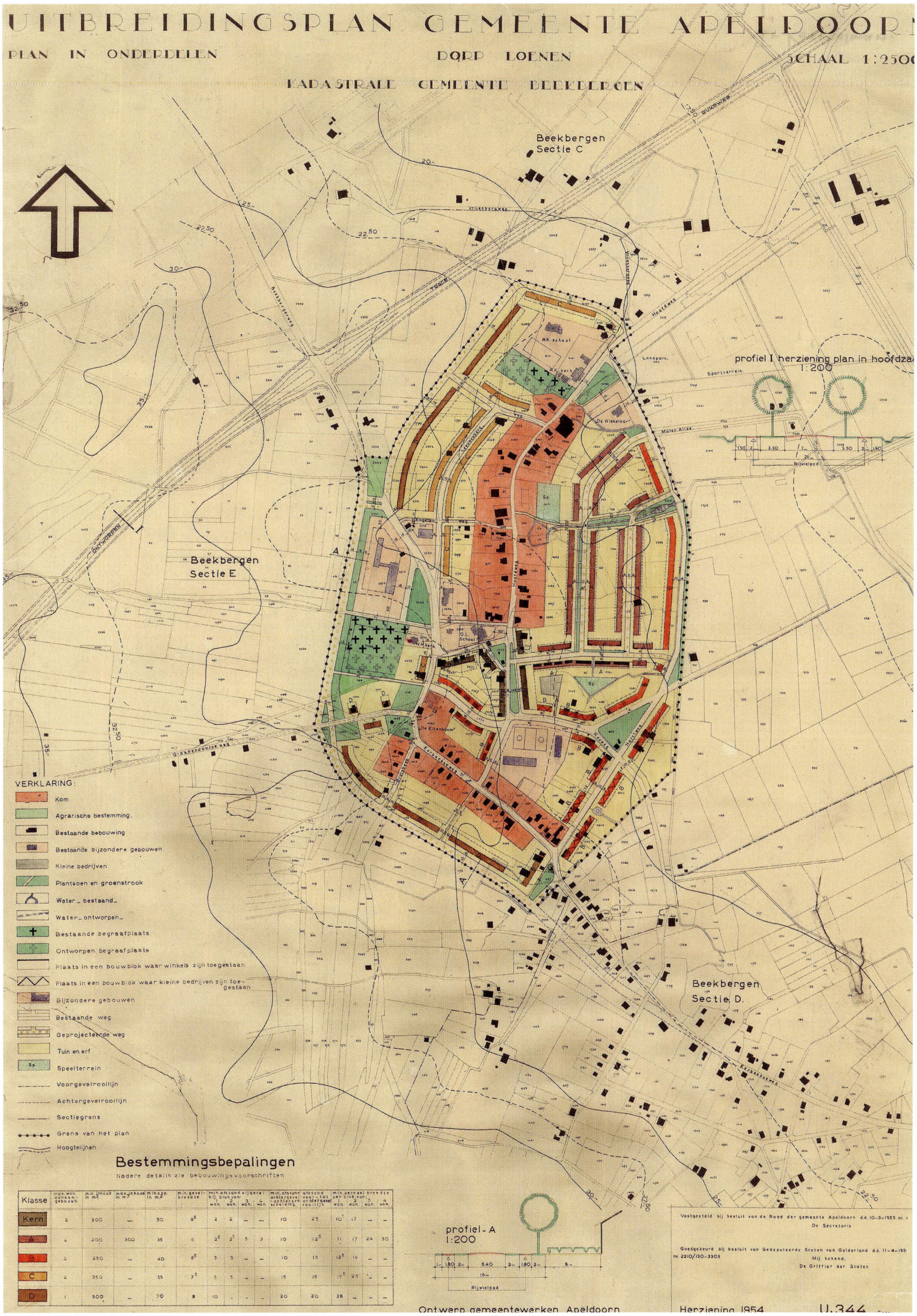

Apeldoorn, the 1954 municipal extension plan for the village Loenen to which Gerrit Brink contributed

In Pretoria in the 1950s and 1960s, there was a network of professional and skilled building industry labour. A Dutch building contractor, Jan Withaar, employed Gerrit's father. After three years he in turn started his own construction company, that later became G.M. Brink en Seuns [Sons] (with Gerrit's brother).

Fluid identities and the influence of religion and Afrikaans

In a country's census, religion is referred to as 'an important element in self-definition and national identity'.[28] Gerrit Brink's identity is largely shaped by his faith. After he had emigrated to South Africa, he attended the *Nederduitsch Hervormde Kerk* (NHK) but changed to the *Nederduitse Gereformeerde Kerk* (NGK) when he lived in the Eastern Cape between 1986 and 1996. The Dutch networks extended into the church and Gerrit designed several NHK churches besides churches for other Christian denominations. He expressed why designing churches was the most meaningful for him as an architect: 'En ek kan sê dat 'n kerk was vir my altyd 'n besonderse opdrag want dit is vir 'n spesifieke gemeente, dit is 'n vereiste wat die gemeente het en jy wil dit graag eintlik *hulle* kerk maak. Ek was geïnspireer deur die moderne beweging in Nederlandse argitektuur. Dit is ook 'n uitbeelding van my geloof' [I can say that to design a church was always a special assignment as it is for a specific community, a requirement for the community and you are keen to make it *their* church. I was inspired by the modern movement in Dutch architecture. It is also a portrayal of my faith].

Pretoria, exterior of the NGK Wapadrand, designed by Gerrit Brink; photo 2020

In South Africa, many Dutch-speaking immigrants anglicised. Language is considered 'one of the most significant criteria in the definition of a nation or nationality'.[29] Despite being born in the Netherlands both Hans Wegelin and Gerrit Brink identify themselves as Afrikaans South Africans and not as Dutch. Dutch origins are evident in the Brinks' Afrikaans accent but not in Hans' accent. Hans' sister, Else, born only a year and a half before him (in 1938) is very much proudly South African. Nevertheless, she still identifies with her Dutch roots: 'sy is anders, sy is nog, ek kan amper sê nog Hollands. Ek weet nie [die rede nie] ek dink ek was net jonger' [she is different, she is still, I can almost say still Dutch. I don't know the reason for this, I think I was just younger].

Not only do the questions in the oral interview provoke responses but the process itself does too. Pauses, in particular, are apt to provoke reflection. Hans reflected on his identity in one of these pauses during his interview and discovered that his embracement of an Afrikaans identity may well have been through his attending an Afrikaans primary school for the first time at the age of seven years. Primary school is an important phase of socialisation and building friendships.[30] His father had remarried and accepted a post at 'Potchefstroom se Universiteit se konservatorium' [Potchefstroom University Music Conservatory]. This predominantly Afrikaans-speaking town suited his father and stepmother as they could not speak English very well. Before this Hans had attended several schools, including an English school in George, even though he could not speak a word of English. At the Afrikaans school in Potchefstroom Hans could not yet speak Afrikaans well and was nicknamed *Kaas* or *Kaaskop*, a generally-used term (at the time) for a person of Dutch descent in South Africa.[31] Hans reflects that this teasing impacted his chosen identity: 'Dus was ek bekend as die Kaaskop nê. Kaaskoppie. En ek dink daar het ek besluit: hoor hier ek wil nie Kaaskoppie wees nie. En toe het ek nou lekker vriende daar begin kry en ek was steeds Kaas, maar jy tel die taal so vinnig op, veral as jy so jonk is' [So, I was known as Blockhead. Little Blockhead. And I think there and then I decided: Listen here, I don't want to be Little Blockhead. After that, I began to make good friends and I was still Block, but you pick up the language very quickly, especially when you are young].

Part of the Afrikaner Nationalism in the C20 included the state's promotion of Afrikaans, not only in legally equalising its use to English, but also 'through the building of infrastructures like Afrikaans-medium schools, universities, and colleges'.[32] Gerrit's interview emphasises how important it was to master Afrikaans for work and a career in South Africa in the 1950s.

28 Christopher, 2011: 9.
29 Christopher, 2011: 10.
30 Yukay Yüksel, 2013.
31 A quolloquialism meaning literally a little 'cheesehead' which refers to his Dutch origins, alluding to the Dutch being known as cheesemakers.
32 Louw, 2004: 45.

Modes of education

While architecture, built or unbuilt, produces an artefactual residue through both documentation and constructed projects, additionally, by way of its subsequent affirmation through publication or critical review, the practice of architecture is intangible knowledge. Both Brink and Wegelin are graduates of the University of Pretoria, but each followed a different career path to become architects, which illustrates the breadth of possibilities at the time. While Brink's route into the profession was circuitous, Wegelin's was more conventional and direct.

Institutional yearbooks of the time may give insight into the factual detail of study and curriculum content, but it is only through interviewing those that have studied at the institution that the ambience and atmosphere of such modes of learning and practice are discovered. Brink relates that he had a personal interview with the then head of the Department of Architecture, University of Pretoria, Professor AL Meiring. Meiring in turn arranged an interview with his counterpart in the University of Witwatersrand, Professor John Fassler, and his colleague Professor Duncan Howie. After discussing Gerrit's experience and capabilities, they granted him matric exemption and direct access to studies in architecture. Hans recalls that his father 'took me to Pretoria for an interview with Meiring, who told us there was a bright future for architects'. This illuminates not only the strong father and son relationships in Dutch immigrants, but also a high level of personal engagement by the senior academics of two institutions, something unlikely today. It perhaps suggests a more leisurely time with a greater degree of social largesse.

Gerrit then further elaborates that it was possible to study while working at the time. The presentation of the syllabus was specifically geared for this. Formal classes were conducted from 7–9am, 1–2pm over lunchtime, and after 4pm, sometimes until 7:30, 8pm or even 10pm in the evening. The Department was located in the extra-mural building in central Pretoria. This locality specifically catered to working students. Brink relates that although studies in architecture required five years, those doing the coursework in diploma studies were allowed eight years. He, however, completed his in the minimum designated time. He also relates that employers were aware of the demands of such a mode of study and accommodated their employees accordingly.

These personal accounts allow for an assessment of the human aspect of the realities of receiving an architectural education at the time. It also gives insight into the social compacts that supported and allowed for these modalities of entering the architectural profession.

Modes of practice – tacit knowledge

When Brink was working in the Department of Public Works at the commencement of his studies, it was a requirement that all government employees be bilingual in English and Afrikaans. Here he was taught to speak English by a Mr Holloway, an English immigrant. He in turn taught the latter his 'Dutch Afrikaans'. This illustrates how bureaucratic directives or social norms might inadvertently foster cultural trade-offs. This personal information also provides an understanding of how legislated injunctions impact personally on practitioners, and how these are addressed in interpersonal relationships.

When asked which practitioner Brink found to be the most influential, without hesitation he cites Hellmut Stauch, for whom he worked from 1956 to 1964, having left the DPW after eleven months—'want ek is eintlik nie 'n staatsamptenaar' [I am not really a civil servant]. Stauch taught him, in particular, the discipline of detailing, but also gave him a wide scope in all aspects of practice. Gerrit was required to do designs, working drawings, contract administration and site management. He says that he is by nature an all-rounder, but Stauch had the good grace to allow him to hone these skills. Thereafter Brink set up his private practice in 1965.

Hans Wegelin recalls that directly after completing his full-time studies in Architecture (a five-year degree) at the University of Pretoria, in 1964, he headed to Cape Town where his wife-to-be, Lucette Greeff, was finishing her nursing studies at the Groote Schuur General Hospital. He worked for the architect Chris Lochner but, finding the pace too slow, and speaking by chance to a university friend of his, Joe Kemp, he decided to move from the Cape. Joe Kemp was looking for a partner in a recently established branch office in Vanderbijlpark which his father, Frik Kemp, had established from his Bethlehem office. Wegelin took the chance and moved to Van der Bijl Park where the firm was busily engaged in housing schemes for the newly-established town of Sasolburg. This work developed into the founding and construction of the town Secunda for Sasol 2 and 3. Hans remembers this time, when he oversaw an entire project from beginning to end, as exciting: 'Dit was alles vir my verskriklik boeiend en lekker. Die Secunda ding veral! Nee, ek kan nie anderster sê nie, my pa het my 'n goeie keuse gegee.' [It was all very fascinating and great. The Secunda part especially! Actually, my father gave me a very good [career] choice].

Aspects of social networks and serendipity in the roles of practitioners are seldom encountered in architectural biographies, and what are merely bland facts are embellished by such personal touches in the conducting and recording of oral narratives. What also emerges from engaging architects in personal interviews is that one discovers genealogies of architectural practitioners and with them the genealogies of modes of practice and ideas: 'the learning environment of future generations of architects... has a clear effect on their spatial experience and outlook, and also because it offers a common point of reference'.[33] Both Gerrit and Danie de Beer worked in Stauch's office and later as empathetic collaborators on occasional projects. Gerrit further recalls the names of some of the students who worked in his office. Here he particularly remembered, amongst others, Abre Crafford, who is currently teaching Building Construction at the University of Pretoria. The work of all these generations of practitioners is marked by an inherent poetic pragmatism and a finesse in the detailing of their work, a legacy with a long lineage.

Ties to the homeland

Gerrit and his wife Hanneke Brouwer, who emigrated to South Africa with her family in 1950, still speak Dutch to each other. Despite the fact that Hans has become Afrikaans he explains: 'Maar ek kan nog suiwer Nederlands praat hoor. Nou en dan praat ek en my vrou Nederlands met mekaar. En snaakse ding, ons het in vroeë jare, toe ons kindertjies klein was, het ons nog heeltyd Hollands gepraat met mekaar in die huis' [But

33 Kuipers, 2010: 9.

Gerrit Brink working on his drawing table with his wife Hanneke Brink at his side, in the late 1950s

Gerrit and Hanneke Brink inside the NHK Pierneef, Pretoria, taken before the interview in 2019

listen here, I can still speak pure Dutch. My wife and I speak Dutch to each other sometimes. Strangely, earlier when our children were young, we used to always speak Dutch to each other at home]. Their children do not speak Dutch.

Both families stay in touch with their Dutch relatives and visits take place in both continents. Hans visited his maternal grandmother for the first time since he had emigrated to South Africa when he was a student on a tour with Strauss Brink. He met his cousins and is still in contact with one of them.

The extensive archive on Dutch anti-apartheid movements that emerged after the Sharpeville tragedy highlights the tensions that existed until the early 1990s.[34] It is evident for Hans Wegelin how much easier it has been since 1994 to have contact with the Netherlands than it was in the period of the cultural boycott. He welcomes 'die verskerpte historiese en kulturele bande met Nederland' [the increased historical and cultural links with the Netherlands].

Mnemonic devices

As highlighted earlier, the interviews took place in locations to which the architects are intimately connected. The Wegelins' home, where his interview was conducted, was designed by the prominent Pretoria architect, John Claassens, as his own family home. Wegelin has meticulously remodelled it to retain its character while personalising its spatial configurations and use. The Brink interviews took place in two churches that he had designed, one being the Pierneef Nederduits Hervormde Kerk of Villieria, Pretoria. The interviews were facilitated by the presence of the architects' works. These acted both as mnemonic devices to stir memory as well as exemplars of points the architect made about attitudes to their modes of practice. A lesson learnt is that it is useful to conduct personal interviews in spaces to which the interviewee relates directly, where they feel familiar and empowered, and not estranged by the whole procedure of being interviewed and recorded. This empowerment aides the depth of recall and the veracity and depth of what the interviewee has to tell.

34 See https://africanactivist.msu.edu/organization.php?name=Anti-Apartheids+Beweging+Nederland.

Pretoria, exterior of the NHK Pierneef, designed by Gerrit Brink; photo 2020

Pretoria, interior of the NHK Pierneef, designed by Gerrit Brink; photo 2020

Omissions

While conducting the interviews both Gerrit and Hans had their wives, if not directly present as was the case with Gerrit, then nearby as with Hans. Although informal discussions were held with both women, regretfully they were not interviewed formally in the manner of oral recording at the time. Both interviewees consulted with their spouses in the course of their interviews. This was done either to aid recall or affirm some factual detail remembered. Both spouses were not only of Dutch descent but were also both intimately involved in their husbands' professional lives. Hans's wife Lucette has been his soulmate and confidant over the many years of friendship and marriage. She has been socially engaged with Hans's work, as well as with his colleagues. Gerrit's wife Hanneke was, for all the years of his private practice, his personal office assistant and office manager. Both women would have added richness to the understanding of peer and social engagement modes of practice. Because of time constraints, they could not be included in this study. This is, in retrospect, a critical omission.

Pretoria, Hans Wegelin's glass collection as currently displayed in his living room, 2020

Reflection

The interviews with Gerrit Brink and Hans Wegelin confirm that, in architecture, there is also a body of intangible heritage. This manifests in the memory, personal reflections on the architect's upbringing, social engagement, education and modes of practice. Such interviews also reveal social networks, embodied intelligences, cultural patrimony and cultural alliances. These aspects, while having their particularities for Hans and Gerrit as educated and articulate architectural practitioners, affirm that such methodologies apply to any heritage study. While the study and recording of the artefactual residue of the architectural profession may reveal the 'What?' and 'When' of the discipline, the addition of their oral histories amplifies the 'How?' and 'Why?' of their physical, artefactual, oeuvre. It also, by way of association, casts light on these aspects of their peers and compatriots' lives.

It is deduced that, while oral histories have been included in the legislation as being imperative in heritage assessments, this should not be seen as only applicable to marginalised or vulnerable peoples. It is also an enrichment of the spectrum for creating the record of architectural endeavour and its archive. This is then not for purposes of the record itself, but for discovering the underlying values embodied in the artefactual residue. As with the vulnerable, it should ever be born in mind that even the privileged, in their shared humanity, have their vulnerabilities. Hence any such information must be garnered with the same high morals and ethical principles to which heritage practitioners, and in this instance oral heritage practitioners, are beholden.[35] As yet there is no codification of this type of engagement for gathering biographical architectural historic material in South Africa.

For South Africa, in its current context, the interviewing of immigrant architects adds sensitivity as to how cultures previously considered as 'outsider' have added to and transformed the practice of local architecture. What this limited survey illuminates is that oral history is intrinsic to the legacy of the South African Built environment. It also broadens the understanding of the diversity of its practice and enriches the value of its production as part of a multicultural shared heritage.

Material residue has no intrinsic value outside of the human context. Only when it embodies human values does it gain meaning. Architecture, as tangible heritage, is no different. In order that its meaning, hence its worth, become accessible, the stories of its practitioners must be considered as intangible heritage, adding incalculable value. It is their stories that enrich the embodied value of architecture for future generations.

35 For example, see the Code of Ethics of the South African Association of Professional Heritage Practitioners. Available at: https://www.aphp.org.za/aphp-code-conduct.

Thaba Nchu, Roman Catholic Church, designed by Edy Payens for Father Frans Claerhout, c1964; photo 2020

12 Reflections and Projections

Ben Mwasinga (South African Heritage Resources Agency - Manager: Built Environment Unit; invited independent reviewer)

Like most South Africans, my understanding of Dutch architecture has always conjured up images of whitewashed walls, thatched roofing, large wooden sash cottage panes fitted with external wooden shutters and long horizontal structures, often with dormer windows. This perception has changed significantly after my first reading of *Common Ground: Dutch-South African Architectural Exchanges / 1902–61*. The book digs deeper to highlight that the Dutch architectural influence permeates larger swathes of the built fabric than previously understood. At a macro scale, this book manages to shift the focus from well-known and celebrated works of famous Dutch architects to the less known but equally important work of Dutch architects in the civil service and private consultancies of South Africa during the early to mid-part of the C20.

These forgotten architects have left an indelible footprint that has had a much larger impact on the everyday lives of many South Africans in the present day than is generally understood. It can be directly traced in the development of civic works and community facilities (see Nicholas Clarke, Chapter 4) or the design of buildings for various communities of faith (Nicholas Clarke, Chapter 5). The impact can be further observed on the Dutch influence on commercial and industrial architectural design, specifically in the banking sector (Catherine Deacon & Marguerite Pienaar, Chapter 6) as well as in large infrastructure developments such as the Cape Town Harbour and Foreshore (Roger Fisher, interlude). While the book uncovers the works of architects that have since faded into obscurity, perhaps one of the most significant contributions of this work is in uncovering the forgotten human stories of life in early C20 South Africa.

Through detailed narrative accounts, one is transported back in time to a period where South Africa was searching for an identity. Two very poignant accounts of life are presented by Mathebe Aphane & Kees Somer (Chapter 8) as well as Roger Fisher & Mary Lange (Chapter 11). The former chapter highlights the inescapable influence of Dutch architecture in a space that was legislated to house the black population of South Africa: the Township. The latter shining a light on the struggles of migration and assimilation into a new and extremely dynamic society.

Marieke Kuipers touches briefly on the Dutch influence on a few series of memorials and cultural fairs (interlude). However, as South Africa grapples with its painful past and considers what level of representation

Stellenbosch, the Cape Dutch 'Blaauwklippen' farm house; photo 2016

Unknown location, eight-sided Roman Catholic church building with freestanding bell tower and people of its community of faith, designed by Edy Payens, photographed shortly after completion

should be incorporated into our collective identity in terms of public memorabilia, it is important to note that shared/colonial heritage is not limited to statues and memorials of Dutch descendants or Afrikaner pioneers. In fact, a major success of this book is in highlighting that shared heritage touches almost every aspect of the spatial realm in South Africa through technology, education, and industrial techniques to name a few, as discussed by Mike Louw (Chapter 9).

However, these structures do not exist in a vacuum and the socio-spatial impact of colonialism and apartheid on the built fabric of South Africa has created a highly contentious heritage landscape where historical structures are viewed as relics celebrating a painful past by large parts of the population. As difficult as these discussions are in a nation not fully healed from its old wounds, the inescapable reality is that South Africa does indeed share a history with its former colonisers.

Common Ground is thus unique in that it manages to achieve something long lost in the general discourse around shared heritage in South Africa's volatile heritage landscape: nuance.

Perhaps the greatest contribution of the book to the national dialogue around heritage and representation in South Africa is its ability to communicate that structures built during colonialism and apartheid are not homogenous in 'celebrating' the painful past. And when separating the context from the structures and separating the structures from their architects, there are human stories attached to each building typology that can resonate with individuals from all backgrounds. As South Africa enters the third decade of democracy, *Common Ground* comes at a perfect moment in time as a body of work that will contribute greatly to our understanding of shared heritage. The book offers a poised and balanced alternative perspective to the 'authorised heritage discourse' in post-apartheid South Africa which tends to polarise colonial and endemic heritage. While normative approaches to heritage management generally emphasise the disjuncture between the colonial (including apartheid) and post-colonial periods, *Common Ground* highlights that there are significant ties to Dutch influences within both epochs.

The above polarisation of heritage resources is largely a result of having 'state led' approaches to heritage throughout the history of South Africa (further discussed below) with the Afrikaner led government celebrating their resistance efforts and commemorating their struggle against British domination, and the newly formed African government celebrating and commemorating their struggle against the Afrikaner led state and apartheid system.

State-driven heritage management is not a uniquely South African feature. Each political regime introduces symbols or memorabilia that capture the hegemonic political zeitgeist. In fact an explicit function of the South African Heritage Resources Agency (SAHRA) is the 'Identification, Promotion and Protection' of national heritage sites (formerly known as National Monuments) in post-1994 South Africa. Under Dutch and British political dominance, early South Africa was an extremely tumultuous period which was reflected in the dynamic shaping of the early heritage landscape; replete with Victorian and Dutch heritage insignia.

State prioritisation of heritage during the apartheid era, post-1948, mainly saw the emergence of the white Afrikaner nation state and the promotion of Afrikaner heritage which was naturally linked with Dutch heritage symbolism through legacy. This period also saw the National Monuments Council, predecessor to SAHRA, proclaim over 4000 structures and areas of significance 'national monuments' (in the official language of the period). Unsurprisingly, the National Estate during that period was characterised by and representative of colonial British and Dutch architecture and design and subsequently sites related to the Afrikaner struggle for independence. Sites representative of the largely African population were generally ignored. This particular feature of both the colonial and apartheid period would prove to have ramifications many years later after the democratization of the state in 1994.

Spatial contexts with a historically oppressive past are generally entangled with the challenge of conflicting heritage as can be seen through the recent calls for the removal of colonial figures from public spaces in the United States of America, United Kingdom and the Netherlands. South Africa is certainly no exception, the recent debates, and controversies around the Steyn Statue at the University of the Free State in 2017 and the Rhodes Statue at the University of Cape Town in 2015 have gained international attention and sparked debate with the year 2020 seeing increased calls for colonial built heritage and public memorials to either be removed, renamed or destroyed all together.

Bloemfontein, mirror with questions about the future of the MT Steyn statue at the right, University of Free State campus, 2020 (since relocated)

Pretoria, Prinsman Place (formerly Impala Building), apartment block designed by Burg Lodge & Burg in 1936; photo 2016

South Africa has one of the most diverse populations in the world. The combined societal diversity which intersects with a deeply painful past for large parts of the population has resulted in virtually all pre-1994 built heritage being 'contested'. They are either seen as sites of oppression and exclusion or historical 'relics' that need to be preserved for the sake of preservation. The 'official heritage discourse' in post-1994 South Africa has uncertainly focused on the many injustices and traumas that subjugated South Africans of colour had endured for a great part of the C20. There remains an ever present need to redress the tragedies of our past and to continuously reflect on our previous injustices while always interrogating what it means to share our heritage with our former colonizers. However, there is an ever present danger of missing an opportunity to harness the immense potential that shared heritage structures may have for an emerging economy such as South Africa's.

The year 2024 will mark 30 years since the end of apartheid, and as we enter our third decade of democracy, it is critical to pause and reflect on the path we have travelled since 1994. There are a few crucial questions that we need to ask ourselves as we move forward into the adolescence of our young nation such as: 'What value can be extracted from colonial infrastructure and buildings?'; 'Can we move past the polarised view of historical structures as colonial or non-colonial?'; 'How can we maximise the potential of these structures to meet our current needs?'; 'How can we utilize these structures to meet our sustainability goals?'; 'Can South Africa use its abundance of cultural heritage to shape its development and secure a sustainable future?'

As South Africa continues on its journey to be a leading economy on the African continent in C21, reflections on these questions are mandatory. Furthermore, maximising the potential of cultural heritage to instigate transformation and categorically promote sustainable development is not only imperative but more urgent now than ever.

South Africa has an abundance of diverse natural and cultural resources. While cultural heritage in South Africa, like many parts of the world, is increasingly being employed as a vehicle for development and sustainability, many forms of heritage resources remain untapped due to their associative histories with a painful past. Two decades after the end of liberation struggles and the demise of apartheid and colonial administrations there has been an emphasis on including liberation heritage in the national estate. This has mainly involved the proclamation of sites related to struggle stalwarts as heritage sites. Expanding our understanding of what constitutes a heritage site (from whatever origins) may be the crucial key in propagating sustainable development in South Africa.

The potential contribution of many historical structures cannot be emphasised enough. However, due to the polarisation of shared heritage sites, a large number of battle sites, detention centres/concentration camps, assembly points and transit bases that may be perceived as colonial heritage in South Africa remain trapped in limbo. Formerly protected and celebrated by previous government administrations these are however shunned by large parts of the population and remain unutilized. This has been the result of many factors that include, but are certainly not limited to, the traumatic effects of colonialism over large parts of the population as well a political dispensation that limits its alliance with structures associated with apartheid and colonialism.

Common Ground is an important volume for an extremely dynamic society and manages to eloquently capture the subtle yet important aspects of the assimilation of Dutch heritage in South Africa during a particularly tumultuous period in time. The book reads like a vintage high definition polaroid of life in the early 1900s and uses the stories of buildings to convey the everyday life of South Africans in the early C20. The repressive context that those architects and civil engineers discussed in this book found themselves understandably evokes a mixed bag of emotions for an extremely diverse population. The duality of the structures built during this period, which are now accessible to all citizens, remains a key issue in contemporary South Africa. For example, conserving Cape Dutch architectural farm houses in Constantia often means conserving the slave quarters associated with them. The beauty and novelty of the structures can easily be lost to a narrative of oppression attached to a significant amount of historical sites.

As the nation continues to define and foster a collective identity that speaks to the values of a democratic South Africa, it is important to remember that we cannot be selective about which aspects of our heritage we consider to be 'colonial'. The general ethos one derives from *Common Ground*, is that shared heritage is more present than we know or at the very least, more present than we would like to believe. It is critical then, that we harness the immense potential that shared heritage may have for advancing the development goals of South Africa and other previously colonized states on the African continent.

Understandably, shared heritage remains highly contentious and a sensitive topic of discussion. The role of the state in defining heritage and leading the discussion on what is desirable and undesirable has been shown to ignore the many layers of history attached to most sites for purposes of achieving the narrow interests of the elected political administration. This has been the case throughout the history of South Africa from colonial times to the present day. It is therefore important to remember that the custodians of all heritage resources in South Africa are the citizens of the country and the communities where these resources find themselves located. Community participation is critical for reaching consensus on what value we will ultimately ascribe to contentious sites from the past. Grass-roots participation in decision-making can avoid the exclusion of socially marginalized groups and understand local needs while sustaining the continuity of the community's unique characteristics and cultural traditions. There is growing recognition that cultural heritage can benefit nation building, especially in the formation of personal or collective identities. Community participation then becomes an indispensable component for a diverse society such as South Africa which is still seeking to come to grips with past traumas, while fostering a new identity for an infinitely hopeful future.

After centuries of state led heritage management which has created a highly polarised heritage landscape, perhaps the time has come for the citizens to lead the direction in shaping our national identity. After all, there are many more layers to all histories than the authorised account. We are reminded of this at a crucial juncture in our journey as country in *Common Ground*.

Cape Town, Tygerberg Hospital designed by Andrews & Niegeman; photo 2020

Bloemfontein, Sacred Heart Cathedral, painted glass window by Sister Piëntia; photo 2020

Sources

This book is the result of research into a previously unexplored field. It made use of many types of sources. The built environment was the primary source, the 'stone repository' and counterpart of the 'paper' archive.
Field surveys were therefore an integral part of the research undertaken. Other sources such as published and archival material elucidate, illuminate, verify, challenge or debunk the reading of the built artefacts. Oral histories were likewise, a vital source to this research. Oral histories were in many cases the only sources apart from the built environment the project had. These oral histories, recollections and opinions facilitated constructing historical narratives and supplemented other historical evidence. They make the chapters and interludes included in the book more inclusive and representative.

During these investigations, various family archives were discovered and consulted. The researchers, where requested to do so, endeavoured to assist the owners of such material to ensure the longer-term conservation thereof either through digitization or through arranging for material to be donated to accredited archives.

In undertaking this research, all persons approached to provide information gave their consent to the use and publication of the information transmitted to the researchers.

Archives

Architecture Archives, University of Pretoria, Department of Architecture, Pretoria.
- Cleland Collection
- Eaton Collection
- Van de Werke Collection

Archival collection Zuid-Afrikahuis, Amsterdam
City of Tshwane, Tshwane Heritage Research Centre, Pretoria
Delft University of Technology, Trésor
Erfenisstigting, Pretoria
- Church Archive of the Nederduitsch Hervormde Kerk

Het Nieuwe Instituut, Rotterdam
- Hanrath Archive [HANR]
- Kammer (and Kret) Archive [KAMM]
- Oud Archive [OUDJ]
- Wijdeveld Archive [WIJD]

Johannesburg Heritage Foundation
Museum Africa, Johannesburg
National Archive of the Netherlands, The Hague
Netherlands South Africa/NedBank Archives, Johannesburg
Special Collections, Library, Nelson Mandela University, Port Elizabeth
Special Collections, Library, University of Cape Town
- JC Jongens Collection
- Andrews & Niegeman/Shapiro Collection
- [Unfortunately, these were partially damaged by the April 2021 Table
- Mountain Fire]

Transnet Heritage Library, Johannesburg
Various private collections

Websites

An essential primary source is:
www.artefacts.co.za.

The following list of references includes the majority of websites that have been consulted for the chapters and interludes, but the list may not be exhaustive. Most of the Dutch digital image collections (often accessible via an online 'beeldbank') have been omitted, while the sources of the selected and printed images in this book are mentioned separately.

www.atomdrisa.co.za
www.atlasofmutualheritage.nl
www.bonas.nl
www.bronberger.co.za
www.canonsociaalwerk.eu
www.claybrick.co.za
www.cultureelerfgoed.nl
www.delpher.nl
www.durasb.co.za
www.dutchfootsteps.co.za
www.gahetna.nl
www.geheugen.nl
www.geheugen.delpher.nl
www.grinaker-lta.com
www.icomos.nl
www.icomos.org
www.ispani.co.za
www.jandijker.nl
www.noord-hollandsarchief.nl
www.rosema.co.za
www.sahistory.org
www.sahris.co.za
www.scnet.co.za
www.stadsarchief.rotterdam.nl
www.theheritageportal.co.za
www.theheritageregister.org.za
www.thepresidencygov.za
www.unesco.org
www.wmbr.org.za
www.zuidafrikahuis.nl

Publications

List of Abbreviations

A&B [SA] = *Architect and Builder* [South African]
ASA = *Architecture South Africa: Journal of the South African Institute of Architects*
SAAR = *South African Architectural Record*
Zuid-Afrika Mbl = *Zuid-Afrika. Maandblad voor de cultureele en economische betrekkingen tusschen Nederland en Zuid-Afrika*

[*A note from the editors:*
Many of the cited published sources are available in digital format. Due to the restrictions on space these have not all been given. Should the reader wish to access these they are advised to enter the title as keywords in a web-browser]

A&B [SA]. 1952. Double-storey shell. *Architect and Builder*, Jun: 38–41.

A&B [SA]. 1953. Dutch firm introduces new building methods. *Architect & Builder*, Aug: 56–58.

A&B [SA]. 1956a. "Here Sewentien" Building. Architects: Chapman & Spoor. Constructors: Miller Bros. (Pty.) Ltd., *Architect and Builder*, Jul: 32–38.

A&B [SA]. 1956b. K.L.M. The planning and redesigning of the Royal Dutch Airlines booking and information office Loveday Street Johannesburg. *Architect & Builder*, Jul: 42–43.

A&B [SA]. 1957a. Nederlands Pavilion, Rand Easter Show. *Architect & Builder*, Jun: 38–41.

A&B [SA]. 1957b. Shell Training Centre, Muizenberg. Architects: Andrews & Niegeman. *Architect & Builder*, Aug: 47–49.

A&B [SA]. 1960a. Nederduitsch Hervormde Church, Cape Town. *Architect & Builder*, Feb: 54–57.

A&B [SA]. 1960b. Curtain-wall facelift for motor showrooms, Cape Town. *Architect & Builder*, Nov: 2–9.

A&B [SA]. 1962a. Netherlands Bank, Johannesburg. *Architect & Builder*, Aug: 20–27.

A&B [SA]. 1962b. Unusual HP roof for factory. *Architect & Builder*, Oct: 10–14.

A&B [SA]. 1963. Hyperbolic paraboloid roof on Stellenbosch house. *Architect & Builder*, Nov: 2–9.

A&B [SA]. 1966. Cape Steel's new premises. *Architect & Builder*, Jun: 9–14.

A&B [SA]. 1967. Natal Plywood and Chipboard Factory, Pietermaritzburg. *Architect & Builder*, Mar: 2–9.

A&B [SA]. 1970. New winery, Epping, Cape. *Architect and Builder*, Mar: 14–19.

A&B [SA]. 1990. Profile of a practice: Andrews & Niegeman attain their half century. *Architect & Builder*, Sept: 20–25.

Advance, 1952. *Govt plan to open concentration camps? Cape Councillors repudiate Pretoria Delegation.* Thursday, Nov 27. [http://www.historicalpapers.wits.ac.za/inventories/inv_pdfo/CULL0001/CULL0001-1-4-01-jpeg.pdf].

Allen, V. 1971. *Kruger's Pretoria: Buildings and personalities of the city in the nineteenth century.* Cape Town: AA Balkema.

Andela, GM. 2000. *Kneedbaar landschap, kneedbaar volk: De heroïsche jaren van de ruilverkavelingen in Nederland*. Bussum: Thoth.

Andrews & Niegeman. 1944. Alma Ata … A house for HTO Niegeman, MIA, of Andrews and Niegeman Architects: Situated at Hout Bay, Cape Peninsula some miles south of Capetown. *SAAR,* Nov: 277–78.

Annema, W. 1973. *Het huis Bouwkunde: De huisvesting van de Afdeling Bouwkunde aan de TH te Delft vanaf 1843–1971: Een bijdrage tot de geschiedenis van de Technische Hogeschool te Delft*. Delft: Technische Hogeschool.

Anon. [1952]. *The Festival in Pictures*. [Cape Town]: s.n.

Anon. 1911. Our prize competition. *The African Architect,* 1(3) Aug: 56.

Anon. 1913. Het "Vrouwenmonument" te Bloemfontein. *Hollandsch Zuid-Afrika: Maandschrift voor de leden der Nederlandsch-Zuid-Afrikaansche Vereeniging en andere belanghebbenden,* 5(1) Jul: 1–6.

Anon. 1926. 'n Gesellige kombuis. (Originally *Die Boerevrou,* August 1926). In Fisher & Le Roux. 1989: 100–01.

Anon. 1928. Protestantsch verzet tegen subsidie aan Katholiek onderwijs, *Overijsselsch Dagblad* (daily newspaper), 14 Jun: 1.

Anon. 1930a. Koninginnedag in Zuid-Afrika. *Zuid-Afrika Mbl,* 7(10): 175.

Anon. 1930b. Anthroposophisch kamp op de Veluwe. *Het Vaderland*, 1930, 7 Aug (Avondblad): 1.

Anon. 1931a. De a.s. Int. Koloniale tentoonstelling te Parijs: De Nederlandsche deelneming, *De Hollandsche Revue*: 59–63.

Anon. 1931b. Nogeens die bediendevraagstuk, *Die Huisgenoot*, 21 Aug: 63, 67.

Anon. 1934. De tewaterlating van het motorschip 'Bloemfontein'. *De Ingenieur,* nr. 25, Jun: 239–40.

Anon. 1935a. M.T.S. voor Bouwkunde. *De Tijd : godsdienstig-staatkundig weekblad* (daily newspaper), 12 July: 10.

Anon. 1935b. Per fiets naar Zuid-Afrika. *De Tijd : godsdienstig-staatkundig dagblad* (daily newspaper), 10 Aug: 10.

Anon. 1936a. Brief uit Pretoria. *Hollands Weekblad voor Zuid-Afrika*, 22 Feb: 6.

Anon. 1936b. Op goed geluk. *Hollands Weekblad voor Zuid-Afrika*, 27 Jun: 7.

Anon. 1936c. Vereeniging van Nederlanders te Johannesburg. *Hollands Weekblad voor Zuid-Afrika*, 27 Jun: 2–7.

Anon. 1937. Emigratie: Bouwbedrijf en wegenaanleg rondom Kaapstad. *Zuid-Afrika Mbl*, 14(11): 150–51.

Anon. 1939. New Provincial Building, Wale Street. *The South African Architect*, June: 91, 94, 177.

Anon. 1944a. Unbreakable spirit of Holland. *Cape Times*, 11 Feb.

Anon. 1944b. Exhibition 'Vrij Nederland'. [exhibition catalogue at National Archive, The Hague, Consulaat-Generaal Kaapstad, 2.05.125, inv.nr. 118].

Anon. 1948. Varia. *Zuid-Afrika Mbl*, May: 78.

Anon. 1952. Grote aanwinsten voor de KLM: Hangar "Kingsford Smith" en DC-B "Jan van Riebeeck" in gebruik genomen. *Het Parool* (daily newspaper), 30 May: 1.

Anon. 1953a. Katholieke groei in Zuid-Afrika : Protestants verzet tegen "Roomse immigratie". *De Tijd: godsdienstig-staatkundig dagblad* (daily newspaper), 13 Feb: 2.

Anon. 1953b. Oude kerk is veranderd in kapel en recreatiezaal: Fraaie aanwinst voor Rooms Katholieke HBS in Bolsward, *Leeuwarder Courant*, 24 March: 3.

Anon. 1954a. Huf terug te Rotterdam. *Algemeen Handelsblad* (daily newspaper), 26 Mar: 11.

Anon. 1954b. Bekend architect in Nederland terug. Bouwer van kerken en kloosters. *De Tijd: godsdienstig-staatkundig dagblad* (daily newspaper), 26 July: 4.

Anon. 1954c. Prins Bernhard te Kaapstad. *Algemeen Handelsblad* (daily newspaper), 6 Oct: 1.

Anon. 1955. Passanten: H. Sikkel: Zeg iets goeds van Zuid-Afrika. *Algemeen Handelsblad* (daily newspaper)*,* 12 March: 17.

Anon. 1957a. Nederlandse industrie exposeert in het buitenland: Handig demonteerbare exportmeccano. *De Maasbode* (daily newspaper), 10 Jan: 6.

Anon. 1957b. Netherlands new pavilion at Rand Show. *Construction in southern Africa*, 2(1/ Apr): 47–49.

Anon. 1960a. Mees besproke kerk in ons land. *Die Huisgenoot*, 12 August: 18–19.

Anon. 1960b. Rassenpolitiek bezorgt Kerk in Z.-Afrika veel problemen : tegenwerking van regering. *Nieuwsblad van het Zuiden* (daily newspaper), 19 Oct: 7.

Anon. 1961. Meer dan puur vakmanschap van architect Sikkel, *Trouw* (daily newspaper), 29 April: 17.

Anon. 1964. Synode wil meer protestanten voor Zuid-Afrika. *De Volkskrant* (daily newspaper), 13 Feb: 3.

Anon. 2012. Hendrik sy tyd ver vooruit met eerste landgoed-ontwikkeling. *Die/The Bronberger*, 26 Sep [www.bronberger.co.za].

APHP. *Code of ethics.* [www.aphp.org.za/aphp-code-conduct].

Army Headquarters, South Africa. 1902. *Treaty of Vereeniging.* [www.sahistory.org.za/sites/default/files/archive-files/peace_treaty_of_vereeniging.pdf].

Attwell, M. 2013. *Cape Town International Convention Centre: Historical background report*. Jan.

B[roekman], JH. 1948. De Hugenoten in Zuid-Afrika, immigratie van nu en vroeger. *Zuid-Afrika*: 57.

B[ruin], W. 1933. De huisvesting der afdeling Bouwkunde te Delft. *Bouwkundig Weekblad*: 117–22.

Bakker, KA. 2014. The Departement Publieke Werken. In Bakker, Clarke & Fisher: 66–89.

Bakker, KA., Clarke, NJ. & Fisher, RC. (eds). 2014. *Eclectic ZA Wilhelmiens: A shared Dutch built heritage in South Africa.* Pretoria: Visual Books.

Barbieri, U., Colenbrander, B. & Engel, H. 1981. *Architectuur van JJP Oud. Catalogue of an exhibition held at the Lijnbaancentrum RKS, Rotterdam, 19 dec 1981 to 31 jan 1982*. Rotterdam: Rotterdamse Kunststichting.

Barker, A. 2012. Cape vernacular interpretations. *ASA,* (57): 36–43.

Barker, A., Van Niekerk, K. & Swart, JJ. 2016. The importance of architectural archives. *ASA,* May/Jun: 6–9.

Barnouw, D. 2015. *Oorlog en bezetting: Nederland in 1940–1945: De geschiedenis in topstukken uit het NIOD-archief*. Amsterdam: Hollands Diep/Over-Amstel.

Baudet, H. 1992. *De lange weg naar de Technische Universiteit Delft 1: De Delftse ingenieursschool en haar voorgeschiedenis*. The Hague: Sdu.

Beelaerts van Blokland, FWA. (ed.). 1989. *Paviljoen Welgelegen 1789–1989. Van buitenplaats van de bankier Hope tot zetel van de Provincie Noord-Holland*. Haarlem: Schuyt & Co.

Berghoef, J. (1954). *Beginselen van kerkbouw: rapport uitgebracht aan de Generale Synode der Nederlandse Hervormde Kerk*. 's-Gravenhage: Boekencentrum.

Bickford-Smith, V. 2016. *The Emergence of the South African Metropolis: Cities and Identities in the Twentieth Century*. Cambridge University Press.

Bijl, A. 2012. *About the background to the Bruynzeel house project.* [www.stellenboschwriters.com/bijla1.html#project].

Bloembergen, M. 2001. *Koloniale vertoningen: De verbeelding van Nederlands-Indië op de wereldtentoonstellingen (1880–1931)*. Amsterdam: Unpublished study, University of Amsterdam. [https://hdl.handle.net/11245/1.199694].

Bock, M., Fluks, M., Van Rossem, V. & Vink, M., 1983. *Groep '32: Ontwerpen, gebouwen, stedebouwkundige plannen 1925–1945*. The Hague: Staatsuitgeverij.

Bokhorst, M. 1953. Oude wijn in nieuwe vaten: Yskor 1928–1953. *Nederlandse Post*, 7(4): 19–21.

Bond van Nederlandse Architecten (ed.). 1941. *Nederland bouwt in baksteen: 1800–1940*. Rotterdam: Museum Boymans-Van Beuningen.

Bonner, P & Segal, L. 1999. *Soweto: A history.* Cape Town: Maskew Miller Longman.

Bosma, K. & Wagenaar, C. (eds). 1995. *Een geruisloze doorbraak: De geschiedenis van architectuur en stedebouw tijdens de bezetting en de wederopbouw van Nederland*. Rotterdam: NAi.

Bosma, K. 1995. *The structural art works by Rijkswaterstaat.* Rotterdam: 010.

Bossenbroek, M. 2012. *De Boerenoorlog*. Amsterdam: Atheneum.

Bot, AK. & Kloppers, PJ. 1949. *Eerste Afrikaanse skoolatlas*. Pretoria: JL Van Schaik.

Bot, AK. 1936. *A century of education in the Transvaal, 1836–1936*. Pretoria: Government Printer.

Botha, NM. 2013. *The gateway of tomorrow: Modernist town planning on Cape Town's Foreshore, 1930–70.* Cape Town: Unpublished study, University of Cape Town. [http://hdl.handle.net/11427/7793].

Bouman, O., Mousavi, B., Berens, H., Mulder, S. & Smit, E. 2012. *Dutch Architecture in 250 Highlights: Preserved by the Netherlands Architecture Institute*. Rotterdam: nai010.

Bratt, JD. (ed.). 1998. *Abraham Kuyper. A centennial reader*. Grand Rapids/Cambridge UK: William B Eerdmans /Carlisle: The Paternoster Press.

Breman, P. 1983. De Dordrechtse Ambachtsschool/Technische School voor Dordrecht en omstreken 1883–1983, *Kwartaal & teken van Dordrecht,* 9(1): 1–3.

Brouwer, JW. & Van der Heiden, P. (eds). 1995. *Drees, minister-president 1948–1958*. The Hague: Sdu.

Buch, J. 1993. *A Century of Architecture in the Netherlands, 1880–1990*. Rotterdam: NAi.

Burg, JR. 1919. Bouwkuns. (Originally *Die Boerevrou*, March 1919). In Fisher & Le Roux 1989: 1.

Burg, JR. 1920. Plan van 'n plaashuis. (Originally *Die Boerevrou*, January 1920). In Fisher & Le Roux, 1989: 2–3.

Calderwood, DM. 1953. *An investigation into the planning of urban native housing in South Africa*. Johannesburg: Unpublished study, University of the Witwatersrand. [http://hdl.handle.net/10539/11249].

Casciato, M. 1996. Notes on the Historiography of Modernism. In Molema: 7–12.

Chiozzi, P. (ed.). 1989. *Teaching visual anthropology*. Florence: Il Sedicesimo.

Chipkin, CM. 1993. *Johannesburg Style: Architecture & Society 1880s–1960s*. Cape Town: David Philip.

Christopher, AJ. 2011. The Union of South Africa censuses 1911–1960: An incomplete record. *Historia,* 56(2): 1–18

City Council of Pretoria Public Relations Office. 1948. Atteridgeville native township, Pretoria. *Public Works of South Africa*: 22–28.

City Council of Pretoria. 1943. Atteridgeville: A model native township. *SAAR,* (Jul): 159–162.

City Council of Pretoria. 1999. *Atteridgeville, Soul City*. Pretoria: Information brochure.

CJ. Beyers (ed.) 1981. *Suid-Afrikaanse biografiese woordeboek : deel IV*. Durban & Pretoria: Butterworth.

Clarke, N. & De Villiers, A. 2015. Church Square. The Old Synagogue and the Old Government Printing Works. In Clarke & Kuipers: 63–83.

Clarke, NJ. & Fisher, RC. 2016. *NZASM-footsteps along the tracks: the identified extant built residue of the Nederlandsche Zuid-Afrikaansche Spoorweg-Maatschappij (1887–1902)*. Pretoria: Visual Books.

Clarke, NJ. & Kuipers MC. 2021. Tracing Tectonic Wilhelmiens: Dutch-South African heritage and modernity. [s.l.]. In Docomomo International 2021: 54–59.

Clarke, NJ. & Kuipers, MC. (eds). 2015. *Re-centring Tshwane. Urban heritage strategies for a resilient Capital*. Pretoria: Visual Books.

Cleghorne, WSH. 1922. *Farm Buildings and Building Construction in South Africa*. London: Longmans Green.

Cloete, E. 1999. Writing of(f) the women of the National Women's Monument, *Literator Journal of Literary Criticism, Comparative Linguistics and Literary Studies,* 20(3) Au: 35–50.

Coertze, RD. 1969. *Atteridgeville stedelike bantoewoonbuurt*. Pretoria: Unpublished study, University of Pretoria. [http://hdl.handle.net/2263/37305].

Coertzen, P. 2011. The Huguenots of South Africa in documents and commemoration. *Dutch Reformed Theological Journal*: 301–24.

Collins, P. 1998. *Changing ideals in modern architecture, 1750–1950*. Montreal: McGill-Queen's University Press.

Corten, J-P. 2015. Shared heritage, joint future. In Clarke & Kuipers: 13–25.

Coyne, R. 2013. Even more than architecture. In Fraser: 185–203.

Cremer, HJS. 1936. Jaarverslag der Nederlandsche Vereeniging te Johannesburg, lopende over het jaar 1935. *Hollands Weekblad voor Zuid-Afrika*, 22 Feb: 3–6.

Crijns, B. 1994. *Het (poly)technisch bouwkunstonderwijs 1864–1916: Een onderzoek naar de kunstzinnige vorming van de bouwkundig ingenieur en het ontstaan van de zogenoemde Collectie Sluyterman ten behoeve van die vorming.* Amsterdam: Unpublished study, University of Amsterdam.

Cross, M. 1986. *The foundations of a segregated schooling system on the Witwatersrand 1900–1924*. Johannesburg, Unpublished study, University of the Witwatersrand.

Cumming-George, L. 1933. *Architecture in South Africa* Vol 1. Cape Town: The Speciality Press.

Cumming-George, L. 1934. *Architecture in South Africa* Vol 2. Cape Town: The Speciality Press.

Curry, TM. 2017. *Form follows feeling: The acquisition of design expertise and the function of aesthesis in the design Process.* Delft: A+BE Architecture and the Built Environment (Architecture and the Built Environment, 06).

De Beurs, JP. 1938. Brieven van lezers in den vreemde: Het slagersbedrijf in Zuid-Afrika. *De Vee- en Vleeschhandel*, 22(104): 10, 13.

De Bie, H. 1951. Bouwen in Zuid-Afrika. *Bouw: Centraal Weekblad voor het Bouwwezen*, 6(1): 4–7.

De Bie, H. 1963. Architect's house, Bloemfontein. *Architect and Builder,* (Nov): 16–21.

De Bie, H. 1965. New bank building: Bloemfontein. De Bie, H & Van Wijngaarden. *SAAR,* (Aug): 18–20.

De Bruin, C. *Johan Christian Meischke (1763–1841): Zijn voor- en nageslacht*. Driebergen: s.n.

De Haan, JA. 2016. *Landhuizen en villa's in Nederland tussen 1840 en 1916*. Amsterdam: Unpublished study, University of Amsterdam. [https://hdl.handle.net/11245/1.541514].

De Jong, C. 1991. Lewenskets van Henk Horstmanshof, argitek, bouer en skilder, 1886–1974. *Pretoriana,* 48 (Apr): 49–61.

De Jong, JJ. 1958. Simposium: 'n Geskikte terrein vir die Pretoriase kunsmuseum, *Pretoriana Commemoration edition 1948–1958,* no's 26 & 27, Apr & Aug: 37–41.

De Jong, RC. 1980. *Die kulturele lewe van die Pretoriase Nederlanders, met besondere aandag aan die 'Nederlandsche Vereeniging', 1890–1918.* Pretoria: Unpublished study, University of Pretoria.

De Mulder, EFJ., De Pater, BC. & Droogleever Fortuyn, JC. (eds) with contributions by De Klerk, LA. & Van Dijk, J. 2019. *The Netherlands and the Dutch: A physical and human geography*. Cham: Springer.

De Vreeze, N. 1993. *Woningbouw, inspiratie & ambities: Kwalitatieve grondslagen van de sociale woningbouw in Nederland*. Almere: Nationale Woningraad.

De Zwarte, I. 2016. *Coordinating hunger: The evacuation of children during the Dutch Food Crisis, 1945. War & Society,* (35)2: 132–149.

Den Dikken, J. 2002. *Liem Bwan Tjie (1891–1966): Westerse vernieuwing en oosterse traditie*. Rotterdam: Bonas.

Den Ouden, A. 1994. *Een hoekstaal van de maatschappij: Constructiewerkplaatsen in Nederland: Van 1840 tot heden*. Eindhoven: Stichting Nederlandse Staalbouw.

Denis, P. 1998. *The Dominican friars in southern Africa: A social history (1577–1990)*. Leiden: Brill.

Department of Arts & Culture. 1999. *The National Heritage Resources Act, Number 25 of 1999*. Pretoria: Government Printer.

Dercksen, A. & Verplanke, L. 1987. *Geschiedenis van de onmaatschappelijkheidsbestrijding in Nederland 1914–1970*. Amsterdam/Meppel: Boom.

Docomomo International (ed.). 2021 The 16th International Docomomo Conference - Inheritable Resilience : Sharing Values of Global Modernities. [s.l.]: Docomomo International.

Donsky, IJ. 1989. *Aspects of the immigration of Europeans to South Africa 1946–1970*. Johannesburg: Unpublished study, Rand Afrikaans University. [http://hdl.handle.net/10210/12294].

Du Bruyn, D. & Oelofse, M. 2019. "A hygienic Native township shall be developed": The founding and development of Batho as Bloemfontein's 'model location' (c. 1918–1939). *Historia,* 64(2): 47–81.

Du Preez, H., Van Oers, R., Roos, J. & Verhoef, LWG. (eds). 2009. *The Challenge of Genadendal*. Delft: IOS Press.

Duncan-Brown, AS. 1991. *The International Style of architecture in southern Africa: A case study.* Port Elizabeth: Unpublished study, University of Port Elizabeth.

Dwars, AWC. 1909. Middelb. Techn. school voor de Bouwkunde te Utrecht. *Bouwkundig Weekblad,* 29(49): 583–85.

Editorial. 1911. A master builder's appreciation. *The African Architect,* 1 (Jun): 10.

Editorial. 1958. Simposium: 'n Geskikte terrein vir die Pretoriase kunsmuseum, *Pretoriana Commemoration edition 1948–1958,* no's 26 & 27, Apr & Aug: 36.

Falize, JJ. 1986. De kerkbouw tussen de wereldoorlogen: De Amsterdamse School. In *Steensma & Van Swigchem*: 75–88.

Feinstein, CH. 2005. *An economic history of South Africa: Conquest, Discrimination, and Development*. Cambridge: Cambridge University Press.

Ferguson, JE. 1925. Drie practische tafeltjes. *De Vrouw en haar Huis*, 11(March): 450–52.

Fienieg, A. 2006. *Gemeenschappelijk erfgoed, gedeeld erfgoed? Een onderzoek naar dissonantie bij gemeenschappelijk cultureel erfgoed in zes landen.* Amsterdam: Unpublished study, University of Amsterdam.

Fisher, RC. & Clarke, NJ. 2014. Wilhelmiens aftermath and legacy: The diaspora of practitioners and hybridity of later styles. In Bakker, Clarke & Fisher: 193–215.

Fisher, RC. & Le Roux, S. 1989. *Die Afrikaanse Woning: Herdrukke uit Die Boerevrou (1919–1931)*. Hammanskraal: Unibook.

Fisher, RC. & Le Roux, S. with Maré, E. 1998. *Architecture of the Transvaal.* Pretoria: University of South Africa.

Fisher, RC. 1998. The third vernacular. Pretoria regionalism – aspects of an emergence. In Fisher & le Roux with Maré: 123–47.

Fisher, RC. 2004. The Union Buildings: Reflections on Herbert Baker's design intentions and unrealized designs. *South African Journal of Art History*, 19: 38–47.

Fouché, EFO. 1923. Gemak en gerief in die huis. (Originally *Die Boerevrou,* Oct and Nov 1923). In Fisher & Le Roux, 1989: 53–58.

Fraay-ten Bokkel Huinink, D. 1921. Zuid-Afrikaansch Hospitaal en Diakonessenhuis. *Neerlandia,* 25(3): 38–39.

Fransen, H. 2004. *A guide to the old buildings of the Cape: A survey of extant architecture from before c1910 in the area of Cape Town, Calvinia, Colesberg, Uitenhage*. Johannesburg: Jonathan Ball.

Fraser, M. (ed.). 2013. *Design research in architecture: An overview*. Farnham: Ashgate.

Freriks, K. 2015. *Echo's van Indië: de onafhankelijkheid van Indonesië in verhalen en herinneringen*. Amsterdam: Athenaeum-Polak & Van Gennep.

Frieze, J. 1986. Abraham Kuyper en het gereformeerde kerkgebouw. In *Steensma & Van Swigchem*: pp 60–66.

Frijhoff, W. & Spies, M. 2004. *Dutch culture in a European perspective: 1900, the age of bourgeois culture*. Basingstoke: Palgrave MacMillan.

Geefu. 1936. De toestand in Nederland. *Hollands Weekblad voor Zuid-Afrika*, 22 (Feb): 9–11.

Geertz, C. 1973. *The interpretation of cultures.* New York: Basic Books.

Geljon, P. 2017. *Een Nederlanse overzeebank: De Nederlandsche Bank voor Zuid-Afrika 1888–1969*. Amsterdam: Boom.

Gerneke, G. 1998. From Brazil to Pretoria. In Fisher & Le Roux, with Maré: 197–230.

Gollom, I. 2001. *The history of the Cape Town Orchestra: 1914–1997.* Cape Town: Unpublished study, University of Cape Town. [http://hdl.handle.net/11427/7846].

Gosselink, M., Holtrop, M. & Ross, R. (eds). 2017. *Good hope? South Africa and the Netherlands from 1600*. Nijmegen: Vantilt.

Greig, D. 1970. *Herbert Baker in South Africa*. Cape Town, Purnell.

Greig, D. 1971. *A guide to architecture in South Africa*. Cape Town: Howard Timmins.

Griffiths, RT. & Van Zanden, JL. 1989. *Economische geschiedenis van Nederland in de 20e eeuw*. Utrecht: het Spectrum.

Grillner, K. 2000. Review. The picturesque. Architecture, disgust and other irregularities. *The Journal of Architecture,* (13)5: 669–73.

Groenendijk, P. & Vollaard, P., with Van Dijk, H. 1992. *Gids voor moderne architectuur in Nederland / Guide to modern architecture in the Netherlands*. Rotterdam: 010.

Groenendijk, P. & Vollaard, P., with Van Dijk, H. 2006. *Architectuurgids Nederland (1900–2000) / Architectural guide to the Netherlands*. Rotterdam: 010.

Grové, S. [n.d.]. *Welcome to SA composers: Wegelin, Arthur Willem* [www.sacomposers.co.za/sacomposers/Wegelin,_Arthur.html].

Guerney, K. 2017. *August House is dead, long live August House! The Story of a Johannesburg atelier.* Johannesburg: Fourth Wall Books.

Haarhoff, E. 2010. Appropriating modernism: Apartheid and the South African township. In Zeren Gülersoy: 229–39. [https://doi.org/10.7480/iphs.2010.2].

Hamilton, LA. 2003. *Dutch resistance to the Nazis during World War Two*. Tennesee: Unpublished study, University of Tennessee. [https://trace.tennessee.edu/utk_chanhonoproj/652].

Harradine, M. [1994] 2002. *Port Elizabeth: A social chronicle to the end of 1945*. Port Elizabeth: EH Walton Packaging.

Harris, CT & Noëth, JG., Sarkady, NG, Schutte, FM & Van Tonder, JM. 2010. *Van seringboom tot kerkgebou: Die argitektoniese erfenis van die gereformeerde kerke.* Krugersdorp: Gereformeerde Kerke in Suid-Afrika.

Harrop-Allin, C. 1975. *Norman Eaton architect: A study of the work of the South African architect Norman Eaton 1902–1966.* Cape Town/Johannesburg: C Struik.

Hartdegen, P. & Terblanche, J. 2007. *A century of building South Africa: Master Builders South Africa.* Johannesburg: Chris van Rensburg.

Heerding, A. 1971. *Cement in Nederland.* IJmuiden: Cemij Cementfabriek IJmuiden.

Henkes, B. 2016. Shifting identifications in Dutch-South African migration policies (1910–1961). *South African Historical Journal*, 68(4): 641–69.

Herbert G. 1975. *Martienssen and the International Style: The modern movement in South African Architecture*. Cape Town: AA Balkema.

Hervormde Emigratie Commissie. 1960. *Van emigrant tot immigrant: Een woord van die Nederlandse Hervormde Kerk tot hen die gaan emigreren*. (4th ed). The Hague: Hervormde Emigratie Commissie.

Hilkhuijsen, JWL. 2001. *Delftse Art Nouveau: Onderwijs en ontwerp van Adolf le Comte (1850–1921), Karel Sluyterman (1863–1931) en Bram Gips (1861–1943)*. Assen/Zwolle: Drents Museum/Waanders Uitgevers.

Hilversum2.clubs.nl. n.d. *Architect Anthonie Pieter Smits 1881–1957 Haarlem-Aerdenhout v.d. Linde.* [https://hilversum2.clubs.nl/nieuws/detail/2086563_architect-ap-smits-1881-1957-haarlem].

Hockins, P. 2014. Discussion: Where is the theory in visual anthropology? *Visual Anthropology*, 27: 436–56.

Hoff, A. 1997. The water snake of the Khoekhoen and /Xam. *South African Archaeological Bulletin*, 52: 21–37.

Hofmeyr, G. 2002. *NG Kerk 350: eenhonderd bakens in die geskiedenis van die Nederduitse Gereformeerde Kerk 1652-2002.* Wellington, Lux Verbi.

Hofstede, BP. 1964. *Thwarted exodus: Post-war overseas migration from the Netherlands.* The Hague: Martinus Nijhoff.

Hofstee, CRG. with Werkgroep Inventarisatie Mijnmonumenten. 1978. *Inventarisatie Mijnmonumenten.* Heerlen: Samenwerkingsverband Sanering Mijnterreinen Oostelijk Mijngebied.

Huisman, J. (ed.). 2000. *Honderd jaar wonen in Nederland 1900–2000*. Rotterdam: 010.

Human, JJ., Cameron, T. & Breytenbach, K. (eds). 1999. *They shaped our century: The most influential South Africans of the twentieth century*. Cape Town: Human & Rousseau.

Human, K. 1999. August Aimé Balkema. In Human, Cameron & Breytenbach: 442–45.

Ibelings, H. 1997. *Americanism: Dutch architecture and the transatlantic model.* Rotterdam: NAi.

IJperlaan, J. & Van der Steur, JAG. 1932. *De Technische Hoogeschool te Delft. Het gebouw der Bouwkunde in gebruik genomen 21 september 1932.* Delft. Waltman.

Isserlis, S. 2009. *Anthem guide to the opera, concert halls and classical music venues of Europe*. London: Anthem Press.

Jansen, E. 2015. *Bijna familie.* Amsterdam: Cossee.

Japha, D. 1998. The social programme of the South African Modern Movement. In Judin & Vladislavić: 422–37.

Jones, S (ed.). 1988. *Banking and business in South Africa.* New York: St Martin's Press.

Jones, S (ed.). 1992. *Financial enterprise in South Africa since 1950*. London: Macmillan.

Jongens, EDJ. 2010. Drie dubbele herenhuizen op de Heemsteedse Dreef. *HeerlijkHeden: Kwartaalblad van de Historische Vereniging Heemstede-Bennebroek*, (38)114: 42–44.

Judin, H. & Vladislavić, I. (eds). 1998. *Blank: Architecture, apartheid and after.* Rotterdam: NAi.

Kaper, L., Mees ten Oever, R. & Schotanus, J. (eds). 1994. *Honderd jaar Fin-de-siècle 1894–1994*. Delft: Stylos.

Katzen, L. 1963. South-African immigration and emigration in the post-war period. *International Migration*, 1(3): 183–91.

Keith, M. 1998. The Baker School. In: Fisher & Le Roux, with Maré: 78–97.

Keuning, D. 2017. *Bouwkunst en de Nieuwe Orde: Collaboratie en berechting van Nederlandse architecten 1940–1950*. Nijmegen: Vantilt.

Koch, L. 2019. *Faculty honoured to welcome daughter of first Dean at 75-Year Gala Dinner.* [www.eng.sun.ac.za/news/faculty-honoured-to-welcome-daughter-of-first-dean-at-75-year-gala-dinner].

Kooijman, D. 1995. *Wortels van het architectuuronderwijs*. Delft: Delftse Universitaire Pers.

Korthals Altes, HJ. 2004. *Tuinsteden, tussen utopie en realiteit*. Bussum: Thoth.

Kuiper, JA. 1991. *Visueel & dynamisch: De stedebouw van Granpré Molière en Verhagen 1915–1950*. Delft: Publikatieburo Bouwkunde.

Kuipers, MC. 1987. *Bouwen in beton: Experimenten in de volkshuisvesting voor 1940*. The Hague: Staatsuitgeverij.

Kuipers, MC. 2010. *Het Architectonisch Geheugen / The Architectural Memory.* Delft: VSSD.

Kuipers, MC. 2017. *Van Nellefabriek Rotterdam: World Heritage of a World Port*. Rotterdam: nai010.

Kuipers, MC. (ed.). 2002. *Toonbeelden van de Wederopbouw. Architectuur, stedenbouw en landinrichting van herrijzend Nederland*. Zwolle: Waanders.

Kuipers, MC. (ed.). 2019. *Interieurs van herrijzend Nederland. Binnenruimten van een opkomende welvaartsstaat*. Zwolle: Wbooks.

Kuyper, A. 1911. *Onze eeredienst*. Kampen: Kok.

Labuschagne, E. 1998. From trekboer to builder: Pioneer builders: Materials, techniques, traditions, types. In Fisher & le Roux, with Maré: 25–54.

Labuschagne, P. 2014. The Women's Monument and memorial complexity in the context of political change: From memorial exclusivity to monument(al) inclusivity. *South African Journal of Art History,* 29(2): 30–43.

Lange, ME. 2011. *Water stories and rock engravings: Eiland women at the Kalahari edge.* Amsterdam: Rozenberg.

Lange, ME., De Wee, J., Van Rooi, M.,Sixaxa, E., Saaiman, G., Malo, M. & HlopeZulu, M. 2014. *Water Stories*. Pretoria: UNISA Press.

Lange, ME., Müller Jansen, L., Fisher, RC., Tomaselli, KG. & Morris, D. (eds). 2013. *Engraved Landscape: Biesje Poort.* Gordon's Bay: Tormentoso.

Langeveld, H. 2004. *Hendrikus Colijn 1869–1944: Schipper naast God.* Amsterdam: Balans.

Law, B. 2015. *Building the Mother City: Cape Town 1880–1913: In the steps of AB Reid, Master Builder and City Councillor*. Cape Town: Beatrice Law.

Le Roux, H. 2019. Designing KwaThema: Cultural inscriptions in the model township. *The Journal of Southern African Studies*, 45(2): 273–301.

Le Roux, SW. 2008. Die soeke van drie argitekte na 'n planvorm vir Afrikaanse Gereformeerde kerkbou, *Suid-Afrikaanse Tydskrif vir Kultuurgeskiedenis,* 22 (2): 20–44, November.

Leigh, RL. 1966. *Port Elizabeth: From a border garrison town to a modern commercial and industrial city*. Johannesburg: Felstar.

Liebenberg, D. 2014. *The use of modernism in Afrikaner Protestant church design in Cape Town's Northern Suburbs.* Cape Town: Cape Peninsula University of Technology.

Lijdsman, P. 1920. Een en ander over Middelbaar Technisch Onderwijs en over opleiding tot aannemer. In Weissman: 206–30.

Lijphart, A. 2008. *Verzuiling, pacificatie en kentering in de Nederlandse politiek*. www.dbnl.org/tekst/lijp001verz01_01/colofon.htm (based on (8th ed). 1990, Haarlem: Becht).

Linstra, M. 2016. *Low-Cost housing in South Africa: The urban changes of west Pretoria*. 2016. Delft: Unpublished paper, Delft University of Technology.

Loedolff, JF. 1960. *Nederlandse immigrante: 'n Sosiologiese ondersoek van hul inskakeling in die gemeenskapslewe van Pretoria.* Cape Town: HAUM.

Logan, W. & Reeves, K. (eds). 2008. *Places of pain and shame: Dealing with difficult heritage*. London/New York: Routledge.

Lotter, AC. 1963. *Bou u eie droomhuis*. Johannesburg: Afrikaanse Pers Boekhandel.

Louw, PE. 2004. Political power, national identity, and language: The case of Afrikaans. *International Journal of the Sociology of Language,* 170: 43–58.

Maas, FN. 1951. *Honderd jaren Academie van Beeldende Kunsten en Technische Wetenschappen*. Rotterdam: AD Donker.

Mabin, A. 1993. The Witwatersrand Joint Town Planning Committee 1932–1940: Of rigour and *mortis*. *Planning History.* (15)2: 49–54.

Mabin, A. 2013. *The map of Gauteng: Evolution of a city-region in concept and plan*. Occasional Paper 05, July. [http://wiredspace.wits.ac.za/handle/10539/16851].

Macdonald, J. 2016. *Tracing the Passion of a Black Christ: Critical reflections on the iconographic revision and symbolic redeployment of the Stations of the Cross and Passion cycle by South African artists Sydney Kumalo, Sokhaya Charles Nkosi and Azaria Mbatha.* Cape Town: University of Cape Town.

MacDonald, S. 2008. *Difficult Heritage: Negotiating the Nazi past in Nuremberg and beyond*. London/New York: Routledge.

Mallory-Hill, S., Preiser, W. & Watson, C. (eds). 2011. *Enhancing building performance*. Hoboken, NJ: Wiley Blackwell. [www.researchgate.net/publication/254644631].

Marius. 1935. Natalsche Pennekrassen. *Nieuwsblad van Friesland,* 4 December: 2.

Marschall, S. 2009. *Landscape of memory: Commemorative monuments, memorials and public statuary in post-apartheid South-Africa*. Leiden: Brill.

Martis, A. 1980. Het ontstaan van het kunstnijverheidsonderwijs in Nederland. In Martis, Miedema & Van Uitert: 79–172.

Martis, A., Miedema, H. & Van Uitert, E (eds). 1980. *Kunstonderwijs in Nederland: Kunsthistorisch Jaarboek 1980.* (Vol 30). Haarlem: Fibula-Van Dishoeck.

Mashabela, H. 1988. *Townships of the PWV*. Johannesburg: South African Institute of Race Relations.

Maylam, P. 1995. Explaining the apartheid city: 20 Years of South African urban historiography. *Journal of South African Studies,* (21)1, Mar: 19–38.

Meek, OC. 1967. Oor die Nederlandse verenigingslewe in ou-Pretoria. *Pretoriana,* 53(1): 4–7.

Meiring, H. 1980. *Pretoria 125.* Cape Town: Human and Rossouw.

Meischke, JC. 1911. De nieuwe Uniegebouwen van Zuid-Afrika. *Bouwkundig Weekblad*: 403–05, 414–16.

Meischke, JC. 1912, The African Architect. *Bouwkundig Weekblad*: 15–17.

Meischke, JC. 1914, Reisschetsen van J. Coenraad Meischke. *Bouwkundig Weekblad*: 488.

Meischke, JC. 1915, Reisschetsen II van J. Coenraad Meischke. *Bouwkundig Weekblad*: 136–39.

Meischke, JC. 1923. Rondavels. *Bouwkundig Weekblad*: 188–90.

Meischke, JC., 1926. Groot Constantia. *Bouwkundig Weekblad*: 47–48.

Mellink, G-J., Saal, P. & Van Schuppen, S. 2017. *Verdreven voor de Atlantikwall: ontruiming en afbraak van de Nederlandse kuststreek, 1942–1945*. Zwolle: WBooks.

Mieras, JP. 1946. Prof Dr Ir DF Slothouwer: 5 November 1884 - 3 December 1946. *Bouwkundig Weekblad*: 289–91.

Miescher, G. 2015. The NE 51 Series Frontier: The Grand narrative of apartheid planning and the small town. *Journal of Southern African Studies,* 41(3): 561–80.

Ministerie van Verkeer en Waterstaat. 1959. *From fisherman's paradise to farmer's pride: The Zuiderzee closed, its bottom reclaimed, the Polderland settled*. The Hague: Regeeringsvoorlichtingsdienst.

Minnaar, EM. 2000. *Grondleggende argitekte van die Departement Openbare Werke in Transvaal tot 1910, hul werk en invloed*. Pretoria: Unpublished study, University of Pretoria.

Moerdijk, G. n.d. *Geskiedenis van Pretoria: soos deur sy geboue vertel.* [https://repository.up.ac.za/handle/2263/1288].

Molema, J with Eaton, LK & Vernon, CD. 1996. *The New Movement in the Netherlands 1924–1936*. Rotterdam: 010.

Morris, D. 2010. *Seeing and knowing: Understanding rock art with and without ethnography.* Johannesburg: Wits University Press.

Morris, D. 2014. Foreword. In Lange *et al*: vii–ix.

Morris, SS. 1959. The Cape Town Wemmershoek Water Scheme. *The Civil Engineer in Southern Africa,* May: 97–120.

Moseneke, D. 2016. *My own liberator: A memoir.* Johannesburg: Picador Africa.

Muller, J. 1995. Influence and experience: Albert Thompson and South Africa's Garden City. *Planning History,* 17(3): 14–21.

Munro, K. 2015a. *Sammy Marks Museum: The survival of a grand century old estate*. [www.theheritageportal.co.za/article/sammy-marks-museum-survival-grand-century-old-estate].

Munro, K. 2015b. *What did Johannesburg look like in 1889?* [www.theheritageportal.co.za/article/what-did-johannesburg-look-1889].

Newall, P. 1993. *Cape Town Harbour 1652 to the present*. Cape Town: Portnet.

Niegeman, HTO. 1936. Staalmeubels, *Die Huisgenoot,* 6 Nov: 73.

Niegeman, HTO. 1937. Het bouwen in Zuid-Afrika. *de 8 en Opbouw,* 14(6): 150–51.

Niegeman, HTO. 1938. My experience as an architect in Soviet Russia. *Architect, Builder, Engineer*, Dec: 7–12.

Niegeman, HTO. 1939. My experience as an architect in Soviet Russia. *Architect, Builder, Engineer*, Jan: 13–19.

Nuij, N-J. 2000. *"Gaat u maar rustig slapen": Colijn en de mythe van mei '40*. Hilversum: Verloren.

Nwati, MP. 2007. *Rex Trueform in the age of Globalization*. Cape Town: Unpublished study, University of Cape Town. Open UCT: thesis_hum_2007_nwati_mp.pdf.

Oldenziel, R. & Bouw, B. 1998. *Schoon genoeg: Huisvrouwen en huishoudtechnologie in Nederland 1898–1998*. Nijmegen: SUN.

Oostindië, G. (ed.). 2008, *Dutch colonialism, migration and cultural heritage*. Leiden: KITLV Press.

Overvoorde, JC. 1910a. Monumenten van Nederlandschen oorsprong in de vroegere nederzettingen buiten Europa. (Rede van Mr. Dr. J.C. Overvoorde op het Ned. Taal- en Letterk. Congres te Maastricht). *Neerlandia,* 14: 204–06.

Overvoorde, JC. 1910b. Uit Zuid-Afrika. *Nieuwe Rotterdamsche Courant*, 6 Dec.

Overvoorde, JC. 1912. Hollandsche monumenten buiten Europa. *Bulletin Oudheidkundige Bond*: 144–50.

Overvoorde, JC. 1913. *Hollandsche herinneringen in Zuid-Afrika, in het bijzonder op het gebied der Monumenten*. Utrecht: Kemink & Zoon.

Overvoorde, PPJ. 2018. *"Als het maar tot iets leidt…". Mr Dr JC Overvoorde (1865–1930). Strijder voor erfgoed en feminist*. Utrecht: IJzer.

Overy, P. 1991. *De Stijl*. London: Thames & Hudson.

Oxley, J. 1994. *Stained glass in South Africa*. Rivonia: Waterman.

Paterson, DE. 1946. The Surrock Graving Dock in Cape Town. *Journal of the Institution of Civil Engineers*, 1946–47: 325–53.

Pather, R. 2017. Twin buildings still echo the changes in Salt River. *The Mail & Guardian,* 21 Dec.

Pavlides, E & Cranz, G. 2011. Ethnographic methods in support of architectural practice. In Mallory-Hill, Preiser & Watson: 299–311.

Pearse, GE. 1957. *Eighteenth century architecture in South Africa*. London: Batsford.

Penders, CLM. 2002. *The West New Guinea debacle: Dutch decolonisation and Indonesia, 1945–1962*. Honolulu: University of Hawaii Press.

Peters, W. & Raubenheimer, H. 2019. The architecture of Henk de Bie & Van Wijngaarden in Bloemfontein of the 1960s: Rooted in purpose, time and place. *Architecture SA*, 95(Jan/Feb): 38–48.

Peters, W. 1998. Houses for Pretoria. In: Fisher & Le Roux, with Maré: 175–95.

Peters, W. 2018. *Tygerberg Hospital Estate (TGB HE): Architectural assessment.* Rondebosch: Unpublished manuscript.

Picton-Seymour, D. 1977. *Victorian buildings in South Africa, including Edwardian and Transvaal Republican styles 1850–1910*. Cape Town: AA Balkema.

Pienaar, EC. 1948. *Die Hugenote-Monument op Franschhoek*. Cape Town: Die Hugenote-Gedenkfeeskomitee.

Pienaar, M. 2013. *The Norman Eaton legacy: a critical architectural appraisal of the documentation of his domestic oeuvre.* Pretoria: Unpublished study, University of Pretoria. [http://hdl.handle.net/2263/41017].

Pienaar, M. 2018. Eaton for Africa: 50 years later. *Architecture SA,* Sept/Oct: 38-49.

Pijzel-Dommisse, HH. 1989. Het Museum en de School voor Kunstnijverheid in de periode 1877–1926. In: Beelaerts van Blokland: 151–72.

Plantenga, JH. 1938. *De Academie van 's-Gravenhage en haar plaats in de kunst van ons land. Gedenkboek van de Academie van Beeldende Kunsten bij de voltooiing van het nieuwe gebouw: 1682–1937*. The Hague: Mouton & Co.

Ploeger, J. 1989. Die argitek Johannes Rienk Burg, 1874–1961, sy werk en sy vennote. *Pretoriana*, 96(Nov): 32.

Ploeger, J. 1994. *Nederlanders in Transvaal 1850–1950*. Pretoria: JL van Schaik.

Pohl, M & Freitag, S (for the European Association for Banking History). 1994. *Handbook on the history of European banks*. Aldershot: Elgar.

Polano, S., Fanelli, G., De Heer, J. & Van Rossem, V. 1989. *Hendrik Petrus Berlage: The complete Works,* New York: Rizzoli.

Posthumus, N. 2019. Hollandse cultuur in Zuid-Afrika: In Johannesburg maakte de Sint voor het laatst zijn opwachting. *Trouw* (daily newspaper), 3 Jan.

Pretorius, E. 2018. *BILD - PIA Centenary talk*. Pretoria: 13 September.

Price, LO. 2015. *Line, shade and shadow: The fabrication and preservation of architectural drawings*. New Castle: Oak Knoll Press.

Rapley, T. 2004. Interviews. In Seale: 15–32.

Rasool, C. & Witz, L. 1993. The 1952 Jan van Riebeeck tercentenary festival: Constructing and contesting public national history in South Africa. *Journal of African History*, 34: 447–68.

Rees, MJ. 1924. Die Boerevrou se yskas (originally *Die Boerevrou,* October 1924). In Fisher & Le Roux 1989: 108–09.

Remery, M. 2011. *Mystery and matter: On the relationship between liturgy and architecture in the thought of Dom Hans van der Laan OSB (1904–1991)*. Leiden-Boston: Brill.

Rennie, J. 1978. *The buildings of central Cape Town 1978. Vol 2: Catalogue*. Cape Town: Cape Provincial Institute of Architects.

Rex Trueform Clothing Company Ltd. 1947. A record of achievement: The story of the House of Rex Trueform, merchant manufacturing tailors. *The Buyer*, July (Supplement).

Rex, H.M. 1975. 'Bylae tot die pleitskrif: 'n Nuwe waardering van die historiese en kuns- historiese betekenis van die drie belangrikste geboue van die Wesfasade van die Pretoria se kerkplein na aanleiding van nuwe feite en gesigspunte wat in die afgelope tyd deur navorsing aan die lig gekom het en by gevolg vantevore nie voldoende beklemtoon is nie. *Pretoriana,* 72(Dec): 223–244.

Ringer, A. 1980. The School of Architecture in Haarlem. In Willinge & Schnitker: 111–17

Rodd, DH. 1989. *Early corrugated iron construction in South Africa: 1820–1920*. Johannesburg: Unpublished study, University of the Witwatersrand. [http://hdl.handle.net/10539/19220].

Roelofs Heijermans, HHR. (ed.). 1906. *Gedenkschrift van de Koninklijke Akademie en van de Polytechnische School 1842–1905: Samengesteld ter gelegenheid van de oprichting der Technische Hoogeschool*. Delft: J Waltman jr.

Roodt, L. 1981. Louw, Wynand Hendrik. In Beyers: 340–41.

Rosenthal, E. 1952–53. South Africa's 300th Birthday: The Van Riebeeck Festival of 1952. *South African American Survey*: 59–70.

Rossouw, T. 2005. *Die Erasmuskasteel (1903) in Pretoria: 'n Kultuurhistoriese studie*. Pretoria: Unpublished study, University of Pretoria, Pretoria. [http://hdl.handle.net/2263/28714].

Rotterdam: BONAS.

Rouw, K. 2014. *Sybold van Ravesteyn. Architect*. Rotterdam: nai010.

Ruby, J. 1989. The teaching of visual anthropology. In Chiozzi: 9–18.

SAAB. 1944. Provincial Building, Cape Town. *The South African Architect & Builder*, 22(11): 37–43.

SAAR. 1961. Total Garages in South Africa. *SAAR,* 46(9/10): 20.

Schilt, J & Van der Werff, J. 1992. *Genootschap Architectura et Amicitia. 1855–1990*. Rotterdam: NAi.

Schippers, H. 1989. *Van tusschenlieden tot ingenieurs. De geschiedenis van het hoger technisch onderwijs in Nederland*. Hilversum: Verloren.

Schoemaker, RLA. 1924. *Utiliteitsbouw.* [Inaugural address 11 Nov] Delft: Technische Hoogeschool Delft.

Schoemaker, RLA. 1931. De a.s. Intern. Koloniale Tentoonstelling te Parijs. *Het Bouwbedrijf*: 17–27.

Schoeman, C. 2011. *Brothers in arms: Hollanders in the Anglo-Boer War*. Cape Town: Random House Struik.

Schutte, GP. 2020. *Beelden uit het archief: Wonderfontein* (8 May 2020). [www.zuidafrikahuis.nl/2020/04/28/beelden-uit-het-archief-wonderfontein].

Schuur, FP. 1913. Bloemfontein. *Neerlandia,* 17(9): 233.

Schuyt, K. & Taverne. E. 2004. *Dutch culture in a European perspective 4: 1950: Prosperity and welfare*. Assen: Royal Van Gorcum/Basingstoke: Palgrave Macmillan.

Scott, TW. 1964. The servantless house in South Africa. *Lantern,* 14(2): 59–65.

Seale, C. (Ed). 2011. *Qualitative research practice*. London: Sage.

Shorten, JR. 1963. *Cape Town*. Cape Town: City Council of Cape Town.

Simons, GJM. 1937. Naar aanleiding van een nieuwe kerk te Haarlem: Architekten: G.J.M. Simons en A.J.C. Voorvelt. *Het R.K. Bouwblad* 9(20): 305–11.

Siraa, HT. 1989. *Een miljoen nieuwe woningen. De rol van de rijksoverheid bij wederopbouw, volkshuisvesting, bouwnijverheid en ruimtelijke ordening (1940–1963)*. Den Haag: Sdu.

Slater, R. 2005. *'Die Maatskappy vir Europese Immigrasie': A study of the cultural assimilation and naturalisation of European immigrants to South Africa, 1949–1994.* Stellenbosch: Unpublished study, University of Stellenbosch. [http://hdl.handle.net/10019.1/1633].

SLN/NZAV. 1939. *De Unie van Zuid-Afrika – Als bestemmingsland van den Nederlandschen emigrant.* s.l.: Stichting "Landverhuizen Nederland" & Nederlandsch Zuid-Afrikaansche Vereeniging.

Slot, PI. 2003. *Bydraes van enkele Nederlandse immigrante tot Suid-Afrika op akademiese, kulturele en ekonomiese gebied, 1945–2002.* Pretoria: Unpublished study, University of Pretoria. [http://hdl.handle.net/2263/51269].

Sluyterman, JKT. 1917. *Het huis van ouds genaamd Portugal te Delft ingericht voor het onderwijs in de decoratieve kunst aan de Technische Hoogeschool.* Delft. Inaugural address, Institute of Technology, Delft.

Stakesby Lewis-Ferguson, JE (ed.). 1953. *Harvest, an anthology of lectures delivered in South Africa.* Pretoria: Institute for Theosophical Publicity.

Stals, M. 1998. *Fragmentation and unity: The search for the design of a "Model Township": The case of Atteridgeville.* Leuven: Unpublished study, Post Graduate Centre for Human Settlements, Katholieke Universiteit Leuven.

Stark, F. 1955. *Pretoria: One hundred years, 1855–1955.* Pretoria: Municipal Public Relations Bureau.

Steenhuis, M. 2007. *Stedenbouw in het landschap: Pieter Verhagen (1882–1950).* Rotterdam: NAi.

Steensma, R. & Van Swigchem, CA. (eds). 1986. *Honderdvijftig jaar Gereformeerde kerkbouw.* Kampen: Kok.

Stempels, C. 1958. *Keukens, indeling en uitrusting.* Amsterdam: Van Holkema & Warendorf (series Wooncomfort en Woontechniek, Stichting Bouwcentrum Rotterdam).

Stieber, N. 1998. *Housing design and society in Amsterdam: Reconfiguring urban order and identity, 1900–1920.* Chicago: Chicago University Press.

Stoloff, CA. 1947. The old banks of Johannesburg. *SAAR*, (Sept): 254–59.

Swanepoel, R. 2008. *Pretoria nuusbrief, 2008.09.* [http://hdl.handle.net/2263/7457].

Swart, J. 2020. *Hidden Pretoria.* Cape Town: Struik / Penguin Random House.

Taverne, E., Wagenaar, C. & De Vletter, M. 2001. *JJP Oud: Poetic functionalist, 1890–1963: The complete works.* Rotterdam: NAi.

Technische Hoogeschool Delft, [1925]. *Programma der Lessen 1925–1926*, Delft: Technische Hoogeschool.

Teeger, E. 1965. Domestic architecture in South Africa from 1930–1965. *SAAR,* (Jun) Supplement: 5–8.

Teeuwen, MAJ. 2016. *De Chaletstijl in Nederland. De toepassing van de chaletstijl op Nederlandse monumentale landhuizen (1837–1915).* Utrecht: Unpublished study, University of Utrecht.

Templer, CF. 1962. The advantages of folded roof plates. *Architect and Builder,* (Jul): 26–29.

Th[unnissen?]. 1931. Bij een tweetal villa's van mevr. Ir. Van Everdingen-Ferguson, *Klei: Tijdschrift gewijd aan de belangen van de klei-industrie,* 23(2): 13–21.

Thuis in Zuid-Afrika. Pretoria: State Information Services. Church Archive of the Nederduitsch Hervormde Kerk Pamphlet Collection: Nr 1953.

Tillema, JAC. 1967. ir JC Meischke. *Rotterdams Jaarboekje.* Rotterdam: 193–96.

Timmer, H. 1997. *Henri Evers 1855–1929. Architect, geschiedschrijver, hoogleraar.*

Town Clerk of Pretoria. 1940. Memorandum on construction of economic houses at Atteridgeville: 26 Sep. [unpublished document at National Archives & Records Service of South Africa, Pretoria].

Tuinstra, W & Petermeyer, H. 1987. *De geschiedenis van de architectenopleiding in Tilburg. 50 jaar architectuuronderwijs.* Tilburg: Akademie voor Bouwkunde.

Tummers, N. 1974. Carboonkolonisatie. *Wonen-TA/BK,* (11): 4–28.

Tunbridge, JE & Ashworth, GJ. 1994. *Dissonant heritage: The management of the past as a resource in conflict.* Chichester/New York: Wiley.

Union of South Africa, Public Works Department. 1912. *Quarterly reports for the financial year 1911–1912.* (Manuscript in collection NJ Clarke).

Union of South Africa. 1945. *New graving dock and the port and harbour of Cape Town.* Cape Town: South African Railways and Harbours Administration.

Union of South Africa. 1947. *The Cape Town Foreshore Plan 1948. Final report of the Cape Town Joint Technical Committee* (Jun). Cape Town: The Government Printer.

Van Adrichem, J. 2016. *To be continued. Een geschiedenis van de Gerrit Rietveld Academie.* Amsterdam: Gerrit Rietveld Academie.

Van Balen. WJ. 1936. *Het werkende land: Opbouw van Nederland in moeilijke tijden.* Haarlem: HD Tjeenk Willink & Zoon.

Van der Bank, DA. 1966. Poskoetse van die Van Riebeeck-fees (1952). *Navorsinge van die Nasionale Museum*: 102–38.

Van der Ham, W. 1999. *Heersen en beheersen: Rijkswaterstaat in de twintigste eeuw.* Zaltbommel: Europese Bibliotheek

Van der Heijden, C. 2009. *Grijs verleden: Nederland en de Tweede Wereldoorlog.* Amsterdam: AtlasContact.

Van der Lans, J. 2009/2016. 1918 Woonschool Zeeburgerdorp: Van opvang van asocialen tot Tokkie-amusement. [www.canonsociaalwerk.eu/woonschool Zeeburgerdorp].

Van der Merwe, FH. 1988. *Die Geskiedenis van die Nederlandsche Bank voor Zuid-Afrika, 1903–1945.* Johannesburg: Unpublished study, Randse Afrikaanse Universiteit. [http://hdl.handle.net/10210/10264].

Van der Meulen, J. 1963. Northern European origins of South African colonial architecture. *Journal of the Society of Architectural Historians*, 22(2): 51–61.

Van der Ploeg, K. 2017. *De Ploeg, het expressionisme en de architectuur*, Zwolle: Wbooks.

Van der Pluijm, C. 2014. *Radio Kootwijk: Biografie van een zendstation en een dorp in het hart van de Veluwe.* Barneveld: BDUmedia.

Van der Waal, G-M. 1987. *From mining camp to metropolis: The buildings of Johannesburg 1886–1940.* Pretoria: Chris van Rensburg.

Van der Wal, C. 1997 *In praise of common sense: planning the ordinary. A physical planning history of the new towns in the IJsselmeerpolders.* Rotterdam: 010 Publishers.

Van der Woud, A. 2017. *The art of building: International ideas, Dutch debate 1840–1900.* eBook: Routledge.

Van Dijk, H. 1992. Introduction. In Groenendijk & Vollaard: 7–35.

Van Duijn, JC. 1920. Huishoudkunde (originally in *Die Boerevrou,* August 1920). In Fisher & Le Roux, 1989: 48–49.

Van Es, E (ed.). 2018. *Van den Broek & Bakema: Vigorous protagonists of a functionalist architecture at the TH Delft: Inaugural speeches in the Built Environment: Global and Contextualised (Issue 3).* Delft: TU Delft Open.

Van Essen, LRz. 1902. *Ambachtsschool Utrecht 1877–1902. Gedenkschrift uitgegeven bij de herdenking van het 25-jarig bestaan der school.* Utrecht: Stoomdrukkerij LB Bosch & Zoon.

Van Gelderen, J. 1996. De gereformeerde kerken in Nederland. In *Steensma & Van Swigchem*: 8–15.

Van Ginkel, AJ. 1936. Hollander eenigheid. *Hollands Weekblad voor Zuid-Afrika,* 22 Feb: 22.

Van Graan, A. 2011. *Negotiating Modernism in Cape Town: 1918–1948. An investigation into the introduction, contestation, negotiation and adaptation of modernism in the architecture of Cape Town.* Cape Town: Unpublished study, University of Cape Town. [http://hdl.handle.net/11427/11100].

Van Heuvel, WJ. 1992. *Structuralism in Dutch architecture.* Rotterdam: 010.

Van Ledden, W-P. 2005. *Jan van Riebeeck tussen wal en schip: een onderzoek naar de beeldvorming over Jan van Riebeeck in Nederland en Zuid-Afrika omstreeks 1900, 1950 en 2000.* Hilversum: Verloren.

Van Loghem, JB. 1932. *Bouwen, Bauen, Bâtir, Building. Nieuwe Zakelijkheid.* Amsterdam: Kosmos.

Van Maanen, C. 1940. De nieuwe haven van Kaapstad. *Tijdschrift voor Economische Geografie*, 15 Aug: 214–23.

Van Rensburg, J. 2012. *Die Boerevrou 1919–1931: 'n Kultuurhistoriese studie oor die eerste Afrikaanse vrouetydskrif.* Pretoria: Unpublished study, University of Pretoria. [http://hdl.handle.net/2263/24176].

Van Schaik, P. 2018. *Publieke Werken. Hoeksteen van de Amsterdamse School 1915–1935*. Amsterdam: Stokerkade.

Van Schoor, MCE. 1993 *Die Nasionale Vrouemonument*. Bloemfontein: Oorlogsmuseum van die Boererepublieke.

Van Selms, A. 1954. *Beginsels van Protestantse kerkbou*. Kaapstad: HAUM.

Van Veen, J. 1955. *Dredge, drain, reclaim: The art of a nation* (4th ed). The Hague: Martinus Nijhoff.

Van Welderen Rengers, Th. & Faber, J. 1913. *Friesland en de woningwet 1902–1912*. Leeuwarden: Meijer & Schaafsma.

Van Zinderen Bakker, [EM]. 1959. Bloemfontein heeft een Holland-huis. *Emigratie: Drie-maandelijks tijdschrift gewijd aan emigratievraagstukken,* 1(3): 34–35.

Veerman, W. 2002. De Jan van Riebeeck-feesten in 1952 te Culemborg. Een nationaal en internationaal gebeuren op lokaal niveau, met verstrekkende gevolgen. *Culemborgse 'Voetnoten'*: 27, 29–40.

Venturi, R., Scott-Brown, D. & Izenour, S. 1972. *Learning from Las Vegas.* Cambridge (MA): MIT Press.

Verhoef, G. 1987. *Die geskiedenis van Nedbank 1945–1973.* Johannesburg: Unpublished study, Rand Afrikaans University. [http://hdl.handle.net/10210/13283].

Verhoeven, HAJ. 2007. *De verwondering van het maken: De bouwopleiding van gilde tot opleidingsbedrijf*. Bergeijk: Eyckehorst Livre.

Vestbro, DU. 2012. *Housing in the apartheid city*. [www.diva-portal.org/smash/get/diva2:578181/FULLTEXT01.pdf].

Wagenaar, C. (ed.). 2015. Town planning in the Netherlands since 1800: Responses to Enlightenment ideas and geopolitical realities. Rotterdam: nai010.

Wattjes, JG. 1931. *Moderne kerken in Europa en Amerika: Fotografieën, teekeningen, plattegronden: Eglises modernes: Moderne kirchen*. Amsterdam: Kosmos.

Wegelin, HW. (1990/1992/1994) 1998. *Model building specifications and standards guide for architects*. s.l.

Wegelin, HW. (2009) 2017. *Construction primer for southern Africa*. Pretoria: (Visual Books) Protea Boekhuis.

Wegelin, HW. 2010. *Construction specifications and standards for southern Africa*. Pretoria: Wegelin.

Weissman, AW. (ed.). 1920. *Gedenkboek: Uitgegeven door den Nederlandschen Aannemersbond ter herdenking van zijn vijf en twintig-jarig bestaan 1895–1920*. Bussum: Uitgeversmaatschappij v/h Paul Brand.

Weltens, A., Marx, R., Den Dikken, A. & Cramer, M. 2002. *Kathedralen en luchtkastelen van de omroep in Hilversum*. Zwolle: Waanders.

Wendt, D. with Van 't Klooster & Winters, P. 2008. *Academie van Bouwkunst Amsterdam*. Rotterdam: 010.

Westendorp, F. (ed.). 1930. *De Technische Hoogeschool te Delft van 1905 tot 1930*. Delft: J Waltman jr.

Wielenga, JWF. 2009. *Nederland in de twintigste eeuw: Geschiedenis van Nederland vanaf de late negentiende eeuw tot en met 2008*. Amsterdam: Boom.

Williams, HH. 2006. *J.A. Heyns en die Nederduitse Gereformeerde Kerk en apartheid*. Bloemfontein: University of the Free State.

Willinge, M. & Schnitker, M. (eds). 1980. *Het Nieuwe Bouwen: Voorgeschiedenis/Previous History.* Delft: Delft University Press.

Witz, L. 2003. *Apartheid's Festival: Contesting South Africa's National Pasts*. Bloomington & Indianapolis: Indiana University Press/David Philip.

Wolff, I. 2014. *Unstitching Rex Trueform: Exploring apartheid modernity and architectural modernism through the Rex Trueform garment manufacturing factory, Salt River, 1937–2013*. Cape Town: Unpublished study, University of Cape Town. [http://hdl.handle.net/11427/13371].

Wolff, I. 2017. *Unstitching Rex Trueform: The Story of an African Factory*. Rome: L'Erma Di Brettschneider.

Woltjer, JJ. 2001. *Recent verleden: De geschiedenis van Nederland in de twintigste eeuw*. Amsterdam: Balans.

Worm, P. [1952]. *Die verhaal van Jan van Riebeeck: Hierdie boekie is vertel en geteken deur Piet Worm bij geleentheid van die herdenking van die feit dat 'n Hollander 300 jaar gelede 'n nedersetting aan die Kaap gestig het*. Amsterdam: De Nederlandsche Bank voor Zuid-Afrika.

Yukay Yüksel, M. 2013. An investigation of social behaviors of primary school children in terms of their grade, learning disability and intelligence potential. *Educational Sciences: Theory and Practice*, 13(2), Spring: 781–93.

Zeijlstra, HH. (ed.). 1931. *Nederland te Parijs 1931: Gedenkboek van de Nederlandsche deelneming aan de Internationale Koloniale Tentoonstelling*. Deventer: Vereeniging "Oost en West".

Zeren Gülersoy, N. (ed.). 2010. *Urban Transformation: Controversies, contrasts and challenges: Vol. 14 no. 2. Proceedings of the 15th International Planning History Society Conference Istanbul, Turkey, July 12–15, 2010*. Istanbul: 229–39. [https://doi.org/10.7480/iphs.2010.2].

Zuid-Afrika Mbl. 1952, April (special on the Van Riebeeck Festival).

Acknowledgements

The editors and authors express their heartfelt gratitude to the following individuals and institutions for their valuable assistance and support during our explorations of the shared South African-Dutch built heritage of the early C20. We hope to have included all our collaborators and, should we have invertedly overlooked anyone, we sincerely apologize while acknowledging that this book is the product of multifaceted cooperation by a continuously expanding group of people.

We dedicate this book to those of our collaborator-friends who passed away before they could see the result in print.

South Africa

Cape Institute for Architects
Brent DE WAAL

Cape Town Heritage Trust
Laura ROBINSON

City of Cape Town
James EKSTEEN
Leonie PIETERSEN

City of Tshwane, Tshwane Heritage Research Centre, Pretoria
Ishmael MBHOKODO
James BOALE
Caren JANSEN

DRC Harmonie, Pretoria
Elise STEENKAMP
Francina SIKANKA

DRC Sonnekus, Cape Town
Colette DE WET

DRC Wellington-Noord, Wellington
Marita COETZEE

Jan Kriel Institute, Kuilsriver
Fanie HERHOLT

Embassy of the Kingdom of the Netherlands in South Africa, Pretoria & Cape Town
Han PETERS
Marisa GERARDS
Bonnie HORBACH
Jan HUESKEN
Daniel SMIT

Erfenisstigting/Heritage Foundation, Pretoria)
Cecilia KRUGER
Zabeth BOTHA
Johan NEL
Estelle PRETORIUS
Nándor SARKADY

National Archives of South Africa, Pretoria
Alexio MOTSI
Dan MOYANE
Gerrit WAGENER

Parliament of the Republic of South Africa, Cape Town
Lila KOMNICK

Pretoria Institute for Architecture
Mauneen VAN WYK
Marlize DE KLERK

Queenspark, Cape Town
Gordon BRADLEY
Adam SNITCHER

RC Pretoria-Noord, Pretoria
Willem KIRSTEN

South African Centre for the Netherlands and Flanders, Pinelands
Eureka BARNARD

South African Heritage Resources Agency, Cape Town
Dumisani SIBAYI
Clinton JACKSON

Suid-Afrikaanse Akademie vir Wetenskap en Kuns, Pretoria
Dionē PRINSLOO
Linda BRINK

Transnet Heritage Library, Johannesburg
Yolanda MEYER

United Reformed Church, Die Ark, Beaufort-West
Deon SCHARNECK

University of Cape Town Libraries/Special Collections
Clive KIRKWOOD
Michal SINGER

University of Pretoria
Chrisna DU PLESSIS
Karlien VAN NIEKERK
Sherona LOYKISOONLAL
Tara DU PLESSIS
Elmar VAN WYK
Helga FERNANDES
Aimee SIMEON

University of the Witwatersrand, Johannesburg
Kathy MUNRO
Hannah LE ROUX
Bongi MPUTHI

Netherlands

Cultural Heritage Agency of the Netherlands, Amersfoort
Jean-Paul CORTEN
Jinna SMIT

Delft University of Technology
Wido QUIST
Abel STREEFLAND

DutchCulture, Amsterdam
Josine BACKUS
Veysel YUCE

Het Nieuwe Instituut, Rotterdam
Staff of Het Nieuwe Instituut - Collection

Linoleum Krommenie Archive, Krommenie
Marijke GRIFFIOEN

Zuid-Afrikahuis, Amsterdam
Angelie SENS
Simon SCHOLTE TER HORST
Jamie VAN BAARSEL
Corine DE MAIJER
Judith CALMEYER MEIJBURG-VAN REEKUM
Guido VAN DEN BERG
Isabelle VERMEIJ

Nicoline ALMA
Alexander ANDREOU
Alexander ANTONITES
Motshidisi APHANE
Piet BAKKER
Elsa BERENTZEN
Abigail BISOGNO
Lawrence BREEDVELD
Marja BREMER
Elsabé BRINK
Gerrit and Hanneke BRINK
Bruce BRINKMAN (1945–2021)
Bryan BRINKMAN
Matilda BURDEN
Clive CHIPKIN (1929–2021)
Paula and Michelle CHIPPS
Fran CLARKE
Karen CRAMÉR
Mario CUPIDO
Larramie and Quinton DAMSTRA
Bart DE GRAAFF
Koos DE JONG
Marianne DE JONG
Elzaan DE VILLIERS
Tanja DE VILLIERS
Kobus DU PREEZ
Adriaan DU TOIT
Gabiël (1925–2020) and Gwen FAGAN
Eric FERGUSON
Theo FERGUSON
Johan FOURIE
Frank GAYLARD (artefacts.co.za)
Shaughnie GEYSER
Patsy GOWER
Kim GURNEY
Margaret HARRADINE (1942–2020)
Engela HECHTER
Gerald HUMPHREY
Adrian, Sharon and Nicoline JONGENS
Elsbeth JONGENS
Vester LANGELER
Stella LEDWABA
Schalk LE ROUX
Katherine LOVE
Noortje LOVEDAY
Eugenie MARINCOWITZ
Sam 'Po' MOTAU
David MOSTERT and William RAATS
Sheilagh NATION (1930–2021)
Isaac NTABANKULU
Martha MTHAMANE (1929–2019)
Walter PETERS
Eddie PRETORIUS
Terri RONDI
Beatrice SALES
Brigitte van SCHOUWENBURG
Bernard SHAPIRO
Dennis SHAW
Gary SHAW
Noziphiwo SIGWELA
Arnold SIKKEL
Ivar SIKKEL
Sister Elizabeth (Franciscan Sisters of SIESSEN)
Mary SMAL
Erica SMEETS-KLOKGIETERS
Ron SMIT
Jerian SPAANS
Dianne STEELE

Alta and Renier STEENKAMP
Michael and Julian STEKHOVEN
Dirk TALJARD
Hubert THOMAS
Irma VAN DE WERKE
Pieter VAN DER BIJL
Jack VAN DER LECQ
Charlotte VAN EMSTEDE
Colette, Jack, Mariette and Syann VAN NIFTRIK
Eugene VAN RENSBURG
John VOORENDIJK
Anthony and Denise VOORVELT
Hans and Lucette WEGELIN
Charles WHYTE
Lloyd WILLIAMS
Heidi ZÖLLNER
...and many others.

Authors

Nicholas J CLARKE [Ed] is an architect and lecturer at the Delft University of Technology in the Department of Heritage & Architecture, where he obtained his PhD in 2021. A graduate of both University of Pretoria and Cambridge University, he practiced as architect and built heritage specialist while lecturing at the University of Pretoria in South Africa before relocating to the Netherlands. He is actively involved in built heritage management and documentation in South Africa and has completed a number of awarded studies and books on shared South African-Dutch built heritage (with Roger Fisher and Marieke Kuipers). Nicholas is a World Heritage advisor to ICOMOS International and serves on commissions for scientific and cultural institutions in both South Africa and the Netherlands.

Roger C FISHER [Ed] is an architect and Emeritus Professor in the Department of Architecture, University of Pretoria, where he was awarded a PhD in 1993. As heritage practitioner he has been engaged in various surveys and documentations of heritage places and sites, most recently the built residue of the NZASM railway lines in South Africa. He has acted as editor and author of publications on the history and culture of the South African built environment, where his interest is in cultural hybridity as well as shared heritage and assimilation. He currently acts as editor and content curator for the website artefacts.co.za which focuses on the South African built environment.

Marieke C KUIPERS [Ed] is Emeritus Professor of Cultural Heritage at Delft University of Technology and Maastricht University and has also worked as a specialist in 'young' built heritage with the Netherlands Cultural Heritage Agency and its predecessors (1977–2018). She obtained a PhD at the State University Groningen in 1987 for a study on experiments in concrete housing. She has widely lectured and published about the identification, valuation and conservation of architectural heritage, and has led various missions related to shared built heritage in Russia and South Africa. Currently she is internationally active as an expert in C20 heritage, Shared Heritage and World Heritage (ICOMOS, DOCOMOMO).

Annie R ANTONITES worked as the Senior Manager: Research and Information Services at *Die Erfenisstigting* [Heritage Foundation] in Pretoria. She holds a PhD in Anthropology from Yale University and is a Research Fellow in the Department of Anthropology and Archaeology at the University of South Africa. Her research focuses mainly on studying the past through people's food and eating habits. It is this general fascination with people, specifically from a historical perspective, that led to an interest in contextualizing the broader political, economic and social milieu of C20 Dutch immigrant architects. As of April 2021 she is the Curator of the Archeo-zoological and Large Mammal Collection with the Ditsong National Museum of Natural History (formerly Transvaal Museum).

Mathebe R APHANE is an architect and an academic currently working at the University of Johannesburg in the GSA. She holds a Bachelor in Politics & Public Administration from the University of Fort Hare, a BCom(Hons) from the Rand Afrikaans University (now University of Johannesburg), and an MArch (Prof) from the University of Pretoria. She has lectured at the University of Pretoria, Tshwane University of Technology and now at the University of Johannesburg in both the undergraduate and postgraduate programmes. She serves on the South African Council for the Architectural Profession's Validation Committee. Her research focuses on the production of Black spaces in South African townships with specific reference to Atteridgeville.

Arthur BARKER is an architect and academic at the Department of Architecture, University of Pretoria, where he coordinates the Professional Master's program while teaching aspects of the history of architecture in the undergraduate program. He chairs the Department's Research Committee while coordinating design teaching in the Department. He also chairs the Pretoria Institute of Architect's Education Committees as well as being a member of its Environmental Committee. He is a National Research Foundation C2 rated researcher and serves on the South African Council for the Architectural Profession's Validation Committee as well as being a member of the Canberra Accord's Architectural Accreditation Board.

Catherine DEACON completed her Master of Architecture degree at the University of Pretoria and obtained a second Master's degree in Heritage Conservation at the University of Minnesota (USA). She has spent much of her career since graduation in private practice working on both architecture and urban design projects, as well as heritage consulting, while also lecturing at the University of Pretoria. Currently she is working for an NPO that focuses on inner city regeneration in Johannesburg. Apart from her written contribution, Catherine also provided research support and archival assistance to this Shared Heritage project.

Esther DE HAAN is a heritage specialist, studying historic interiors and living culture in the Netherlands and shared heritage countries. She works as a self-employed researcher and publicist for several heritage foundations. She also lectures at the University of Amsterdam Master's programme for Conservation of Historic Interiors and is a member of the ICOMOS-Shared Built Heritage International Scientific Committee.

Mary E LANGE is an independent arts, culture and heritage practitioner and researcher. She chairs ARROWSA, an arts, culture and heritage for peace non-profit-organisation and is an honorary lecturer at the Centre for Communication, Media and Society, University of KwaZulu-Natal. Her heritage interest focuses on oral heritage and public archaeology, particularly for fostering intercultural understanding.

Michael LOUW is a Senior Lecturer at the Department of Architecture, Planning and Geomatics at the University of Cape Town, South Africa. He holds a BArch degree from the University of Pretoria, and both BPhil and MPhil degrees in Sustainable Development from the University of Stellenbosch. He is currently registered for his PhD studies at the University of Cape Town, with a focus on architectural technologies in Africa.

Ben MWASINGA holds a Master's degree in City and Regional Planning from the University of Cape Town and is currently the manager of the Built Environment Unit at the South African Heritage Resources Agency (SAHRA). This role gives him the unique advantage of being directly involved with key developments relating to the transformation of the national estate. He is also directly responsible for developing policies and procedures that relate to the management of structures, spaces and landscapes that are declared National Heritage Sites. His background in city and regional planning has also provided him with a unique insight into the spatial context of South Africa today.

Marguerite PIENAAR is an awarded professional architect. She is curious about all things relating to the production of space: across scales, types, experiences, histories, cultures and continents. She is a serial place-making enthusiast, and continues to be involved as researcher, lecturer, studio teacher and external examiner at various institutions. She completed a postgraduate Master's degree on the work of the modern movement architect Norman Eaton (1902–66) at the University in Pretoria and was subsequently awarded for the best completed post-graduate study through research.

Kees SOMER studied architectural history at the University of Amsterdam. He obtained his PhD in 2007 with a research project on The Functional City and the contribution of Cornelis van Eesteren to it. Formerly a Policy Advisor for cultural heritage for the Dutch Ministry of Education, Culture and Science, Kees currently works as a specialist of C20 architecture and built heritage at the Cultural Heritage Agency of the Netherlands. He is editor-in-chief of the Bulletin KNOB, a peer reviewed academic journal on architectural and building history, urban planning history, cultural landscape and heritage.

Johan SWART holds a Masters degree in both architecture and heritage studies. He lectures at the University of Pretoria, where he teaches architectural history and leads a heritage focused design studio for postgraduate students. As curator of the architecture archives at the University, he is also responsible for the safeguarding and interpretation of significant historical drawing collections. His academic interests include the history of design, archival practice, cultural landscapes and adaptive re-use.

Lizette VAN DER WAL studied art history and architectural history & heritage conservation at the Utrecht University and the Delft University of Technology. She has worked since 2017 as a researcher at the Cultural Heritage Agency of the Netherlands, particularly on the national register of protected monuments and advises on boundary registration matters to external parties. She has a special interest in the history of architectural education and C19 and C20 architecture and built environment of the Netherlands.

Image Credits

Numbers refer to page numbers;
b = bottom; c = centre; l = left; r = right; t = top

Agephotostock, Tomo
- Manfred Capale 101
- Glyn Spencer 201b

AHN, Amersfoort 23l
Alamy Limited, Oxon
- Eric Nathan 205b

Aphane, Mathebe 172b, 176tl&tr&c
Architectural Archives University of Pretoria
- Cleland Collection 171t, 192b, 192b, 215br, 216t
- DPW ZAR Collection 208tl
- Eaton Collection 126tl, 127, 209b, 211, 212
- Pearse Collection 207
- Van de Werke Collection 16b, 50br, 145br, 146t&b, 148b, 154, 166, 217, 218, 219t, 220
- Van der Waal Collection 75tr, 80, 158b, 159tl, 171br, 172tl

Barker, Arthur 138, 141t&b, 142t, 143t&b, 144c&bl&br, 147b, 148t, 149b, 150t&b, 151, 152, 153, 155, 219b
Bothma, 144tr
Brink/Snyman family collection 236l
Brinkman family collection 129br
Chipps/Payens family collection 15t, 78r, 110br, 113cl, 114cl, 242
City of Tshwane, Tshwane Heritage Research Centre, Pretoria 13l, 162, 162, 163, 164, 165, 168, 171bl
Clarke, Nicholas 7b, 69bl&br, 70tl, 76t, 78l, 82, 84tl, 85cl, 88t&b, 89t, 99, 100t, 102tl&tr, 103tl, 104l&cr, 106l&r, 107l, 109, 110bl, 112, 113tl&tr, 114t, 119, 170, 186, 187, 240
CODA Archief, Apeldoorn 233
Corten, Jean-Paul 77tr
Damstra family collection 14b, 63, 81tl, 213cl&bl
De Villiers, Tanya 213br
Erfenisstigting, Pretoria 65tl, 65r
- Church Archive of the Nederduitsch Hervormde Kerk

Fisher, Roger C 128, 132t
Forder, Cameron 11t&b, 19, 126tr, 228, 234, 236, 238
Gelders Archief, Arnhem 42cr
Groninger Archieven, Groningen 50cl
Haags Gemeentearchief, The Hague 49
Hardman, Theresa 15b, 83, 85bl, 130b
Het Nieuwe Instituut, Rotterdam 26r, 35l, 36t, 52tr&cr, 53l, 126cl, 145cr, 209t
- [Johan Swart] 208tr

Het Utrechts Archief, Utrecht 50tl, 110cl
Hextex collection, Worcester 17cl
Historiek.net 29bl
Internationaal Instituut voor Sociale Geschiedenis, Amsterdam 22
Jacx Vastgoedpresentatie – www.jacx.nl 42cl
Karol, Eitan, 72cl
Kuipers, Marieke 4, 7t, 8, 9, 10, 12bl, 12br, 13r, 16t, 18, 21, 33t, 42tl, 67cr, 68tr, 73br, 79, 87tl, 93t, 98, 103cl&r, 105, 107r, 108, 110tr, 111, 115, 131t, 132cr, 133t&cl, 142br, 145l, 161,169tl, 174t, 175, 180, 182br, 184br, 185r, 190cr, 195, 197, 241, 246
Lange, Mary 230, 236r
Louw, Michael 181l, 184bl, 185l, 194tl
Matiyane, Titus/De Kler, Annemieke 178–79
Museum Africa, Johannesburg 123tl
Nationaal Archief, The Hague 27l, 45r, 72cr, 199l
- Anefo/Joop van Bilsen 30r
- Anefo/De Nijs 232tl
- Anefo/Piet van der Ham 29cl
- Anefo/Van Duinen 95br
- Anefo/Winterbergen 29r
- Klaas van Buiten 30l

National Archives of South Africa, Pretoria
- [Art2motion/Thania Louw] 167t&b

Nederlands Instituut voor Militaire Historie, The Hague 55br, 64tr
Pienaar, Marguerite 191t
Proust, Alain 75, 118
R1, Johannesburg 68b
Raubenheimer, Hein 114cr
ReclameArsenaal, Laren 6, 25
Rijksdienst voor het Cultureel Erfgoed, Amersfoort 12tl, 28r, 38tl, 40t, 42tr, 51cl, 52l
- Chris Booms 31r, 44
- Gerard Dukker 66, 181r
- Paul van Galen 39br, 42br
- Flying Focus 37
- Thea van den Heuvel 38b
- Nanette de Jong 40br
- Joop de Koning 71cl
- Kris Roodenburg 41b, 182l
- Louk Tangel 32tl
- Sergé Technau 43, 50tr
- Ronald Tilleman 39t
- Ton van der Wal 33br, 73tr

Rijksmuseum, Amsterdam 28l
Rijkswaterstaat, The Hague 24, 30cr, 32tr, 32b, 89b
RKD - Nederlands Instituut voor Kunstgeschiedenis, The Hague 48
Schuurmans Stekhoven family collection 14t
South African Heritage Resources Agency, Cape Town, 92
Spaarnestad Photo, The Hague 200bl
Stadsarchief Amsterdam 23r, 31l, 36br, 57br, 87bl, 94tl, 132tr, 192tr
- JM Ansath 45l

Stadsarchief Rotterdam 35r, 51tl, 194br
Somer, Kees 177
Suid-Afrikaanse Akademie vir Wetenskap en Kuns 12tr
Swanepoel, François 20, 77bl&br, 81b, 86, 183t, 191bl&br, 245
Swart, Johan 229br, 239
Tetteroo, Tom 169tr&b
Transnet Heritage Library, Johannesburg 77tl, 122tl, 198, 199r, 202t&b, 203t

University Cape Town, Libraries
- Andrews & Niegeman/Shapiro Collection
  - [Alain Proust] 85tl 134–35, 135–37, 224, 255, 226–27
- Isandora Repositories/Vallie, Zubeida 156
- JC Jongens Collection 71t, 71cr, 76b, 87tr&br, 96r, 222, 223
  - [Alain Proust] 90–91, 93cr, 184t, 200t, 204b, 206 214tr&br, 215tl, 224t, 225

University of the Free State, Bloemfontein 243
University of Southern California Libraries, 149cr
University of the Witwatersrand, Johannesburg 173, 216b
Van As family collection 140tr
Van Niftrik family collection 17tl, 17tr, 97tl&tr&b, 160cr, 189, 213cr, 214tl&br, 221
Voorvelt family collection [Nicholas Clarke] 70tr
Wegelin family collection 232tr
Wikimedia Commons 27r, 46–47, 100cr
- Wutsje 104br

Wikipedia, 94tr,
- Romke Hoekstra 26t

Zuid-Afrikaansche Hospitaal 85tr, 204t
Zuid-Afrikahuis, Amsterdam 55br, 56bl&cr&br, 59, 60t&cl&cr, 61, 62, 64b, 94cr, 95t, 96tl&cl, 121l, 122tr, 123cl&tr, 124, 125tr, 126cr, 201t, 204t

Register

General references to The Netherlands, South Africa, Cape, Gauteng, Natal, Mpumalanga, Orange Free State or Transvaal are omitted. Buildings and places in the Netherlands, South Africa, Lesotho and Namibia are listed under their respective countries/towns. Those located in other places are indicated in italics.

Acronyms

AAUP Architecture Archives of the University of Pretoria 208, 210, 211, 215, 218, 221
BBC British Broadcasting Company 64
BNA Bond van Nederlandse Architecten [Association of Dutch Architects] 49
CCA Canadian Centre for Architecture 207
CCP City Council of Pretoria 78, 163, 164, 168, 169, 170, 171, 172, 174, 175, 215, 221
CHB Central Housing Board 172, 174, 192, 215, 217
CIA Cape Institute of Architects 133
CNO Algemene Kommissie tot behartiging van het Christelik Nasionale Onderwijs [Christian National Education] 59, 60, 78
CSB Cape Schools Board 81, 82
CSIR Council for Scientific and Industrial Research 61, 168, 196
DPW Dienst Publieke Werken ZAR [Department of Public Works, South African Republic] 75, 76, 78, 100, 139, 151, 235
GK Gereformeerde Kerk – *see* individual building entries under Reformed Church
HAM Hollandsche Aannemings Maatschappij 31, 199, 200, 201, 202, 203
HNI Het Nieuwe Instituut 71, 84, 125, 208, 21
IMC Instrument Manufacturing Company 190, 191
ISCOR South African Iron and Steel Corporation 12, 56, 78, 128, 164
LTS Lagere Technische School [Lower Technical School] 49
MBA Master Builders Association 170, 195
MTS Middelbare Technische School [Medium Technical College] 48, 49, 51, 52, 218
NAD Native Affairs Department 172
NASA National Archives of South Africa 193, 208, 215
NBCV Nederlandsche Bank en Credietvereeniging 119
NBRI National Building Research Institute 168, 172, 175, 196
NBZA Nederlandsche Bank voor Zuid-Afrika [Netherlands Bank of South Africa] 19, 59, 119, 120, 125, 128, 129, 189, 210
NGK Nederduits Gereformeerde Kerk – *see* individual building entries under Dutch Reformed Church
NHK Nederduits Hervormde Kerk van Afrika – *see* individual building entries
NHO National Housing Commission 174
NHPC National Housing and Planning Commission 152, 163, 172, 173, 174
NISM Nederlandsch Indische Spoorweg Maatschappij
NZASM Nederlandsch-Zuid-Afrikaansche Spoorwegmaatschappij [Netherlands South African Railway Company] 62, 71, 75, 84, 139, 142, 143, 149, 150, 151, 152, 154, 199, 208
NZAV Nederlands Zuid-Afrikaanse Vere(e)niging [Netherlands South African Association] 45, 57
PS Polytechnische School Delft [Polytechnical School Delft] 51, 52, 53
PWD Public Works Department 34, 39, 74, 75, 78, 79, 84, 85, 100, 101, 103, 121
RC Roman Catholic Church – *see* individual building entries under Roman Catholic
RWS Rijkswaterstaat 33
SAHRA South African Heritage Resources Agency 61, 196, 241, 242
SABS South African Bureau of Standards 61, 242
SAR&H South African Railways and Harbours 69, 200, 203, 204
TH Technische Ho(o)geschool [Delft Institute of Technology] 18, 31, 52, 53, 67, 68, 72, 76, 144
TUD Technische Universiteit Delft [Delft University of Technology] 31
VHBO Voortgezet en Ho(o)ger Bouwkunst Onderricht [Continued and Higher Architectural Education] 52
VNS Vereenigde Nederlandsche Scheepvaartmaatschappij [United Netherlands Navigation Company] 57
VOC Vereenigde Oost-Indische Compagnie [Dutch East India Company] 8, 53, 55, 76, 94, 99, 207
WJTPC Witwatersrand Joint Town Planning Committee (WJTPC) 166
ZAR Zuid-Afrikaansche Republiek [South African Republic] 8, 55, 75, 76, 78, 83, 99, 100, 139, 142, 143, 151, 152, 163, 164, 208
ZHESM Zuid-Hollandsche Electrische Spoorweg-Maatschappij 31

Abercrombie, P 166
Adams Thompson & Fry 166, 168
Algemeene Maatschappij van Levensverzekering en Lijfrente [General Life Insurance Company] 59
Ambon, Indonesia 29
Amsterdam Academie van Bouwkunst [Amsterdam Academy of Architecture] 52
Andrews & Niegeman 17, 71, 72, 83, 86, 131, 137, 159, 185, 186, 187, 189, 190, 191, 193, 194, 222, 224, 245
Andrews, ED;17, 159, 222
Anglo American Corporation 109
Antilles 11, 23
Atteridge (née Wood), MP 164, 165
Auer, A 33
Australia 45, 58, 61

Baker, H 12, 59, 75, 76, 143, 183
Baker, Kendall & Morris 76
Baldinelli, A 111, 112, 113
Balkema, AA 13
Bandung Institute of Technology 53
Bartholomew, BV 121
Bauhaus, Dessau, Germany 51, 71, 134
Beatrix, Princess of the Netherlands 32
Berlage, HP 23, 34, 38, 39, 46, 181, 208, 210
Bernhard, Prince of the Netherlands 96
Bijl, A 194, 197, 235
Bijl, Green & Todeschini 194
Black, B 201
Blauw, J 60
Bloem, H 57
Blokland, P 33
Boeken, A 41
Boeyinga, BT 104
Bongers, FM 77
Borbereki, Z 114
Borel, A 149
Botbijl, W 61
Bouwkunst en Vriendschap, Rotterdam 71
Bowling, PJ 166, 168, 175, 176
Brandts, WJ 140
Brink (née Brouwer), H 235, 236
Brink, GH 20, 228, 229, 230, 231, 232, 233, 234, 235, 236, 237, 238, 239
Brink, GM 231, 232, 234
Brinkman (née Siemerink), GH 15, 121, 130, 189, 194
Brinkman & Van der Vlugt 37, 132
Brinkman, JF 121
Bron System 192
Brouwer, J 31, 42, 235

Bruply Doors 12, 196
Brussels, Belgium 96
Bruynzeel 12, 60, 194, 196, 197
Bruynzeel, C 12, 60, 194, 196, 197
Buijs, JWE 52
Bulawayo, Zimbabwe/Rhodesia 120
Burg & Lodge 122
Burg Lodge & Burg 11, 19, 20, 244
Burg, JR 84, 85, 122, 142, 143, 149, 150, 151, 152, 157
Burg, JS 121

Calabar, Nigeria 211
Calderwood, DM 168, 174, 175
California, United States of America 131
Camberley, United Kingdom 69
Canada 45, 58, 61, 86
Cape Town City Orchestra 232
Chandigarh, India 207
Chapman & Spoor 70, 71, 128, 186, 188, 189, 190
Chick, HE 121
Chipkin, CM 103, 122
City Engineer's Department, Cape Town 77, 190, 221
Claassens, J 236
Claerhout, F 21, 24
Cleland, JS 193, 215, 217
Colijn, H 28, 57
Committee for Non-European Affairs, City Council of Pretoria 164
Congo 72
Cooke & Spicer 123
Cooke, PR 122, 123
Corobrick 195
Cort van der Linden, PWA 27
Crafford, A 235
Cramer, BJK 67
Cripple Care Fund 86
Cuypers, EGH 144
Cuypers, JTJ 25, 39, 51, 140
Cuypers, PJH 38

D'Ory 229
DAF 96
Damstra, L 213
Damstra, MG 14, 45, 63, 80, 210, 211, 213, 215, 222, 226
De 8 17, 34, 40, 189
De Beer, D 235
De Bie, H 58, 88, 123, 124, 186, 187, 188
De Geer, DJ 28
De Jong, J 195
De Jong, J (sr) 75
De Jong, JJ (jr) 13, 19, 75, 78, 158, 159, 163, 165, 166, 168, 169, 170, 171, 174, 175, 176, 193, 215, 216, 217, 222
De Klerk, M 35, 39, 40, 144, 181
De la Quellerie, M 19, 96
De Lange, E 79
De Ploeg 26
De Ridder, J 104, 105
De Stijl 26, 40, 79
De Vries Robbé 60, 189
De Vrije Wapenbroeders 62
De Zwaan, W 119, 149, 150, 151, 152
Delagoa Bay Railroad 208
Delfos, C 56, 128
Department of Architecture of the University of Pretoria 13, 232, 235
Department of Public Health, National 172, 192, 215
Department of Public Health, City Council of Pretoria 164
Deurvorst, TT 42
Dey, J 79
Dijker, J 17
Dommisse, J 51, 120, 128
Drees, W 30, 31
Dudok, WM 35, 36, 42, 77, 79, 103, 121, 125, 134
Duiker & Bijvoet 182
Duiker, J 40, 83, 181, 182, 186
Duncan, P 20, 129, 142, 143, 198, 199, 200, 202, 235
Dura Construction Company/Piling/Soletanche Bachy 188, 195
Duram Paints 194
Dutch Chamber of Commerce 62
Dutch Pavilion(s), International Colonial Exhibition 1931, Paris, France 72
Dutch State Forest Service [Staatsbosbeheer] 24
Dutch State Mines 31, 35
Dwars, AWC 49, 52
Dykstra/Dijkstra, PS 83, 84, 102, 104, 105, 193, 215, 217, 222

Eastern Cape Provincial Health Services 86
Eaton, NM 118, 120, 121, 125, 126, 127, 128, 142, 145, 146, 153, 210, 211, 212, 222
Edinburgh, United Kingdom 96
Egan & Sikkel 193, 194, 195
Egan, JE 193, 194, 195
Elliott, A 68
Engelenburg, FV 12, 83, 143
Era Bricks 195
European Mediterranean Academy, Cavalière, France 72
Evers, H 53

Fair, AC 150
Fassler, J 210, 235
Ferguson (née Boerrigter), WP 68
Ferguson & Stakesby-Lewis 68
Ferguson Stakesby-Lewis & Sayce 69
Ferguson, JE 18, 67, 68, 69, 73
Ferguson, TTH 68
Fiji 144
First Factory Shops 195
Fokker, JP 147
Ford Motor Car Company 129, 130
Freyssinet 195
Friedhoff, G 41, 42, 93, 94
FW Braat 84

Geddes, P 166
Geers & Geers 7, 102, 103, 105, 106, 122, 180, 185
Geers Koelewyn & Moors 105, 106
Geers, GMJ 103, 105, 122
Geers, LM 75, 100, 103, 105, 122
General Motors (SA) 129
Gerretsen & Wegerif 73
Gerretsen, F 72, 73
Gijlswijk, BA 109
Glennie, FM 76, 183, 187
Granpré Molière, MJ 34, 41, 53
Gratama & Versteeg 23
Greig, B 75, 86, 114, 133
Greiner, D 192
Grinaker-LTA 195
Groen, J 42
Grosny, Russia/Soviet Union 71, 72
Group '32 61

Haarlem School voor Bouwkunde, Versierende Kunsten en Kunstambachten [Haarlem School for Building, Decorative Arts and Crafts] 51
Hamdorff, WC 33
Hanrath, JW 38, 84
Harare/Salisbury, Zimbabwe/Rhodesia 69, 120, 125
Heidemij 27
Hellberg, HC 76, 77
Hertzog, JBM 57, 199
Hesse, F 76, 77, 81, 99, 101
Hesse, FW 101
Heyns, JA 106, 107
Hitler, A 28
Hobhouse, E 93
Hoekstra, H 88
Hofman, PJC 75
Holland-Afrika Lijn 6
Hollanderkorps [Dutch Corps] 8
Hollandsche Voetbal Vereeniging 62
Hollandse Mannenkoor 63
Holsboer, B 120
Howard, E 166
Howie, D 235
Hugo, H 152

International Federation of Hospital Engineering 194
Isaacs, H 156

Johannesburg Heritage Foundation 208
Jongens, A 194, 213
Jongens, JC 17, 18, 20, 45, 65, 67, 70, 71, 73, 76, 77, 87, 88, 89, 90, 93, 94, 96, 128, 183, 184, 185, 187, 188, 189, 190, 191, 194, 204, 206, 210, 211, 213, 214, 215, 221, 222, 223
Jongens, N 195
Jongens, S 213

Josephus Jitta, JP 87, 89
Judge Clothing Manufacturers 72
Juliana, Queen of the Netherlands 29, 96

Kaal, H 196
Kahn, A 129
Kakebeeke, JP 120
Kano, Nigeria 211
Katholieke Afrikanersentrum [Catholic Afrikaner Centre] 109
Kazachstan 71
Kemp, F 235
Kemp, J 235
Kenya 69
Keuning, J 30, 12
Klinkhamer, JF 53
KLM Royal Dutch Airlines 17, 57, 95, 221
Knuppe, B 194
Koelewyn/Koelewijn, J 105, 106
Kotera, J 67
Kraan & Wijers/Wyers 125, 126, 140, 209, 235
Kraan, J 12, 78, 100
Kramer, PL 39, 40, 181
Kret, J 52, 53
Kröll, R 107
Kromhout, W 67
Krommenie Linoleum 84
Kroon, PHJ 28
Kropholler, M 39
Kruger, SJP 8, 55, 83, 84, 163
Kuijers, A 13
Kumalo, S 111, 113
Kuyper, A 27, 45, 100, 102, 106, 107

L Smit & Co 199
Lagos, Nigeria 211
Landbank (now Land and Development Bank of South Africa) 120
Lansdorp, N 50
Lawrence, HG 165
Le Corbusier 150, 168, 186, 207
Le Sextant, Mathes, France 150

LESOTHO
National University of Lesotho/Catholic University College/Roma Campus 70, 78, 79
Roman Catholic Cathedral Maseru – Our Lady of Victories 110, 111
Seboche Mission Hospital, Seboche 85

Lewis, S - *see* Stakesby(-)Lewis 68, 69
Liem Bwan Tjie 144
Lochner, C 235
Lockwood Hall, GH 152, 163
Lodge, CS 11, 19, 20, 121, 122, 244
London, United Kingdom 28, 100, 120, 157
Longstreth Thompson, F 166
Louw & Louw 105, 106
Louw, W 5, 20, 76, 77, 100, 101, 102, 105, 106, 125, 181, 234, 242
Lubinov, Russia/Soviet Union 71
Luitingh, HC 76
Lürsen, JB 52
Lutyens, EL 207
Lyon, J 81

Maaskant, HA 42, 182
Mandela, NR 10
Mansergh, BGL 205
Martienssen, RD 130, 168
Matiyane, TT 177, 179
May, E 71
McIntosh, WG 183, 21
Meiring Eaton & Naudé 126
Meiring, AL 125, 126, 140, 209, 235
Meischke & Schmidt 66
Meischke, JC 18, 66, 67, 73
Meischke, MCA 75, 182, 195
Mendelsohn, E 71, 13
Metropolitan Tabernacle/Spurgeons Temple (London) Reformed Baptist Church 100
Michels, J 6
Milner, A 77, 78, 96, 151, 152
Moerdyk & Watson 79
Moerdyk/Moerdijk, GLP 100, 101, 103, 105, 106, 142, 149, 150
Molkenboer, THAA 27
Moojen, PAJ 72, 73
Moors, JAM 105, 106
Morris, SS 76, 87, 229, 230
Moscow, Russia/Soviet Union 71
Muller, KJ 33, 166
Munnik, Visser & Black 194
Mussert, AA 28

NAMIBIA (formerly South-West Africa)
Keetmanshoop Primary School 70
Keetmanshoop State Hospital 70
Walvis Bay 199

Nasionale Party [National Party] 58, 77, 109, 165
National Monuments Council 242
Nauta, J 196
Nectar Tea and Coffee Company 128
Nederlandsche Aannemersbond [Dutch Contractors Association] 49
Nederlandsche Linoleumfabriek Krommenie 185
Nederlandsche Zuid-Afrikaansche Landbouw Maatschappij [Netherlands South African Agricultural Company] 59
Nederlandse Emigratiedienst [Netherlands Emigration Service] 58
Nederlandse Vereeniging [Dutch Association] 62

NETHERLANDS
Aerdenhout
  Adventskerk [Advent Church] 44
Afsluitdijk [Closure Dyke] 31
Amerongen
  Weirs 32, 33
Amsterdam
  Betondorp [Concrete Village] 36, 192
  Beurs [Stock Exchange] van Berlage 38, 39, 181
  Effectenbeurs [Stock Exchange] (Jos Cuypers) 38
  Gerrit Rietveld Academy 51
  Het Schip housing estate 35
  Javakade 45
  Middenweg, shop-house 70
  Municipal MTS Dongestraat 48, 49
  National Aviation Laboratory [Nationaal Luchtvaart Laboratorium] 182
  Olympic Stadium 26, 87
  Openluchtschool [Open Air School] 186
  Orphanage [Burgerweeshuis] 44, 45, 83
  Rijksmuseum 140
  Rijksmuseum Chief Director's Residence 140
  Scheepvaarthuis 39, 181
  Spaarndammerplantsoen 37
  Technical School Patrimonium 44
  Transvaal district/buurt 23
  Van Heutszmonument/Nederland-Indië Monument 93, 94
  Watergraafsmeer 36, 70
  Zaanhof 35, 37
Amsterdam-Rhine and Lek canal
  Beatrix Lock 33
  Prince Bernhard Lock 33
Apeldoorn
  Ambachtsschool 232
  Paleis Het Loo [Palace] 231
Arnhem
  Provincial Administration Building 42, 76, 183
  Rhine Bridge 30
  Atlantikwall 29
Baarn
  Florence Grove 142
Bereplaat
  Rotterdam drinking water factory 194
Bergen
  Gereformeerde Kerk [Reformed Church] 104
Bolsward
  Roman Catholic High School Chapel of the St Martinus Church 70
Bosch en Duin
  Sunnyside 68
Brunssum
  State Mine Emma 32
Capelle aan den IJssel
  Storm Flood Barrier 33

Culemborg
Market Square 94, 95
Town Hall 95
Delft
Bouwkunde (Faculty Building) 53, 76
Former VOC premises, Oude Delft 53
Portugal House 53
Delta Works 23, 33
Den Bosch/'s-Hertogenbosch 42, 50
Den Haag/'s-Gravenhage/The Hague
Academy of Arts [Academie van Beeldende Kunsten] (1839) 52
Academy of Arts [Academie van Beeldende Kunsten] (1937) 52
House Winjewanje 72
Nirwana Flat 40, 182
Peace Palace [Vredespaleis] 25
Vrije School 72
Dordrecht 50
Driel
Weirs 33
Emmeloord 35
Emmen 44
Enschede
Town Hall 41, 42
Flevopolders 32
Friesland 34, 35
Goeree 30
Groningen
MTS & Crafts School 50
Haarlem
Teekenschool voor Kunstnijverheid [Haarlem Drawing School for Applied Arts] 70
Roman Catholic Church – Onze Lieve Vrouw van Zeven Smarten [Maria Church] 69
Gereformeerde Kerk [Reformed Church] – Haarlem-Noord 104
Hagestein
Weirs and hydro power installation 33
Heemstede
Heemsteedse Dreef, semi-detached houses 70
Heerlen 50
Hengelo
Kleine Driene 33, 34
't Lansink 44
Heusden
Town Hall 42
Hilversum
House JL Bool 147
Municipal Housing Scheme 35
Town Hall [Raadhuis] 42, 77, 103
Zonnestraal Sanatorium 83, 182, 186
Hoek van Holland [Hook of Holland]
Housing 150
IJmuiden
Noordzeekanaal lock 203
Kinderdijk 23, 24
Kollum
Gereformeerde Kerk [Reformed Church] 26, 104
Kootwijk
Radio station 26
Laren
Villa Cradalis 73
Leeuwarden 34
Lelystad 34, 44
Loenen 233
Maastricht
Pietersberg 24
Middelburg 28, 42
Nagele 34, 44
Nieuw Amsterdam
Noorderkerk 104
Nijkerk
De Neude 70, 71
North-East Polder 32
Renkum
Heveadorp 34
Rhenen 42
Rotterdam
Academy of Visual Arts and Technical Sciences [Academie voor Beeldende Kunsten en Technische Wetenschappen] 51, 53
Arts Academy [Academie voor Beeldende Kunsten] 67
Bergpolder 34
Bergpolderflat 37, 38
Blijdorp 34
Customs Office [Douanekantoor/Woongebouw Puntegale] 88
Groothandelsgebouw 42
Heyplaat 34
Hofpleinlijn Viaduct 31
Huf Building 123, 125
Kiefhoek 125
Lijnbaan ensemble 42
Laurens Church 28, 67
Maastunnel 30
Pendrecht 37, 38
Prinsekerk 66
Spangen 34
Town Hall 53, 67
Van Nelle Factory 41, 186
Vreewijk 34
Scheveningen – *see* The Hague
Schiphol 24, 95, 96
Schoonebeek 24, 30
Schoten - *see* Haarlem
Slochteren 24
Sneek 50
Tilburg 52
Utrecht
Diaconessenhuis 84
House Van Ravesteyn 145
MTS Croeselaan 50
Schröder House 40
Vaals-Lemiers
Sint Benedictusberg Abbey Church 43
Veluwe 72, 231
Voorthuizen
House Schermbloem 72
Vorden
De Wiersse 70
Wageningen
De Huif 68
Geodetic Laboratorium 42
Westerbork
Transit Camp 29
Woonoord Schattenberg 29
Wieringermeer 32
Zaandam 196
Zeeland 25, 33, 231

Netherlands Bank of South Africa (now Nedbank) 119, 120, 189, 210
Nicolas, JAHF 69
Niegeman, HTO 17, 18, 67, 71, 72, 73, 83, 84, 85, 86, 129, 130, 131, 132, 133, 134, 137, 159, 160, 185, 186, 187, 189, 190, 191, 193, 194, 222, 224, 225, 245
Niegeman, JCH 71
Nixon, R 87
NV Volkswoningbouw 38

Oud, JJP 125, 126, 150, 209, 210
Overvoorde (née Gordon), J 11
Overvoorde, J 11, 12

Payens/Paijens, EHA 7, 14, 15, 21, 45, 78, 79, 109, 110, 111, 113, 114, 210, 240, 242
Pearse, GE 207, 208
PG Bison 196
Philips 60, 84, 96, 188
Picton-Seymour, D 13, 139, 140
Pienaar, JJ 5, 19, 64, 119, 183, 210, 241
PJ Olivier School 190
Plantenga, JH 52
Ploeger, J 44, 55, 58, 59, 60, 61, 63, 65, 75, 76, 79, 102, 128, 150, 151, 195
Pocock, W 100
Polak, L 42
Policansky, M 72, 125, 130, 131
Potchefstroom University Music Conservatory 234
Prague Academy, Czechia 67
Preller, A 211
Pretoria Country Club 143, 152
Pretoria Gymnastic Vereeniging 62
Pretoria Iron Mines 128

Pretoria Master Builders Association 170
Primrose Brick Company 147
Prinses Irene Brigade [Princess Irene Brigade] 64, 70, 213, 214
Quellinus Applied Arts School, Amsterdam 51, 70

Quist, WG 194

Rabie, J 13
Rand Easter Show 19, 97, 188, 189
Reckitt & Colman Group 193
Reitsma, E 26, 104
Reitz (née Mulder), C 76
Reitz, FW 76
Reitz, H 76, 77
Rienk, J 122, 142, 150
Rietveld, GT 40, 51, 210
Rijksacademie van Beeldende Kunsten Amsterdam [Royal/National Academy of Arts Amsterdam] 51
Ringers, JA 28, 35
Roentgen, FE 42
Roosenburg, D 32
Rosema & Klaver/Rosema Group 195
Rotterdam Building Inspectorate 67
Ruysch & Co 22

Sasol 2&3 235
Sayce, CH 69
Schallies, JA 75
Scheffer, LSP 88, 89
Scheltema 195, 196
Scheltema, C 195, 196
Schimmel, F 114
Schmidt, P 66, 67
Schoemaker, RLA 53, 73
Schutte, GJ 60, 61
Schuurmans Stekhoven, JZ 14, 15, 45, 60, 61, 73, 76, 81, 183, 194
Sebök, E 114
Sedgwicks 193
Selhorst (Sister Piëntia) 113, 114
Seyss-Inquart, A 28
Shanghai, China 68
Shapiro, B 72, 86, 185, 194, 222, 224
Shell Oil Company 134
Siemerink & Brinkman 15, 86, 121, 130, 191
Siemerink & Walker 83, 129
Siemerink, H 15, 75, 82, 83, 85, 86, 120, 121, 129, 130, 191, 194
Sikkel & Partners 194, 196
Sikkel, A 98, 115,
Sikkel, H 106, 107, 193, 194
Simons, GJM 69
Skotnes, C 111, 114
Slothouwer, DF 70, 71
Sluyterman, TKL 53, 146
Smit, HF 42, 199
Smith, JA 105, 121
Smits & Van de Linde 147
Smits, AP 62
Smuts, JC 57, 64
Soff, FW 12, 83, 84, 85, 92, 93, 143
Soletanche Bachy/Soletanche-Freyssinet 195

SOUTH AFRICA
Algoa Bay 129
Assumpta 114
Beaufort West
  Dutch Reformed Church/Nederduits Gereformeerde Kerk [NGK] – Beaufort West 115
  Dutch Reformed Church/Nederduits Gereformeerde Kerk [NGK] – Gamka-Oos 105
  United Reformed Church, Rustdene – Die Ark 98, 115
Benoni
  Netherlands Bank of South Africa branch/Mahube House 122
  Reformed Church [GK] 103
Berg River Valley 93
Bethlehem
  Netherlands Bank of South Africa branch 113
Bloemfontein
  Adelaide Tambo Public Library 86, 87
  Batho 172
  Bochabela 110
  Ember El Mar 188
  Glen Road Total Service Station 190
  Holland House 88
  House De Bie 187
  Netherlands Bank of South Africa branch 123, 124
  Roman Catholic Cathedral – Sacred Heart 113
  Roman Catholic Church – St Rose of Lima 110
  St Mary's Primary School 110
  Steyn Statue 242, 243
  Vrouemonument [Women's memorial] 93
  Waaihoek 172
Camphill Village 73, 84
Camps Bay
  Rottingdean Court/Crownebay 193
Cape of Good Hope/Kaap de Goede Hoop 55, 99
Cape Town
  Arderne Scott Timbers, Epping 189
  Artscape Theatre 204
  Athlone Waste Treatment Plant 87
  Bakebo/House Sorensen 71
  Bellville 227
  Boere Saamwerk Beperk Wool Warehouse 128, 129
  Breda Court 14
  Cape Provincial Administration Building 76, 183, 187
  Cape Steel Construction 189, 190, 233
  Cape Town Waterfront 196, 204
  Casteel [Castle of Good Hope/Cape Castle] 95
  Civic Centre 204, 222
  Claremont 71
  Clifton 194
  Constantia Waldorf School 84
  Culemborg Railways Complex/SA Railways and Harbours Warehouses 204, 205
  Culemborg, Market Square replica 95
  Duncan Dock 20, 198, 199, 200, 202
  Dutch Reformed Church/Nederduits Gereformeerde Kerk [NGK] – Sonnekus 106
  Dutch Reformed Church/Nederduits Gereformeerde Kerk [NGK] – Ysterplaat 106, 107, 108
  Epping 189, 193, 194, 195, 223
  Foreshore 20, 87, 94, 96, 128, 199, 200, 203, 204, 205, 211, 241
  Foschini Department Store 72, 134
  Gateway to Africa (project) 96, 204
  Green Point Stadium 87, 90, 91
  Groote Schuur General Hospital 235
  Here Sewentien Building 187
  House Georgeu 194
  House Palermo 14, 213
  House Thögersen 194
  Instrument Manufacturing Corporation Building (IMC)/Plumstead Municipal Offices 133
  International Convention Centre 204
  Jan van Riebeeck Statue 94, 96
  Judge Clothing Factory 72, 130, 131
  Kewtown/Kewtown 87
  Langa 163
  Leeuwendal Maternity Home 83
  Liberty Cavalcade 214, 215
  M Bertish & Co/House of Monatic 131, 137, 222
  Maria de la Quellerie Statue 19, 96
  Multifunctional building 227
  Nederduitsch Hervormde Kerk [Church, NHK] – Kaapstad 188
  Netherlands Bank of South Africa branch – Buitenkant Street 125
  Netherlands Bank of South Africa branch – harbour 119
  Netherlands Bank of South Africa branch – Salt River 120
  Netherlands Club 88
  Newlands Public Swimming Pool 20, 190, 191, 221
  Oranjezicht Gardens Caretakers Cottages 14
  Pinelands 106, 107
  Plumstead 133, 190, 191
  Reckitt & Colman Group Factory 193
  Reformed Church/Gereformeerde Kerk [GK] – Kaapstad 105
  Rex Trueform Factory 19, 72, 186, 187, 189, 222
  Rhodes Statue 242
  Salt River 120, 129, 130, 131, 132, 133, 186, 190
  Sea Point Fire Station 77
  Sea Point Promenade 87
  Sedgwicks Winery/CTP Cartons and Labels 193
  Stanley Porter Building 187
  Sturrock Graving Dock 20, 199, 202
  Table Bay Harbour 199, 202, 203

Tokai 185, 194
Tygerberg Hospital 72, 86, 185, 194, 245
Van Riebeeck Festival venue 19, 31, 65, 96, 109
Victoria & Alfred Waterfront 196
Victoria Basin 199
Westbrooke/Genadendal (official residence) 10
De Doorns
Dutch Reformed Church/Nederduits Gereformeerde Kerk [NGK] – Murray (former) 99
Durban
Lamontville 163
Netherlands Bank of South Africa branch (1934) 121
Netherlands Bank of South Africa branch (1960) 126, 128
East London
Netherlands Bank of South Africa branch 121, 128
Fordsburg 182
Fort Savage
Assisi Mission 7
Franschhoek
Huguenot Monument 17, 18, 70, 93, 94, 183, 184, 206, 214, 215
Town Hall 76
Genadendal
Assembly Hall of the Moravian mission 10
Germiston 120
Graaff-Reinet
Town Hall/Victoria Hall 96, 97
Grahamstown 190, 222, 224, 226
Hanover Road
School (former) 82
Harrismith
Dutch Reformed Church /Nederduits Gereformeerde Kerk [NGK] – Kerkenberg 103
Heidelberg
CNO Volksskool 78
Hermanus
Camphill Farm 84
Hex River Valley 99
Hout Bay
Alma Ata (House Niegeman) 92, 159
Humansdorp
Stulting Primary School 82
Johannesburg
Art Gallery 207
August House 68, 69
Belen Bakery 69
Bienvenue Shelter 69
Braamfontein 182
Brixton 7, 18
Catholic Centre 70, 111
City Hall 182
Constitution Hill 9, 10
Diamond Cutting Works 69
Dutch Reformed Church/Nederduits Gereformeerde Kerk [NGK] – Kensington 103
Dutch Reformed Church/Nederduits Gereformeerde Kerk [NGK] – Melville 102, 103
Fordsburg Post Office 182
Fort 9
Guildhall Pub 67
Jeppe Post Office 182
KLM Booking Office(s) 17, 221
Malvern – *see* Kensington
Maryvale 111, 112, 113, 185
Meischke's Building 67
Milner Park 96
Motor Centrum 128
Nedbank Centre 128
Netherlands Bank drive-through branch 125
Netherlands Bank of South Africa branch Fox/Simmonds Streets 122
Netherlands Bank of South Africa branch Von Brandis 122
Netherlands Bank of South Africa Johannesburg Headquarters 123
Netherlands Pavilion Rand Easter Show Pavilion 96, 97, 188, 189
Orchards 69
Orlando 174
Post Office [Post- en Telegraafkantoor] 182, 208
Reformed Church/Gereformeerde kerk [GK] – Johannesbrug-Noord/Melville 102
Rissik Street Post Office 182
Roman Catholic Church – St Mary of the Wayside 111, 112, 113
Royal Court 70
Sharpeville 10, 174, 194, 236
St Benedict's College 70, 113
Sterling House 69
Washington House 69
West Campus Witwatersrand University 96
Westcliff 69
Klerksdorp
Reformed Church/Gereformeerde Kerk [GK] 102
Knysna 76
Komatipoort 150, 151
Kroonstad
Catholic Afrikaans boys' school 109
Roman Catholic Cathedral – St Patrick's 114
Roman Catholic Church – St Peter Claver 111
Seeisoville 111
Kuils River
Jan Kriel Institute 83, 85
Limpopo 55, 56, 85
Mosselbay 109
Muizenburg
Shell Staff Training Centre/SA Naval College 133, 134
Paarl
Town Hall 76, 77
Pietermaritzburg
House Knuppe 194
Natal Plywood and Chipboard Factory 194, 196
Pietersburg/Polokwane
Netherlands Bank of South Africa branch 120, 122
Pinelands
Dutch Reformed Church/Nederduits Gereformeerde Kerk [NGK] 106, 107
Port Elizabeth/Gqeberha
Aquarium 129
Cummingham Primary School/Quest School 82, 83
Dr Viljoen Primary School 82
Dutch Reformed Church/Nederduits Gereformeerde Kerk [NGK] 101
Ford Motor Car Company – Highland Park Plant 129, 130
General Motors (SA) 129
McNamee Township 163
Mobbs Factory 130, 189, 190, 191
Netherlands Bank of South Africa North End branch 121
North End Public Library 15
Provincial Hospital 85
Ridgewood (House AL Stockelbach/GFI Art Gallery) 130
South End 82
Walton Orthopaedic Home 86
Porterville
High School/Hoërskool 82
Primary School/Laerskool 82
Potchefstroom 60, 76, 78, 234
Pretoria
Agriculture Building Univeristy of Pretoria 74, 79
Amanda Court 11
Arcadia 143, 144, 153
Atteridgeville/Oustad 12, 19, 78, 158, 159, 162-179, 193, 215, 216
Bantule 164, 165, 174
Botany Building University of Pretoria 79
Brooklyn 139, 140, 141, 142, 143, 144, 145, 146, 147, 151, 153, 218
Burgers' Park Park Keeper's Residence 140
CBD/Church Square 8, 99, 119, 164
Clubview 153
Danville 12, 13, 78, 163193, 215
Dutch Reformed Church/Nederduits Gereformeerde Kerk [NGK] – Grootekerk 100
Dutch Reformed Church/Nederduits Gereformeerde Kerk [NGK] – Harmonie 108
Dutch Reformed Church/Nederduits Gereformeerde Kerk [NGK] – Wapadrand 228, 234
Eastwood 152, 164
Engelenburg House 12, 143
Erasmus Castle 19, 138, 139, 140, 141, 142
Erasmuskloof 139, 149
Garstfontein 147
General Hospital 85, 235
Hillcrest 143, 146, 150, 154
House Ackerman 154
House Arnold 153

House Botha 220, 221
House Burg (Duxbury Street) 150
House Burg (Lunnon Road) 150
House Coetzee 221
House Cohen 220, 221
House De Kock 154, 155
House De la Hunt 147, 154, 220, 221
House De Moor 145
House Falcke 153
House Goldstein 147, 220
House Grobler/Lydia 12
House Grové 147, 148, 219
House Harrison 147, 148, 219
House Horstmanshof 144
House Lorentz 152
House Poole 154
House Smal 160, 161, 220, 221
House Sturdy 152, 153
House Van Boeschoten 152
House Van den Heever 217
House Van Reenen 152
Houses for J Corbishly 143
Hove's Ground 164, 165, 172, 174
Huis Voortrekker/Glaskas/Xayata Hostel 16, 79, 80
Impala Building/Prinsman Place 244
Irene 152
JJ de Jong School 78
Kirkness Sandfontein Works 154
Kruger Memorial 8
Lady Selborne 164
Loreto Convent School 113
Louis Botha Memorial Home for Children 83
Lynnwood 218
Marabastad 164, 165, 172, 175
Mea Vota 139
Metro Building 144
Moedersbond [Mothers Union] 84, 85
Mooiplaas 165
Motsemogolo 165
Muckleneuk 154, 218
Nederduits Hervormde Kerk [Church] – Pierneef 30, 236, 237, 238
Nederlandsche Bank en Credietvereeniging (NBCV) second head office 119
Neethlinghuis 140, 142
Nellmapius House 152
Netherlands Bank of South Africa Pretoria 118, 125, 126, 127, 210, 211, 212, 222
OK Bazaars 11
Oost-Eindschool 60, 78
Osbourne House 142, 144
Ou Raadsaal 8
Reformed Church /Gereformeerde Kerk [GK] – Brooklyn 104, 105
Reformed Church /Gereformeerde Kerk [GK] – Pretoria-Noord 104
Roman Catholic Church – Pius X 111
Rondawel houses (Duncan Street) 142
Pres. Kruger Children's Home 84
Pretoria Normal College 70
Pretoria Teachers College 16
Proclamation Hill 12, 152, 163, 215
RDP (Reconstruction and Development Program) Houses 177
Roman Catholic Church (Parish) – Immaculate Conceptions, Pretoria Gardens 189
Sammy Marks House 152
Saulsville 165
Savelkoul Building 19, 20
Schoolplaats 164
St John Vianney Seminary 109, 110
Station Gardens and WW1 Memorial 70
Sunnyside 78, 144
Superstadium Atteridgeville 176
Trianon/Tiny Town 144
Union Buildings 67, 75, 121, 144, 183
United Reformed Church – Melodi Ya Tshwane 100
Villieria 236
Vlakfontein/Mamelodi 174
Voortrekker Monument 93
Waterkloof 109, 110, 111, 139, 143, 152, 153, 154, 155, 185, 218
Westerlig Primary School/Laerskool 78
Zuid-Afrikaansche Hospitaal 84, 85
Zwartkops 152
Rawsonville
Goudini High School/Hoërskool 82
Robben Island
Murray's Bay Harbour 202
Roggebaai 128
Rustenburg
Reformed Church/Gereformeerde Kerk [GK] 105, 106
Sasolburg 235
Schweizer-Reneke
Medium High School/Hoërskool 15, 17, 78
Secunda 235
Somerset West
Morgenster 207
Springs
Netherlands Bank of South Africa branch 122
Stellenbosch
Blaauwklippen (district) 241
Bloemhof Meisiesskool [Girls School] 81
Bruynzeel Factory/BruPly 12
House Bruynzeel/Stormvogel 194, 197
Natural Sciences Building, University of Stellenbosch 81
Town Hall 76
Welgelegen 194
Swartruggens
Dutch Reformed Church/Nederduits Gereformeerde Kerk [NGK] 101, 102
Reformed Church/Gereformeerde Kerk [GK] 102
Swellendam
Dutch Reformed Church/Nederduits Gereformeerde Kerk [NGK] 101
Table Bay 95, 199, 200, 201, 202, 203
Table Mountain 107
Tshilidzini Hospital 85
Tshwane - *see* Pretoria
Type House designs
NZASM (A, B and C) 150, 151
'Non-European', Central Housing Board of the Department of Public Health 174, 192, 193, 215, 217
'Type C', City of Pretoria 216, 216
'Four-room house for Non-Europeans, Type 288' 215
'Non-European', National Planning Commission (51/6; 51/7; 51/8; 51/9; 51/12) 163, 172, 173, 174, 177, 192, 216, 217
Unknown
Roman Catholic Church 114, 242
Flat-roofed single storey house 225
Utrecht
Town Hall 76, 77
Uvongo 144
Vanderbijlpark 235
Vereeniging
Reformed Church [GK] 104
Villiers
Dutch Reformed Church/Nederduits Gereformeerde Kerk [NGK] 103
Vrede 15
Vryheid 153
Welkom 109
Wellington
Netherlands Bank of South Africa branch 128
Westbrooke 10
Westminster 114
Wolmaransstad
Daeraad School/Skool 70
Wonderfontein 60
Woodstock Beach 199
Worcester
Hextex 17, 132, 133
Netherlands Bank of South Africa branch 128
Wynberg
Groot Constantia 12
Public Library 87

South African Department of Environmental Affairs 229
South African Mining and General Investments Company 128
South African Post Office 123, 170, 208
South African Theosophical Society 69
South African Township & Mining Company 152
Spaans, A 195
Spaans, J 195
Spaans, JH 195
Spaansbou CC 195

Spicer, HW 122, 123
Spoor, H 70, 71, 128, 186, 188, 189, 190
Springbok Kitchen Equipment 160
Staal, A 41
Stakesby Lewis, S 69
Stakesby-Lewis (née Ferguson), JE - *see* Ferguson;
Stam-Beese, CIA 38
Stam, M 38, 51
Stauch, HWE 123, 153, 210, 235
Steiner, RJL 72, 84
Stekhoven, MM (Schuurmans) 73, 76, 194
Steyn (née Fraser), RI 93
Steyn, MT 93, 243
Steynberg, C 18, 93, 94, 183
Stockelbach, AH 130
Stork, CT 33, 34
Studiegenootschap voor Nederlandsche Belangen [Society for the Study of Netherlands Interests] 64
Sturrock, FC 20, 199, 202
Stuyt, J 38, 39
Suid-Afrikaanse Vrouevereeniging [South African Women's Association] 84
Sukarno 29
Sumner, M 115
Surabaya 199
Surinam 11, 23
Switzerland 73

Te Water, FK 194, 196
Templer, CF 190, 193
The Stained Glass Studio 70
Thompson, FL 166
Tilburg Academie voor Bouwkunst [Tilburg Academy of Architecture] 52
Tivoli Society, Utrecht 231
Transvaal Education Department 78
Transvaal Group 168
Transvaal Provincial Administration 61
Transvaal University College 79
Troelstra, PJ 28
Tuynman & Snellebrand 31

Uganda 211
University of Cape Town 94, 115, 196, 213, 242
University of Pretoria 13, 15, 16, 74, 79, 80, 104, 120, 125, 193, 196, 208, 210, 231, 232, 235
University of Stellenbosch 76, 81, 86
University of the Free State 242
University of the Witwatersrand 207
Unwin, R 166

Van Beijma, WFGL 65, 163, 173, 174, 193, 216, 217, 222
Van de Werke, J 15, 16, 50, 59, 78, 79, 80, 85, 108, 144, 145, 146, 147, 148, 150, 152, 153, 154, 155, 160, 163, 210, 217, 218, 219, 220, 221
Van den Berg, J 88
Van den Broek & Bakema 53, 123, 125
Van der Ben, F 76, 138, 139, 140, 141, 142
Van der Laan, H 42, 43
Van der Laan, N 42
Van der Leeuw, CH 41
Van der Mey, JM 181
Van der Sluys Projects/Strukture 195
Van der Sluys, J 195
Van der Steur, JAG 53
Van der Vlugt, LC 37, 38, 41, 50, 132
Van der Waal, G-M 13, 67, 103, 122, 157
Van Doornik, W 142
Van Eesteren, C 34
Van Everdingen - *see* Ferguson, JE
Van Eyck, AE 45
Van Gemert, JW 109, 111, 113, 114
Van Gendt, ADN 40, 181
Van Gendt, JG 40, 181
Van Hall, FJ 93, 94
Van Houten (née Wegerif), A 73
Van Kretschmar van Veen, C 199
Van Kretschmar van Veen, JA 199
Van Lent, C 58
Van Loghem, JB 36, 182, 189
Van Lokhorst, J 51
Van Moorsel, CM 110
Van Niftrik, C 213
Van Niftrik, JJ 15, 17, 45, 78, 96, 97, 188, 189, 190, 210, 211, 213, 214, 215, 221, 222
Van Ravesteyn, S 41, 145
Van Riebeeck Festival/Tercentenary 19, 31, 95, 96, 109, 204
Van Riebeeck, JA 13, 17, 19, 31, 45, 55, 65, 81, 82, 94, 95, 96, 109, 117, 119, 120, 204
Van Rijsse, K 67, 1
Van Selms, A 107, 108
Van Straten, W 104
Van Tijen & Maaskant 182
Van Tijen, W 37, 38, 42, 182
Van Velsen, GMF 109, 111, 113, 114, 115
Van Voorst, JJ 86, 87
Van Wijngaarden, W 58, 123, 124
Van Wouw, A 8, 92, 93
Vegter, JJM 42
Vereeniging voor Vrouwenkiesrecht [Women's Suffrage Association] 27
Verhagen, P 34
Vermooten, H 105
Verwoerd, H 10
Villa, E 14, 15, 41, 42, 72, 73, 114, 139, 140, 142, 146, 151
Vinci Group 195
Visser, L 48, 194
Vixseboxse, JE 67, 115
Vladivostok, Russia/Soviet Union 71
Voorvelt, AJC 14, 18, 45, 64, 67, 69, 70, 73, 78, 109, 110, 111, 112, 113, 185
Vrije Universiteit Amsterdam 106

Walgate & Elsworth 70, 77
Walker, AH 121
Walker, J 13
Wattez, P 33
Wegelin (née Greeff), LE 232, 235, 239
Wegelin (née Zoetelief Tromp), WJ 232
Wegelin, AW 231, 232
Wegelin, E 234
Wegelin, HW 20, 196, 229, 230, 231, 232, 234, 235, 236, 239
Wegerif (née Gravestein), AJ 72
Wegerif, C (jr) 18, 67, 72, 73, 82, 84
Wegerif, C (sr) 72
Welschen System 193
Wentink, DE 67
West Guinea 30
Westmaas, P 140, 141, 142
Wiebenga, JG 40, 5
Wierda, SW 8, 208
Wijdeveld, HT 39, 71, 72, 125
Wilhelmina, Queen of the Netherlands 8, 23, 24, 25, 28, 29, 122, 231
Wils, J 26, 87
Winkelman, HG 28
Withaar, J 234
Witwatersrand Brick and Tile Company 147
Wolbers, DJ 96
Workers Club, Grosny, Russia/Soviet Union 71, 72
Worm, PJFM 117, 119, 120
Woudstra & De Ridder 104, 105
Woudstra, J 104, 105
Wright, FL 144, 147
Wyers/Wijers, J 12, 78, 100

Yarolslavl, Russia/Soviet Union 71

Zijlstra, J 96
Zuid-Afrikahuis 45, 96
Zweedijk, WJG 72, 73

Colophon

LM Publishers
Voorhaven 129
1135 BP Edam
The Netherlands
+31 85 8772 397
info@lmpublishers.nl
www.lmpublishers.nl

Graphic design: Erik Rikkelman & Ad van Helmond
Production: Hightrade BV

ISBN: 9789460225338
NUR: 648

Cover image: Newlands Swimming Pool, Cape Town, designed by JC Jongens & R Nixon; photo: Francois Swanepoel
Back cover image: Amanda Court, Pretoria, designed by Burg Lodge & Burg; photo: Cameron Forder
Inner cover: Sketch for the Cape Town Foreshore, JC Jongens

All chapters and interludes in this book have been triple-blind peer-reviewed by independent researchers located in both South Africa and the Netherlands in order to verify that they meet the academic and scholarly standards of research in the disciplines of architecture and architectural history.

This book has been realized with support from:

Embassy of the Kingdom of the Netherlands
University of Pretoria
Cultural Heritage Agency of the Netherlands
DutchCulture

Kingdom of the Netherlands
UNIVERSITEIT VAN PRETORIA
UNIVERSITY OF PRETORIA
YUNIBESITHI YA PRETORIA
ENTERPRISES University of Pretoria
DutchCulture
Cultural Heritage Agency
Ministry of Education, Culture and Science